Textures of the Sikh Past

Textures of the Sikh Past
New Historical Perspectives

edited by
Tony Ballantyne

OXFORD
UNIVERSITY PRESS

OXFORD
UNIVERSITY PRESS

YMCA Library Building, Jai Singh Road, New Delhi 110 001

Oxford University Press is a department of the University of Oxford.
It furthers the University's objective of excellence in research, scholarship,
and education by publishing worldwide in

Oxford New York
Auckland Cape Town Dar es Salaam Hong Kong Karachi
Kuala Lumpur Madrid Melbourne Mexico City Nairobi
New Delhi Shanghai Taipei Toronto

With offices in
Argentina Austria Brazil Chile Czech Republic France Greece
Guatemala Hungary Italy Japan Poland Portugal Singapore
South Korea Switzerland Thailand Turkey Ukraine Vietnam

Oxford is a registered trade mark of Oxford University Press
in the UK and in certain other countries.

Published in India
by Oxford University Press, New Delhi

© Oxford University Press 2007

The moral rights of the authors have been asserted
Database right Oxford University Press (maker)

First published 2007

ISBN-13: 978-0-19-568663-0
ISBN-10: 0-19-568663-2

Typeset in Plantin 10.5/12.5
by Eleven Arts, Keshav Puram, Delhi 110 035
Printed in India by De-Unique, New Delhi 110 018
Published by Oxford University Press
YMCA Library Building, Jai Singh Road, New Delhi 110 001

Contents

Preface

The chapters in this volume emerged out of the symposium hosted by the University of Otago's History Department and Asian Studies Research Centre at St Margaret's College in December 2003. Early in 2003, it was decided to shift this event from Santa Barbara to New Zealand after it became clear that W. H. (Hew) McLeod was not well enough at that point to travel overseas. In mid-December 2003, 25 scholars travelled from around the world to meet in Dunedin, joining members of the local University, the Punjabi communities, and the McLeod family. The symposium's theme was 'New Directions in Sikh and Punjab Studies' and over three days, many papers were shared and there was robust discussion of the new research and the existing historiography.

This volume grows out of the symposium and, like that gathering, it has a two-fold purpose. First, the chapters gathered here are reflective in nature. In their own way, each offers an assessment of Sikh studies as it stands today, but also looks forward and offers new perspectives on Sikh culture and history. Second, the symposium and this volume are a recognition and celebration of the tremendous contribution of Hew McLeod to the field of Sikh studies. A pioneering scholar in the field and now its elder statesman, Hew's influence has shaped the development of Sikh studies in a multitude of ways. His scholarship has blazed new paths and there is no doubt that his substantial oeuvre has radically transformed how we understand Sikh history. But he has also been a great mentor, friend, teacher, referee, examiner, and reader. Never dogmatic, Hew has watched Sikh studies grow and encouraged a wide range of scholars to follow their interests in a myriad directions. The Otago symposium provided an opportunity to reflect on Hew's momentous contribution and to hear about his ongoing research (which is included in this volume).

This volume brings together 11 chapters that have been expanded from the initial papers presented in Dunedin. While Verne Dusenbery, Mark Juergensmeyer, Ainslee Embree, Shinder Singh Thandi, and Rashmere Bhatti have not contributed to the collection, their presence was crucial to the success of this gathering. Each of these scholars will see that their work and participation at Otago has imprinted the chapters that follow. It is important to note that some scholars who wished to participate in this symposium were unable to attend for various reasons. It was especially sad that both Professor J. S. Grewal and Professor Indu Banga, two scholars who have profoundly shaped both Punjabi and Sikh historiography, were unable to travel to New Zealand. We also greatly missed Gurinder Singh Mann, who had to withdraw from the conference at the last minute. Gurinder was a moving force behind the conclave and his impetus to this project is greatly appreciated.

As the organizer of the symposium, I gratefully acknowledge the support of the History Department at Otago as well as the Asian Studies Research Committee in providing the core funding for the event. The British Council was generous in enabling Amrit and Rabinda Kaur Singh's visit to Dunedin. In terms of planning the symposium, the History Department's support staff were invaluable. Sue Lang helped with the arrangements for the gathering and oversaw the finances, while Kyle Matthews and Frances Couch assisted in preparing the printed materials for the speakers. Karen Henderson, the events manager at St Margaret's, ensured that the three days went smoothly. The Mayor of Dunedin, Sukhi Turner, was also a generous host to the visiting speakers and their families. In her official capacity, she opened the symposium and also hosted a reception for the participants and members of Dunedin's South Asian community. That reception was a very special occasion where members of the Otago Sikh community presented Hew with a *pounamu* (jade) plaque which was engraved with the *khanda*. In combining distinctive symbols of New Zealand and the Panth, this gift was a special recognition of the ways in which Hew has brought New Zealand and Punjab together, and these chapters are also offered in that same spirit of celebration.

Introduction

Tony Ballantyne

O ver the past four decades Sikh studies has come of age. In the early 1960s, there was only a very small body of scholarship relating to Sikhism and limited work undertaken on Sikh history. In the wake of the decolonization of South Asia and the Partition of India, nation building was the primary concern of most scholars and the construction of the history of nationalism was the paramount project for historians of India. While regional history remained popular in provincial urban centres, drawing significant support from local literary elites who were committed to fortifying regional languages and identities, professional historians were deeply concerned with the project of 'Indian History' and the construction of a history for the new nation-state.

If the drive to construct a national political history overshadowed long standing traditions of regional history within South Asia as a whole, the project of constructing a national history of India including Punjab, also marginalized Sikhism. In the immediate post-war period, histories of nationalism were framed as the story of the struggle against imperial administrative systems and the development of indigenous high politics at an all-India level. Within this secular rendering of the national past, there was little space for consideration of the place of religion in moulding the language and symbolic repertoire that South Asians drew upon in responding to colonial rule, let alone its place in everyday life. When religion did enter narratives of Indian history, it was read primarily in terms of the rivalry between Congress and the Muslim League. Given the power of this binary and the more general opposition that was assumed between Hindus and Muslims, Sikhism was rarely a prominent element in the histories of India.

Around 1960 Ganda Singh, Fauja Singh, and Harbans Singh were the most notable of a small cadre of historians who were actively researching Sikh history within Punjab itself. At that same point in time, even fewer non-Punjabis, whether scholars from other regions of South Asia or elsewhere, were drawn to Punjabi and/or Sikh history. A British or American undergraduate in 1960 would have found few sophisticated works on Sikhism in their university library. They would certainly have struggled to locate works published in Punjab and would have found only limited western scholarship on Punjab that was not produced by the printing presses of missionary organizations or the intellectual residue of the colonial state. In effect, the history of Sikhs and Sikhism remained largely unknown outside India.

In the late 1960s, however, a historiographical revolution was enacted by a new generation of scholars. Substantial new bodies of scholarship invigorated interest in the distinctiveness of Punjabi history and transformed received understandings of Sikhism. Within India, J. S. Grewal, who completed his postgraduate training in England, emerged as a leading expert on both Punjabi and Sikh history. A significant cohort of international scholars, primarily from North America, also produced a large corpus of high-quality research in the late 1960s that broadened and deepened understandings of Punjabi history. Some of these scholars, most notably Tom Kessinger, worked within the new framework of village-based historical research that characterized the 'area studies' approach that transformed humanities scholarship in North America during the Cold War. Kessinger's *Vilyatpur*, a longitudinal of the transformation of one Punjabi village, revealed much about the demographic, economic, and environmental patterns that moulded Punjabi life.[1] In a different domain, N. G. Barrier produced detailed assessments of colonial policy-making and Punjabi politics.[2] His work on the intersections between local politics and the voluminous print culture that Punjabis fashioned under colonialism and local politics was crucial in connecting religion and politics within the Punjabi context, at the very moment when members of the so-called 'Cambridge school' were attempting to uncouple religion and politics once and for all. Barrier's work on the urban reformers of the Singh Sabha nicely complemented Kenneth Jones's landmark studies of the Arya Samaj and communal politics in Punjab under colonialism.[3]

But at the heart of the transformation of historical understandings of Sikhism was the work of one scholar: W. H. McLeod. A New Zealander trained in history, McLeod arrived in Punjab in 1958 to serve in the New Zealand Presbyterian Church's North Indian mission. McLeod developed a rich understanding of Punjabi language and history before pursuing postgraduate studies in history at the School of Oriental and African Studies, London. His PhD thesis on the traditional sources for the life of Guru Nanak laid the foundations for his paradigm-shifting *Guru Nanak and the Sikh Religion*. Published in 1968, just prior to the five-hundredth anniversary of Guru Nanak's birth, this monograph rigorously applied textual criticism to Sikh sources and history. McLeod cast doubt on the veracity of many traditional narratives relating to Guru Nanak, producing a short, stripped-down biographical summation of Nanak's life, effectively demarcating the 'Nanak of history' from the 'Nanak of faith'. While this radical re-interpretation of the life of Sikhism's founder was at odds with some of the other publications that marked the quincentenary and was quickly contested by some Sikhs, McLeod's careful and sympathetic exposition of Nanak's teaching has proved to be tremendously influential amongst Punjabi and Western scholars alike. Most crucially, it was this work that finally punctured the long-established belief amongst Western scholars that Sikhism was essentially a syncretic tradition and emerged as a synthesis of Hinduism and Islam.

In the 1970s, McLeod extended this initial research using the *janam sakhis*, the narratives that record the life of Guru Nanak, to trace the development of Sikh tradition and as a window into the social composition of the Sikh Panth. At the same time, Indu Banga was undertaking a path-breaking research on the agrarian history of Punjab and Ranjit Singh's state, highlighting the regional context of Sikhism's development.[4] Taken collectively, these historians were producing a substantial body of scholarship that was producing a new vision of Sikh history. This new history was characterized by its complexity. It was interested in the relationships between religious texts and their social contexts, examined the connections between communication and politics, and, most of all, reconstructed the dynamic development of the Sikh community from the time of Nanak.

By the 1980s and 1990s, the field of Sikh studies was growing and diversifying. Mark Juergensmeyer's important work on the intersections between religion, caste, and access to socio-political power was published, providing important insights into the place of Dalits within the Panth.[5] Harjot Oberoi's paradigmatic work on social change under British rule revolutionized our understandings of Punjabi cultural and intellectual history, and still stands as a landmark study of late nineteenth-century cultural change within the historiography of South Asia as a whole.[6] The research of Pashaura Singh and Gurinder Singh Mann produced increasingly nuanced understandings of the making of the Sikh 'canon'.[7] Louis Fenech authored an innovative study of the place of martyrdom in the Sikh tradition and, like Jeevan Deol, has produced important work on the relationship between Sikhism and Punjabi literary culture.[8] Verne Dusenbery, Parminder Bhachu, Karen Leonard, and Darshan Singh Tatla opened new perspectives on the histories of Punjabi migration and the construction of Sikh diasporic communities, themes that McLeod, Barrier, and Pashaura Singh have also addressed.[9] Nikky-Guninder Kaur Singh and more recently Doris Jakobsh have also focused our attention on the place of gender within the Sikh tradition and have revealed the power of gender as an analytical category for Sikh studies.[10]

As we enter the twenty-first century, we have a much greater appreciation of the richness and complexity of Sikh history than we had three decades ago. Robust debate remains a key feature of the field and these exchanges are carried on in a growing stack of monographs, edited collections, and academic journals. Thanks to these exchanges, many old theories have been disproven, modified, and reworked, while new approaches are tested, contested, and defended. Most important, scholarship on Sikhs and Sikhism remains strongly engaged with Sikh communities. Sikhs from various social backgrounds and in a wide array of locations have energetically engaged with this scholarship, meaning that Sikh studies are unlikely to ever become a rarefied and inaccessible field.

This volume is an attempt to both reflect on this large body of scholarship and to look ahead to new ways of imagining the Sikh past. The chapters roam over a wide analytical terrain, examining sacred texts and popular culture, the transformation of Punjab under British rule and contemporary developments, local histories, and social issues that concern the Panth as a whole. They are united, however, by a deep concern with what we might term the 'texture' of Sikh history: the ways in which space, time, social structures, and political systems have shaped the development of the Panth. Many of the chapters are concerned with very specific issues—a single text, internet list server, author—or with the history of

Sikh communities in particular locations, at particular points in time. This interest in specificity is very important as regards the production of carefully contextualized studies that require us to appreciate the forces, processes, and structures that have conditioned Sikh history. There is no denying the very real power of the fundamental beliefs and practices that provide Sikhism with its distinctiveness and coherence, but we must understand the ways in which the experiences of different Sikh individuals and communities have been shaped by the specificities of time, place, and prevailing social structures. Most important, this collection underlines the widely divergent social formations that members of the Panth have experienced through the broad sweep of Sikh history and the ability of these diverse Sikh communities to adapt to these circumstances while maintaining their commitment to the teachings of the gurus. In bringing together this range of carefully researched perspectives, this volume highlights some key features of the complex fabric of Sikh history. In assessing these multiple histories, the authors of these chapters not only communicate much about the texture of Sikhism's history, but also identify new archives and novel approaches that may provide new and valuable vantage points for future research.

The volume begins with N. G. Barrier's keynote address that opened the Otago symposium. Here Barrier offers a synoptic view of the development of Sikh studies, locating the emergence of Sikh studies as a distinctive area of expertise in a variety of contexts. He ultimately locates the origins of Sikh studies in the work of the scholars and politicians of the Singh Sabha movement, those energetic leaders whose pamphlets, novels, and religious commentary continue to function as both a foundational archive and a key analytical reference point for work on Punjabi and Sikh history. But, in tracing the growth of the field, Barrier also emphasizes the conjuncture between personal and institutional histories. A new generation of western scholars were drawn to work on Punjabi history in the 1960s for a variety of reasons: for some, like Hew McLeod, scholarship grew out of living and working on Punjab from 1958, while others 'discovered' the region during their travels in South Asia or were intrigued by the profuse documents relating to the region produced by both Punjabis and Britons during the colonial period. This cohort of scholars shaped Sikh studies in the West during the 1970s and the 1980s, producing a substantial body of work that covered the wide span of Sikh history, from sacred texts to Punjabi migration, from community politics to Sikh literature. During the 1980s and 1990s, Barrier argues, the field faced a crisis. Although a new generation of scholars emerged whose work challenged both the approach and arguments of the work produced in the late 1960s and 1970s, scholars of Sikhism now found themselves operating within a highly charged political environment. The struggle to attain a Sikh 'homeland' (Khalistan), Operation Blue Star, the assassination of Indira Gandhi, and the widespread violence directed against Sikhs within India in the mid-1980s drew international attention to Sikhs, both in India and abroad. Sikhs themselves were increasingly sensitive to how they were represented by non-Sikhs and many Sikhs began to contest the ability of 'Western' disciplines and scholars to understand *their* history.

From this basis, Barrier moves on to critically reflect on the state of Sikh studies today. He highlights the real and potential points of conflict between Sikh communities and experts in Sikh studies. He provides several anecdotes that succinctly communicate the nature of these faultlines and the ways in which one leading American academic reads these conflicts. But while Barrier is firm in his defence of Sikh studies, he notes the great potential for productive engagement between 'insiders' and 'outsiders', members of the Panth and scholars trained in 'Western' disciplines such as history and religious studies. Barrier's essay is a lively and provocative opening to the volume, and his chapter captures the verve of his presentation in Dunedin.

It is entirely appropriate that the main body of the volume begins with contributions by two leading scholars, Pashaura Singh and Louis Fenech, who completed their PhD research under Hew McLeod's guidance and whose work casts new light on the textual tradition that has been at the heart of Sikh studies. The first of these chapters is Pashaura Singh's examination of the *Vanjara Pothi*. Singh, whose research has extended our understanding of the making of the Sikh canon, assesses a recently discovered text which he believes casts new light on the production of the Adi Granth. Singh argues that the various compositions that eventually made up the Adi Granth were produced collaboratively through a series of working drafts that were prepared under the direct supervision of Guru Arjan himself. This text, belonging to the nomadic Vanjara trading community, stands alongside MS 1245 and the *Bahoval Pothi* as one of these working drafts. The *Vanjara Pothi* was produced by a range of scribes and does not fit the standard sequence of compositions that would come to characterize the Adi Granth. Here Singh details the 'physiognomy' of the text, assesses the sequence of the compositions, and reads the *Vanjara Pothi* against the other texts that stand as precursors to the Adi Granth. More broadly, Singh argues that this *pothi* reveals the important role that Vanjara Sikhs played as scribes and as guardians of highly valued texts. But Singh suggests that this text raises important questions about the social composition of the early Panth. While some Vanjara Sikhs enjoy considerable prominence in Sikh memory—such as Makhan Shah Labana, the supporter of Guru Tegh Bahadur, and the eminent scribe Bhai Mani Singh—the broader history of Vanjara Sikhs, especially Vanjara communities in central and south India, remains under-researched and under-appreciated.

With Louis Fenech's chapter, we move forward in time to assess the life and career of Bhai Nand Lal 'Goya'. As well as serving as the *mir munshi*, chief scribe, of Prince Muhammad Muazzam (the future emperor Bahadur Shah), Nand Lal was a scribe and renowned poet in the circle of Guru Gobind Singh. Although he was prominent in the cultural imagination of the Panth during the nineteenth century, Nand Lal remains an elusive figure who has received limited attention from Sikh studies scholars. Displaying the same close attention to language and the nuances of meaning that characterize the textual criticism pioneered by McLeod's work on Guru Nanak, Fenech reconstructs two Nand Lals. The first is the Nand Lal of history. As Fenech makes clear, reconstructing the historical Nand Lal is a tremendously challenging project, as the sources are limited and accounts of his life only began to be elaborated from the late eighteenth century. Fenech is sceptical of the value of these texts as accurate guides to the life of Nand Lal, preferring instead to tease out the biographical fragments contained in the Persian texts he authored.[11] Fenech handles these texts carefully but deftly, judiciously weighing what the terminology, idiom, and style of these texts reveal about their author. He then assesses the 'second' life of Nand Lal, assessing his posthumous reputation amongst the members of the eighteenth- and nineteenth-century Panth. He guides us through the large body of texts in which Nand Lal appears, figuring as a constant questioner of the tenth guru, Gobind Singh, engaging him on a wide range of issues from the Bhagavad Gita to the nature of Kaliyuga. Fenech suggests that both Nand Lal's Persian texts and these later references to Nand Lal were in wide circulation amongst Sikhs, who understood Nand Lal as a beloved disciple of the tenth guru. Fenech's reading of the two lives of Bhai Nand Lal 'Goya' is of particular significance because Nand Lal was a rare character, positioned at the interstices of the developing Sikh Panth and Mughal courtly culture.

Where the chapters by Singh and Fenech offer new vantage points on largely neglected aspects of the Sikh textual tradition, the next pair of chapters focus on the issue of caste. In a typically careful yet wide-ranging assessment, McLeod offers an overview of the place of caste within the scholarship on Sikhs and Sikhism. As ever, he is attentive to questions of language and translation, reflecting on the concepts that underpin the operation of social hierarchies in Sikhism. In particular, he highlights the limitations of the English word 'caste' as he explores the very distinct meaning of two key terms within South Asian understandings of social differentiation: *varan* and *jati*. He then outlines Sikh teachings on caste and summarizes the state of our knowledge of key Sikh castes: Jats, Ramgarhias, Dalits, Khatris, and Aroras. The final section of the chapter identifies future avenues for research, highlighting 10 key issues that require careful exploration if we are to assemble a richer assessment of the operation of caste within the Panth.

As McLeod emphasizes, caste has of course been pivotal in structuring understandings of South Asian communities and their histories since the advent of British rule, if not before. A substantial body of recent scholarship has revealed the profound extent to which British visions of Indian history were shaped by their Brahmanical informants and the ways in which the *varna* model of caste, which of course privileged Brahmans, was consolidated as the primary model of social organization under British rule. There has been a growing realization, however, amongst historians and anthropologists alike that the dominance of the varna model is profoundly problematic. In many regions, most notably Punjab itself, the pattern of caste relationships and the shape of social hierarchies diverge markedly from the Brahman–Kshatriya–Vaishya–Shudra model. Moreover, it is increasingly clear that various reformist religious movements and a range of social groups produced alternative readings of social organization as they rejected the authority of the four-fold varna division. This is most clear in the work of historians who work with Adivasi and Dalit communities. Ajay Skaria's outstanding *Hybrid Histories*, for example, rematerializes the Dangi's very different social vision and their particular understandings of colonialism, modernity, and history. In reconstructing this worldview, Skaria produces a new kind of history, one that works against traditional Western forms of historical narration and also against the dominant understandings of social organization produced from within Hinduism.[12]

John Webster's chapter in this volume explores the possibilities of producing a similarly new vision of Sikh history: a Dalit Sikh history. Webster, of course, is a pioneering historian of Dalit Christians and his 1992 volume on the history of Dalit Christians was a significant landmark in the developing Dalit historiography.[13] Webster moved beyond the narrow focus on evangelization and conversion to place the Dalitness of Dalit Christians at the heart of his narrative rather than privileging the perspectives of Christian missionaries and indigenous elites. Here Webster assesses whether such a Dalit-centred approach can be fruitful within the Sikh context. His chapter opens with a powerful assessment of the existing work on Dalit Sikhs, highlighting the ways in which 'Sikh history' approaches have marginalized the importance and experiences of the Dalits within the Panth. He then sketches a vision of a Dalit Sikh history, one which is based around the agency of Dalits, emphasizing their agency as historical actors who were able to contest their position in society and shape their own vision of the world. He also suggests that any convincing reading of Dalit Sikh history needs to recognize the centrality of conflict between caste groups in shaping Sikh history and he therefore attaches much greater weight to caste within the Panth than has been characteristic of the work produced by either social scientists or historians who work on Sikhism. Webster's chapter is a powerful reminder of the complexity of the Panth's internal social structure and of the social divisions and struggles that co-exist with the coherence provided by the guru's teaching. Most of all, however, it is a compelling challenge for those of us who work on Sikhism to be self-reflexive about the politics of our analytical strategies and to search for new ways to narrate Sikh history.

Where Webster highlights the changing position and status of Dalits under British rule, Ian Kerr's chapter is firmly fixed on the transformation of Punjab in the wake of the East India Company's annexation of the Lahore kingdom in 1849. Kerr uses a woodcut by a Punjabi artist from 1870 which shows a train standing at a station to read the broad cultural changes unleashed by the colonial state's pursuit of modernity. While this Punjabi artist's train, like the trains that were powerful instruments transforming the fabric of Punjab from the 1860s, was under the control of a British driver, it also depicts the broad cross-cultural engagement with the new modes of transport and communication that were so vital to the British imperial project. This image is, as Kerr shows, a potent symbol of the innovative social formations that emerged out of the encounter between the colonial state and Punjabi culture. While the woodcut was a well-established and popular genre by 1870, here it was not used to represent its 'traditional' subjects, the Sikh gurus and great heroes like Baba Dip Singh, but rather was extended to grapple with one of the key elements of the 'modernizing' forces that reshaped the material basis and cultural forms of life in Punjab between 1849 and 1947. Kerr reminds us that this modernizing project was underpinned by the highly unequal power relations that characterize colonialism: in other words, technologies like the railways, canals, and the telegraph were instruments that the British deployed in their efforts to assert their mastery over Punjab and its peoples.

Most important, Kerr stresses that these technologies were central in the transformation of space in Punjab. They provided new pathways through and across space, structured the dissemination of ideas and information, provided the vectors for the movement of migrants and microbes, and enabled the enactment of colonial authority. These new road systems, railway lines, canal networks, and telegraph lines were not only powerful sinews that connected markets and facilitated the movement of commodities, capital, and troops, but they also provided key structures for new forms of Punjabi intellectual production and political organization. In the final third of the nineteenth century, the emergent Punjabi public sphere roared into life as printing presses sprang up in all of the region's significant urban centres. These presses were fed by an increasing flow of news and a rekindled enthusiasm amongst Punjabis for critical reflections on local politics, religious practice, the nature of community identity, the value of Western knowledge, and the nature of colonial rule. Kerr's chapter provides us with a rich appreciation of the material and cultural basis for this period of extraordinary intellectual energy.

This critical reflection on the period of colonial rule is extended by Ian Catanach's examination of Sikh responses to the plague. A pioneering social historian of western India and a leading authority on the history of disease in South Asia, Catanach here uses the plague as a prism through which he can read the development of Sikh politics. In this chapter, he shows that there seems to have been a significant connection between the impact of epidemic disease and political change, particularly between the consequences of the plague and the agitations against the Colonization Bill during 1906–7. More broadly, Catanach's chapter is of significant historiographical value because it interrogates some of the assumptions that govern Sikh and Punjab studies. While the substantial regional

historiographies that have re-emerged as a key feature of work on South
Asian history are incredibly rich, they can begin to reify the supposedly
unique characteristics of any region. In this case, historians of Punjab
and scholars of Sikhism have not engaged consistently with the patterns
of other regional histories, nor do they use their work on Punjab to
engage in the broader debates within South Asian history as a whole.
Here Catanach adopts the position of an outsider to urge Sikh studies
to draw a wider methodological and theoretical net, suggesting that it
could be enriched by a greater willingness to draw upon the work of
subaltern studies and feminist historians, as well as the insights produced
by sociologists and anthropologists. His chapter suggests, moreover,
that moments of crisis—which can be environmental, agrarian, or
epidemiological crises as well as political crises—provide particularly
valuable insights into the nature of social formations and religious
traditions, including those of Sikhism.

Himadri Banerjee's chapter addresses many of the themes that these
first six chapters deal with: the relationship between texts and community
formation, the politics of caste and social hierarchies, the role of
communication in shaping social and religious institutions, and the place
of British rule within the transformation of Sikh communities. In Banerjee's
chapter, however, we travel out of Punjab, to the south and to the east—
to Orissa. Banerjee here provides a detailed synoptic history of place of
Orissa in Sikh history, reconstructing the reach of Sikh networks into
eastern India and the development of a Sikh minority community within
the plural, cultural, and religious worlds of Orissa. Banerjee's chapter is
of historiographical significance for three reasons. First, in rematerializing
the history of Sikhs in Orissa, he builds upon his pathbreaking research on
Sikhs and Sikhism beyond Punjab, drawing attention to a relatively unknown
chapter in the broad history of the Panth. Second, he demonstrates the
ways in which Sikhs in Orissa were incorporated into the world of Oriya
popular culture; and third, he highlights some of the strategies they used
to find a space for themselves in this non-Punjabi world. These are issues
that the scholarship on the Sikh diaspora in the late nineteenth and
twentieth centuries has begun to deal with, but here we have a fascinating
study of the culture of mobile and migrant Sikhs within South Asia.
Banerjee is aware that the material he is handling is sensitive, as it reveals
the very real geographic reach and cultural diversity of the Panth in pre-
British times; but he is committed to recording this fascinating history, a
story that adds much to our understanding of the texture of Sikh history.

Banerjee's interest in the extended spatial domain of Sikh history establishes a concern that is carried through the final three chapters in the collection. In my own chapter, I explore the ambivalent and contested relationship between Bhangra and both Punjabi and Sikh identities. Although Bhangra performers have become visible and influential embodiments of a certain type of Punjabi identity within global culture during the last two decades, I suggest that the equation of Bhangra with Punjabi-ness originally emerged in the wake of Partition. Prior to this, Bhangra was a highly localized performative tradition that had developed as an important element of the rural culture of the Sialkot-Gurdaspur region. In tracing the place of Bhangra in the projection of *Punjabiyat* in newly independent India, this chapter highlights the ways in which this important form of cultural production was territorialized. I show, however, that the growth of a large Punjabi diasporic community in Britain from the 1950s sowed the seeds for the further transformation of Bhangra. The distinctive demography of Punjabi communities in major British urban centres such as London and Birmingham, together with the strong engagement between British South Asians and Britons from Afro-Caribbean backgrounds in the late 1970s and 1980s, created a cultural context where the sound, content, and style of Bhangra was radically re-invented. While British Punjabis retreated from this identification with blackness during the mid-1990s, the music of Alaap, Apache Indian, and Bally Sagoo drew large international audiences and circulated widely within the Punjabi diaspora. The chapter concludes by highlighting the hostility of some Sikhs to these new forms of Bhangra and the efforts of other Sikh leaders to shore up elements of religious and artistic 'tradition' in the face of the cross-cultural engagements implicit within contemporary Bhangra.

There is no doubt that music has played an important role in the production of both Punjabi identities and has provided some of the important connections that have linked mobile Punjabis to their homeland. In the 1980s and 1990s, the primary medium for these cultural flows was that most vital technology for South Asian soundscapes: the cassette.[14] In the late 1990s, CDs began to compete with cassettes and the internet became an increasingly significant means of connection. N. G. Barrier's chapter focuses on the role of the internet in shaping debates over Sikh politics, history, and religion. Barrier, of course, is the leading expert on the history of Sikh print culture and the use of the printing press as a political tool in colonial Punjab. Here Barrier highlights the Sikhs' enthusiastic embrace of the internet, as his chapter begins by documenting the various types of web-pages and list servers that are used to produce and disseminate information about Sikhism. The bulk of the chapter focuses on one particular list, 'Sikh Diaspora'. This has emerged as a particularly significant forum where Sikhs (in Punjab itself and the diaspora) and non-Sikhs engage with each other. On 'Sikh Diaspora', they are able to share news reports relating to the global Panth, explicate important elements of the gurus' teachings, and discuss key elements of Sikh culture and history. Barrier assesses the nature of some of these exchanges, stressing the important role of this new medium in connecting Sikhs across a wide range of locations. He also stresses the importance of this list as a forum where Sikh studies scholars, particularly Barrier himself, Hew McLeod, Doris Jakobsh, and Pashaura Singh, participate in discussions and share their ideas with a wide range of Sikh individuals who articulate a diverse array of opinions. Barrier's chapter is a valuable contribution to our understanding of the connections between communications and community formation, and suggests the value of the internet as an archive for scholarship on contemporary Sikh community.

The volume ends with an illustrated chapter produced by Amrit and Rabindra Kaur Singh. Highly regarded British contemporary artists, the Singh twins have exhibited their work widely in North America, the United Kingdom, and India. While the twins resist the tendency to be read as simply 'ethnic' artists within a broader British art scene that remains strongly rooted in Euro-American visual culture, there is no doubt that their work is grounded in the aesthetic traditions of South Asia. In their chapter, Amrit and Rabindra discuss the development of their work over the past 12 years, reflecting on its relationship to South Asian arts (especially the Mughal miniature); but they also locate their artistic output within the contexts of the British art world, the cultural challenges facing South Asian Britons, and their own personal concerns. In discussing a wide range of their works, the twins explore the style, themes, and iconography that have become characteristic of their work and reflect on the ways in which their repertoire is conditioned by their Sikh heritage. Ultimately the paintings of Amrit and Rabindra Kaur Singh are a potent reminder of the power and flexibility of Sikh artistic production and of the close relationship between Punjabi creative arts and the rich visual cultures of South Asia as a whole.

It is very apposite to conclude this volume with the twins' exploration of the visual arts for two reasons. First, the art of the Singh twins is a compelling manifestation of the complexity, richness, and sophistication of Sikh culture and history. While their ability to stage a productive dialogue between long-established South Asian aesthetic conventions and the world of contemporary art gives their work a distinctive quality, their humane perspectives on family, contemporary culture, and global politics reflect the ethical and spiritual basis of Sikhism. For scholars of Sikhism, their work has particular value when read as a form of diasporic cultural production. The paintings of the Singh twins are powerful statements about the negotiation of Sikh and South Asian identities outside South Asia. We encounter arresting juxtapositions of kilts and turbans, William Wallace and Maharaja Ranjit Singh. We also learn about the struggles that are frequently embedded in the experience of diasporic communities. In 'Wedding Jange II', for example, the neighbour's newspaper recounts legal battles over the status of the turban within the United Kingdom and the twins' own battle over their degrees. That same painting suggests the kinds of cross-cultural engagements that are commonplace within the diaspora, as the neighbours are intrigued by the wedding party while the British Punjabis themselves have embraced certain elements of 'Western culture', including the video camera that is capturing the proceedings. At a fundamental level, this image also reminds us of the ways in which British Punjabis have transformed Britain itself: under the Liverpool skyline the road becomes patterned like a Persian carpet and this northern city bears a discernible Punjabi imprint. To my mind, there is no more powerful representation of the texture of contemporary diasporic Sikh life.

Second, the Singh twins' discussion of the relationship between the arts and Sikhism suggests some fertile avenues for future research and critical reflection. But any new work on Sikhism and arts, as in so many areas in Sikh studies, will be produced in the wake of the pathbreaking work of Hew McLeod. In 1991, McLeod produced a pioneering study of representations of the Sikh past in Punjabi bazaar prints.[15] Although the volume opened with a slightly apologetic introduction where McLeod justified his focus on an art form that was unabashedly popular, *Popular Sikh Art* stands as an extremely important contribution to South Asian historiography. It not only provides a valuable snapshot of Punjabi bazaar art around 1990, but embeds this late twentieth-century form of cultural production within both the long-established artistic traditions of Punjabi and a distinctively Sikh popular culture. In so many areas of inquiry within Sikh studies—the teachings of the gurus, the study of prescriptive texts, the history of diasporic communities, popular understandings of the Sikh past, and the history of the Khalsa itself—the story is the same: Hew McLeod either opened that field of critical scholarship or has produced a foundational assessment of an issue and its attendant conceptual problems. The challenge that lies ahead is to submit this existing scholarship, including McLeod's own landmark works, to critical scrutiny as well as developing new ways of imagining the Sikh past. The challenges and possibilities that lie ahead are tremendous, but we are building on a substantial and dense foundation of scholarship, much of which was laid by the efforts of one scholar: Hew McLeod. The chapters that follow mark his enormous contribution to Sikh studies and build upon the many insights that he has offered since the mid-1960s.

Notes

1. Tom G. Kessinger, *Vilyatpur 1848–1968: Social and Economic Change in a North Indian Village* (Berkeley: University of California Press, 1974).

2. N. G. Barrier, 'The Formulation and Enactment of the Punjab Alienation of Land Bill', *Indian Economic and Social History Review* 2, 2 (1965), pp. 145–65; 'Mass Politics and the Punjab Congress in the Pre-Gandhian Era', *Journal of Indian History* 50, 149 (1972), pp. 459–70; *The Sikhs and their Literature: A Guide to Tracts, Books, and Periodicals, 1849–1919* (Delhi: Manohar, 1970).

3. Kenneth W. Jones, 'Communalism in the Punjab: the Arya Samaj Contribution', *Journal of Asian Studies* 28, 1 (1968), pp. 39–54; 'Ham Hindu Nahin: Arya-Sikh Relations 1877–1905', *Journal of Asian Studies* 32, 3 (1973), pp. 457–75.

4. Indu Banga, *Agrarian System of the Sikhs: Late Eighteenth and Early Nineteenth Century* (New Delhi: Manohar, 1978). J. S. Grewal and Indu Banga (trans. and eds), *Early Nineteenth Century Panjab: From Ganesh Das's Char bagh-i-Panjab* (Amritsar: Department of History, Guru Nanak University, 1975). J. S. Grewal and Indu Banga (eds), *Maharaja Ranjit Singh and His Times* (Amritsar: Department of History, Guru Nanak Dev University, 1980).

5. Mark Juergensmeyer, *Religion as Social Vision: The Movement against Untouchability in 20th-century Punjab* (Berkeley: University of California Press, 1982).

6. Harjot Oberoi, *The Construction of Religious Boundaries: Culture, Identity and Diversity in the Sikh Tradition* (Delhi: Oxford University Press, 1994).

7. Gurinder Singh Mann, *The Goindval Pothis: The Earliest Extant Source of the Sikh Canon* (Cambridge, Massachusetts: Department of Sanskrit and Indian Studies, 1996); *The Making of Sikh Scripture* (New York: Oxford University Press, 2000). Pashaura Singh, *The Guru Granth Sahib: Canon, Meaning and Authority* (Delhi: Oxford University Press, 2000).

8. Jeevan Deol, 'Eighteenth Century Khalsa Identity: Discourse, Praxis and

Narrative', Christopher Shackle, Gurharpal Singh and Arvindpal Singh Mandair (eds), *Sikh Religion, Culture and Ethnicity* (Richmond: Curzon, 2001); 'Surdas: Poet and Text in the Sikh Tradition', *Bulletin of the School of Oriental and African Studies* 63, 2 (2000), pp. 169–93; 'The Minas and Their Literature', *Journal of the American Oriental Society* 118, 2 (1998), pp. 172–84. Louis E. Fenech, *Martyrdom in the Sikh Tradition: Playing the 'Game of Love'* (Delhi: Oxford University Press, 2000); 'Contested Nationalisms; Negotiated Terrains: the Way Sikhs Remember Udham Singh "Shahid" 1899–1940', *Modern Asian Studies* 36, 4 (2002), pp. 827–70.

9. N. Gerald Barrier and Verne A. Dusenbery (eds), *The Sikh Diaspora: Migration and the Experience beyond Punjab* (Delhi: Chanakya Publications, 1989). Parminder Bhachu, *Twice Migrants: East African Sikh Settlers in Britain* (London: Tavistock, 1985). Rashmere Bhatti and Verne A. Dusenbery (eds), *A Punjabi Sikh Community in Australia: from Indian Sojourners to Australian Citizens* (Woolgoolga: Woolgoolga Neighbourhood Centre, 2001). Verne Dusenbery, 'A Sikh Diaspora? Contested Identities and Constructed Realities', Peter van der Veer (ed.), *Nation and Migration: the Politics of Space in the South Asian Diaspora* (Philadelphia: University of Pennsylvania Press, 1995). Karen Isaksen Leonard, *Making Ethnic Choices: California's Punjabi Mexican Americans* (Philadelphia: Temple University Press, 1992). Darshan Singh Tatla, *The Sikh Diaspora: the Search for Statehood* (London: UCL Press, 1999).

10. Doris R. Jakobsh, *Relocating Gender in Sikh History: Transformation, Meaning and Identity* (Delhi: Oxford University Press, 2003). Nikky-Guninder Kaur Singh, *The Feminine Principle in the Sikh Vision of the Transcendent* (Cambridge: Cambridge University Press, 1993).

11. Fenech discounts the Punjabi texts attributed to Nand Lal, suggesting that they are the product of another Nand Lal who has been conflated with the Nand Lal who authored the Persian texts. See Louis E. Fenech, 'Bhai Nand Lal "Goya" and the Sikh Tradition', Pashaura Singh and N. G. Barrier (eds), *Sikhism and History* (New Delhi: Oxford University Press, 2004), pp. 111–34.

12. Ajay Skaria, *Hybrid Histories: Forests, Frontiers and Wildness in Western India* (Delhi: Oxford University Press, 1999).

13. John C. B. Webster, *The Dalit Christians: a History* (Delhi: Indian Society for Promoting Christian Knowledge, 1992).

14. Peter Manuel, *Cassette Culture: Popular Music and Technology in North India* (Chicago: University of Chicago Press, 1993).

15. W. H. McLeod, *Popular Sikh Art* (Delhi: Oxford University Press, 1991).

Hew McLeod and the Development of Sikh Studies

N. G. Barrier

This chapter provides an understanding of how modern Sikhism has evolved. Particular attention is paid to historical documents, changes in the colonial period, the varied yet intertwined experiences of Sikhs in the diaspora, and, finally, a concern for contemporary changes and issues facing both academicians and the Sikhs as a community. Woven into the narrative is a celebration of the life and works of Hew McLeod whose contributions have been invaluable to the study of Sikhism. This chapter also discusses and evaluates major themes and developments affecting Sikhs throughout the world. This discussion is built upon a rich history of evolving scholarly attention to Sikh tradition, personal life, and public activities. In a sense, it tries to project the responses to issues and sources generated over hundreds of years of Sikh experience.

It is fitting that this chapter takes into account the Singh Sabha project—particularly in the period from 1875 to 1920—that framed the meaning of Sikhism in a changing and modern world. Sikhs in the nineteenth century found themselves having to untangle the past and deal with pressing identity issues, to a large extent as a response to processes and ideas associated with colonialism. They worked in new structures, addressed Western constructs, and attempted both to consolidate the community as well as champion its interests in an expanding political system. In doing so, the Singh Sabhas produced the intellectuals, the institutions, and the documents that influence discussions of Sikh history and identity even today. That late nineteenth-century age of tracts and scholarship produced the Mohan Singh Vaids, the Ditt Singhs, and the Teja Singh Bhasaurs who rose to address perceived dangers confronting the Panth and whose pens produced so many influential statements of Sikh ideals. In their efforts to fortify Sikhism they were joined by institution builders such as Sundar Singh Majithia and scholars represented most notably by Kahan Singh Nabha. All of these influential leaders shared a sense of living through a pivotal point in history. Their efforts to communicate led to a new network of journals and newspapers as well as major institutions such as the Chief Khalsa Diwan and the Sikh Educational Conference.

In addition to raising questions that are still central for those of us interested in Sikhism, these unusual individuals have left us a rich documentary legacy. Without those records, we could not really understand the divisions and the spirit involved in the initial Sikh efforts to address tradition and the challenges of a rapidly changing world. On a personal note, in the late 1960s, Ken Jones and I spent a lot of time roaming the Punjab involved in an intellectual treasure hunt for documents, papers, and journals. Ken found a significant number and based his work on Hindu revivalism and the Arya Samaj on those scattered records that he brought together. I had a much easier time with Sikh history, because Sikhs had already done the job for me. Mohan Singh Vaid and especially Bhai Takht Singh preserved virtually every printed document from approximately 1890 onward. The joy of opening the almirahs and warehouse doors at the Sikh Kanya Mahavidyalaya in Ferozepur remains with me to this day, and the documents from there are now preserved along with sister collections in Patiala.

In the post-1947 period, a new generation of Sikh specialists grew up in east Punjab. Most notable was Ganda Singh, the editor of *Panjab Past and Present* and a major scholar. He preserved documents and books, and held on to them tightly. For fledgling students such as myself, the road to understanding Sikhism ran through his personal library and many cups of tea. Again, without Ganda Singh's fearless scholarship and academic standards, mirrored in many ways by excellent colleagues such as Fauja Singh, the scholarly legacy of the period would have been less impressive. Newer scholars joined them, such as S. S. Bal and J. S. Grewal, who in turn expanded Sikh studies in Chandigarh and Amritsar. Mohinder Singh continues the tradition at the National Institute of Panjab Studies in New Delhi, as do noted scholars such as Harish Puri and Kashmir Singh.

Then came Hew McLeod, initially as a missionary scholar, but very soon moving away toward secular scholarship. From the 1960s onward, much of Sikh scholarship and historical understanding of the community has had its roots in Hew's work and influence. He has written a personal and intellectual account of his journeys, scholarship, and often controversies in his *Discovering the Sikhs*.[1] Like Hew, many of us starting out in the same period were 'accidental scholars' in the sense that we did not set out to work on the Sikhs but rather, because of opportunity and documents, moved in that direction. Each has his own story. Mark Juergensmeyer's work on South Asia, and Punjab in particular, was built on a personal interest in religion, non-violence, and ethnicity, and a concern with the place and experience of the downtrodden.[2] Ian Kerr developed a doctoral programme based on understanding nineteenth-century urban Punjab, which led him to discussing Sikh history, while never giving up interest in his first intellectual love: communications and especially the railroads.[3] Personally, I discovered the Sikhs because of the persistence of Nahar Singh M. A., who finally convinced me to make a midnight train trip to Ferozepur. That experience with the treasure troves of the Takht Singh collection, along with the sudden opening of the Home Political Files in the National Archives (which lasted at that juncture only a few months), created an opportunity to blend the Sikhs' views of their experience with those of the colonial power and I thus began a three-decade exploration of things Sikh.

The development of Sikh studies was not only shaped by these documents, but also by the changing institutional base for Sikh and Indian studies in North America. The 1976 Sikh conference set a standard for bringing together scholars and informed members of the community. The fruitful sessions resulted from Mark Juergensmeyer's entrepreneurial work with the Ghadar project[4] and other efforts in the Bay area, combined with the inputs of Narinder Singh Kapany and the Sikh Foundation. This landmark event was followed by more conferences as Sikh studies developed as a distinctive area of expertise within the broader world of South Asian scholarship, a development that encouraged several North American Sikh communities and universities to develop chairs in Sikh studies. Initially, departments and universities adopted a positive approach to Sikh studies, often seeing the nascent programmes as part of a widening network of area studies programmes. Soon, however, the early cooperation between scholars and the local Sikhs, who often funded such activities, gave way to suspicion and sometimes open conflict. The primary reason was the growth of Sikh militancy in the Punjab, which in turn heightened diasporic Sikh concerns with protecting traditions and maintaining control of institutions.

The year 1984, of course, was the tipping point. After that, for at least a decade Hew McLeod, Harjot Oberoi, and other scholars came under heated attack. Pashaura Singh soon became a target, as did Piar Singh. Conferences became battlegrounds, often with picketing, threats of violence, and even police presence. An even more serious round of conflict occurred among Sikhs themselves as those supporting particular political agendas, especially the call for Khalistan, often took over the gurdwaras and local institutions. Things have now cooled a bit, but the damage done to Chairs and Sikh studies programmes in Vancouver, Toronto, New York, and Ann Arbor has been appreciable. Similarly, in the United Kingdom, interest in Sikh and Punjab studies has waxed and waned, often without a significant institutional base or fiscal commitment. Nevertheless, new scholarship continues to emerge and Sikh studies gains energy from those recent enterprises that have been more successful, most notably the programmes at Santa Barbara, Riverside and Hofstra University. Community-supported programmes for teaching Sikh history and Punjabi have popped up again, but the long-term success of such ventures remains to be seen.

Several Sikh studies scholars have either trained with Hew or have been associated with him on a regular basis. Mark Juergensmeyer and Ainslie Embree participated in the first Sikh conference in California, and have maintained close contact with Hew through the programmes at Santa Barbara and Columbia University. John Webster has been associated with Hew for decades. Hew helped launch Pashaura Singh and Louis E. Fenech toward distinguished careers of teaching and research. Hew's relationship with Verne Dusenbery, Ian Kerr, and me similarly goes back almost to the beginning of his adventures in things Sikh. Shinder Thandi represents the significant group of Sikh and Punjab scholars in the United Kingdom, most of who could not attend the conference because of exigencies of cost and timing. The twin artists Amrit Kaur Singh and Rabindra Kaur Singh bring with them a unique blend of creative arts and historical reinterpretation. From New Zealand, Andrew Major and Ian Catanach have been involved in Punjab studies for some time. Rashmere Bhatti from Australia represents the new and refreshing blend of activist-academic concerns spreading among Sikhs. The successor to Hew at Otago who made these meetings possible, Tony Ballantyne became involved in Punjab and Sikh studies while an undergraduate at the University of Otago before going on to advanced study at Cambridge.

Sometimes those of us with ties to Hew McLeod are identified as a cohesive group intent on undermining Sikh tradition and falsely using 'Western' concepts in trying to understand Sikhism. Although these charges are false and do not take into account the divergence of questions and use of material, in a sense we all accept the McLeod badge with a sense of thanks and honour. The rigorous scholarship and the cultural sensitivity reflected in Hew McLeod's work have been a beacon to us that functions as a benchmark as we go about our work as researchers and teachers.

As scholars of Sikhism, we are now facing much more diverse and nuanced environment. In light of the experience in the West, diasporic Sikhs have begun to assume leadership in evaluating the nature of Sikhism and have been at the forefront of assessing the nature of Sikh tradition. The global reach of the Panth and the international attention to Sikhism over the past two decades has once again forced Sikh intellectuals and public leaders to become respondents and spokespersons in the public sphere. And as happened over a century ago, Western paradigms, assumptions, and political agendas are helping frame how Sikhs look at themselves. This in turn has helped foster new political patterns and an intense examination of the interaction between religious belief and academic study. Within this context, the question of identity remains a central concern. Sikhs struggle among themselves and against outsiders in public arenas and new communication networks, such as the internet, over the nature of Sikh identity and the boundaries of the community.

So it is not surprising that the interfaces between scholarship and the Sikh community have a unifying theme in earlier Sikh studies conferences: it will be so here as well. Although sometimes central to debate, the issue of 'insiders versus outsiders' in Sikh studies has now been placed in a broader context that includes personal belief, methodology, and underlying assumptions of discourse. Many scholars of Sikhism have already been engaging a range of Sikh individuals in formal settings, such as the 1996 Michigan conference on Sikh identity, in addition to participating in a range of discussion groups, list serves, and even in the judicial process as expert witnesses. We are also aware of how the tone and nature of exchanges can be influenced by an event or a set of responses to traumatic experiences, such as the events of 1984, in much the same way that American politics has moved in new and sometimes disturbing directions since 9/11.

Pashaura Singh's two books on the Guru Granth Sahib and the formulation of canon evoked few attacks, a response quite dissimilar to the often violent rhetoric concerning his dissertation.[5] Similarly, Lou Fenech's potentially controversial assessments relating to changing Sikh views of martyrdom went almost unnoticed.[6] But since December 2003, that seems to have changed. Specific organizations and individuals have launched various attacks on Doris Jakobsh's book, charging her with unprofessional conduct and an anti-Sikh attitude once again associated with the 'McLeodian' views of Indian tradition.[7] Following the pattern of trying to mobilize academics and university administrations that was used against Harjot Oberoi, Hew McLeod, and Pashaura Singh, a small group claiming to represent all Sikhs sent resolutions and documents to Jakobsh's home institution, the University of Waterloo. Most recently, in the spring of 2005, the University of California-Riverside's search for a new Chair in Sikh studies has again evoked a mobilization against the 'McLeodians' and especially Pashaura Singh. The same pattern persists, with public denunciations and personal attacks. Apparently none of the senior Sikh scholars competing for the chair fits the ideological and political expectations of the vocal opponents. Whether any academic programme can generate and fill a Sikh studies position in such a climate remains doubtful.

However, the most intense conflicts between a particular religious community and Western scholars have involved Hindus, not Sikhs. In the last two years, NRI organizations have combined with political activists to denounce scholars, some of whom have even received warnings of physical retaliation over their allegedly 'anti-Hindu' research. The size and organization of the Hindu community in North America and its close ties with radical groups in South Asia help account for the marked differences between the responses of Hindus and Sikhs to perceived threat. Also, the widespread networks espousing Hindu nationalism and events such as the controversy over the Babri Masjid and the Gujarat killings fuel great discontent. Western specialists have become embroiled in such struggles as part of battles over key religious symbols or because their work has been associated with alleged insensitivity toward Hinduism in Europe and North America.

Such encounters point out lessons for Sikh scholars engaging with groups and institutions in the Sikh diaspora. Our choice of words matters, as Sikhs are sensitive to ways in which the community is represented. Probably a greater danger for scholars is being seen as insensitive to evolving Sikhism. Correcting a record or presenting an alternative explanation is generally acceptable, but not an insistence that our methodology and worldview are superior and should become norms. As one Hindu scholar noted in print and during a panel discussion at the American Academy of Religion, 'we do not care about this criticism or that, or a comment on our gods, but we do resent deeply the assumption that academic paradigms and a Western worldview are only the correct ones, and that our beliefs and understandings are second-rate or worse.' Ultimately, of course, there are limits to compromise and efforts to reach common ground. Thus far, the continuing efforts of scholars such as Hew McLeod and Pashaura Singh to engage with opponents has done little to resolve fundamental differences in assumptions and worldviews.

Sikhs struggle with these issues in meetings and in cyberspace, and we should too. Personally, this has meant that over the last year, I have been rethinking my presuppositions and how I handle documents. The Singh Sabha period involved many complex issues and conflicting views, and while ultimately assessments must be made, one should be careful. Specifically, I sometimes have gone too far in casting developments in terms of power struggles and political machinations, although the polemics in papers and tracts support such a slant. I forgot, and will highlight in future research, the fact that before every major *diwan*, Sikhs gathered sometimes for a whole day to pray, listen to *gurbani* and music, and meditate. Trying to understand the most accurate context and communicate the meaning of an event is difficult, but it should be possible.

Let me share one experience that raises questions and puts interaction between academics and Sikh individuals in perspective. Pashaura Singh, Nikky Singh, Arvind Mandir, Doris Jakobsh, and I attended a small conference on Sikhs and inter-faith dialogue in Birmingham, October 2003. At the outset, it looked like yet another academic enterprise, and but it quickly moved from a set of academic position papers to a happening, an exciting and intense exchange of ideas and feelings that proved uplifting and challenging. Perhaps it was one of those unique situations coloured by the constant inputs of Sikhs, both scholars and public figures, interested less in making points than in expanding a base of mutual understanding. Certainly contributing to the quality and tone was the role of a local (Sikh) individual of note, Baba Sahibji Mohinder Singh, head of the Guru Nanak Sewak Nishkam Jatha. He opened and closed sessions, all the while providing funds and floods of sustenance, which were happily showered upon us by youths immersed in a culture of service, *sewa*. He participated in all discussions, bringing over seventy years of wisdom, personal experience on the world stage, and thoughtful ideas to the dialogue.

But I doubt that this was just a one-off affair, because I think all of us who interact regularly with members of the Sikh community, either directly or in discussion groups, have had similar experiences. Delightful interactions with informed and responsive Sikh individuals involve both teaching and learning from all sides. My essay on the Sikh internet experience discusses such dynamics in more detail. Striving for meaning and developing common bonds takes work, but I am convinced it is a goal well worth pursuing.

Feelings and scholarship, learning and teaching, role models and friendship—that brings us back in a circle to where I began some time ago, back to the person we respect and love, Hew McLeod. Perhaps the sharpest critics of Hew and his alleged group of conspirators have a point. We do not think alike, but we all have been influenced by the academic style, the wisdom, and the courage of Hew McLeod. Personally, without his counsel and criticism, I would have made grievous errors and acted even more impetuously than I often do. I know everyone has their Hew stories, and I will share in this chapter two stories that are burnt into my consciousness. Many years ago, Harjot Oberoi, Hew, and I found ourselves in a panel session at the American Academy of Religion. There we were confronted by militant Sikhs. After a very tense panel discussion, we were invited to a party where the attacks came fast and furious. Just recovering from his stroke, Hew argued points valiantly, but the charges and manipulation of facts came fast and caught all of us somewhat by surprise. Margaret McLeod jumped in and shamed her hosts as being unfair and inhospitable (she had learned much about Punjab culture during her sojourn in India). Harjot then got several of the antagonists in a back room and denounced them roundly, as one can only do in Punjabi. A fascinating evening, reflecting both the hospitality of Sikhs but also the poisonous mixture of religion and politics that inflamed discourse at that time.

Both these instances reflect Hew's central role in how ideas and discussions have been framed in the world of Sikh studies over the last thirty-five years. This volume celebrates his life's work and we can only hope that our scholarship and our commitments measure up in some small way to who he is and the meaning it has for all of us.

Notes

1. W. H. McLeod, *Discovering the Sikhs* (Delhi: Permanent Black, 2004).
2. Mark Juergensmeyer, *Religious Rebels in the Punjab: The Social Vision of Untouchables* (New Delhi: Ajanta, 1988). Also noteworthy has been Mark's

contribution to the study and preservation of documents on the Ghadar party. A short bibliography of his research in that area is in an excellent new bibliography, Rajwant Singh Chilana, *International Bibliography of Sikh Studies* (Dordrecht: Springer, 2005).

3. Kerr's dissertation focussed on Lahore and Amritsar, and he subsequently contributed several articles and chapters on the Sikhs. Again, a full record is in the Chilana bibliography.

4. Juergensmeyer, 'The International Heritage of the Ghadar Party, A Survey of Sources', N. G. Barrier and Harbans Singh (eds), *Punjab Past and Present: Essays in Honor of Dr Ganda Singh* (Patiala: Panjabi University Press, 1976). Also, 'Ghadar Syndrome', Juergensmeyer and Barrier, *Sikh Studies*, pp. 173–90.

5. Pashaura Singh, *The Guru Granth Sahib: Canon, Meaning, and Authority* (New Delhi: Oxford University Press, 2000); *The Bhagats of the Guru Granth Sahib: Sikh Self-Definition and the Bhagat Bani* (New Delhi: Oxford University Press, 2003).

6. Louis E. Fenech, *Martyrdom in the Sikh Tradition: Playing the 'Game of Love'* (New Delhi: Oxford University Press, 2000).

7. Doris R. Jakobsh, *Relocating Gender in Sikh History: Transformation, Meaning and Identity* (New Delhi: Oxford University Press, 2003).

Vanjara Pothi: A New Source in the Formation of the Sikh Canon

Pashaura Singh

> This Granth is a copy of Fateh Chand's Granth, which is a copy of the Pushkar Granth. The Pushkar Granth has been corrected by comparing it with the Great Granth (*vadda granth*), which was inscribed by Gurdas Bhalla at the dictation of the Fifth Guru. A Granth corrected against the Great Granth becomes correct (*sudh*). Even if someone still wants to correct one's text, one should do so by comparing it with Jagana Brahmin's Granth. Jagana Brahmin's Granth is more correct than others, and the Pushkar Granth is also corrected against Jagana Brahmin's text.[1]
>
> Adi Granth manuscript (1692)

The primary aim of textual study of the Sikh scripture is to reconstruct its history by addressing a fundamental question: how did the text of the Adi Granth come into being? By doing so, one can come to understand the redaction process that was at work behind the whole operation of formulating a canonical text of the Adi Granth. One can also come to determine the scribal errors or the introduction of both intentional and unintentional textual changes. In the context of the present discussion, the term 'canon' has two meanings—norm and list—both of which connote definitive and authoritative writings. A canon not only distinguishes between what is to be accepted and what is to be rejected but also differentiates between two kinds of scriptural authority in a religious tradition. We can characterize this difference in terms of absolute and relative authority: the absolute authority of the canonical scriptures over and against the relative authority of other works from the same tradition.[2] Thus the concept of a canon may be defined in terms of the element added to the text by a religious community—sacredness, authority, value, prestige, and so on.[3]

Sikh tradition maintains that the fifth guru, Arjan (1563–1606), produced the 'first canonical text' of the Adi Granth in 1604.[3] The manuscript bearing this date is still in existence at Kartarpur, in Jalandhar district of Punjab. That is why it is commonly known as the Kartarpur bir ('recension') of the Adi Granth. The manuscript evidence has also brought to light another recension that was prepared in 1610, during the period of Guru Hargobind (1595–1644). It is popularly known as Lahori bir because it was found at a shrine in Lahore. The Lahore recension differs from the Kartarpur version only in its concluding section. It has a different order, sometimes ending with the saloks ('couplets' or 'stanzas') of Kabir and Farid, and sometimes with the panegyrics by the Sikh bards in praise of the gurus. In 1642, a Sikh named Banno traditionally prepared another recension of the Adi Granth at Khara Mangat in Gujrat district. The Banno bir consists of the Kartarpur text plus some unauthorized additions. In the last decades of the seventeenth century, the tenth guru, Gobind Singh (1666–1708), added the works of his father, Guru Tegh Bahadur (1621–75), to the original compilation at Damdama Sahib in Anandpur and closed the canon. This final text is popularly known as the Damdama bir, a version that provides the text of the modern Guru Granth Sahib.[4]

Recent research has made us aware of the two divergent views on the process of canon formation in the Sikh tradition. The first view is primarily based upon the traditional sources. According to this view, when Guru Nanak (1469–1539) lived at Kartarpur ('Creator's Abode') for the last two decades of his life, there came into being a single codex of his writings, which he bestowed on his successor Guru Angad (1504–52). The updating of this early scriptural corpus continued under the care of successive gurus, through Guru Arjan's 'first' canonical text to Guru Gobind Singh's 'final' closing of the Sikh canon. Thus a 'mother tradition' of sacred writings had flourished 'under the watchful eyes' of the Sikh gurus.[5] The transmission of the bani ('divine Word') was, therefore, a linear process that began with a single source and then diversified into separate textual strands with minor variations that we encounter in the available manuscripts of the Adi Granth. In this context, Gurinder Singh Mann makes the following assertion: 'Because these manuscripts grew out of a single source, there are no substantive variations within their contents.'[6] He focuses on the evolution of the Sikh sacred text from the pre-canonical stage, represented by the Guru Har Sahai pothi ('volume'), the Goindval pothis, and the Guru Nanak Dev University MS 1245, through the Kartarpur pothi, to the final compilation of the Adi Granth by Guru Gobind Singh in the last decades of the seventeenth century.[7] Mann accepts the authenticity of the Kartarpur recension but maintains that the 'issue of the [Kartarpur] *pothi's* contents, however, is open to debate'.[8]

The second view lays emphasis upon the development of 'independent' textual traditions in different geographical areas in isolation from one another in the process of repeated copying and correction over generations of scribal activity. They are distinguished especially by different sets of readings, but also by other features, including orthographic and grammatical peculiarities. For instance, certain early manuscripts such as MS 1245 and the Bahoval pothi display all kinds of variant readings that must have originally come from different oral repertoires of the bani used in a singing tradition. Not surprisingly, Piar Singh emerged as an advocate of the second view of canon formation in the Sikh tradition. He stressed the development of the sacred text through a complex series of manuscripts until eventually it finds finality in the Damdama recension of the Adi Granth. He was primarily driven by the quest to identify the original bir that had been prepared by Bhai Gurdas at the behest of Guru Arjan. He emphasized independent collections and sporadic compilations that throw 'a flood of light on the proclivities—preferences, insights, and modalities—of their compilers'.[9] Following a 'sceptical approach' in his analysis, Piar Singh became obsessed with the idea of rejecting the authenticity of the Kartarpur *bir* through the extensive use of manuscript evidence even though he was not able to get the opportunity to examine that manuscript personally. More recently, Jeevan Deol has followed Piar Singh's lead to offer his analysis of the manuscripts of the Adi Granth as follows: 'The earliest manuscripts appear to be independent compilations, including of course the Kartarpur text.'[10] This approach is largely based upon the works of scholars working on the oral and written transmission of contemporaneous north Indian devotional literature of both *nirguna* ('without attributes') and *saguna* ('with attributes') schools of thought.[11] There was, however, no check from any central authority against the innovative tendencies in the Bhakti literature. It was a common practice among the rural bards to add verses in the names of celebrated Bhakti poets. The examples of such textual additions may be seen in the *Sursagar*[12] and the various Kabir collections. In fact, no other contemporary or near-contemporary religious compilation can be compared with the doctrinal consistency and complexity of the Adi Granth structure.

These two approaches to understand the process of canon formation represent two extreme viewpoints. The major weakness of these approaches is that textual problems are dealt with in isolation, without any reference to Guru Arjan's overall editorial perspective, by means of which he produced the first canonical text of the Adi Granth in 1604. In order to arrive at a more balanced perspective, we need to look at the making of Sikh scripture as the result of a 'collaborative approach' based upon the 'theory of working-drafts' prepared under the supervision of Guru Arjan.[13] This is an approach that duly acknowledges the role played by other human actors in the complex process of canon formation. In this context, Bhai Gurdas is universally regarded as Guru Arjan's amanuensis in the making of the scripture. His extended visits to Varanasi and Agra were intended to study the various conventions of the Sanskritic learning. His 39 ballads and a series of Braj poems clearly indicate his background knowledge of Indian scriptural traditions and philosophical systems. Moreover, there was Jagana Brahmin, a resident of Agra, who had his own training in the study of Sanskrit and Hindu scriptures. He was a devout follower of Guru Arjan and a scribe of repute for 'correct' copies of the Adi Granth.[14] Thus both of them were well versed in the various conventions of the Sanskrit literature, Braj bhasha, and the Indian literary traditions. In addition, tradition also records the names of four other scribes—Bhai Sant Das, Bhai Haria, Bhai Sukha, and Bhai Mansa Ram—who were equally involved in the making of Sikh scripture.[15] Incidentally, there are at least four different handwritings discernible at different places, although the major portion of the Kartarpur bir is by the primary scribe. Thus the preparation of the scripture was the result of teamwork under the direct supervision of Guru Arjan at Ramsar in the central place of Amritsar.

The Evidence of Pre-canonical Texts

The process of the formation of the Sikh canon began with the use of Guru Nanak's hymns in Sikh liturgy, originating during the later years of his life when he settled down at Kartarpur (now in Pakistan) as the head of a nascent Sikh Panth ('community').[16] These hymns were committed to memory by his first disciples, who passed them on to the next generation through oral transmission of a singing tradition. It is no wonder that

Guru Nanak himself wrote these down in a pothi in the newly emerging Gurmukhi script, that is, a script of business shorthand (lande/mahajani) that he undoubtedly used as a professional Khatri. Originally, Guru Nanak's pothi was intended as an aide-mémoire, a mnemonic device to facilitate the memorization of his inspired utterances by singers and the early Sikhs. This was a common practice in north India among the professional singers—to prepare repertoires for their musical performances.[17] In fact, the initial impetus for the preparation of this original pothi must have been to preserve the bani as a legacy for future generations. Later on, the preservation of the written tradition became popular as a devotional activity within the newly emerging religious community. Thus oral and written transmission of the bani have taken place simultaneously within the Sikh tradition since the last years of Guru Nanak's life at Kartarpur. Guru Angad further refined the Gurmukhi script for recording the compilation of the Guru's hymns and composed 62 saloks, some of which are found independently recorded in the Guru Har Sahai pothi.[18]

Recent research on the two available copies of the Goindval pothis has shown the pre-canonical stage of the evolving Sikh scriptural tradition. By establishing the traditional understanding skilfully, Gurinder Singh Mann regards these volumes as the earliest extant source of the Sikh canon, whereas Pritam Singh does not subscribe to this viewpoint.[19] In his analysis of the Ahiyapur pothi, Pritam Singh has strongly rejected the so-called 'borrowing theory', which states that Guru Arjan had to acquire the Goindval pothis from Mohan on loan for the purpose of the compilation of the first canonical text of the Adi Granth. Nevertheless, these two volumes must be regarded as based upon the original Goindval pothis or some other genuine sources. They are still the oldest manuscripts at our disposal. They contain the earlier forms of the compositions of the first three gurus and the bhagats as recorded by scribes prior to the compilation of the Adi Granth in 1604. Their structure reveals that the key organizing principle was based on ragas, keeping in mind the needs of the singers. The Gurmukhi script of these two volumes represents the early stage of orthography when vowel signs were not yet fully developed. However, these two volumes do not contain all the compositions of the first three gurus. Presumably, there were two additional volumes of the Goindval pothis that have not survived.

The index of the Kartarpur bir states that Guru Nanak's Japji was copied from the manuscript written in Guru Ram Das's own hand. Although no manuscript of his works has survived, Guru Ram Das (1534–81) frequently encouraged the professional class of scribes to write *gurbani* ('guru's utterances') for the purpose of distribution among the various Sikh *sangats* ('congregations').[20] Indeed, Guru Arjan inherited a large body of sacred verse when he assumed the office of guru in 1581. He was filled with admiration when he found 'priceless gems' and 'inexhaustible treasure' in what has been preserved by his predecessors (*'piu dade ka khajana'*).[21] In fact, the written works of his predecessors were the source of inspiration for Guru Arjan right from the beginning of his ministry. He carried the spiritual authority of Guru Nanak that provided him with every right to revise the received tradition in order to establish the final arrangement of the hymns in the canonical text.

In order to understand the preparation of the authoritative text during Guru Arjan's period, however, we need to have a fresh look at the available set of early manuscripts, including the 'Vanjara pothi'. This newly discovered manuscript belonging to the nomadic class of Sikh traders, known as Vanjaras, illuminates the complex textual process underlying the formation of the Sikh canon. In addition to MS 1245 and the Bahoval pothi, the Vanjara pothi must be regarded as one of the 'working drafts' prepared by different scribes under the direct supervision of Guru Arjan. In my earlier work, I have examined the place of MS 1245 in the process of canon formation in detail.[22] The Bahoval pothi is another such document, preserved in the library of Bhai Vir Singh Sahitya Sadan, New Delhi. In his description of this manuscript, Giani Mahan Singh treats it as a 'preliminary draft' that was used in the compilation of the Adi Granth.[23] Indeed, the volume is known for its variant readings and does not follow the standard sequence of compositions. It represents the fluid state from which the various structures of organization and the final form of various hymns emerged in the first canonical text of the Adi Granth. There are at least five handwritings to be seen in this pothi.[24]

For about four centuries, the Vanjara pothi has been a sacred possession in the hands of Vanjara leaders who trace the origins of their lineage to the period of the sixth guru, Hargobind.[25] Mahant Parsann Singh received it as a token of spiritual inheritance when he became the leader of approximately one million Vanjara Sikhs, roaming around the area of the principal Sikh centre in South India, Takhat Sri Hazur Sahib in Nander. Notably, Vanjara (or Banjara) Sikhs, akin to the Labana Sikhs of Punjab, are found scattered throughout central and south India as well as in Uttar Pradesh and Rajasthan.[26] Although they were de-notified as 'tribals' in the northern Telengana region in 1956, they have been recognized officially as 'tribals' since 1976. Being on the margins of society, they have not received much scholarly attention. A brief report appeared in 1986 in the *India Today* news magazine that took notice of the phenomenon of a community of three million Banjaras embracing Sikhism in Andhra Pradesh: 'The banjaras are a community in search of itself and the growing ranks of converts suggest that their search has ended at the doors of the gurdwara.'[27]

Although the manuscript of the Vanjara pothi is still intact in the original binding without the external hardcovers, it has become so brittle that it requires the immediate attention of experts for its proper care and preservation. For this purpose, Mahant Parsann Singh had given it to the late Sant Sucha Singh of Jawaddi Taksal (Ludhiana) in 1988 so that it could be laminated and microfilmed. I examined the manuscript during my research trip to India in the months of June and July 2002. I have in my possession a number of photographs of certain folios that are quite significant from the perspective of this study. Not surprisingly, during our conversation I found that Sant Sucha Singh did not know the historical importance of this document. He considered it just another collection of gurbani that has remained with Vanjara Sikhs for centuries. The Vanjara pothi is now preserved at Guru Hargobind Library, Jawaddi Taksal, Gurdwara Gur Gian Prakash, Ludhiana.[28]

A careful examination of the physiognomy of the Vanjara pothi reveals the following facts. All the 820 folios of this volume are made up of light brown Kashmiri paper. They are 8.5 inches long and 6.5 inches wide, and their total thickness in the book form is 5 inches. A border of two vertical lines is drawn on the left and the right sides of each folio. There is, however, no horizontal border on the top or the bottom of any folio. An average of 18 lines are written on each page. The manuscript is very neatly written, has few corrections, and appears to be in a single hand throughout. The pen does change at certain points, shown by the change in the thickness of writing. Deletion by means of a yellow-greenish paste (*hartal*) is used very sparingly at places where duplication of certain lines has occurred (folios 375b and 451b). The scribe has skillfully pointed out with the symbol of a plus sign ('+') where a word or verse has been left out. Corrections of such missing lines or words may be seen in the margins of folios 178a, 196b, 568b, 573a, 646b, 698a and 706b. In one particular instance, folio 258b, the page is left blank because ink has seeped through from the back. Only at one place, in the margin of folio 543b, is the scribal formula '*vah guru ji*' ('praise to the guru') inscribed vertically. I have seen the use of this formula in another manuscript, MS Or. 2747, preserved at the British Museum Library in London, which received much attention in the media in 2002 as the 'oldest manuscript' of the Adi Granth outside of India.[29] On the whole the Vanjara pothi is indeed the work of an accomplished scribe and is written *ad seriatim*.

Fortunately, all the numbered folios (1–820) of the Vanjara pothi are still intact, and the content of these folios is luminously clear. The folio number is written in the top right-hand corner in the standard way. There is no colophon showing the date of its writing, and no index is to be found in the beginning. There are two blank folios (ff. 719a–720b) after Kabir's 81 saloks, and two unnumbered blank folios are to be found at the end of the volume. Despite the fact that a number of folios show signs of water damage, the writing on these folios is still very clear. The place of the Vanjara pothi in the process of canon formation will emerge only from a careful examination of its contents.

Thus it is extremely important to look closely at the sequence of the various compositions in this document. It is described in seven tables in this essay, which are discussed in the following sections. The serial number of any composition is given according to its place in the Vanjara pothi. That is, the folio numbers correspond exactly to the content of various compositions that are assigned particular serial numbers. The tables are arranged according to the themes in our analysis. On the whole, the sequence of the compositions follows the actual pattern of the Vanjara pothi except where we have brought similar material from one table to another on the basis of a common theme. For instance, Table 1 contains the compositions of 1–8 and 31–4, bringing together the liturgical compositions and longer works. Similarly, the sequences of the compositions in Table 5 and Table 6 are determined on the basis of common themes.

Fixing the Divine Word

A close examination of early manuscripts reveals that Guru Arjan worked on a number of pre-canonical texts to finally produce an authoritative text of the Adi Granth in 1604. The process does not seem to involve a linear mode of operation in any way, that is, copying directly from one codex to another. Rather, a number of codices were being used simultaneously during the redaction process to establish the canon. The texts were read and re-read frequently to arrive at the final reading. In the following sections, therefore, we will examine this complex process through which the various compositions and structures of the Adi Granth achieved their final form. Throughout our discussion, we will focus our attention on the sequence of the Vanjara pothi, along with frequent references to the Bahoval pothi and MS 1245. The examination of the contents of these manuscripts places them in the following chronological order: MS 1245 (c. 1599 CE) is the oldest, followed by the Bahoval pothi and the Vanjara pothi. It is highly likely that there were other such manuscripts that have not survived. Here, we will collate certain textual readings from these manuscripts with those of the Kartarpur bir and the standard version of the Adi Granth. This procedure will certainly help us understand the emerging structure of the Adi Granth.

Fixing the Liturgical Texts and Longer Works

The liturgical sections of both MS 1245 and the Bahoval pothi represent the pre-canonical stage. In MS 1245, the morning prayer contains Guru Nanak's *Japu* and the evening prayer consists of '*Sodaru* and four hymns' ('*Sodaru thatha chare sabad*'). The late evening prayer, *Sohila* ('Song of Happiness'), is not to be found in MS 1245, while it is present in the Bahoval pothi. Both these manuscripts show remarkable text variants in the spellings of certain words of the *Japu*.[30] The situation of liturgical texts in the Vanjara pothi is shown in Table 3.1.

Table 1: Liturgical Texts and Longer Works

No.	Composition*	Verses	Folios
1.	*Japu*		ff. 1–11b
2.	*Sodaru Panch Sabad*		ff. 11b–14a
3.	*So Purakhu*		ff. 14a–16b
4.	*Sohila*		ff. 16b–18b
5.	*Ragu Ramakali Dakhani Oankar* M1		ff. 18b–30b
6.	*Ragu Ramakali* M1 *Sidh Gosti*		ff. 30b–43b
7.	*Ragu Gauri Bavan Akhari* M5		ff. 43b–61a
8.	*Ragu Gauri Sukhmani* M5		ff. 61a–109b
...	...		...
31.	*Ramakali Anandu* M3		ff. 402b–412a
32.	*Ragu Tukhari Barah Maha* M1		ff. 412a–416a
33.	*Ragu Majh* M5 *Barah Maha*		ff. 416b–421b
34.	*Ragu Maru Solahe* M1, M3, M4, M5	62	ff. 421b–525a

*'M' stands for the code word Mahala, which with an appropriate number, identifies the compositions of each guru. The works by Guru Nanak, Guru Angad, Guru Amar Das, Guru Ram Das, and Guru Arjan are indicated by the notations 'M' 1, 2, 3, 4 and 5 respectively.

A careful look at the sequence (1–8, 31–4) of the Vanjara pothi compositions in Table 1 indicates that the readings of the liturgical texts and other longer works were fixed first to achieve the final forms of these compositions. It is no wonder that the title 'Sodaru panch sabad' in this volume is the same as found in the Kartarpur manuscript.

In my earlier work I have discussed in detail the fixing of the 'Basic Invocation' (Mul Mantar), the early morning prayer (Japu, 'Recitation'), the evening prayer (So Dar Rahiras, 'Supplication at That Door') and Guru Amar Das's Anand ('Hymn of Bliss') in the Ramakali mode.[31] At that time I used caution in suggesting that the liturgical text of So Purakh ('That Being') became part of the evening order possibly during the last two years of Guru Arjan's life. The reason for this caution was the absence of this text in the introductory section of the Kartarpur bir. But this text is present in the beginning (#3) of the Vanjara pothi. This raises an important question of its absence in the Kartarpur manuscript.

The Bahoval pothi does not have the normal set of Sodar and So Purakh texts in its liturgical section. Even the So Purakh hymn does not come immediately after the Sodar hymn in the beginning of the compositions in Asa mode, as it comes in the standard version of the Adi Granth. Not surprisingly, Piar Singh made the following remark: 'The writer of this [Bahoval] pothi has not allowed the so purakh hymn of Asa Raga to interfere in between the first, so daru and the second suni vada hymns in Raga Asa, as does in the version that is current at present. This shows a deep consciousness of the format on the part of the compiler.'[32] Here, Piar Singh has missed the opportunity to closely examine Guru Arjan's editorial interventions in the process of canon formation. There is no doubt that the fifth guru consciously diverged from the normal pattern of arrangement of hymns by the gurus according to chronological sequence of their authors when he took the decision to include the So Purakh hymn after the Sodar text. But he did so to achieve a theological coherence, since the So Purakh text reveals the nature of the Supreme Being, who answers the prayers of His devotees seeking divine grace by singing eternally at His door (sodar).[33]

The issue of the absence of the So Purakh text from the Kartarpur manuscript may be addressed as follows. The writing of the Kartarpur volume was done in a discontinuous manner, moving between sections rather than strictly seriatim. The cluster of the five hymns of the evening prayer ('Sodaru panch sabad') were written on folios 50/1–51/2 in one sitting, followed by the inscription of the scribal formula 'by the grace of the true guru' ('satgur prasadi') at the completion of the text at the end of the page.[34] The original form of the evening prayer contained only these five hymns of the Sodar text, three of them by Guru Nanak and one each by the fourth and the fifth gurus.[35] Bhai Gurdas testifies to the tradition of its singing in Sikh worship during the Kartarpur period of Guru Nanak's life.[36] In the Kartarpur bir, the writing of the five hymns of the Sohila text ('sohila thatha arati panch sabad') began on folio 52/1 and concluded on folio 52/2 with the scribal formula 'satgur prasadi' at the end. These liturgical texts were apparently written much earlier, when the project of the making of Sikh scripture was first undertaken. The addition of the So Purakh text to the evening prayer was done much later, at the instance of Guru Arjan.[37] It was written in the Vanjara pothi in the final sequence, but it was not possible to include it in the Kartarpur manuscript because there was no space left between the Sodar and the Sohila texts. This is the only possible explanation for its omission. An early seventeenth-century manuscript of the Kartarpur tradition (Punjabi University Museum MS #8) contains the liturgical text of So Purakh, signifying that it was written at a time when the expanded version of the evening order had come into vogue.[38] Notably, the So Purakh text is also to be found in Baba Ram Rai's bir (1659), which belongs to the Kartarpur tradition.[39] Similarly, the Amritsar pothi (1654) of the Lahore tradition, which was copied from the manuscript written by Bura Sandhu (1605), contains the So Purakh text in its expanded version of the liturgical section.[40]

Most interestingly, the standardization of the text of Bavan Akhari (#7) is quite illuminating when we look at the variant readings of MS 1245, Bahoval pothi and the Vanjara pothi. It is Guru Arjan's composition on 'fifty-two letters'('bavan akhari'), the traditional number of Sanskrit vowels, single consonants, and diphthongs. It is in the form of an acrostic, propounding philosophical and religious themes and doctrines. In its basic structure, this composition comprises 55 stanzas (pauris) of eight lines each, preceded by saloks, all of which are couplets except the one preceding the last stanza, which is of four lines. Besides, there is an additional couplet following the first stanza that serves the purpose of a refrain (rahau).[41] In the standard version of the Adi Granth, there is an opening salok of nine lines that is repeated at the end of this composition as well. An editorial note by Guru Arjan instructs the reader specifically to recite the opening salok at the end of the composition as well, since it is recorded in both places. The editorial note reads: 'Read this salok at the beginning and at the end (*ehu salok adi anti parhana*).'

The opening salok of *Bavan Akhari*, beginning with the line '*gurdev mata gurdev pita gurdev suami paramesura*' ('the Divine Guru is my mother, the Divine Guru is my father, the Divine Guru is my Transcendent Lord and Master'), is not to be found in the beginning of the Bahoval pothi. Later on, a different scribe inserted this salok at the end of the text (f. 305) along with the editorial note. Notably, the handwriting of this salok and the editorial instruction tallies exactly with the writing style of the primary scribe of the Kartarpur bir.[42] Evidently, Bhai Gurdas wrote it under the direction of Guru Arjan. In contrast with the standard version, this composition comes after Guru Arjan's *Sukhmani* ('Pearl of Peace') in the Bahoval pothi. In MS 1245, however, the opening salok is not repeated at the end on folio 272b. Obviously the decision to repeat the first salok at the end of the composition was taken by Guru Arjan when he fixed the final reading of this composition. This standard version of *Bavan Akhari* may be seen in the Vanjara pothi and the Kartarpur bir. Talib has suggested that the opening salok is repeated at the close of the composition because 'it has an incantatory quality as a mantra'.[43] The thematic analysis of this salok in the total context of the *Bavan Akhari*, however, reveals that by repeating it Guru Arjan put emphasis on the reality of the Divine Guru ('*gurdev*', the keyword of the opening salok), in contrast with the unreality of worldly relations such as father, mother, friends, and so on. Traditionally, the *Bavan Akhari* is recited at the time of the death of a dear one to console the bereaved family members. The repetition of the opening salok awakens people to the reality that the Eternal Guru is the only true support at the beginning as well as at the end of life.

The Vanjara pothi contains 62 *solahas* ('16-stanza compositions') in total: 22 by Guru Nanak, 24 by Guru Amar Das, two by Guru Ram Das, and 14 by Guru Arjan. These are the exact numbers and order to be found in the standard version of the Adi Granth. There is the striking textual issue of one such hymn beginning with the opening line '*kudarati karanaiharu apara*' ('The Creator is limitless in His power'). This hymn is recorded under the symbol of Guru Arjan in MS 1245 (f. 1001a). Similarly, it appears in the Bahoval pothi under the title '*Maru Pandrah Mahala 5*' on folio 544, signifying that the number of stanzas in this hymn is 15 rather than 16. The standard version also has only 15 stanzas to this hymn. There is a marginal note in the Kartarpur bir (f. 778/2) specifying that 'the right place of twenty-second *solaha* belongs to Guru Nanak's hymn which is currently located in folio 800' (*'22 baihavan solaha pati 800 sahi hai/ mahale 1/pahale ka'*). The editorial comment in the index on folio 16/1 further clarifies that the 'hymn (*kudarati karanaiharu apara*) of folio 799 should come at number 22'. Clearly, these editorial notes indicate that it was Guru Arjan who took the decision to assign the authorship of this hymn to Guru Nanak. I have examined this issue in detail in my earlier work.[44] In the Vanjara pothi this hymn comes at number 22 among Guru Nanak's hymns (ff. 456b–458a). Thus the canonical forms of the '*Maru Solahas*' were established by the time this pothi was written.

Fixing the 22 Vars ('Ballads')

A *var* ('ballad') may be defined as an old form of Punjabi narrative poetry highlighting exploits and acts of heroism and chivalry. On the psychological plane, the struggle is between the good and evil propensities in human nature.[45] The var of the Adi Granth is a distinctive genre, which is constituted of a series of stanzas (pauris). Each pauri is preceded by a number of subsidiary stanzas called salok. The Adi Granth salok is normally a two-line classical prosodic form allowing a variety of metrical arrangements, including variation in number of the lines.[46] The vars contained only the stanzas (pauris) to which saloks were affixed during Guru Arjan's period. On the issue of fixing the vars, Piar Singh has made an important observation: 'The compilation of the vars, it appears, took place separately and thereafter they were assigned to their respective ragas.'[47] Presumably, the sequence of the vars in the Vanjara pothi reflects the standard pattern established for the first time, which is shown in Table 2.

Table 2: 22 Vars ('Ballads')

No.	Composition	*Dhuni*	Folios
9.	*Asa ki Var* M1	Yes	ff. 109–129a
10.	*Malar ki Var* M1	Yes	ff. 129–148a
11.	*Majh ki Var* M1	Yes	ff. 148a–68b
12.	*Var Gujari ki* M3	Yes	ff. 168b–182a
13.	*Var Ramakali ki* M3	Yes	ff. 1821a–96b
14.	*Var Suhi ki* M3		ff. 196b–206b
15.	*Var Maru ki* M3		ff. 206b–217a

(*contd...*)

(Table 1 continued)

No.	Composition	Dhuni	Folios
16.	*Var Sarang ki* M4	No	ff. 217a–237a
17.	*Var Sorathi ki* M4		ff. 237a–255b
18.	*Var Siri Ragu ki* M4		ff. 255b–269b
19.	*Var Vadahans ki* M4	Yes	ff. 269b–284a
20.	*Var Bihagare ki* M4		ff. 284a–96b
21.	*Var Kanare ki* M4	Yes	ff. 296b–306b
22.	*Var Bilaval ki* M4		ff. 306b–316a
23.	*Var Gauri ki* M4		ff. 316a–343a
24.	*Maru ki Var* M5 *Dakhane*		ff. 343a–356a
25.	*Var Ramakali ki* M5		ff. 356a–371a
26.	*Var Gujari ki* M5		ff. 371a–81b
27.	*Var Jaitsiri ki* M5		ff. 381b–389b
28.	*Gauri ki Var* M5	Yes	ff. 389b–398a
29.	*Var Basant ki* M5		ff. 398a–398b
30.	*Var Rai Balvand tatha Sattai Dum akhi*		ff. 398b–402b

There are some significant textual issues related to the strategy of fixing the *vars* in the Adi Granth. In the first place, the vars in MS 1245 are still in their pre-canonical stage. For instance, the saloks preceding the pauris—such as M1, M2, M3, M4, and M5—are not assigned their proper authorship. In certain cases, the saloks have yet to be selected for the pauris. The most striking examples may be seen on folios 482b, 483a, and 483b of MS 1245, where there are blank spaces to be filled in with the saloks for the pauris numbering 18, 20, and 21 respectively in Guru Amar Das's *Var Gujari*. These blank spaces clearly illuminate the textual process of the vars being fixed for the first time in MS 1245. There is another significant editorial instruction in Guru Nanak's *Var Malar*—to shift a new stanza of Guru Arjan's, numbering 28, to the place of Guru Nanak's stanza, numbering 27, and vice versa—showing the work in progress towards fixing the final reading of this text.[48]

Second, only four vars in the Bahoval pothi—namely, Guru Nanak's *Var Asa* (ff. 44956), Guru Amar Das's *Var Maru* (ff. 546–54), Guru Arjan's *Maru Var Dakhane* (ff. 554–63), and Guru Ram Das's *Var Bihagara* (ff. 597–602)—are to be found in the appropriate raga sections. The remaining 17 vars are put together in one cluster (ff. 774–930) before the epilogue of the volume. Guru Amar Das's *Var Suhi* is not to be found in this pothi, since the whole raga section is missing in the volume. The scribe of the Bahoval pothi normally adds the formula 'mukki' ('[the var] has ended') at the end of the var, signifying that the task of fixing the final reading of this text has been accomplished. This he does to other works as well when all the compositions in a particular section have been put together at their proper places.

Third, there are only four vars in the Bahoval pothi that are assigned the specific heroic tunes (dhuni) to which they are supposed to be sung. These are as follows: Sikandar Biraham ki Var ki Dhuni for Guru Amar Das's Var Gujari, Rai Mahame Hasan ki Dhuni for Guru Ram Das's Var Sarang, Ranai Kailas ki Dhuni for Guru Nanak's Var Malar, and Jodhai Vire Purbani ki Dhuni for Guru Amar Das's Var Ramakali. In the case of MS 1245, seven vars are assigned the heroic tunes, although most of the time they are mentioned only in the index. In the two cases of Guru Nanak's Var Malar and Guru Ram Das's Var Vadahans, however, the tunes are specifically stated at the beginning of their texts in addition to the index entries.[49] In the Vanjara pothi, however, eight vars are assigned the heroic tunes. The only missing heroic tune is that of Guru Ram Das's Var Sarang, which leaves the Vanjara pothi one short compared the Kartarpur bir and the standard version of the Adi Granth, both of which have nine specific heroic tunes assigned to nine different vars.[50]

Fourth, there is no recording of such words as sudh ('correct') or sudh kichai ('make corrections') at the end of the vars in the Bahoval pothi, MS 1245, and the Vanjara pothi, reflecting the pre-canonical nature of these documents. This convention was used for the first time in the Kartarpur manuscript by Guru Arjan to mark his personal approval of the content, form, and organization of the vars in particular raga sections. This is quite evident from the inscription of 'sudh' in the margins at the end of 16 vars in the Kartarpur bir.[51] It also highlights the editorial process through which the blank spaces in the vars of MS 1245 and the missing heroic tunes of both the Bahoval pothi and the Vanjara pothi were duly filled in in the Kartarpur volume. Even the titles of saloks (M1, M2, M3, M4, and M5) were inserted in the Kartarpur manuscript in between the lines later on with a fine pen.[52]

Finally, the sequence of the vars in the Vanjara pothi is an indication of the order in which they were fixed for the first time. The celebrated Asa ki Var of Guru Nanak has always enjoyed a prominent place in Sikh liturgy. It was thus natural to fix its canonical form first by assigning to it the heroic tune of the popular ballad of the stump-armed (tunda) Asraj, the son of a king named Sarang, who fought a battle against his stepbrothers to win the throne of his father. It is instructive to note here that this heroic tune is not to be found in the text of *Var Asa* in the Bahoval pothi. Clearly, the tradition of singing of *Var Asa* to the heroic tune of the 'ballad of stump-armed Asraj' (*Tundai Asrajai ki Dhuni*) became popular during Guru Arjan's period. After fixing the gurus' ballads in a chronological order, Guru Arjan composed his *Var Basant* at the end. Unlike the other vars of the gurus, this var consists of only three stanzas. It was followed by a ballad in the Ramakali mode by two Sikh bards, Rai Balwand and Satta Dum. In fact, Guru Arjan's *Var Basant* provided the model for the 'Ballad of Coronation' (*'Tikke ki Var'*) by Balvand and Satta in much the same way as his 20 panegyrics provided the model for the panegyrics by the bards (*Bhattan de Savayye*) in praise of the gurus. This final sequence of 22 ballads became current among the Sikh scribes, who took extraordinary care to copy them down in that order in their collections of gurbani. This fact may be noted from the index folio of the Adi Granth manuscript, written by Ram Rai in Sambat 1749 (1692), where the same sequence is described under the title of *Bandhej Varan ka* ('the fixed order of ballads').[53] This is, however, not the order in which they occur in the standard version of the Adi Granth. There they are recorded according to their proper place in different raga sections.

Fixing the Raga Sections

The most significant point about the structure of the Adi Granth relates to the fact that the divisions in the bulky middle section have been made on the basis of ragas or melodic patterns. The fundamental question that arises is the rationale behind this organizing principle. In order to find the answer to this question, we need to examine closely the sequence of the ragas in the available pre-canonical texts. The final sequence of the raga sections was certainly established before the Vanjara pothi was written. It is described in Table 3.

Table 3: Sequence of the Ragas

No.	Composition	Folios
35.	*Ragu Siri Ragu* M1 *Chaupade Gharu* 1	ff. 525a–29a
36.	*Ragu Majh* M4 *Chaupade Gharu* 1	ff. 529a–32a
37.	*Ragu Gauri Guareri* M1 *Chaupade Gharu* 1	ff. 532a–34a
38.	*Ragu Asa* M1 *Gharu* 1 *Chaupade*	ff. 534a–37b
39.	*Ragu Gujari* M1 *Gharu* 1 *Chaupade*	ff. 537b–40b

(contd...)

(Table 3 continued)

No.	Composition	Folios
40.	Ragu Devagandhari M4 Dupade Gharu 1	ff. 540b–42b
41.	Ragu Bihagara M5 Chaupade Gharu 1	ff. 542b–48b
42.	Ragu Vadahansu M1 Chaupade Gharu 1	ff. 548b–52a
43.	Ragu Sorathi M1 Chaupade Gharu 1	ff. 552a–55b
44.	Ragu Dhanasari M1 Gharu 1 Chaupade	ff. 555b–58b
45.	Ragu Jaitsiri M4 Gharu 1 Chaupade	ff. 558b–62a
46.	Ragu Todi M4 Gharu 1 Chaupade	ff. 562a–64b
47.	Ragu Bairari M4 Gharu 1 Dupade	ff. 564b–66b
48.	Ragu Tilang M1 Gharu 1 Chaupade	ff. 566b–569a
49.	Ragu Suhi M1 Chaupade Gharu 1	ff. 569a–71b
50.	Ragu Bilavalu M1 Gharu 1 Chaupade	ff. 571b–74b
51.	Ragu Gond M4 Chaupade Gharu 1	ff. 575a–78b
52.	Ragu Ramakali M1 Chaupade Gharu 1	ff. 578b–81b
53.	Ragu Nat Naraian M4 Chaupade Gharu 1	ff. 581b–84b
54.	Ragu Mali Gaura M4 Chaupade	ff. 584b–87b
55.	Ragu Maru M1 Gharu 1 Chaupade	ff. 587b–90a
56.	Ragu Tukhari M1	ff. 590a–95b
57.	Ragu Kedara M4 Gharu 1	ff. 595b–97b
58.	Ragu Bhairau M1 Chaupade Gharu 1	ff. 597b–600b
59.	Ragu Basant M1 Chaupade Gharu 1	ff. 600b–3b
60.	Ragu Sarang M1 Gharu 1 Chaupade	ff. 603b–6a
61.	Ragu Malar M1 Gharu 1 Chaupade	ff. 606a–9b
62.	Ragu Kanara M4 Chaupade Gharu 1	ff. 609b–12b
63.	Ragu Kaliyan M4 Chaupade	ff. 612b–5b
64.	Ragu Bibhas Parbhati M1 Chaupade	ff. 615b–8a

The raga sections of both MS 1245 and the Bahoval pothi reflect the pre-canonical stage, showing a different order of the ragas. Although a total number of 30 major ragas are to be found in MS 1245, certain ragas such as Sorathi, Kalayan, and Nat-narain are placed as eleventh, twelfth, and thirteenth in the present sequence while they appear as ninth, twenty-ninth, and nineteenth in the standard version of the Adi Granth. The Bahoval pothi does not even contain all the 30 major ragas. Its sequence runs as follows: Siri-ragu, Majh, Gauri, Ramakali, Asa, Maru, Tukhari, Kedara, Jaitsiri, Bairari, Mali-gaura, Bihagara, Kalayan, Nat-narain,

Devgandhari, Gond, Bilaval-gond, Tilang, Todi, Basant, Hindol, Kanara, Vadahans, Prabhati, and Sorathi, followed by the available vars and the compositions of the epilogue. Evidently, Guru Arjan established the sequence of the ragas after working on a number of early traditions. The Vanjara pothi contains all the 30 ragas in the order of the standard sequence except the final raga, Vibhas Prabahati, a combined (*sankar*) raga which is common with the Kartarpur manuscript but appears as Prabhati Vibhas in the standard version of the Adi Granth. This is, however, a minor reversal of the order of two ragas in a combined melodic pattern. Once the sequence of the ragas was fixed in the first canonical text, it was not possible for the scribes to alter it in any way in the later manuscripts of the Adi Granth.

Guru Nanak and the succeeding gurus laid great emphasis on the performance of those ragas that produced a balanced effect on the minds of both listeners and performers. Any raga that aroused passion of any kind was not selected as the carrier of their message. For instance, there are still some musicians who believe that Dipak raga generates fire if correctly performed. Whether it is true or not, this raga is not used independently in the Adi Granth. It is, however, used as Gauri-dipaki in the mixed form (a sankar raga), so that its extreme effect is toned down. The resulting form is most suitable for the creation of a reflective mood.[54] In particular, Gauri-dipaki is employed in the opening hymn of the bedtime prayer, Sohila ('song of praise'), thereby conjuring up a sense of light that flickers in darkness, of mystery and apprehension (in the context of an immanent death, symbolized as a wedding in the text) which is steadied by faith and fearlessness.[55] Similarly, Hindol is not used independently in the Adi Granth but appears in the mixed form as Basant-hindol. Whereas the Basant raga is associated with the coming of the spring season, Hindol expresses a jubilant mode, creating an atmosphere of passion and joy. Literally, the word *hindol* means 'swing' and it refers to the 'swing' of Krishna. In the musical setting of this raga, the *gopis* ('cowherd girls') move the swing with passion while Krishna plays his transverse flute to create a mood of amorous love. A considerable number of hymns in the Bahoval pothi are recorded independently under the title of Hindol: (1) *Ragu Hindolu Mahala 5* ('*Hoi ikattar milahi mere bhai...*'), (2) *Ragu Hindolu Mahala 5* ('*Teri kudarati tuhai janahi avar na duja janai...*'), and (3) *Ragu Hindolu Mahala 5* ('*Mul na bujhai andh na sujhai...*').[56] These three hymns appear under the title of Basant-hindol in the final version of the Adi Granth.[57]

These changes in the titles illuminate the implicit editorial principles, reflecting Guru Arjan's choice of only those ragas that produced a gentle tonal effect in one's mind.

It is no wonder that a gender-based classification of the Goindval pothis was not accepted in the first canonical text of the Adi Granth. Indeed, the final sequence of the ragas was carefully worked out after blending a number of popular forms and regional varieties from the existing musical system of north India at that time. In doing so, Guru Arjan created a theological and musicological coherence in the very structure of the Adi Granth. The division of the first canonical text into 30 ragas may have been inspired by the system of 30 *gramaragas* developed in the musical treatise *Brhad-desi* by sage Matanga in the late tenth century.[58] Further, the time theory of the Indian musical system divides day and night into eight *pahirs* or watches. Each pahir is further divided into seven-and-a-half *ghari*, thereby dividing each day and night into 60 gharis. The time-unit of a ghari being equal to 24 minutes, the performance of 30 ragas during a day and night thus offers each raga the set time of two gharis or 48 minutes.[59] Furthermore, Frederic Pincott suggested in the late nineteenth century that the arrangement of the hymns of the Adi Granth into 30 major ragas 'exactly correspond with the 30 semitones of the Indian *stabaka*, or musical staff, reckoning the minor intervals as single tones'.[60]

Let us now closely look at the raga sections of the Vanjara pothi. Each raga section contains a set of six hymns (*chaupadas*, 'four-verse compositions') by Guru Nanak (M1) or Guru Ram Das (M4) in the musical category of *gharu* 1 ('house 1', that is, 'drum beat / clef 1') in the style of the particular performance used in devotional singing. The plan was thus laid out to organize the hymns in 'clusters of sixes' (*chhakas*) according to the ascending order of 17 musical categories (gharu 1, 2, 3, 4,.... 17) in the process of canonization. It is no wonder that at a number of places in the Kartarpur bir and the Bahoval pothi the totals are found indicated in chhakas. The order of the six hymns in each raga section of the Vanjara pothi tallies exactly with the order found in the standard version of the Adi Granth.

It should be emphasized here that the final version of the Sikh scripture contains 31 major ragas, along with an equal number of regional varieties. The last raga, Jaijavanti, is the contribution of the ninth guru, Tegh Bahadur. No other guru has employed this raga for his compositions.

The final position of the Jaijavanti raga was fixed only after experimentation with two different positions in the raga sequence of the Adi Granth. In certain manuscripts, Jaijavanti comes after the Jaitsari mode, while in some other instances it comes after the Gauri mode.[61] Jaijavanti is a highly majestic raga that is assigned to the night hours. Its performance is associated with the feelings of victory (jai) over temptations. With its final position in the raga sequence, the cycle of time is complete.

Fixing the Titles of Certain Works

The Vanjara pothi reflects the earlier sequence of certain titles arranged on the basis of common themes. Some of these titles deserve special attention. For instance, the titles *Dhamal* and *Vichar* do not occur in the standard version of the Adi Granth. The first title refers to the musical style of *dhamal*, in which the drumbeats followed a particular rhythm of Dhamar *tal*. It was a popular folk style in those days in north India. This folk style is commonly used at the time of weddings or on other happy occasions. The second title refers to the *khayal* style with its allowable freedom. Both these musical styles are much more jubilant compared to the *dhurpad* style, which is slower, much less ornamented and more sedate than the khayal style. In Sikh musicology, the word 'dhurpad' is a combination of two words, *dhur* and *pad*, signifying 'melodious vibration of divine origin'.[62] It refers to the sacred context of devotional 'singing of the hymns' (*shabad kirtan*) in Sikh worship.

The primary objective of Sikh kirtan is spiritual discipline. That is why it is kept free of secular characteristics that may be in vogue at any given time. Any kind of music that might contribute to the arousal of sensuality has no place in the Sikh tradition. In fact, devotional music 'gradually washes the inner consciousness' and one becomes 'holy and spotless through the power of *kirtan*'.[63] In this context, Guru Arjan proclaims: 'Blessed are the notes of those ragas which put the mind in a tranquil mood'.[64] Evidently, music is a divine gift that finds an echo in the hearts and minds of the people. As such, it is used with the divine word as an aid to ethical and spiritual development. Thus any musical style that arouses passion of any kind was not acceptable to Guru Arjan. That is why the titles *Dhamal* and *Vichar* were not retained in the Adi Granth, although the texts (*Ragu Bilaval Mahala 5//prabh janam maran nivar//* ...and *Ragu Bilaval Mahala 3//adi purakh ape sarishat sajje//*...) under these titles were included in the Bilaval mode.[65]

Table 4: Titles of Certain Works

No.	Composition	Folios
65.	*Ragu Bilaval M5 Dhamal*	ff. 618a–26b
66.	*Ragu Gauri M5 Thiti*	ff. 626b–33a
67.	*Ragu Bilavalu M3 Var Likhe*	ff. 633a–34b
68.	*Ragu Bilavalu M3 Vichar*	ff. 634b–36a
69.	*Ragu Asa M4 Gharu 2*	ff. 636a–42b
70.	*Ragu Asa M1 Patti Likhi, M3 Patti*	ff. 642b–48a
71.	*Ragu Asa M4 Chhant Gharu 4*	ff. 648a–56a
72.	*Ragu Suhi Chhant M1, M4 Gharu 1*	ff. 656a–65b
73.	*Ragu Majh M5*	ff. 665b–73a

The title *Var Likhe* ('days written') was changed to *Var Sat* ('seven days') in the Bilaval raga, while the heading *Thitin* ('lunar dates') appears in the Gauri mode. The remaining two titles of *Patti Likhi* ('thus was slate written') and *Patti* ('acrostic song') were recorded in the Asa raga in the standard version of the Adi Granth. The changes made in the headings of these works clearly indicate the minute details of the redaction process. Moreover, there are minor textual variations in the lyrical hymns recorded under the title *Ragu Suhi Chhant Mahala 1* (no. 72 in Table 4). For instance, read the opening verses of the following three hymns by Guru Nanak in the original:

Suhi Lalat Mahala 1 (ff. 662a–62b)

Kaunu taraju kaun tola tera kaunu sarafu bulava//
Kaunu guru jai pahi dikhia mangaun kai pahi mulu karava//1//
Lal ji mai tera antu na jana//
Tun jali thali mahiali bharpuri lina tun ape sarab samana//
Manu taraji chitu tola teri sev sarafu kamava//
Ghati hi bhitari so sahu toli ini bidhi chitu rahava//2//... [66]

Which is the scale, which the weight-measure? Which gold-tester may I call to test you? Who is the Guru from whom I may receive instruction? Whom do I approach to evaluate you? (1) O Beloved! I cannot know your extent. You are all-pervasive on water, land, and on the entire surface of the earth. My mind is the scale, consciousness the weight-measure, and I earn the gold-tester by your service. Weighing the Lord in my self I restrain my mind this way. (2)...

Suhi Kuchajji Mahala 1 ('uncultured woman') (ff. 662b–663a)

Manj kuchajji amavani dosare hau kium sahu ravani jau ji//
Othai ikk du ikki charandhian kaun janai mera nau ji//1//
Jina sakhian sahu ravia tina ambarian chhavariasu ji//
Se gun mujhai na avani kai ji dosarre dosu dhareu ji//2//
Kia gun tere bitharan kia kia ghinna tera nau ji//
Ikkatu toli na appran sada kurbane tere jau ji//3//...[67]

Cherished Friend! I am an uncultured woman, endless blames are cast on me.
How can I enjoy the bliss of my spouse? Cherished Friend! There are females,
each better than the other. Who would even make mention of me? (1) Cherished
Friend! Those of my sister-friends who are having bliss with the spouse are resting
under the shade of mango-tree. Cherished Friend! I do not possess the qualities
like theirs. On whom may I lay the blame? (2) Cherished Friend! What power
do I have to recount your merits? By which method shall I recall your Name?
Cherished Friend! I cannot have access to even one of your merits. May I be a
sacrifice to you forever! (3)...

Suhi Suchajji Mahala 1 ('cultured woman') (ff. 663a–663b)

Ja tun tan mai sabh koi tun sahib meri rasi ji//
Tudhu antari hau sukhi vassan tun antari sabasi ji//1//
Bhanai takhati vadiaian bhanai bhikh udasu ji//
Bhanai thal siri saru vahai kaval fulle akasi ji//2//
Bhanai bhavajalu langhana bhanai manjh bhariasu ji//
Bhanai so sahu rangula sifati rata gunatasu ji//3//...[68]

Cherished Friend! In your company I am possessed of all boons. O Lord! You
are my capital. Cherished Friend! When you are on my side I live in joy, With
your blessings I am approved. (1) Cherished Friend! In your sweet will you may
grant me a throne and exaltation. If it pleases you I may go about begging,
leaving my home. Cherished Friend! In your sweet will an ocean may flow on
dry land. If it pleases you a lotus flower can bloom in the sky. (2) Cherished
Friend! In your sweet will may the ocean of existence be crossed! If it pleases
you the ship of life may sink in mid-ocean filled with water. Cherished Friend!
In your sweet will you are suffused with joy. May I be absorbed in the treasure-
trove of your virtues! (3) ...

The reading of the first hymn is closer to the reading of the first volume
of the Goindval pothis and that of MS 1245. In particular, the use of the
common word *tola* (weight measure) in the three documents establishes

a clear relationship between them. A comparison of this hymn with its standard version reveals certain linguistic variations. For instance, the Punjabi expression 'kaunu guru jai pahi dikhia mangaun' ('who is the guru from whom I may receive instruction?') is replaced with 'kaunu guru kai pahi dikhia leva' in the final version for metrical purposes. There is no difference in the meaning. Similarly, the first line in the refrain of the standard version, 'mere lal jiu tera ant na jana' ('I cannot know your extent, my dear Beloved!') is written in the Vanjara pothi as 'lal ji mai tera antu na jana' ('O Beloved! I cannot know your extent.'). The use of the honorific particle jiu in referring to the divine Beloved (mere lal jiu) acts as a singing device, which makes the hymn more musical. The same revision was done in the next two hymns when 'ji' was replaced with 'jiu' at the end of each line. The following expression from the Sindhi language, 'jina sakhian sahu ravia tina ambarian chhavariasu ji' ('Cherished Friend! Those of my sister-friends who are having bliss with the Spouse are resting under the shade of mango-tree'), was modified to 'jinni sakhi sahu ravia se ambi chhavariehi jiu' for metrical purposes. Evidently Guru Arjan's literary talent was at work behind this whole process of refinement.

Fixing the Bhagat Bani

The inclusion of the Bhagat Bani ('the utterances of the poet-saints') in the Adi Granth illuminates the process of scriptural adaptation in the Sikh tradition. The selection logic favours those poems of the medieval Bhagats that stress the notion of nirguna religiosity and social equality, and are in general conformity with the Sikh gurus' line of thinking. It should, however, be pointed out that this selection was not made exclusively on the basis of identity with the teachings of the gurus, for there is difference as well as identity. This is quite evident from the verses of the poet-saints that received direct comments from the gurus at certain points. For instance, the gurus differ from both Kabir and Shaikh Farid on the issue of the primacy of divine grace over personal effort in spiritual progress. The Sikh view of divine grace requires one to believe that the whole of one's spiritual progress is a matter of divine grace, not of one's efforts alone. Thus, in their comments on the verses of the poet-saints, the gurus emphasize that God's gifts are not ultimately dependent upon the merit of an individual. Divine grace is ultimately fundamental but is a mystery. Similarly, the gurus did not accept the ideals of self-mortification and asceticism held by Shaikh Farid. These additional reflections of the gurus were crucial for shaping the emerging Sikh identity. They play an important role in defining what it means to be a Sikh in relation to the commonly held Sant, Sufi, and Bhagat ideals. These points become clear from the gurus' comments on the verses of Shaikh Farid, Kabir, Dhanna, and Surdas. In fact, the net effect of the gurus' comments on the Bhagats is to cement firmly the Bhagat Bani in the Sikh scripture.[69]

Let us look carefully at the situation of the Bhagat Bani in the Vanjara pothi as given in Table 5. The hymns of the Bhagats are still in their pre-canonical stage in the Vanjara pothi. They are not arranged in any set order. As compared to the 243 saloks of Kabir in the standard version of the Adi Granth, only 81 saloks are to be found in this volume, followed by two blank spaces. However, Shaikh Farid's 130 saloks are recorded completely. Most interestingly, Guru Arjan's comment on Surdas is recorded under the title *Sarang Surdas Ji Mahala 5* ('*har ke sangi basse hari lok//tanu manu arapi sarbasu sabhu arapio anad sahaj dhuni jhok//...*, 'The devotees of the Lord abide with Him alone. They dedicate their mind, body and everything else to him and remain joyously intoxicated by the divine music of the Word...') on folios 765a and 765b. However, a single line of Surdas's hymn ('*chhadi mani hari bimukhan ko sang*', 'Soul, turn your back on those who shun the Lord') is not to be found there. This omission throws an interesting light on the textual problem of the incomplete nature of Surdas's hymn, the first line of which is recorded in the Kartarpur manuscript in the Sarang mode, followed by Guru Arjan's comment on Surdas. Clearly, Guru Arjan took the decision to include the single line later on to provide the context for his comment.[70]

Further, Mira Bai's hymn is another textual problem in Adi Granth studies that has drawn great scholarly attention. This hymn is not to be found in the Maru raga section in the Vanjara pothi, although it appears in the Bahoval pothi (f. 566). It found its place in the Kartarpur manuscript much later. However, it was subsequently deemed unworthy of inclusion and was deleted with a pen. Not surprisingly, it is not to be found in the earliest extant manuscript of the Kartarpur tradition (Punjabi University Museum MS 8) that was apparently prepared during Guru Arjan's period.[71]

Finally, there is Guru Arjan's hymn (M5, '*Gobind gobind gobind sangi namdeu manu lina//Addh dam ko chhiparo hoio lakhina//*', 'In Gobind, Gobind, Gobind was Namdev's *man* ['heart-mind-soul'] absorbed. A calico-printer worth half a farthing became worth many hundred thousands!') inserted between the two hymns of Dhanna in the standard version of the Adi Granth. It is included in a section marked *Asa Bani Bhagat Dhanne Ji ki* ('Bhagat Dhanna's utterances in the Asa mode') and

Table 5: Bhagat Bani

No.	Composition	Saloks	Folios
74.	*Ragu Prabhati Arati Kabir Ji*		ff. 673a–73b
75.	*Ragu Gauri Guareri Bhagatan ki*		ff. 673b–678a
76.	*Ragu Sorathi Bani Bhagatan ki*		ff. 678a–83a
77.	*Ragu Suhi Bani Bhagatan ki*		ff. 683a–85a
78.	*Ragu Bilaval Bani Bhagatan ki*		ff. 685a–87a
79.	*Ragu Ramakali Bani Bhagatan ki*		ff. 687a–89a
80.	*Ragu Asa Bani Bhagatan ki*		ff. 689a–696b
81.	*Ragu Basant Bani Bhagatan ki*		ff. 696b–99b
82.	*Ragu Kedara Bani Bhagatan ki*		ff. 699b–701a
83.	*Ragu Parbhati Bani Bhagatan ki*		ff. 701a–4a
84.	*Ragu Siri Ragu Bani Bhagatan ki*		ff. 704b–5a
85.	*Ragu Bhairau Sabad Kabir Ji ke*		ff. 705a–708b
86.	*Ragu Tilang Bani Bhagatan ki*		ff. 708b–709a
87.	*Ragu Dhanasari Bani Bhagatan ki*		ff. 709a–12a
88.	*Ragu Bhairau M4*		ff. 712a–712b
89.	*Salok Bhagat Kabir Jiu ke*	1–81	ff. 713a–718b
90.	*Salok Shaikh Farid Jiu ke*	1–130	ff.721a–731a
...	...		...
97.	Bilaval *Kabir Ji* and other Bhagats		ff. 755a–757b
98.	*Ramakali Bani Bhagatan ki*		ff. 757b–761a
99.	*Maru Kabir Ji and Ravidas Ji*		ff. 761a–762b
100.	*Sarang Kabir Ji*, other Bhagats & M5		ff. 762b–65b
101.	*Malar Ravidas Ji*		ff. 765b–766a
102.	*Ragu Kanara Namdev Ji*		ff. 766a–766b
103.	*Ragu Asa Dhanna Ji, Shaikh Farid Ji*		ff. 766b–768b

therefore, it is understood as a comment on Dhanna. The position of this hymn in the Vanjara pothi is, however, slightly different. The hymns of the poet-saints in the Asa mode appear at two different places as shown in Table 5 (no. 80 ff. 689a–96b, no. 103 ff. 766b–8b). Guru Arjan's hymn is recorded at the end of *Ragu Asa Bani Bhagatan ki* (ff. 696ab) without attribution after Ravidas's hymn. Dhanna's two hymns appear separately (ff. 766b–7b) along with Shaikh Farid's hymns. Obviously, Guru Arjan took the conscious decision to place his hymn in between Dhanna's two hymns in the Asa mode in the Kartarpur bir. On the whole, the Vanjara pothi offers important insights with regard to the integration of the Bhagat Bani in the Adi Granth.

Fixing the Chhants and Astapadis

In the structure of any given raga section, the hymns of the gurus in the standard version of the Adi Granth are divided into subsections of chaupadas ('four-verse compositions'), astapadis ('eight-verse compositions'), chhants ('six-verse lyrical songs'), longer works, and vars ('ballads'). This sequence is different from the two available Goindval pothis where chhants come before the astapadis. Similarly, the Vanjara pothi reflects the earlier convention of the Goindval pothis as shown in Table 6. Clearly, the criterion of length is followed in this early arrangement where chhants are followed by the longer astapadis and karahale ('10-verse compositions to camel tunes').

In the context of present discussion, Gurinder Singh Mann raises an important question: 'In the Kartarpur Pothi, unlike the Goindval Pothis, the chhants are placed after ashtpadis. It is not clear why this was done, since the ashtpadis (eight stanzas of four verses each) are longer than the

Table 6. Chhants and Astapadis

No.	Composition	Folios
91.	Vadahansu M1, M5, M4, M3 Chhantu	ff. 731a–735b
92.	Ragu Gauri Guareri M5	ff. 736a–38a
93.	Asa M1 Gharu 4 and M3 Gharu 4	ff. 738a–740b
94.	Ragu Gujari M5 Chaupade Gharu 1	ff. 740b–742b
95.	Ragu Gauri Chhant M3 and M5	ff. 742b–48b
96.	Ragu Bilavalu M4 Astapadian	ff. 748b–755a
...	...	...
104.	Ragu Tukhari M5 Chhantu	ff. 769a–71a
105.	Ragu Bhairau M5 Gharu 2 Astapadian	ff. 771a–772b
106.	Tilang M4, M5 and M1, M4 Astapadian	ff. 772b–76b
107.	Ragu Maru M1 Astapadian	ff. 777a–83a
108.	Ragu Bibhas Parbhati Astapadian	ff. 783b–788a
109.	Ragu Malar M1 Astapadian	ff. 789a–791b
110.	Ragu Gauri Purabi M4 Karahale	ff. 792a–792b

chhants (four stanzas of six verses each), and, given the criterion of length, should have followed them.'[72] The reason for this change seems to be linked with the concern to create a balance between classical and folk traditions. Since chaupadas and astapadis are sung in the classical ragas, they are put together in the beginning of the raga. The last part belongs to the folk tradition in which chhants and vars are put together along with longer works which are meant to be recited. It is not simply the criterion of increasing length of compositions that is followed in the structure of the Adi Granth. Rather, it is the question of creating a theological and musicological coherence in the final sequence. That is, the classical and folk tunes were employed side by side so that both styles of singing are balanced in the musical performance. It was done keeping in mind the sociological significance of the folk tradition. The primary intention of the gurus was to reach out to various audiences from different parts of India through the medium of different styles of singing that were popular among those audiences.

Further, Mann raises another significant point about the position of Guru Amar Das's *Anand* after the astapadis in the Ramakali raga:

> The most noticeable such shift is that of the *Anand* of Guru Amardas, in *rag* Ramkali. This composition is included in the grouping of the longer compositions in the Goindval *Pothis* (folio 80) and MS 1245 (folio 881) but is recorded at the end of the subsection on the *ashtpadis* in the Kartarpur *Pothi* (folio 697). The reason for this alteration is not clear.[73]

The 'reason for this alteration' is intimately linked with Guru Arjan's editorial perspective. First, the text of *Anand* commands a particular prominence in Sikh ritual and liturgy. The first five and last stanzas of this text are sung at the conclusion of every Sikh ceremony. In particular, the Sikh musicians (*ragis*) sing the first stanza in Ramakali raga in its classical form while the remaining ones are sung to folk tunes.[74] This is the main reason for placing this liturgical text immediately after the astapadis. Second, Guru Amar Das's composition of 'Bliss' (*Anand*) is juxtaposed with the text of the *Saddu* ('call'), that is, Sundar's dirge on the third guru's death. This juxtaposition illuminates Guru Arjan's editorial insight, stressing the 'ideal of balanced life' in which the sad and the joyous are subtly interwoven with the moods of yearning and rejoicing.[75] Third, *Saddu* is a folk genre that is followed by lyrical songs of joy (chhants) to cultivate an optimistic spirit. Finally, the position of Guru Amar Das's *Anand* in the Ramakali raga section highlights the most significant point:

that even the seemingly straightforward structure of the Adi Granth can hold big surprises if one fails to pay close attention to the liturgical and literary context of the texts in which they are used.

Fixing the Epilogue

The concluding section of the Vanjara pothi is not yet fixed, nor is its content determined. It reflects the early fluid stage in the textual process when the decision to include the panegyrics by the Sikh bards and some other compositions was not yet taken. Indeed, the epilogue is still in the process of evolving. Interestingly, the last composition, *Sahansar Nama* (#116), was added later on with a different pen. It consists of 82 stanzas that are extracanonical. It enlists the different names of God frequently used in the Vaishnava and Nath traditions. It was certainly taken from the text of the *Pran Sangali* ('chain of breath') attributed to Guru Nanak.[76] Originally, it was written under the title of M1, but later on it was covered with the deletion paste (hartal) and number '6' was written over the number '1'. It was consciously done to attribute this composition to Guru Hargobind. However, the number '1' can still be seen under the paste. The Sikh hagiographical accounts, particularly the Puratan *janam sakhis*, do refer to the *Pran Sangali* as composed by Guru Nanak in Sri Lanka (Cylone). Each of its chapters contains the guru's response to a question raised by Raja Shivnabh of Singladip (Sri Lanka).[77] The major part of this text, however, is an exposition of the *hatha yoga* technique, which obviously cannot be the work of Guru Nanak.

Tradition records that when Guru Arjan was compiling the Adi Granth, he came to know about this composition of Guru Nanak. He dispatched a learned Sikh, Bhai Paira Mokha, to Singladip to bring back a copy of the manuscript of *Pran Sangali* in the possession of the descendants of Raja Shivnabh. The copy Bhai Paira Mokha brought was scrutinized by

Table 7: Epilogue

No.	Composition	Verses	Folios
111.	*Chaubole* M5	1–11	ff. 793a–793b
112.	*Phunahe* M5	1–23	ff. 793b–797a
113.	*Savayye Sri Mukhvak* M5	1–20	ff. 797–802a
114.	*Salok Sahaskriti* M5	1–67	ff. 802b–11b
115.	M5 *Gatha*	1–24	ff. 811b–13b
116.	*Sahansar Nama Dakhani* M1/6	1–82	ff. 814a–820b

Guru Arjan and adjudged spurious.[78] Interestingly, the title *Pran Sangali Mahala 1* has been inscribed in Arabic letters in the Kartarpur bir on folio 963 / 1, but there is no such text to be found there.[79] The rest of the page is totally blank. The presence of the text of *Sahansar Nama* in the Vanjara pothi throws an interesting light on the strength of the popular tradition that some portions of the *Pran Sangali* were indeed available to Guru Arjan. He made the final decision to exclude the 82 stanzas of *Sahansar Nama* from the first canonical text of the Adi Granth.

Finally, it is instructive to note that the Bahoval pothi contains the *Raga-mala* ('garland of ragas') at the end, signifying that this text was on the agenda much earlier than the tradition would have us believe. It was included in the Kartarpur bir with the intention of highlighting the distinctiveness of the ragas of the Adi Granth in the context of the prevailing musical tradition. It certainly helps to illuminate certain characteristic features of the Sikh approach towards the ragas. For instance, its text follows the *raga–ragini–putra* classification of six–five–eight (six head ragas, each having five female raginis and eight sons, that is, 6+30+48 = 84), giving rise to a total of 84 ragas. There is no such system in the Adi Granth, where all the major ragas appear under the same title of raga, not under the title of ragini. Only one-fourth of the *Raga-mala* list is accepted in the Sikh tradition. Therefore, the exclusion of the 63 ragas of the *Raga-mala* that are not employed in the Adi Granth may reveal the choices made by the gurus. An understanding of the musical system of the *Raga-mala* enables one to explore the spiritual ethos of the Adi Granth.[80] Further, the apocryphal texts of the Banno version of the Adi Granth (two sets of saloks attributed to Guru Nanak, *Ratan-mala* and *Hakikat Rah Mukam*) are not to be found in the Bahoval pothi. Although *Ratan-mala* appears in MS 1245 (f. 1257a), it was not included in the Kartarpur bir due to its emphasis upon hatha yoga ideals.[81]

Quest for a Letter-perfect Text of the Adi Granth

The creation of the Adi Granth evidently owes much to the enormous energies of Guru Arjan. He prepared an authoritative text in response to the process of consolidation of the Sikh tradition taking place within the larger context of doctrinal and institutional developments of his times. He used the best possible words to crystallize the divine message. Indeed, his intention was to create a letter-perfect text for the Sikh community.[82] He carefully directed the whole operation of recording the Adi Granth.

This is quite evident from his personal approval of the content, form, and organization of the bani in particular raga sections, as indicated by the use of the word 'sudh' ('correct') in the margins of the text. The issue of textual accuracy is, however, in many ways relative, not absolute. We live in an age of photographic reproduction and expect that a copy of an original will resemble it in virtually every way, but this is really not the case with the manuscripts of the Adi Granth. The available manuscripts display all kinds of scribal errors of omission and commission. The Vanjara pothi illuminates the textual process through which Guru Arjan meticulously followed a carefully laid-out plan to achieve the final readings of the compositions of the Adi Granth. He devised certain checks and balances that made it extremely difficult for anyone to interpolate extraneous matter in the text without being identified. Each entry in the Adi Granth is numbered and its position is further determined by its raga, authorship, and metrical form. Guru Arjan's achievement can be seen from the remarkably consistent structure of the Adi Granth. There are, however, certain instances where he consciously departed from consistency, in order to provide a deeper theological coherence to the text, a coherence that is not visible on the surface. It becomes meaningful only when one explores the contextual depth of the relevant text. For this purpose, Guru Arjan sometimes added his own couplet or stanza to the celebrated works of his predecessors.

The Vanjara pothi, MS 1245, Bahoval pothi, and certain other documents (such as Painda Sahib's Granth) played a significant role as 'working drafts' in the complex process of redaction under the direct supervision of Guru Arjan. All these pothis were kept in the Guru's archives at Amritsar. Baba Bachittar Singh Bedi (who was a descendant in the lineage of Guru Nanak's son, Baba Lakhmi Chand, and who exchanged the Bahoval pothi with Bhai Vir Singh's set of publications in 1956) preserved the family tradition that the pothi was given to Baba Sri Chand when he visited Guru Arjan at Amritsar.[83] It stayed with the Bedi family for more than three centuries before it became the precious possession of the Bhai Vir Singh Sahitya Sadan, New Delhi. Similarly, other pothis survived as scriptural relics.

Without understanding the real nature of these documents, Jeevan Deol makes the following assertion: 'Early pothis such as the Bahoval, Goindval and Guru Nanak Dev University MS 1245 texts would still represent independent oral and textual traditions that failed to proliferate in the ways that the traditional Adi Granth recensions did.'[84] One must understand that working drafts do not normally proliferate. They serve their specific purpose and survive as scriptural relics in the possession of particular families to whom they were handed over as gifts from the guru's archives. There was no need to copy them when the updated versions of the Adi Granth were available. In this context, Gurinder Singh Mann's adroit observation is much more accurate, when he remarks: '...MS 1245 was prepared in the central Sikh community'.[85] Interestingly, the main scribe of the Kartarpur bir, Bhai Gurdas, had written one hymn in the text of the *Bavan Akhari* in the Bahoval pothi, highlighting the fact that the latter document was being used in the process of canon formation at Amritsar. If certain pothis had distinguished origins during the period of the gurus, they were preserved as sacred relics. This is how the Vanjara pothi and other documents have survived. Some of these pothis may have even remained within the families of the descendants of early scribes who worked in the court of Guru Arjan. Historically, the pothis of gurbani have always remained prized and frequently used ritual objects, and Sikh scribes have continually worked as carefully as possible to copy them, always holding dear the belief that they were producing as accurate and correct ('*sudh*') text as they could. These volumes were discarded only through 'sacred cremation' when they became too brittle and old.[86]

From the perspective of this study, the Kartarpur bir itself emerges as the 'master draft' which was frequently revised in the process of canon formation. There are ample signs of deletions, crossings, and blank spaces that throw enough light on the nature of this document. In fact, Guru Arjan had not yet closed the canon and he intended to add more hymns to the evolving corpus of the Sikh scripture. Both Gurinder Singh Mann and I have discussed in our works that certain hymns were added after 1604. Note the entry of the date of its completion recorded at the head of the table of contents: 'Having completed the pothi, [the scribe] has reached [to the indexing of it] on sambat 1661 *miti bhadau vadi ekam* 1' (1 August 1604). The Punjabi phrase '*pothi likhi pahunche*' points in the direction of the ongoing operation of canon formation at that particular stage. A simple recording of the date of its completion would have been sufficient if the canon was closed.

The citation at the head of this paper clearly indicates that various scribes used the great granth ('*vadda granth*') of the fifth guru as a touchstone to authenticate their own copies of the Adi Granth. Throughout Sikh history, the Kartarpur bir has served as a benchmark for later scribes. Scholars have raised questions about its authenticity by focusing on certain 'grave errors' in this document, because they expect it to be a 'letter-perfect' text prepared by Bhai Gurdas under the direct supervision of Guru Arjan. Its real significance, however, lies in understanding its true nature as a 'master draft', not as a liturgical canon. Here, one can raise an objection: why would the Kartarpur manuscript proliferate while the other working drafts, in the form of early pothis, failed to do so. As a 'master draft', the Kartarpur bir must be distinguished from other 'working drafts'. By calling it a 'master draft' as well as the 'first canonical text', I acknowledge its historical significance from two angles. First, this was the bir where final readings of various compositions were established. Second, this bir functioned as a master draft to control the activity of canon formation. Its blank folios and other deletions point in this direction. Anyone who has seen the Kartarpur bir can testify that it is a huge volume with a total of 974 folios (of which 226 are entirely blank and some others partly blank). It was thus not possible to use it as a liturgical canon in the Darbar Sahib, Amritsar.[87] There were some accomplished scribes in Guru Arjan's court who prepared copies of the Kartarpur volume. One such bir that was written *ad seriatim* was installed in Darbar Sahib in 1604.[88]

In spite of Guru Arjan's remarkable editorial achievement in establishing the first canonical text in 1604, there emerged three different recensions of the Adi Granth in the course of time. The principal reason for this development was the unstable situation created by Guru Arjan's execution in 1606 under the orders of the Mughal emperor Jahnagir. This event became the turning point in the history of the Sikh tradition, creating a new situation that was conducive to sectarian tendencies within the Panth. Not surprisingly, the Lahore recension was prepared in 1610 when Jahangir imprisoned Guru Hargobind in the Gwalior fort. Similarly, the Banno recension originated in 1642 in the area of Khara Mangat in Gujrat district when the main centre of Sikh activities shifted from Amritsar to Kiratpur under Guru Hargobind, who had to withdraw to the Shivalik Hills due to the pressure of Mughal authorities. The central place of Amritsar fell into the hands of the 'Minas' ('scoundrels'), the followers of Prithi Chand and his descendants. In many instances, the later scribes and their groups within the Panth failed to understand the editorial insights of Guru Arjan and struggled with problematic texts. Some of them made some intentional changes in the text to reflect the changed historical situation of the Panth.[89] In order to prevent the circulation of three different versions of the Adi Granth, the tenth guru, Gobind Singh closed the canon after adding the works of his father, Guru Tegh Bahadur, during the last decades of the seventeenth century at a place called Damdama Sahib in Anandpur. There still exist a number of manuscripts of this standard Damdama version around the Anandpur and Bhatinda areas, the main centres of Sikh activities in the late seventeenth and early eighteenth centuries.[90]

Conclusion

This study has examined the place of the Vanjara pothi in the formation of the Sikh canon. This newly discovered manuscript provides us with a window through which to look into the complex process of the making of Sikh scripture. It offers new data to illuminate the emerging structures and final forms of various compositions in the Adi Granth. It highlights a collaborative approach based upon the theory of working drafts prepared under the direct supervision of Guru Arjan at Ramsar, in the central place of Amritsar. It provides a new direction in the field of Sikh studies, suggesting that it is more fruitful to reconstruct the textual history of the Adi Granth than to decide prematurely what the original reading was. In fact, it is the 'final reading' that is of utmost significance in the Sikh tradition. In a certain sense, this study offers a fresh perspective on the early history of the Sikh Panth, in which Vanjara Sikhs played important roles as the scribes and custodians of the Sikh scriptural relics.

There is a need to explore new avenues of research into the social constituency of the early Sikh Panth: When did Vanjara Sikhs enter the Panth? Were they acquainted with Guru Nanak during his missionary travels? Did they become Sikhs during the period of Guru Hargobind for the purpose of making weapons for the Sikh army? If the Vanjara pothi had come down from generation to generation in the family of the scribe who originally wrote it, then Vanjara Sikhs were already an integral part of the Sikh Panth during the period of Guru Arjan. Thus, we need to investigate the history of the movement of the Vanjara pothi further. It is no coincidence that Makhan Shah Labana and Lakhi Shah Vanjara were associated with the life of Guru Tegh Bahadur, the former for identifying and supporting the 'real guru' in the face of the severe threat posed by pretenders and the latter for cremating his headless body at Delhi in 1675. Indeed, both have become an integral part of the cultural memory of the Sikh Panth for their roles at crucial moments of Sikh history. Similarly, Bhai Mani Singh was an accomplished scribe whose five sons— Ude Singh, Bachittar Singh and others—received the Khalsa initiation in

VANJARA POTHI 59

1699 and laid down their lives fighting for the guru. All these eminent Vanjara Sikhs must have had a long association with the Sikh Panth. They were sufficiently armed for self-defence, and some of them were engaged in maritime trade. In particular, the culture of the Vanjara Sikhs of central and south India needs further exploration.

Notes

Acknowledgements: I am grateful to Professor W. H. McLeod for providing me with his valuable feedback in his response to my paper at the Dunedin conference. I am also thankful to other participants, including N. G. Barrier, Verne Dusenbery, and Louis Fenech, for their useful comments.

1. A note from a manuscript written by a Sikh, Ram Rai, son of a goldsmith named Uttam Chand, in *sambat* 1749 (1691–92 CE). The note is on folio 27b, now bound at the end of the volume. This manuscript was originally at Patna Sahib, but recently it has been moved to Guru Granth Sahib Bhavan, Goindval Sahib and numbered as MSS Bir 36. I saw this manuscript on 14 July 2002 during my visit to Goindval Sahib.

2. Rein Fernhout, *Canonical Texts: Bearers of Absolute Authority: Bible, Koran, Veda, Tipitaka*, Henry Janson and Lucy Janson-Hofland (trans.) (Amsterdam and Atlanta, GA: Editions Rodopy B.V., 1994), pp. 2–7.

3. Two contemporary sources, *Sri Gurbilas Patashahi 6* (1840) and *Suraj Prakash* (1843), provide detailed accounts of the compilation of the Adi Bir in 1604. These authors had seen the Kartarpur manuscript.

4. For details on different recensions of the Adi Granth, see Pashaura Singh, *The Guru Granth Sahib: Canon, Meaning and Authority* (New Delhi: Oxford University Press, 2000), chapters 2 and 7.

5. Balwant Singh Dhillon, *Early Sikh Scriptural Tradition: Myth and Reality* (Amritsar: Singh Brothers, 2000), p. 281.

6. Gurinder Singh Mann, *The Making of Sikh Scripture* (New York: Oxford University Press, 2001), p. 123.

7. Ibid., pp. 32–85.

8. Ibid., p. 67.

9. Piar Singh, *Gatha Sri Adi Granth and the Controversy* (Grandledge, MI: Anant Educational and Rural Development Foundation, Inc., 1996), p. 35.

10. Jeevan Singh Deol, 'Text and Lineage in Early Sikh History: Issues in the Study of the Adi Granth,' *Bulletin of the School of Oriental and African Studies* 64, 1 (Cambridge University Press, 2001), p. 48.

11. For details, see ibid., p. 34, n. 3.

12. For the growth of the 'Sursagar', see John Stratton Hawley, *Surs Das: Poet, Singer, Saint* (Seattle and London: University of Washington Press, 1984), pp. 35–63.

13. For details, see my *Life and Work of Guru Arjan: History, Memory, and Biography in the Sikh Tradition* (New Delhi: Oxford University Press, 2006), pp. 134–71.

14. Harbans Singh (ed.), *The Encyclopaedia of Sikhism* 2, (Patiala: Punjabi University, 1996), p. 315.

15. Piara Singh Padam (ed.), *Bhai Kesar Singh Chhibar Krit Bansavalinama Dasan Patashahian Ka* (Amritsar: Singh Brothers, 1997), p. 76.

16. Gurdas Bhalla, *Varan Bhai Gurdas*, Giani Hazara Singh and Bhai Vir Singh (eds) (Amritsar: Khalsa Samachar, 1962), 1: 38.

17. Winand M. Callewaert, 'Singers' Repertoires in Western India,' R. S. McGregor (ed.), *Devotional Literature in South Asia: Current Research, 1985–1988* (Cambridge: Cambridge University Press, 1992), pp. 29–35.

18. For a brief discussion on the stolen Guru Har Sahai pothi, see Pashaura Singh, *The Guru Granth Sahib*, pp. 32–4.

19. Gurinder Singh Mann, *The Goindval Pothis: The Earliest Extant Source of the Sikh Canon* (Cambridge, MA: Harvard Oriental Series, 1996). Pritam Singh, *Ahiyapur Vali Pothi: Part I—Introduction* (Amritsar: Guru Nanak Dev University Press, 1998). Also see Pashaura Singh, 'Competing Views of Canon Formation in the Sikh Tradition: A Focus on Recent Controversy,' *Religious Studies Review* 28, 1 (January 2002), p. 3–9.

20. M4, *Bihagara Chhant 4*, Adi Granth, p. 540.

21. M5, *Gauri 31*, Adi Granth, pp. 185–6.

22. See Pashaura Singh, *The Guru Granth Sahib*, pp. 41–53, 106–14.

23. Giani Mahan Singh, 'Bahoval vali *Pothi* Sahib: Pavittar Adi Bir te Samkalin ikk Puratan *Pothi* Sahib,' *Khera* 1, 4 (March 1980), pp. 13–6.

24. I examined the Bahoval Pothi at Bhai Vir Singh Sahitya Library on 29–30 May 2002. The manuscript is now laminated in four volumes. I had earlier seen this pothi in 1999, when it was still in its original brittle condition and needed immediate attention for preservation.

25. Kirpal Kazak, *Sikligar Kabile da Sabhyachar* (Patiala: Punjabi University, 1990), pp. 17 and 97.

26. For details, see Harbans Singh (ed.), *The Encyclopaedia of Sikhism* 4, (1998), pp. 405–6.

27. Amarnath K. Menon, 'Banjaras Embracing Sikhism,' *India Today* (31 May 1986), p. 139.

28. Vanjara Pothi, MSS # 1. The librarian, Bhai Sohan Singh, helped me with the examination of its contents during intermittent periods between June 8 and 12 July 2002. Louis Fenech was with me when I re-examined the pothi on 12 July 2002.

29. 'Centuries-old Sikh Relic Found in UK Library,' *The Hindustan Times* (24 September 2002). It was not any new discovery as claimed in the report, but a new hypothesis on an old document offered by Jeevan Deol. I had examined this document during my research trip in 1990. This manuscript was purchased by

the British Museum in 1884 from Reverend A. Fisher, who placed it there in the nineteenth century. Deol pushed the date of the writing of its early portion to the middle of the seventeenth century. The final two thirds of the document, being no doubt worn out with use, were rewritten on new folios during the nineteenth century. The media coverage of this story prompted the Akal Takhat Jathedar, Giani Joginder Singh Vedanti, to visit the British Library for investigating the truth of this matter. Being himself an expert on the Adi Granth manuscripts, Vedanti categorically refuted the authenticity of this manuscript, adding that 'such propaganda was being carried out by Anti-Panthic circles in the name of research'. Jeevan Deol immediately retracted from his early claims and supported Jathedar Vedanti's assertion: 'British Bir: Cambridge Scholar Backs Vedanti', *Indian Express* (14 December 2002).

30. Piar Singh, *Gatha Sri Adi Granth* (Amritsar: Guru Nanak Dev University, 1992), pp. 123–4, 137–40.

31. Pashaura Singh, *The Guru Granth Sahib*, pp. 84–102.

32. Piar Singh, *Gatha and the Controversy*, p. 22.

33. For more details, see Pashaura Singh, *The Guru Granth Sahib*, pp. 97–8.

34. See Bhai Jodh Singh, *Sri Kartarpuri Bir de Darsan* (Patiala: Punjabi University, 1968), p. 46.

35. The *Sodar* cluster has the following five hymns in the Adi Granth: (1)–(3) M1, Asa 1, 2/1 and 3/2, Adi Granth, pp. 8–10, 347–9; (4) M4, Gujari 4/1, Adi Granth, pp. 10, 492; and (5) M5, Gujari 5/1, Adi Granth, pp. 10, 495.

36. *Varan Bhai Gurdas* 1:38.

37. The *So Purakh* group has the following four hymns in the Adi Granth: (1) M4, Asa 1/2, Adi Granth, pp. 10–11, 348; (2) M4, Asa 2/53, Adi Granth, 11–12, 365; (3) M1, Asa 3/29, Adi Granth, pp. 12, 357; and (4) M5, Asa 3/29, Adi Granth, pp. 12, 378.

38. For details of this manuscript, see Pashaura Singh, *The Guru Granth Sahib*, pp. 61–4.

39. Ibid., pp. 64–6.

40. Gurinder Singh Mann, *The Making of Sikh Scripture*, p. 77.

41. For details, see *The Encyclopaedia of Sikhism* 1, p. 300–2.

42. I have a photograph of this folio in my possession. I have also examined the Kartarpur bir personally. Also see Giani Mahan Singh, 'Bahoval vali *Pothi Sahib*', p. 15.

43. G. S. Talib (trans.), *Sri Guru Granth Sahib* 1 (Patiala: Punjabi University, 1984), p. 508.

44. Pashaura Singh, *The Guru Granth Sahib*, pp. 155–7.

45. *The Encyclopaedia of Sikhism* 4, p. 252.

46. Ibid.

47. See *Gatha and the Controversy*, p. 39.

48. For details, see Pashaura Singh, *The Guru Granth Sahib*, p. 48.

49. Ibid., pp. 48–9.

50. For details, see ibid., pp. 209–10.

51. Ibid, p. 49, n. 70.

52. Ibid., p. 48, n. 67.

53. I have a photograph of this index folio of Ram Rai's bir (1692) that I took at Goindval Sahib when I examined this manuscript on 14 July 2002. Another manuscript of the Adi Granth (1705) in the library of Dr Trilochan Singh/Anurag Singh has a similar entry at the end of the index.

54. Pashaura Singh, *The Guru Granth Sahib*, p. 145.

55. Gopinder Kaur, *Understanding Shabad Kirtan in its Sikh Context: Why is it so Important to Sikh Religious Experience and in what Ways does Gurbani Convey This?* (MA thesis, School of Oriental and African Studies, University of London, 2001), p. 20.

56. Bahoval Pothi, ff. 661b–62b.

57. M5, *Basant Mahala 5 Gharu 2 Hindol*, 19–21, Adi Granth, pp. 1185–6.

58. Pashaura Singh, *The Guru Granth Sahib*, p. 138.

59. Gurinder Singh Mann, *The Making of Sikh Scripture*, p. 94.

60. Frederic Pincott, 'The Arrangement of the Hymns of the Adi Granth,' *Journal of Royal Asiatic Society* 18 (1878), p. 440.

61. For details, see Pashaura Singh, *The Guru Granth Sahib*, p. 140.

62. The pad ('word') is of divine origin ('dhur') in much the same way as *dhur ki bani* ('word from the beginning') is considered revelation in the Sikh tradition. The term *dhrupad* ('fixed word') stands for a musical style that became popular in north India during the fifteenth and sixteenth centuries. Interestingly, Abu'l Fazal uses the word dhurpad in his *Ain-i-Akbari*. See Bonnie C. Wade, *Imaging Sound: an Ethnographic Study of Music, Art and Culture in Mughal India* (Chicago: University of Chicago Press, 1988), pp. 95–6, 144, and 191.

63. Gobind Singh Mansukhani, *Indian Classical Music and Sikh Kirtan* (New Delhi: Oxford and IBH, 1982), p. 78.

64. M5, *Ramakali ki Var*, 1 (4), Adi Granth, p. 958.

65. M5, *Ragu Bilavalu Asatapadi 2 Ghar 12*, Adi Granth, pp. 837–8 and M3, *Bilavalu 2*, Adi Granth, pp. 842–3.

66. M1, *Suhi 2*, Adi Granth, pp. 730–1.

67. M1, *Suhi Kuchajji*, Adi Granth, p. 762.

68. M1, *Suhi Suchajji*, Adi Granth, pp. 762–3.

69. For issues related to the Bhagat Bani, see Pashaura Singh, *The Bhagats of the Guru Granth Sahib: Sikh Self-Definition and the Bhagat Bani* (New Delhi: Oxford University Press, 2003).

70. For an analysis of this textual problem, see Pashaura Singh, *The Guru Granth Sahib*, pp. 195–8. Also see Pashaura Singh, *The Bhagats of the Guru Granth Sahib*, pp. 143–5.

71. For details, see ibid., pp. 193, n. 55.

72. Gurinder Singh Mann, *The Making of Sikh Scripture*, p. 95.

73. Ibid., pp. 95–6.

74. The late ragi Bakhshish Singh used to sing the first stanza of *Anand* in 'pure' ('*sudh*') Ramakali raga after his kirtan performance. I myself have followed this ancient tradition in my kirtan performance.

75. For details, see Pashaura Singh, *The Guru Granth Sahib*, pp. 161–5.

76. See the text of *Sahansar Nama* under the title *Raga Maru Mahala 1* in Jagjit Singh Khanpuri (ed.), *Pran Sangali* (Patiala: Punjabi University, 2nd edn, 1999), pp. 279–84.

77. See *The Encyclopaedia of Sikhism* 3, pp. 354–7.

78. Ibid., p. 355.

79. See Pashaura Singh, *The Guru Granth Sahib*, p. 64, n. 102. Also see Bhai Jodh Singh, *Sri Kartarpuri Bir de Darsan*, p. 121.

80. Ibid., pp. 145–8.

81. Ibid., p. 51.

82. The phrase 'letter-perfect text' comes from B. Barry Levy, *Fixing God's Torah: the Accuracy of the Hebrew Bible Text in Jewish Law* (New York: Oxford University Press, 2001).

83. Giani Mahan Singh, 'Bahoval vali *Pothi* Sahib', pp. 14–15.

84. Jeevan Deol, 'Text and Lineage in Early Sikh History', *Bulletin of the School of Oriental and African Studies* 64, 1 (Cambridge: Cambridge University Press, 2001), p. 45.

85. Gurinder Singh Mann, *The Making of Sikh Scripture*, p. 58.

86. Both Louis Fenech and I watched the most interesting ritual of the 'sacred cremation' of the old volumes of the Guru Granth Sahib and pothis of gurbani at Goindval Sahib on Sunday, 14 July 2002, when thousands of Sikhs participated in this devotional activity under the guidance of Baba Narinder Singh of Prabhu Simaran Kendar, Ludhiana.

87. The volume of the Adi Granth installed in the Darbar Sahib (Golden Temple) is opened at random every morning for 'taking the Divine Word' (*vak*) for inspiration. How can a volume with blank pages serve this purpose?

88. Traditionally, shortly after Shahjahan's accession in 1628, the first skirmish between Mughal troops and Sikh soldiers occurred when the Emperor was hunting near Amritsar. A hawk of his happened to be captured by Guru Hargobind's followers. This led to fighting, in which Mughal troops assaulted the Darbar Sahib. This happened when the marriage of Guru Hargobind's daughter Bibi Viro was about to take place. The Mughal soldiers disrupted the wedding and ate the sweets reserved for the groom's party. The Guru immediately rushed to his residence to take the Kartarpur bir to safety on horseback. It is highly likely that the volume installed in the Darbar Sahib was destroyed during this skirmish. The present Kartarpur bir was then taken to Kartarpur (Jalandhar). One surviving bir of the Kartarpur tradition is the Punjabi University Museum manuscript # 8. See Pashaura Singh, *The Guru Granth Sahib*, pp. 61–4.

89. Pashaura Singh, ibid., chapters 2 and 7.

90. Ibid., pp. 81, 222–4.

The Two Lives of Bhai Nand Lal 'Goya'

Louis E. Fenech

Among all the Sikhs Nand Lal ji [glows like] the [full]
moon [at night].[1]

We begin our discussion of Bhai Nand Lal with a quotation from
the practically unknown *Gur-pādhantī*, a late eighteenth or
early to mid nineteenth-century manuscript. The *Gur-pādhantī* is a record
of a conversation in Anandpur Sahib between Nand Lal, Mani Singh,
and Guru Gobind Singh in which Nand Lal questions the guru about
the nature of the Nirmala Sikh Panth.[2] The guru's answers briefly detail
Nirmala history and that of the first nine gurus and in the process
elucidate, among other things, the Panth's relationship with the three *gunas*
or constituent qualities of matter.[3] Of course it is not this text as such with
which we are concerned, but rather with its allusion to Nand Lal.

For most critical scholars of the Sikh tradition, such blatant references
to illustrious Sikhs such as Nand Lal (and Mani Singh and Guru Gobind
Singh)[4] like the one with which we begin this chapter add genuineness
to the account in question, thereby increasing the reputation of both the
text itself and its subject.[5] In the case above, for example, the allusion seems
to authorize Nirmala existence to the larger Panth.[6] But it is important
to note that these conclusions take a number of things for granted, in
particular Nand Lal's position as a revered Sikh. For our purposes, it would
be more advantageous to work backwards. It is not Nand Lal who
substantiates the Nirmala text, in other words, but the text which validates

Nand Lal. This therefore suggests what is today a common Sikh claim, namely that by placing such questions in the mouth of Nand Lal, the *Gur-pādhantī* makes clear that the latter was probably understood in this period as Sikh tradition tersely describes him today: an exceptionally pious, learned, and well-known devotee of the tenth guru. Indeed, the epigraph with which we begin seems to support this contention easily.[7]

This praise is, in retrospect, nevertheless ironic, as over time Nand Lal has become more like the moon than the author of the *Gur-pādhantī* probably intended. We will in a moment see that during the time in which the *Gur-pādhantī* was produced, Nand Lal waxed to his ultimate extent, shining like the full moon, a calming and beautiful sight at night, eclipsing all other Sikh 'stars' of note. But as the moon waxes, so too must it wane. Today, despite the fact that Nand Lal's Persian compositions are occasionally sung at the Golden Temple, Nand Lal is granted far less attention by both the Sikh community and the scholars of the tradition, and as a result, both his writings and history are little known.[8] This is not at all surprising if we examine evident trends in Sikh historiography (indeed, in any historiography) from the seventeenth to the early twentieth centuries, evincing a demotion of certain important figures such as Nand Lal or Bhai Bidhi Chhand Chhina, for example, or allowing other once-famous Sikhs to simply disappear.[9]

These comments notwithstanding, it may be that the time for Nand Lal's resurgence is at hand. Thanks in part to the recent fascination of regular Sikhs all over the world with the history of their people and their tradition and the vibrant discussions which this has engendered in both electronic print and newspapers, Sikh interest in Nand Lal is today rising.[10] This concern is principally focused upon the Punjabi *rahit-nāmās* or 'codes of conduct', which Nand Lal is believed to have authored, a focus which is in turn fuelled by current Sikh inclination to better understand what 'proper Sikhs' believe (an issue which is outside the scope of this present paper) and what it means to be Sikh in both India and the multi-ethnic Sikh diaspora. Welcome as this development is, however, it has little to do with the historical Nand Lal, his image in Sikh history, or even his Persian poetry. But this growing interest nevertheless brings to the surface a theme which I have already briefly touched and which pervades late eighteenth- and early nineteenth-century narratives of Nand Lal's life and poetry, and merits serious consideration.

The first step in uncovering this important theme is to realize that Nand Lal is in many interrelated ways a very rare character in Sikh historiography. I am not strictly speaking here of Nand Lal's ability as a Persian littérateur. Such knowledge may have been exceptional amongst Sikhs of the late seventeenth and early eighteenth centuries, but it was by no means unique.[11] A familiarity with the Persian and Arabic languages was, according to tradition, shared by many Sikhs, including Guru Nanak, Guru Gobind Singh, and Bhai Gurdas, as well as some other members of the tenth guru's court (to which Nand Lal belonged), such as Diwan Nand Chand.[12]

Nand Lal is one of the very few Sikhs who throughout the span of Sikh history occupied a space in which Sikh aspirations and desires intersected with Mughal court policies and procedures. In fact, Nand Lal's very person is the site of this congruence. We do hear of a small handful of seemingly similar Sikhs in the eleventh vār of Bhai Gurdas,[13] but even taking into consideration the brief narratives of their lives which we discover in the later Sikhān dī Bhagat-mālā attributed to Bhai Mani Singh, claiming that some of these Sikhs were initially employed by the Mughal army, none of these devotees have lives as relatively detailed in nineteenth-century sources as Nand Lal's and, as well, none of these characters were as intimate with Mughal nobility as Sikh tradition claims of our poet.[14] Very little may therefore be said about them, a point to which the silences in Sikh tradition bear ample testimony. The accounts of Nand Lal's life as the munshī and then mīr munshī, or 'scribe' and 'principal scribe', of the future emperor Bahadar Shah, Prince Muhammad Mu'azzam (who was also known as Shah 'Alam, a title he was bequeathed by the Emperor Aurangzeb in October 1676),[15] then, make Nand Lal unique in traditional Sikh history.

Symbolically related to this privileged position is the fact that Nand Lal is also one of the very few Sikhs besides the gurus whose popular narrative extends back into his childhood. As far as I can recall, the only other famous Sikh of whose youth we possess a singular account is Baba Buddha.[16] Although the allusion in question may, like the story of the child Baba Buddha, be an early verification of Nand Lal's brilliance, wisdom, and piety, I believe it has a structural importance which extends beyond the figure of Nand Lal himself. Indeed, the narrative of Nand Lal's childhood is very significant in understanding the Sikh–Mughal space to which I allude above and Nand Lal's position within it. Examining the conjunction of these rare features as they are brought together in the early to mid-nineteenth century will tell us a great deal about how Sikhs conceptualized themselves, their tradition, and the nature of Mughal power over that of individual emperors, and should ultimately expose the unnamed theme to which I alluded above: authority and legitimacy, not just for individual segments of the Sikh Panth like the Nirmalas but rather for the Panth as a whole. Fleshing out this theme and accounting for the construction of Nand Lal's particular image during the nineteenth century will be the principal purpose of the second part of this chapter. Tracing the historical Nand Lal and integrating him into the image will occupy the first. These are what I refer to as the two lives of Nand Lal, the actual and the posthumous. Let us begin this chapter with an account of what we can know about the first life of Nand Lal.

Life One

The difficulty in reconstructing the life of the historical Nand Lal is immense, as there are simply no sources outside the Sikh tradition in which he figures. Even Sikh tradition itself, as we shall see, does not allocate space to Nand Lal's life until the very late eighteenth to mid-nineteenth century. Both of these facts should most certainly cause one to question the many grandiose claims about Nand Lal put forth by Sikh tradition, but it should not lead us to reject these assertions outright. Indeed, a modified version of this Sikh tradition may in some instances be buttressed by circumstantial evidence, which will allow us to partially rebuild the life of our poet. To do this, we must once again begin by working backwards, taking as our point of departure not the actual life of Nand Lal but rather the products which remain at the end of his life, the works attributed to him—in particular, the Persian works.

I single these out for good reason. I have shown elsewhere that it is highly unlikely that the Punjabi works attributed to Nand Lal are the product of the same Bhai Nand Lal 'Goya' under discussion.[17] If there were indeed two Nand Lals (or more), they have been purposely conflated in Sikh history since, one may assume, the appearance of Bhai Nand Lal as an important figure in the early eighteenth century.[18] We have therefore no reason for the time being to dispute Hew McLeod's oft-repeated claim that the authors of the many rahit-namas attributed to Nand Lal probably used his name to grant authority to their texts and the ideas contained therein in the same way as with the Gur-pādhantī above.[19] It seems likely that the anti-Islamic/Islamicate injunctions in works like the Tankhāh-nāmā/Nasīhat-nāmā were attributed to Nand Lal to add a particular force to this enmity.[20]

Assuming that it was in fact the Persian-writing Nand Lal who was a figure in the court of Guru Gobind Singh is both a sensible and well-contextualized conclusion. It is very likely that Nand Lal's initial fame would in all probability have rested upon his very good Persian works rather than the pedestrian Punjabi ones attributed to him. And in this light, moreover, it seems highly plausible that it was Nand Lal's skill as a poet which would have initially attracted the attention of the guru.[21] Such may have engendered the Guru's love for Nand Lal, a rare affection which has informed later developments in Sikh history and which is strongly implied in many eighteenth- and nineteenth-century Sikh manuscripts. According to a tradition which comes to us from the descendents of Nand Lal, for example:

Bhai Nand Lal ji so enjoyed [taking] the [tenth] guru's darshan that he was not satiated even though he did so every day. Guru Gobind Singh likewise remained very pleased with [Nand Lal] and was exceedingly happy to hear the poet's words of wisdom.[22]

Such a conclusion is easily borne out by making reference to the standards that court poets of the various Persian courts of the Indo-Islamic period were expected to exhibit. Many of the anecdotes we possess of Nand Lal, for instance, demonstrate him to manifest these traits. Such qualities are defined by the famous twelfth-century Persian court poet and prosodist Nizami-'i 'Aruzi-'i Samarqandi:

...[the court poet] must be of a tender temperament, profound in thought, sound in genius, clear of vision, quick of insight. He must be well versed in many divers [sic] sciences, and quick to extract what is best from his environment; for as poetry is of advantage in every science, so is every science of advantage in poetry. And the poet must be of pleasing conversation in social gatherings, and of cheerful countenance in social gatherings, of cheerful countenance on festive occasions...[23]

I do not of course mean to caricature Nand Lal by reducing him to a series of qualities or characteristics in the way that Gibb and Browne often do to both the Ottoman and Iranian poets of their famous histories, but if Nand Lal was cognizant of such ideals (a likely conclusion since the Mughal cultural environment in which he lived valued and sought these in its poets), he may have cultivated such in his professional life which would, we may assume, have easily endeared him to his patron, in this case Guru Gobind Singh. The famous Nirmala Sikh author of the early to mid-nineteenth century, Santokh Singh, may therefore be on the mark when, as we will see, he claims as much of Nand Lal.[24]

I have here tacitly answered the first question one must pose in any analysis of Nand Lal: were such works in fact written by the Nand Lal 'Goya' of Sikh tradition? This to be sure is a difficult question (one which, incidentally, Sikh tradition never asks) as the Persian works of Goya possess no internal evidence which suggests that the Goya of the texts is the Nand Lal of today's accepted Sikh history.[25] This difficulty is compounded by the fact that there are other Indo-Persian poets who took the sobriquet 'Goya' ('the speaker').[26] But recent fieldwork has led me to believe that it is more likely than not that a substantial portion of the Persian texts attributed to Nand Lal 'Goya' were in fact written by one such figure. My reasons for this are three, all of which are as interrelated and unexpectedly straightforward as they are circumstantial. First, Sikh tradition's claim to them since at least the mid-eighteenth century has been contested by no other poet, group, or scholar over the last 250 or so years; second, not one couplet or *bait* appears in either the many exhaustive *tazkirahs* of the late seventeenth century and onwards (in India or elsewhere) or within the numerous contemporary biographies of poets which would help us identify them as the product of an author other than Nand Lal 'Goya';[27] and third, in some cases internal evidence seems to suggest a Sikh author or, to be more precise, a non-Muslim poet who was associated with the court of Guru Gobind Singh. Two baits, one from the *Zindagī-nāmah* and another from the *Dīvān-i Goyā* hint as much:

In the language of India (*hindavī*) the name [of the community of the faithful] is *sādh sangat*. O Maulavi! All those [who belong to it] praise the Lord.[28]

That person [who has seen the face of the Beloved] becomes a sacrifice to the dust of those who traverse the path of the sangat. Goya's heart desires this very same thing.[29]

The terms 'sādh sangat' and 'sangat' (not Persian words) are of course used in the Adi Granth and explicated in the vars of Bhai Gurdas.[30] Though the reference here and the term 'sangat's' appearance elsewhere in both the *Zindagī-nāmah* and the *Dīvān-i Goyā* may not be specifically Sikh, it is a good chance that it does indeed allude to the nascent Panth. What one can assume with certainty in this regard however is that the term does not refer to a Muslim or Sufi congregation/community as the word very often employed for these (among many others) is the

Persian *sohbat*.[31] In fact, as far as I know, the term 'sangat' appears in no other Persian poetry in India apart from that attributred to Nand Lal.[32] Of course this conclusion must be tempered, since such non-Muslim references also find their place within the conventions of Muslim-Persian ghazal poetry. It is commonplace for Muslim mystic poets to find salvation in features of contemporary society which legalistic Islam considers *haram* or forbidden, such as the tavern, the idol, the wine cup, and the brahman's *janeū* (sacred thread). Such inclusion, moreover, may have also simply been an attempt to consciously infuse this bait with an easily recognizable 'regional idiom'.[33] These facts notwithstanding, the cumulative effect of such seemingly 'Sikh' terminology throughout the works attributed to Nand Lal seems to dictate otherwise. Indeed, as Christopher Shackle reminds us in another context, 'the use of Islamic terms [or poetic norms in this case] does not guarantee an Islamic content'![34] The irony here is quite apparent.

To these three reasons, we may now add a related point which I will describe in more detail later on: the sheer frequency of both eighteenth-century Sikh manuscripts in which Nand Lal figures and mid to late eighteenth-century manuscripts of his Persian poetry, especially the *Dīvān-i Goyā* and the *Zindagī-nāmah*. Although all of these factors do not provide one with an incontrovertible conclusion, they nevertheless allow one to assume that it is unlikely that Nand Lal's Persian texts are the product of some other writer with the sobriquet 'Goya' or 'Lal'.[35] Let us proceed by keeping in mind that this is a tenuous conclusion at best.

As both the *Dīvān* and the *Zindagī-nāmah*, amongst other Persian Nand Lal texts, are sources of relatively good quality, one can be assured that they indicate considerable training in both Arabic and Persian, and a keen knowledge of the great Persian works which infused Indo-Islamic culture.[36] The possibility that the poet of these works was employed by the Mughal administration (or perhaps some other Indian administration modelling itself along the same lines as the hegemonic Mughal one) is strong, as Persian in particular was the language of high culture and thus in the late seventeenth century, the formal language of the eastern Islamicate of which India was a formidable part.[37] Though Sikh tradition makes it clear that Nand Lal was indeed a clerk of the Emperor Aurangzeb's son, Prince Mu'azzam, and that after the evacuation of Anandpur in late 1704–early 1705, he had managed to once again procure employment in the Mughal court, Mughal sources say nothing in this regard. Such silence should not compel us to deny tradition's claim, but rather to amend it.

Since it is implausible to believe that every clerk in the empire's employ would have been noticed and mentioned by its Persian chroniclers, it may be that Nand Lal served the Mughal administration as a minor scribe or in an as-yet-to-be-determined capacity. However, one must indeed be cautious here, for it is also very likely that such a royal pedigree was an apocryphal one, appropriated in order to increase the reputation of this poet and in turn that of the court of the tenth Sikh master to which he was most likely pledged at one point in his life.

To continue: that such literary skills as we find in these Persian texts could only come about through long, perhaps a lifetime of study is a point worth repeating, particularly when we combine this with the contention that internal evidence suggests a non-Muslim poet. This leads one to assume that the author of these sources would probably have belonged to those Hindu or (though less likely) Sikh castes which valued literacy and whose traditional occupations tended towards bureaucratic employment such as the Kayastha or the Khatri (in some cases the Brahman).[38] Such extensive training would have benefitted no other non-Muslim group, though to be fair Sufis and, rarely, Hindu Bhagats would also have possessed knowledge of Persian and so too would other non-Muslim traders throughout northern India have had at least a remedial knowledge of the language. Sikh tradition easily supports this inference since it holds that Nand Lal was a Khatri, member of a group generally associated with trade. This is a point, moreover, which we may reinforce with a bait from the first ghazal of Nand Lal's Persian *Dīvān*. Here we are told that:

I will sacrifice my life, heart, and body to the dust of the feet of the *muqaddam*, [who is] anyone who shows me the way to You.[39]

The reference to the 'muqaddam', the village headman in the Punjab and other parts of northern India, is an unusual one as it is rarely if ever encountered in Persian ghazal poetry in India or elsewhere. The muqaddam in the period under discussion would most likely have been a Khatri, though there are examples of other groups becoming one.[40]

Now that we have inferred from our evidence that the author was most likely a Khatri, that he was perhaps employed by the Mughal administration at one point in his life (in Multan, according to a Sikh tradition, which seems based on evidence supplied by Nand Lal's descendants, though of course this claim cannot be substantiated)[41] and certainly by the Sikh court (as we will see) at another, the obvious question one must ask is: were these texts the product of a Sikh? Here we are on surprisingly unstable ground and not simply because the line separating Sikhs and Hindus in the period under discussion was a rather fuzzy one. It would be folly to claim that Nand Lal's *Dīvān*, easily his best work, was principally inspired by the bani of Guru Nanak, the central motivation behind the vars and *kabitts* of Bhai Gurdas and the hymns of the Sikh gurus we discover in the Guru Granth Sahib.[42] It is of course impossible to show with Nand Lal's poetry the type of hymn for hymn correspondence we recognize between the hymns of Guru Nanak and his successors to the guruship[43] because Nand Lal's work is not written in what Christopher Shackle terms 'the Sacred Language of the Sikhs'.[44] The ghazals in the *Dīvān-i Goyā*, as I have shown elsewhere, may certainly be interpreted as Sikh, but only insofar as there exists in many cases a general affinity between both the Sufi and Sikh traditions of the seventeenth and eighteenth centuries.[45] More than simply affinity may be the case, however, when we examine the other works attributed to Nand Lal.

Sikh tradition certainly claims that Nand Lal was not an ordinary Sikh disciple, but one of the Guru's most revered devotees, whose literary acumen was exceeded only by his humility and his capacity for selfless service or *sevā*. The earliest Sikh narratives of Nand Lal's life make this utterly clear. Such a picture of Nand Lal, moreover, receives strong support from certain Persian couplets attributed to him, which do seem to indicate that the author is a Sikh. The *Sultanat Dahamm* or the 'Kingdom [of the] Tenth [Lord]', which is the concluding chapter of the *Ganj-nāmah* ('Treasure Book'), for example, suggests as much. Here we have a collection of 17 couplets in the first portion of the text and 56 couplets in the second.[46] As the *radīf* or 'word(s) repeated after an end rhyme' of the final portion of the *Sultanat Dahamm* is 'Gobind Singh', let me provide the first three couplets and the last one by way of example:

Guru Gobind Singh protects [the world] and is [himself] protected by the Lord. Chosen by the Lord himself is Guru Gobind Singh [who] is the treasury of [the Lord's] Truth and the sum of divine light effulgent. The knower of God's truth is Guru Gobind Singh, the king of the greatest of kings... Let it be that this one's life is a sacrifice to Guru Gobind Singh at whose feet he places his head.[47]

Most likely written after the creation of the Khalsa in 1699 CE (according to tradition) these lines certainly suggest a fondness for the Guru and, perhaps, an attempt to undermine the grandeur of the Mughal emperor, Aurangzeb 'Alamgir.[48] Add these to other couplets we find in Goya's works, especially those within the *Ganj-nāmah*, *'Arz-ul Alfāz*, *Zindagī-nāmah*, and the Persian *Jot Bigās* and *Dīvān-i Goyā*, and one could easily claim (as many tacitly do) that Sikh authorship is simply beyond doubt. But doubt nevertheless exists. Does such praise necessarily mean that the author was in fact a Sikh? What it certainly does suggest (and what to my mind is beyond doubt) is that the author was a poet in the court of the tenth guru. The list of terms associated with the guru above would not seem out of place in many a panegyric written for the patron of any number of Persian poets in Mughal India and elsewhere in the Islamicate. One need only observe the work of perhaps the most noted Persian writer in the history of Mughal India, Akbar's vizier or informal secretary, Abu'l-Fazl 'Allami (d. 1011/1602), author of the celebrated *Akbar-nāmah* and its *Ā'in-i Akbārī*, who, based on Chingisid/Timurid precedent develops a fabulous chronology for his most beloved emperor, tracing the divine light which penetrated the legendary Mongol queen Alankuva and which sustains the universe through the emperor's bloodline to finally become manifest in him.[49] To this we may add the Mughal court poet 'Urfi's qasidah in praise of the then Shah-zada Salim (the future Emperor Jahangir).[50] Both of these descriptions are easily as magnificent as the *Ganj-nāmah*'s praise of Guru Gobind Singh. Indeed, the last line of the *Sultanat Dahamm* brings to mind the practice of *kurnīsh* made popular during the reign of the Emperor Jalaluddin Akbar (d. 1604 CE) and continued in the courts of Jahangir and Shahjahan.[51] With this in mind, we may allude to precedents set in earlier Persian courts, along which the Mughal court of Akbar in particular was in part purposefully modelled. Although the following quotation applies specifically to the Samanid court of Persia, circa tenth century, it would nevertheless hold a certain amount of truth for court poets of Mughal India regardless of the darbar in which they wrote:

The presence of a poet at court was an ancient [Persian] tradition of royalty, an essential part of the pomp and circumstance attaching to it. At the Persian courts he not only occupied himself in celebrating his master's triumphs but also performed a very practical function which corresponds in some measure with that of the press attaché or 'public relations officer' of today. The ode, intended to flatter the prince by an elaboration of his noble virtues and magnificent exploits in the field, might serve a secondary purpose by being distributed among rivals as a challenge, among potential usurpers as a warning, and among the general population subject to the prince as a manifesto of his greatness.[52]

Now of course this does not discount the belief that Nand Lal was a Sikh. Sikh tradition makes this claim vociferously and we have no need to challenge it in light of our earlier arguments; we seek merely to problematize the traditionally accepted narratives with questions as to its veracity and suggest an intriguing answer to the problem which has plagued many a scholar of Sikhism this last century (well, at least those scholars interested in Bhai Nand Lal, like me): why did Nand Lal not become a member of the Khalsa, especially since so many Khalsa rahit-namas lay claim to him as their putative author? There are of course some Sikhs who contend that despite the lack of evidence, Nand Lal did indeed join the Khalsa. Their opinion is, however, shared by very few scholars of Sikh history and may be dismissed forthwith.[53] From a traditional point of view, Nand Lal's failure to join may be inferred from statements found in the early eighteenth-century *gur-bilās* text of the poet Sainapati, *Srī Gur-sobhā*: that is, Khatri Sikhs (like Nand Lal apparently) were not overly happy at the creation of the Khalsa, as its regulations, particularly keeping one's hair uncut, violated their traditional practices.[54] In the light of my observations above, however, one could speculate that Nand Lal did not seek admission to this august assembly because he was not a Sikh to begin with and perhaps had no intention of becoming one. Let us never forget that much of the poetry attributed to Nand Lal suggests that our writer was first and foremost a poet in the employ of the Guru's court. Sikh tradition strongly implies that the Guru had kept a poetic entourage not just to translate Sanskrit and Persian poetry for the benefit of a Punjabi-speaking audience but because it doubtlessly added grandeur to his court, a splendour which, incidentally, contemporary Persian sources substantiate.[55] Here we may allude to certain cultural ideals and values which pertained to the Uzbek-Timurid courts of sixteenth-century Central Asia. Although the following observation is Central Asian to be sure, it is nevertheless relevant to the point at hand, especially since the Mughal emperors were also, like the Uzbeks, particularly cognizant of their descent from both Amir Timur and Chinghis Khan (despite the fact that the Mughal emperors collectively despised the Uzbecks) and that it was the Mughals who provided the dynastic model with which the Sikh gurus were most familiar:

Poetry was a cultural staple that no self-respecting court could afford to do without and it was the determining factor in the assessment of its ultimate worth.[56]

And so in this light, although it is very likely that Guru Gobind Singh inherited a 'court of poets' and a fondness for their productions from his father, Guru Tegh Bahadar,[57] one may also assume that like the Mughal emperor himself, the Guru kept many poets not so much for their religious allegiance but simply because of their skill. Indeed, it is abundantly clear that the Mughal emperors allowed non-Muslim poets to write in their courts without personally expressing loyalty to Islam, the emperor's religious tradition.[58] In the case of the *Ganj-nāmah*, therefore, Nand Lal's reasons for writing may have simply been professional ones:

The poet himself benefitted [from writing elegant poetry for a patron] in more than one way.... Copies might be sent to neighbouring courts... to [perhaps] provide him with alternative markets for his wares should the first patron fail to provide rewards that came up to expectation... It was not unknown for a poet to hawk his compositions about from one court to another, changing a name here and a line there as circumstances made expedient...[59]

Let me state categorically that this is simply speculation, but in light of the commonly held belief that Nand Lal returned to the employ of the then Mughal emperor, Bahadar Shah, sometime in the first decade of the eighteenth century or perhaps earlier[60] and continued to serve the Mughals under the latter's successors, Jahandar Shah and Farrukh Siyar, it is merited conjecture.[61] All the above may seem tentative, and indeed parroting what Sikh tradition has been claiming for many years, but it is very much a step forward for critical historians who wish to reconstruct the life and career of Nand Lal, one of the more enigmatic characters of Sikh history.

Life Two

There is further conjecture one could sustain by an examination of Nand Lal's poetry, but let us be cautious: relying on this material is problematic as what poets generally left to posterity was not an account of their historical times but rather a testament to their skill and to the spiritual concerns which were foremost in their minds.[62] With some dexterity, historians can reconstruct prevalent contemporary attitudes and ideals (and of course criticisms) from these accounts but rarely actual events. More to the point, however, we have at this time simply exhausted all that we can really know about Nand Lal's 'first life', his historical life.

We are fortunately on more firm ground when we attempt to reconstruct Nand Lal's 'second life', his posthumous reputation amongst eighteenth- and nineteenth-century Sikhs. It is without doubt that Nand Lal possessed an extraordinary one in this period. The sheer number of eighteenth and early to mid nineteenth-century manuscripts in which Nand Lal emerges are alone a testament to such esteem.[63] In many of these he appears to be constantly questioning the tenth guru, as in the many versions of the rahit-namas attributed to him and in the *Gur-pādhantī* noted above;[64] in others he is conversing with the tenth master about subjects as wide-ranging as the Bhagavad Gita,[65] magical and curative hymns from the Adi Granth, and the benefits accrued from 'broken' (literally, 'ordinary' or *sādhāran pāth*) and unbroken readings (*akhaṇḍ pāth*) of the text,[66] and as well the nature of the Kaliyug,[67] to name but a few; and in still more Nand Lal appears as the Guru's emissary, sent to deal with the concerns of Brahmans irate at the creation of the Khalsa.[68] To such manuscripts one must add the frequency of other eighteenth and nineteenth-century texts containing Nand Lal's Persian *Divān-i Goyā* and *Zindagī-nāmah* the majority of which are in Gurmukhi script,[69] though one does find the occasional *nastaʿlīq* version, at least in India.[70]

These Gurmukhi–Persian manuscripts merit further consideration as these possess features which add weight to Nand Lal's appeal to Sikhs of this period and allow us to draw out some more tentative conclusions. First, just below the Gurmukhi–Persian text of MS 115123 held by Punjabi University, Braj translations in both Devanagri and Gurmukhi scripts appear.[71] In light of the fact that most Sikhs of the eighteenth century did not understand the now-classical Persian of the Mughal court one could assume that the translations indicate that the texts were indeed read, heard, and perhaps studied by pious Sikhs or others. The second feature of these texts which seems to also emphasize this point is their size. Many manuscripts of the *Divān-i Goyā* and *Zindagī-nāmah* are small, compact, and *gutka*-like, signifying breviaries.[72] Size in this case does matter for a number of interrelated reasons: it generally allows us to date the manuscripts to the mid- to late eighteenth century, as this was the period in which Khalsa Sikhs were generally mobile and they often carried with them their sacred literature. As these texts were most likely shuttled from place to place easily (and so their size) we may assume that these were, once again, read by literate Sikhs.

The number of such manuscripts therefore implies that the baits and ghazals of Nand Lal were circulating throughout the Punjab in the late eighteenth and early nineteenth century and may well have been a part of the repertoire of the many travelling professional singers who used the hymns of the gurus and other Sufis and Bhagats in congregational singing or kirtan.[73] That the majority of manuscripts are written in Gurmukhi, the script of the Adi Granth, Dasam Granth, and the vārān of Bhai Gurdas, supports such a contention, highlighting in effect the oral nature of transmission in the Punjabi culture of this period.[74] The recitation of such works in Persian, moreover, would most certainly have required a giānī (traditional Sikh intellectual) or kathākār (exegete) to elucidate both the meaning of individual couplets as well as their 'subtle' or paramārath meaning to gathered Sikhs. As the kathakar's discussion of passages from scripture involved supporting his interpretation with, among other things, 'anecdotes from the lives of the Gurūs [sic]',[75] it seems likely that in the case of both Bhai Gurdas and Bhai Nand Lal, a 'history' of their lives would have been required for a well-rounded exegesis of their more demanding poems.[76]

Although in light of the manuscript evidence presented above it is clear that Nand Lal was generally understood to be a beloved disciple of the tenth guru by the Sikhs of the eighteenth century, it is not until the mid-eighteenth century, at approximately the time that the Sikh court of Maharaja Ranjit Singh begins, that the first narratives of Nand Lal's life are written down. These initial narratives supply only bits and pieces of our poet's biography / hagiography, but these are nevertheless the basis on which later narratives will be situated. We will begin in the year 1797 with the gur-bilas text attributed to Sukha Singh, the Gur-bilās Pātshāhī 10, a hagiography narrating the semi-legendary events associated with the tenth guru. The specific portion we have in mind regards the journey of Prince Mu'azzam to the Punjab in 1696 (the prince's entry into the suba is briefly noted in the thirteenth chapter of the Bachitar Natak)[77] to deal with Raja Bhim Chand of Kahlur and the other troublesome hill rajas who had occasionally withheld their tribute to the emperor and who had as well been frustrated by the guru's apparent success (and perceived defiance) at Paonta, Makhowal, and later Anandpur Sahib. We are told that it was through the intercession of Nand Lal that the prince ultimately excused Guru Gobind Singh and concentrated his punitive efforts solely on the hill rajas:

A Khatri Sikh [who was] a resident of Delhi [named] Nand Lal was the first among the [prince's] wise counselors [mat-rāsī, literally, 'one who has a hold of the reins of the mind, i.e. opinions/ideas']. He advised the emperor's son in a number of ways. Through his conversation he successfully accomplished the task [of pleading on the guru's behalf].

[Nand Lal's] good advice appealed to [Prince Mu'azzam's] heart. [As a result the prince] loved him dearly. As his heart [was] stolen by this devotee of the [true] Lord [the prince] took the word of the Sikh [Nand Lal] as true.[78]

The evidence here is of course historically questionable, as is the entire text itself, stamped as it is with a strong Udasi Sikh flavour.[79] Its lack of historical veracity notwithstanding (nowhere else do we hear of Nand Lal as a resident of Delhi, for example), the text does suggest one of two possibilities. Nand Lal may either have not joined the court of the tenth guru (which seems very unlikely in light of the evidence we have thus far marshalled) or Nand Lal shifted his residence between the two courts. As we have already noted, such is claimed by some scholars of the Sikh tradition.[80] As we shall see, this double allegiance will become significant for later developments regarding Nand Lal; but for now let us state that this text also demonstrates that as early as 1797, some Sikhs were convinced of Nand Lal's (continued) involvement in the affairs of the prince who would become the Emperor Bahadar Shah. adding support perhaps to the contentious evidence one discovers in the Persian *Amar-nāmah* of Dhadhi Nath Mal noted above. This passage in *Gur-bilās Pātshāhī 10* is incidentally the first time in Sikh literature that we hear of Nand Lal's connection with the Mughal administration and of Prince Mu'azzam's affection for him although earlier sources imply this.[81]

It would not be until Ranjit Singh's kingdom was well underway, however, that we would hear more of the Nand Lal narrative. That it appears more fully in this period may have something to do with the role of the Persian language in the court of the Sikh maharaja. As Persian was the language of elite culture and the principal language of the Sikh court and of its coinage, an erudite figure from Sikh history proficient in Persian such as Nand Lal would perhaps have enhanced the reputation of the Sikhs and of Ranjit Singh's darbar, which at least according to some scholars was consciously fashioned along the same lines as the Mughal court.[82] Such a connection, moreover, may have established a more determined link to both the court of Guru Gobind Singh, a point which the Gobindshāhī couplet on the Sikh coins minted during Ranjit Singh's rule no doubt attempted to elicit, and the earlier Mughal court to which Nand Lal was connected.[83] For this reason perhaps the earliest nineteenth-century Nand Lal narrative, the *Gurū kīān Sākhīān* of Svarup Singh Kaushish, refers to Nand Lal only in his capacity as a gifted Persian poet:

At this time, [during] the year Sambat 1739 (1682 CE) . . . a great (*changā*) writer and poet of Persian and Arabic [named] Bhai Nand Lal 'Goya' of Multan came to the sangat at 'Chakk Nanaki' (Anandpur).[84]

This to be sure is all the *Gurū kīān Sākhīān* says of Nand Lal, but it is enough, for it confirms what most Sikhs of the period knew of our poet and connects the court of the Guru to the high culture of the Mughal court by virtue of Nand Lal's ability in the languages of Islam, notably Persian.

The next text in which we find reference to Nand Lal is the *Sau Sākhīān* of 1834, attributed to Guru Gobind Singh himself. Although the relevant passage fails to mention Nand Lal's erudition, it implies it, along with underscoring his intimacy with the tenth guru:

[One day in Kesgarh the tenth guru] ordered that the sangat direct the questions [which would normally be asked of the guru] to [Bhai] Nand Lal. When Nand Lal heard this order, he gathered together [all of] the writers [in the guru's entourage from the] centre[86] [at which they were stationed]. He summoned [all of] the royal writers and poets. [Nand Lal often performed this task of summoning poets] into the presence of the True Guru for sessions of poetry [because their recitals] pleased the tenth master.[85]

The text may exclude reference to Nand Lal's skill in Persian as it was generally well enough known to be taken for granted, though in regard to a later passage we find in the *Sau Sakhīan* in which Persian-knowing Sikhs are disparaged, it seems that the author may have purposefully excluded this fact to ensure that no negative light is cast upon this most devoted disciple.[87] An interesting feature of this passage is the tacit equation between the guru and Nand Lal, a feature we will see elsewhere in a different context.

Although the two texts mentioned earlier make reference to Nand Lal, it is thanks to two somewhat later mid nineteenth-century sources that we are indebted for a large part of the standard Nand Lal narrative which is still followed by scholars of the Sikh tradition today.[88] Let us take each one in turn. The first is Ratan Singh Bhangu's famous *Gur-panth Prakāsh* of 1841 CE. Although Bhangu's narrative is relatively brief, it is significant, for here Nand Lal will adopt the role which he will play repeatedly in other nineteenth-century texts, namely that of messenger and emissary shuttling instructions and requests from the royal camps of either Bahadar Shah or, as in Bhangu, Farrukh Siyar to the camp of the tenth guru and, after 1708, to that of Mata Sundari.[89] We first see him summoned by the Mughal emperor Farrukh Siyar, who instructs Nand Lal to go and petition Mata Sundari to put an end to Banda's incursions into the Punjab.[90] The Mata ji then deputes Nand Lal to do this very thing:

After [having heard the request to persuade Banda to end his campaigns] Mata ji spoke to Nand Lal, '[Nand Lal] send a letter in our name [to Banda] conveying [my] order.' She continued, 'Now please write it [for me] and affix the seal of the [House of] Guru [Gobind Singh] onto the letter.' Bhai Nand Lal did exactly this, [writing down] that which the [wife of the true] king requested. Bhai Nand Lal hurriedly dispatched the Guru's command [to Banda].[91]

Here Nand Lal is emissary to both the Mughal emperor and the house of the guru as represented by Mata Sundari. In the person of our poet, Bhangu allows the interests of both parties to in a sense merge together. Nand Lal is thus a figure who appears at home in both worlds and, while so positioned, bestows legitimacy on the two at least from Bhangu's perspective. Now we once again do not hear of Nand Lal's Persian ability, but it is nevertheless implied by virtue of his situation in the court of the Mughal emperor. We infer that his position is a privileged one since Farrukh Siyar immediately summoned only Nand Lal after reminding his courtiers that it is to the family of the guru that the descendents of Babur are indebted. Such is also the case in the second appearance of Nand Lal, when the emperor's courtiers instantly implore Farrukh Siyar to summon our poet to once again deal directly with Mata ji and Banda.[92]

In all four of the accounts thus far noted we have yet to hear of Nand Lal's life before meeting with Guru Gobind Singh. Much is implied in these and we may assume taken for granted, but an early connection with the gurus and with the Sikh tradition has not materialized at this point. If one were to demonstrate such a connection, one in which Nand Lal is portrayed as a pious Sikh from a very early period in his life, here is how one would do it, from Santokh Singh's celebrated text of 1843 CE, *Gur-pratāp Sūraj Granth* (ritu 3, ansu 24):

There [once] was a very wealthy Khatri. [Into] his very learned/religious (*mativantā*) household was born [a son whom he named Nand Lal]. [As] the family was Vaishnavite, the father instilled within his son [a] love [for this tradition]. One day during [the son's] twelfth year of age, the father wandered over and looked at him. [He said,] 'Now is the proper time for you to be invested with the sacred thread.' Having consulted his heart (ur bichār kiya) [the father] summoned his [Vaishno] guru.

[When the guru had arrived the father said to Nand Lal,] 'Be seated beside [the guru] so that you may be instructed [in the ways of all Vaishnos].' The son was then told, 'We are the servants of the Lord Hari and as such you must pay heed (dhāran karo) to the Vaishno guru and always abide by his commands. Tie this sacred thread around your neck and become a member of the Vaishno dharam.' Having spoken these words, he summoned the ascetic.

[Hearing his father speak so] Nand Lal [became very unhappy as he did] not [want to] become a devotee [of a tradition which placed such value on the external forms of religion]. The [Vaishno] guru [then] spoke, 'Adopt this dharam and put the sacred thread around your neck.'

Nand Lal pressed [his palms] together and spoke, 'This sacred thread does not bring one [the] joy [of liberation]. Recognize that the bānī, the sacred utterance of the guru, is the most beautiful of sacred threads. This is the very thread which you should put on my neck. The glory of the guru who is the highest lord resides within one who bears such a thread. [But keep in mind, pandit ji, that] making statements of this sort [alone] will not lead to contentment. [Indeed, know that] on every neck there exists this very beautiful thread. It captivates the hearts of all people [but may be recognized only] through reciting and hearing [the True Name]. For a thousand years it will continue to increase and [the true devotee's] glory within the world will come forward and he will secure the knowledge leading to salvation. Always praise the [True] Guru; [always] utter the glory of the highest Lord who is pure.'

Hearing this the Vaishno [guru] became delighted and said, 'Glory to this self-accomplished child! I [unfortunately] do not possess such a thread. One must obtain it from him beside whom it is found. This child [is one such person, one who] is profoundly intelligent (sumti-vanti). Throughout his heart is strung the thread made up of the name of the Lord Hari.'[93]

This early narrative is especially important for a structural reason: it is purposefully modelled along the same lines as a popular eighteenth-century janam sakhi account of Guru Nanak in which the first master is about to be fitted with the sacred thread.[94] Although the report of Guru Nanak's investiture takes place after the Guru's ninth birthday rather than at his twelfth, both accounts provide their respective protagonists the opportunity to censure external rituals and verify the inward acceptance of the sacred utterances which communicate the divine name.

Here, in other words, Nand Lal conveys that same message we have heard the first master enunciate on numerous occasions in both the Adi Granth and his hagiographic narratives. A more subtle connection is implied, however, through which Santokh Singh relates Nand Lal even more intimately to Guru Nanak, fortifying our poet's bond to the Sikh tradition on the one hand and indeed making him into the image of the first master on the other. It is true that both Nand Lal and the Guru are Khatris. But, as well, Nand Lal (like Guru Nanak) achieves his insight into the transcendent Lord and interior religion intuitively, without the assistance of a guru or teacher. This I believe marks Nand Lal as a Sikh of exceptional character, a trait which may explain why the early twentieth-century Sikh poet and theologian Puran Singh eulogizes Nand Lal so eloquently in his poem, 'Addhī mītī akkh bhāī nand lāl jī dī' or 'The half-closed eyes of Bhai Nand Lal ji', emphasizing the more mystical inclinations of our poet.[95] For Santokh Singh it seems only natural therefore that Nand Lal's innate ability to discern the truth would attract Muslim disciples to him[96] and ultimately compel him to seek out Guru Gobind Singh at Anandpur, which he does very soon after having secured employment with Prince Mu'azzam.[97] Although Max Arthur Macauliffe fails to note the similarity between the two investiture narratives in his Sikh Religion, most of Santokh Singh's contemporaries would no doubt have done so.[98]

Now with this in mind we turn to that other rare feature of Nand Lal's narrative I mentioned earlier, his intimate association with the Mughal court. How this is related to our discussion of Nand Lal's childhood earlier will become clear. Although there can be no doubt that the Sikhs had had their differences with the Mughals during the seventeenth century, Mughal rule was nevertheless authenticated by Guru Nanak who, according to tradition, bestowed sovereignty upon Babur, a point to which we made reference in the notes above.[99] There is moreover tentative evidence to suggest that Guru Gobind Singh himself recognized and accepted the suzerainty of the Timurid line of which Aurangzeb was most certainly a part.[100] For Ratan Singh Bhangu (easily the most famous of the gur-bilas authors), as I have shown in another context, the Mughals rejected Baba Nanak's gift by executing both Guru Arjan and Guru Tegh Bahadar, a rejection which ultimately led to the Mughal downfall of the mid-eighteenth century.[101] Nand Lal, who (as we have implied) is a symbolic representation of Guru Nanak at the Mughal court, is made to buttress this point. In order to understand the process at work here, let me provide some background.

Santokh Singh's Nand Lal, it is clear, embodies those other qualities of the Mughals to which the Sikhs have been privy since Akbar's meeting with Guru Arjan in 1598: the munificent, erudite, and tolerant characteristics represented by the Emperor Akbar and elucidated in the bani of Guru Nanak and his successors. We noted earlier the features that Persian court poets were assumed to embody. Santokh Singh describes Nand Lal with these in mind. We are told for example that

[As time went on] Nand Lal went to the *maktab* [for his education] on a daily basis. Here he was made to study Persian and all forms of Islamic knowledge (*ilm*; Persian: *'alm*).[103] His brilliance (*tīcchan* 'sharpness') and wisdom improved through steady practice (*punahi abhbhayāse*). The great light of knowledge began to shine within him through his relentless learning. [Nand Lal] read large collections of books and as a result became knowledgeable / very accomplished in the subject of Islamic literature and learning. Within society [Nand Lal] was quick-witted and spoke on important subjects intelligently. [In this way] his excessive knowledge in all things became most apparent.[102]

What we see at this point therefore is a very rare Sikh who manifests that same insight as Guru Nanak and who is as well an accomplished scholar of the various Islamic disciplines and an ideal Mughal scribe.

But this array of expertise is not enough for the author of the *Sūraj Prakāsh*. Santokh Singh goes a step further to ensure that his readers and listeners know beyond doubt that Nand Lal is indeed the full moon of the Mughal court. Here we have the first reference of which I am aware to the famous story in which Nand Lal is the only scholar in the entire assembly of Aurangzeb's very learned maulanas who can interpret an *āyat* (literally, 'a [miraculous] sign', a single verse of the Qur'an) to the satisfaction of the Emperor.[104] This story provides an interesting twist to a familiar theme we discover in the janam sakhis, a theme which Hew McLeod titles Guru Nanak's 'Triumph over Islam' and whose standard pattern shows Guru Nanak defeating both in debate and through a display of miracles various Muslim religious personnel.[105] Nand Lal too triumphs over these personnel: not through miracles or an elucidation of Sikh doctrine but rather (or so we are led to infer) through Islamic understandings themselves refracted through the personality, erudition, and wisdom of Nand Lal. What makes this story so captivating is that Persian poets in the emperor's entourage did at times present their patron with commentaries on verses found in the Qur'an.[106] It is sad to say, however, that because we are never told the verse upon which Nand Lal excercises his extraordinary exegetical skill nor given his specific interpretation of the unknown ayat, it is likely that this is a story of pure fiction, a creation of Santokh Singh's imagination, whose aim is many-sided.[107] Not only is it a triumph for Nand Lal (and so Guru Nanak), but it is also a victory for the Sikh court of the tenth master, underscoring the legitimacy of Guru Gobind Singh and his court as the true heirs of the empire of Babur, an empire which, let us repeat, was bestowed upon these descendents of Timur by Guru Nanak.

How is this so? What I have not mentioned is that Nand Lal is told of Aurangzeb's quest for the ayat's meaning by the prince, who is initially terrified of his father's wrath if he does not divine a satisfactory meaning. When Nand Lal recognizes the prince's anxiety, he is told of its cause, and after some consideration he provides the prince almost immediate relief by supplying the best possible interpretation. The prince is overjoyed.[108] He goes to his father and recites Nand Lal's commentary. Hearing it, Aurangzeb is naturally amazed.[109] The emperor then questions Prince Mu'azzam about its author and the prince informs Aurangzeb of his very intelligent mir munshi. The emperor proceeds to summon Nand Lal before him. It is only when Nand Lal stands in front of the emperor that Aurangzeb discovers that he is not a Muslim. Aurangzeb then says to his son rather darkly:

So, [Nand Lal] is a Hindu and he is learned. This will not do [literally, 'this is an injustice']; this does not befit me. Bring him inside the faith. By any means necessary (*jayom kayom*) cause him to understand thoroughly.... Bring [Nand Lal] into the faith by any means at our disposal.[110]

Rather than comply, Prince Mu'azzam informs Nand Lal of his father's desire and permits him to leave. Nand Lal does so and flees to the court of Guru Gobind Singh along with his friend and disciple.

By forcing Nand Lal, a pious non-Muslim and learned scholar of all things Islamic, to flee the court for fear of his life, Santokh Singh shows that the authority of Babur really no longer lies at the court of Aurangzeb, a man who we are told:

... treated hundreds of thousands of Hindus cruelly... [a man who was] a sinner ... [who] placed the noose of the Sharia around the necks [of all people].[111]

When Nand Lal leaves the court, it is not only Nand Lal in the image of the first master leaving the court, but also the legitimacy bestowed upon that court by Guru Nanak that departs. It comes full circle when

Nand Lal arrives at the court of the tenth master who is the ninth embodiment of the first guru. This narrative of Nand Lal, in other words, is a symbolic dramatization of both the delegitimization of the Mughal court of Aurangzeb and the authentication of the court of Guru Gobind Singh based on that very feature which legitimized the Mughal court in the first place, Guru Nanak. While Babur bows in humility before Guru Nanak in the *Puratan Janam-sakhi* account of their meeting, the self-righteous Aurangzeb fills both Hindus and his courtiers with dread at his intolerance in the *Sūraj Prakāsh*.[112] He is, it would seem, a twisted version of Babur and thus unfit to don the mantle of Mughal rule from the point of view of Santokh Singh. It would not have been lost on Santokh Singh's audience that the departure of such a learned and illustrious figure from the court of the emperor to that of the guru would have also increased the grandeur and pomp of the tenth master's own court. It would not be until Bahadar Shah was on the throne that the Mughal empire would be somewhat redeemed, redeemed in particular as tradition maintains (and historical sources support this contention) that Guru Gobind Singh helped (and therefore blessed) the then Prince toward securing his claim to the Mughal throne against his brothers. But the Nand Lal we find in Bhangu, the emissary of Farrukh Siyar opposed to the 'innovations' of Banda, is not present in Santokh Singh.

Conclusion

It is perhaps fitting that such an interpretation of Nand Lal comes to the surface during the reign of Ranjit Singh and the Khalsa army. This we may infer was a period of relative turmoil, especially after 1839, in which Sikhs were wary of their position in northern India in the light of the dawning British colonial endeavour, and in which Santokh Singh was wary of post-Ranjit Singh inheritors of the Sikh kingdom. The message Santokh Singh communicates through the figure of Nand Lal in this instance therefore appears to a straightforward one: the Sikhs are the true inheritors of Mughal renown and glory. This message it seems was one encouraged by the Sikh court itself, as it also couched its legitimacy in the very trappings of the imperial kingdom, Persian-inscribed Sikh coins, and chronicles based on those of the Mughals. Such a figure as Nand Lal may perhaps may have been constructed to remind both the new Sikh rulers and the British (who were literally on the Khalsa's doorstep in the early 1840s and even before this date) of past Sikh glory on the one hand and the legitimacy of the early nineteenth-century Sikh empire on the other. I have here covered but two of Nand Lal's many lives. As can be expected with such pivotal figures in the history of the Sikhs, Nand Lal would take on new lives during the era of the Singh Sabha and its inheritors, in particular the Chief Khalsa Diwan. These likewise would be attempts to confer legitimacy and authority, though in this case in the light of the 'reforms' which formed the basis of Tat Khalsa endeavours to elevate their interpretation of the early twentieth-century Sikh/Khalsa tradition. But this is a full moon which will shine on another night and a story best suited for a different conference.

Notes

1. *Gur-pādhantī*, MS 115682, Sikh Reference Library, Punjabi University, Patiala, ff. 1a–b. There are many allusions to the auspicious nature of the glowing full moon in the *Zindagī-nāmah* attributed to Bhai Nand Lal. One such appears in the twelfth couplet:

Anyone who has discovered how to take a turn around the lane of the Lord's devotees (*kū-ye shān*) shines like the sun in the morning and the moon at night in both this world and the next.

Zindagī-nāmah 12, Ganda Singh (ed.), *Kulliyāt-i Bhā'ī Nand La'l Goyā* (Malaka, Malaya: Sikh Sangat, 1963), p. 77. The author of the *Gur-pādhantī* could well be alluding to these.

2. As the Nirmala Sikhs interpreted Sikh theology through a Vedantic lens, it is only fitting that the title of this work is *Gur-pādhantī*, 'the end of the guru's instruction'—alluding, it seems, to the Vedantic Darshanas. A brief description of the Nirmalas and their tradition appears in W. H. McLeod, *Historical Dictionary of Sikhism* (Lanham, Maryland: Scarecrow Press, 1995), p. 155, while a more substantial treatment is found in the various essays of Pritam Singh (ed.), *Nirmal Sampradai* (Amritsar: Guru Nanak Dev University Press, 1981).

3. *Gur-pādhantī*, ff. 1a-13a. Nand Lal begins by asking a question ('*prashan karī*') and the guru begins his reply with 'Well asked, Nand Lal!' ('*bhalī prashan karī nand lal*')—folio 1b, for example. For the Panth, the Nirmala Panth, and the three gunas, see lines 23 and 34–5, ff. 4b and 6b.

4. This will not be the only time that Mani Singh and Nand Lal will join forces in a session of question and answer with the tenth guru. See *sakhis* 155, 161, and 163 of the *Sikhan dī Bhagatmālā*, also known as the *Bhagat-ratnāvālī*, an exploration of the eleventh var of Bhai Gurdas, attributed to Mani Singh. Tarlochan Singh Bedi (ed.), *Sikhān dī Bagatmālā* (Patiala: Punjabi Univ. Publication Bureau, 1994), pp. 145–8, 152–5, and 155–7. Note that the Vir Singh edition does not contain

these supplements to the text. Vir Singh (ed.), *Bhai Gurdās jī dī Yarvhīn Vār dī Tīkā Arthāt Sikhān dī Bhagat Māllā Rachit Sacchkhand Vasī Srī Bhāī Sāhib Shahīd Bhāī Mani Singh jī Gayānī* (Amritsar: Khalsa Samachar, 1966).

5. See, for example, W. H. McLeod, *The Chaupa Singh Rahit-nama* (Dunedin, New Zealand: University of Otago Press, 1987), pp. 29–30.

6. The Nirmalas, though tracing their lineage to Guru Gobind Singh, were a marginal group during most of the eighteenth century. By the latter part of the 1700s, however, their importance was on the rise, peaking during the Sikh kingdom of Maharaja Ranjit Singh (1799–1849 CE) and continuing somewhat afterwards thanks to the generous moral and financial support of the Sikh rulers of Patiala (the city in which we find this manuscript). Darshan Singh, 'How Did the Nirmalas Preach?', *Journal of Sikh Studies* 5 (1978), pp. 147–51.

7. It is interesting to note that the quotation above actually begins with the words '*prashan karī*' [*nand lal jī sabh sikhan mai chand*]. Although the context suggests that the principal meaning of *prashan karī* is 'a question was asked [by]', there may here be a double entendre as *prashankarī*, taken as one rather than two words (in virtually all early Punjabi/Braj manuscripts, breaks between words are nonexistent)—which means 'greater than Lord Shiv himself'. In the light of the epigraph above, this is not an invalid reading. A contemporary retelling of Nand Lal's brief biography and reputation is found in Harbans Singh (ed.), *The Encyclopaedia of Sikhism* 3 (Patiala: Punjabi University Press, 1997), pp. 195–6. Even this entry is not altogether critical of Sikh tradition. A more critical appreciation of Nand Lal's 'biography' is my 'Bhāī Nand Lāl "Goyā" and the Sikh Tradition', in Pashaura Singh and N. G. Barrier (ed.), *Sikhism and History* (New Delhi: Oxford University Press, 2004), pp. 111–34.

8. In fact, Ganda Singh himself begins his *Bhāī Nand Lāl Granthāvalī* implying this much in his discussion of Bhai Nand Lal's regional origins:

At this time nothing definite can be said about the original residence of Bhai Nand Lal's ancestors. Neither historical texts nor family narratives offer us any help whatsoever in this [reconstruction].

Ganda Singh, *Bhāī Nand Lāl Granthāvalī* (Patiala: Punjabi University Press, 1989), p. 1. Such lack of concern may also be inferred from J. S. Grewal and Irfan Habib, *Sikh History from Persian Sources* (New Delhi: Tulika, 2001). I'm well aware of Professor Grewal's choice of sources (p. 48) and of the fact that most of the works attributed to Nand Lal are not history per se, but some mention of Nand Lal as the premiere Persian littérateur of the tenth guru's court would not have been unwarranted, especially since the *Zafar-nāmah* attributed to Guru Gobind Singh is discussed (on pp. 15, 48, and 96).

9. An example of this would be Kuldipak Singh. Virtually unheard of today, in the eighteenth century Kuldipak Singh was a well-known disciple and emissary of Guru Gobind Singh who was given a *siropa* or robe of honour by Bahadar Shah in the weeks leading up to the tenth guru's death. Kuldipak Singh appears

in many manuscript copies of the *Gur-pranālī* (also *Gur-pranāvalī*) available. See for example the *Gurpranālī* of Natha Singh, MS 115786, Punjabi University, Patiala. Also Randir Singh (ed.), *Bābānī Pīrhī Chalī Guru-pranālīān* (Amritsar: Shiromani Gurdwara Prabhandak Committee, 1964).

10. Discussions which appear on the internet chat group Sikh-Diaspora, for example.

11. Prakash Tandon's comments on the Persian language in the Punjab notwithstanding. Prakash Tandon, *Punjabi Century, 1857–1947* (Berkeley: University of California Press, 1961), pp. 14–15. Also Stephen Fredric Dale, *Indian Merchants and Eurasian Trade, 1600–1750* (Cambridge: Cambridge University Press, 1993), p. 11. Some Persian was most certainly known by Hindu-Punjabi Khatri traders. One can only assume that Sikh Khatri traders were also similarly knowledgeable (though such statements to this end in contemporary seventeenth-century sources are not forthcoming, assuming of course that such traders would identify themselves as Sikh rather than Hindu). Such trends may well account for Guru Nanak's and Guru Gobind Singh's familiarity with Persian, as both gurus were born to Khatri parents. Guru Nanak may be particularly singled out here as the janam sakhis make it clear that he was involved in the trade for which Khatris were duly famous. That scribes of the Sikh scripture knew some Persian may also be the case as some such have, it seems, penned into some manuscript copies of the Adi Granth a Braj translation of a Persian couplet from Saʿdi's *Būstān*—a text which (along with the same author's *Gulistān*) enjoyed great popularity during the Mughal period of Indian history—and attributed it to Guru Tegh Bahadur. Although a translation certainly does not suggest a familiarity with the original language, it nevertheless implies the 'pervasive influence of the Persian tradition' in seventeenth-century northern India. Jeevan Singh Deol, 'Non-Canonical Compositions Attributed to the Seventh and Ninth Sikh Gurus', *Journal of the American Oriental Society* 121, 2 (2001), pp. 200–1. Indeed, the most famous couplet of the *Zafar-nāmah* attributed to Guru Gobind Singh (bait 22) is a clear allusion to the eighth admonition ('*hasht pand*') of Saʿdi's *Gulistān*.

12. The Sikh tradition that there was a Nand Lal in the court of the tenth guru is inferred from the earliest manuscript copy of the *Tankhāh-nāmā* attributed to our poet, MS 770 of the GNDU library, dated 1719 CE. For Diwan Nand Chand, see Gian Singh, *Tavārīkh Gurū Khālsā* I (Patiala: Bhasha Vibhag Punjab, 1993), pp. 866–7. In Gian Singh, we are told that while many Sikhs were sent to Varanasi to translate Sanskrit texts for the Guru, Diwan Nand Chand translated Persian ones (interestingly, Nand Chand was not sent to any specific location to do so, which once again implies the ubiquity of Persian traditions in northern India). That both Guru Nanak and Guru Gobind Singh had at the least a remedial knowledge of Persian is commonly understood in Sikh tradition, as too is Guru Arjan's acquaintance with the language. See W. H. McLeod, *Guru Nanak and the Sikh Religion*, p. 36, and Pashaura Singh, *The Guru Granth Sahib*, p. 109. The inclusion

of Bhai Gurdas may seem odd here, but it seems certain that he was familiar enough with Persian to construct the following line:

There is [only] a dot [of difference] between the *maharama* and the *mujaramu*, the friend (*khair*) and the foe (*khuārī*).   [var 11:2:1]

Understanding this hemistich relies upon knowing the orthography of the Persian words *maharam* and *mujaram*, which, as we can see, differ by one diacritical mark or dot (Punjabi: *nukatā*; Persian: *nuqatā*) alone distinguishing the 'h' from the 'j'. Vir Singh (ed.), *Sri Gurū Granth Sāhib dī Kunjī arthāt Vārān Bhāī Gurdās Satīk Bhav Prakāshanī Tīkā Samet Mukammal* (New Delhi: Bhai Vir Singh Sahitya Sadan, 1997), p. 174. Alluding to the dots of specific characters of the Perso-Arabic letter system is not altogether rare in Persian poetry, especially in chronograms.

13. There are well over one hundred devotees of the gurus mentioned in this var but only a small number of these were employed by the Mughal administration or army. Vir Singh, *Bhai Gurdas*, pp. 174–96.

14. A critical edition of this text is Tarlochan Singh Bedi (ed.), *Sikhān dī Bagatmālā*, pp. 61–143. Also Vir Singh (ed.), *Bhai Gurdās jī dī Yarvhīn Vār dī Tīkā arthāt Sikhān dī Bhagat Māllā Rachit Sacchkhand Vasī Srī Bhāī Sāhib Shahād Bhāī Mani Singh jī Gayānī*, pp. 28–165. Most of the Sikh individuals mentioned in var 11 also have very brief entries in Kahn Singh's *Gur-shabad Ratanakar Mahan Kosh* (Patiala: Bhasha Vibhag Punjab, 1983).

15. Background on Prince Muhammad Mu'azzam appears in Jadunath Sarkar, *History of Aurangzeb based on Original Sources* 3, 4 (Calcutta: M.C. Sarkar & Sons, second edition, 1928, 1930), esp. III: pp. 44–7.

16. *Encyclopaedia of Sikhism* 1, pp. 399–400.

17. Louis E. Fenech, 'Bhāī Nand Lāl "Goyā" and the Sikh Tradition', pp. 111–34.

18. According to Sikh tradition, there were other Nand Lals associated with the history of the Sikhs and indeed within the court of the tenth guru. Piara Singh Padam, *Srī Gurū Gobind Singh jī de Durbārī Ratan* (Patiala: Punjabi University Press, 1976), p. 217. For the reasons behind the elimination of this Nand Lal and various other namesakes in Sikh tradition, see Louis Fenech, 'Bhāī Nand Lāl "Goyā" and the Sikh Tradition', pp. 117–18.

19. For example W. H. McLeod, *Sikhs of the Khalsa: A History of the Khalsa Rahit* (New Delhi: Oxford University Press, 2003), p. 16.

20. This assumes of course that the story of Nand Lal's involvement with the Mughals was known at this time, a conjecture for which there is no reliable contemporary evidence.

21. As we see in Hari Ram Gupta, *History of the Sikhs* 1 (Delhi: Munshiram Manoharlal Publishers, 1984), p. 381, prior to presenting himself before the guru, Nand Lal presented his poetry. It was only after this that the Guru invited the poet before him. This tradition has a basis in earlier Timurid / Mughal precedent, as a poem or good turn of phrase did not only increase a poet's prestige (and in

many instances his income) but could also usher him into the royal circle of poets and in turn bestow upon his patron even more renown amongst his peers. According to E. J. W. Gibb, for example:

> For a man of literary ability there is… no better introduction to the notice of the great [ruler] than a skillfully composed qasida or ghazel [sic]; and so we find that from this time [1450 CE] forward nearly all the greater poets are at least nominally either court functionaries or government officials of one class or another. When a clever young poet was brought under the notice of a vezir or other grandee, it was almost a point of honour with the great man to find him some berth where he would be provided with a competence and yet have the leisure to cultivate his talent.

Indeed, in the court of the famous Central Asian ruler Timur Gurgan Barlas (Tamerlane, of whom Babur was a fifth-generation descendant), the poet Ahmedi was requested by the emperor to join his private circle after he had presented him with a particularly enjoyable Persian qasidah.

E. J. W. Gibb, A History of Ottoman Poetry 2 (London: Luzac and Company, 1900), pp. 19–20; and 1, p. 262. Sikh tradition assumes as much of Guru Gobind Singh, who in grand Timurid fashion is said to have rewarded poets lavishly in some instances. See M. A. Macauliffe, The Sikh Religion 5, p. 59, and Ishar Singh Nara, Safarnama and Zafarnama, Joginder Singh (trans.) (New Delhi: Nara Publications, 1985), pp. 39–41.

22. Bhai Megh Raj 'Garib' (apparently a descendent of Bhai Nand Lal), Prem Phulvarī: arthat Srī Gurū Gobind Sigh jī de Annanay Sikh Bhāī Nand Lāl jī Krit 'Divān Goyā' (Amritsar: Bhapedi Hatti, 1912), p. 23.

23. These statements appear in Nizami-'i 'Aruzi's Chahār Maqāla or 'Four Discourses'. Edward G. Browne (ed. and trans.), The Chahár Maqála ('Four Discourses') of Nidhámí-i-'Arúdí-i-Samarqandí (London: Luzac & Co., 1900), p. 49. For the common Turko-Persian culture of the eastern Islamicate (Khurasan and Transoxiana, including Mughal India), see Robert Canfield, Turko-Persia in Historical Perspective (Cambridge: Cambridge University Press, 1991), pp. 1–21, especially pp. 20–21.

24. Vir Singh (ed.), Srā Gur-pratāp Sūraj Granth Kavī Chūrāmani Bhāī Santokh Singh 12 (Patiala: Bhasha Vibhag Punjab, 1989), p. 5076.

25. In an earlier article on Nand Lal ('Bhai Nand Lal "Goya" and the Sikh Tradition', in Pashaura Singh et al. (eds), Sikhism in History, New Delhi: Oxford University Press, 2004, pp. 111–34), I alluded to a series of statements which supported Nand Lal's authorship of the Dastūr-ul-Inshā and other Nand Lal works. On an examination of the manuscript copy from which Ganda Singh drew the information for his Kulliyāt-i Bhā'ī Nand La'l Goyā, however, namely MS 332164/ GS in the Sikh Reference Library at Punjabi University, Patiala, titled Tasnīfat-i Goyā, I found that such authorship must once again be problematized. The statements to which I made reference are all pencilled into the manuscript at a

later time and in a different hand (see f. 26a for example). One must suspend judgement on this later addition at this point, however, as notes along the margins of the folios claim that the scribe had missed some lines and pages of the copy he had used to prepare MS 332164 (as it appears that MS 332164 had been prepared *seriatum* in a very elegant hand, it seems very likely that the scribe worked from a copy). Such is also alluded to in Ganda Singh's handwritten Urdu note (dated 1945 CE) inserted between the third and fourth folios of the *Ganj-nāmah*. Such problems may be moot, however, in the light of my recent fieldwork noted above. Unfortunately, Vir Singh does not mention the manuscript on which he relied for his version of the *Ganj-nāmah*. See Vir Singh (ed.), *Ganj-nāmah* (New Delhi: Bhai Vir Singh Sahitya Sadan, 1966).

26. One such is Kamran 'Goya', brother of the famous Kashmiri poet Mirza Darab Beg 'Juya' (d. 1707). G. L. Tikku, *Persian Poetry in Kashmir 1339–1846: an Introduction* (Berkeley: University of California Press, 1971), pp. 117–8.

27. Failure to mention Nand Lal in these texts, however, may rest with the quality of our poet's verses. Tazkirah (Arabic *tadhkirah*) was a genre of literature which basically provided the biography of a poet and a number of examples of his or her poetry. One could argue that E. G. Browne's monumental *A Literary History of Persia* in 3 volumes (Cambridge: Cambridge University Press, reprint; 1969) is in fact a tazkirah of Persian poets in the English language. The type of tazkirahs I have in mind are similar to Shaikh Dihlawi's (d. 1052 H/1642 CE) delightful *Akhbār al-Akhyār fī Asrār al-Abrār*. M. S. Akhtar, 'An Introduction to the Life and Works of Sheikh 'Abd al-Haqq Muhaddith Dihlawī', in *The Muslim World* 68, 3 (July 1978), pp. 205–14.

28. *Kulliyāt, Zindagī-nāmah* 152, p. 86; also bait 20, p. 78.

29. *Dīvān-i Goyā* 33, *Kulliyāt*, p. 62. In one *Dīvān-i Goyā* manuscript, this is the only *ghazal* preserved. Ms 609, ff. 103b–104b, Guru Nanak Dev University, Amritsar. This manuscript is dated Sambat 1874 or 1817 CE. Indeed, in nineteenth-century narratives of Nand Lal, this ghazal is the one best known as it is said to have been recited during a celebration of the Holi festival in which Guru Gobind Singh himself playfully participated. See Vir Singh, *Santokh Singh*, 12, 3:27, p. 5090 and Gian Singh, *Tavarikh Guru Khalsa*, 1, pp. 891–2. Gian Singh most certainly relies on Santokh Singh's earlier account as the Holi ghazal noted scans incorrectly in the same way as does Santokh Singh's: the first *mesra* (hemistich) of the first bait ends with the word *bishaguft* ('to flower') rather than *bū kard*, 'to make fragrant'. The meaning of the bait is basically unchanged, but the rhyme in the former is faulty. In both cases, moreover, in the place of *'rāh-'i sangat'* (the path of the sangat), in the first mesra of the final bait appears *'sādh sangat'* (the true community).

30. In var 9(1), Vir Singh, *Bhai Gurdas*, p. 141, Bhai Gurdas refers to the *'sadh sangat'* as the *sach khand* or True Realm which marks the height of the spiritual ascent to which Guru Nanak alludes in *Japjī* 37, Adi Granth, p. 8. Also see vars 6(4), 12(20), 16(8), and 22(18). More often than not, we have the term *sat sangati*

in the Adi Granth, though on one occasion Guru Amar Das (*Sirī Rāg* 4:8:41, Adi Granth, p. 29) employs *sādh sangat*:

> Those people who have discovered [the *nām*] have found it within the true congregation of believers. [It is through] this extraordinary fortune that [true] detachment [from the world is obtained].

31. Nand Lal also uses the term 'sohbat' throughout his *Dīvān* and *Zindagī-nāmah*.

32. For more Persian poetry dealing with the Sikhs, see G. L. Tikku, *Persian Poetry in Kashmir*, pp. 207–12.

33. Christopher Shackle, 'Early Vernacular Poetry in the Indus Valley: its Contexts and its Character,' A. L. Dallapiccola, et al. (eds), *Islam and Indian Regions* (Stuttgart: Franz Steiner Verlag, 1993), pp. 264 and 287.

34. Emphasis in the original. Shackle makes this observation in light of Guru Nanak's *Siri Rag* 17, Adi Granth, p. 64. See Christopher Shackle, 'Approaches to the Persian Loans in the *Ādi Granth*', *Bulletin of the School of Oriental and African Studies* 4, 1 (1978), p. 93.

35. There are works attributed to Nand Lal in which the penname is 'Lāl/ La'l' rather than 'Goya'. See *Joti Bigās* 175; 'Arz-ul Alfāz 72, 136, 791, and 1358; and the *Khātimah* of the *Tausīf o Sanā'* 21 in Ganda Singh, *Kulliyāt*, pp. 169, 210, 214, 252, 285, and 158. Although poets did not frequently alter their pennames, such did in fact occur in rare instances. The famous court poet of the Mughal emperor Akbar, for example, Faizi (the brother of Abu'l-Fazl 'Allami) changed his *nom de plume* from Faizi to Fayyzi. See Muhammad Abdul Ghani, *A History of Persian Language and Literature at the Mughal Court: Part III–Akbar the Great* (Allahabad: The Indian Press, Ltd., 1929), p. 44. Similarly, Mulla Muhammad Tahir of Kashmir discarded his takhallus of 'Tahir' for 'Ghani'. See G. L. Tikku, *Persian Poetry in Kashmir*, p. 108.

36. The works attributed to Nand Lal Goya are the *Dīvān-i Goyā* (Persian), *Zindagī-nāmah* (Persian), *Ganj-nāmah* (Persian), *Joti Bigās* (Punjabi), *Joti Bigās* (Persian with Punjabi—the title of this work is in Punjabi, as it is, according to tradition, an attempt in Persian to expand upon the 43 couplets of the Punjabi *Joti Bigās*. Indeed, MS 332164 at Punjabi University, Patiala, titles this Persian work *Tarjumah Joti Bigās* or '[An] Interpretation of the Joti Bigas'), *Tanakhāh-nāmā* (Punjabi), the *Sākhī rahit kī* usually appended to the text of the Chaupa Singh rahit-nama (Punjabi), *Prashan-uttar* (Punjabi), *Dastūr-ul Inshā* (Persian), 'Arz-ul Alfāz (Persian with some Punjabi and Arabic), and the *Tausīf o Sanā'* (Persian). All of these are included in Ganda Singh (ed.), *Kulliyāt-i Bhā'ī Nand La'l Goyā*. For the education required to write such works, see Aziz Ahmad, *An Intellectual History of Islam in India* (Edinburgh: Edinburgh University Press, 1969), pp. 53–7, and 78; and his *Studies in Islamic Culture in the Indian Environment* (Oxford: Clarendon Press, 1964), pp. 234–5.

37. Douglas E. Streusand, *The Formation of the Mughal Empire* (New Delhi: Oxford University Press, 1999), p. 45. Richard Foltz, *Mughal India and Central Asia*

(Karachi: Oxford University Press, 1998), pp. 1–9. For Persian as Mughal India's language of high culture, see Muzaffar Alam, 'The Pursuit of Persian: Language in Mughal Politics,' *Modern Asian Studies* 32, 2 (1998), pp. 317–49.

38. A case in point would be the famous Chandar Bhan 'Brahman', the court poet and mir munshi of Dara Shikoh, author of the *Chahār-Chaman* ('The Four Orchards'). See F. M. Asiri, 'Chandar Bhan Brahman and His Chahar Chaman,' *Visva-Bharati Annals* 4 (1951), pp. 51–64. Also in southern India, particularly the later Maratha homeland, including the district of Bijapur, many Brahmans took to Persian and Islamic learning. See Richard Eaton, *The Sufis of Bijapur 1300–1700* (Princeton: Princeton University Press, 1978), pp. 90–1. Indeed, as James Laine reminds us, to this day, many high-caste Hindus in Maharashtra have the surname Parasnis, indicating 'a former profession as a clerk literate in Persian'. See James W. Laine, *Shivaji: Hindu King of Islamic India* (New York: Oxford University Press, 2003), p. 10. For the role which Khatris and Kayasthas played in Mughal bureaucracy and administration, see Aziz Ahmad, *Studies in Islamic Culture in the Indian Environment* (Oxford: Clarendon Press, 1964), pp. 105–7.

39. MS 332121 (1851 CE), Punjabi University, Patiala, f. 2a. This manuscript copy of the *Dīvān* begins incidentally with the Arabic invocation *bismallah*, 'In the name of God…'. Other versions of this ghazal substitute the word *mardum* or 'man' for *muqaddam*. Although Ganda Singh supplies *mardum* in this spot, he does note that other versions supply *muqaddam*. See *Kulliyāt*, p. 49.

40. C. A. Bayly, *Rulers, Townsmen and Bazaars: North Indian Society in the Age of British Expansion, 1770–1870* (Delhi: Oxford University Press, 1993), pp. 140–1 and 240. J. S. Grewal and Indu Banga (eds), *Early Nineteenth Century Punjab: From Ganesh Das's Chār Bāgh-i-Panjāb* (Amritsar: Guru Nanak Dev University, 1975). Irfan Habib, *The Agrarian System of Mughal India 1556–1707* (Delhi: Oxford University Press, second revised edition, 2002), pp. 160–8.

41. Ganda Singh, *Bhāī Nand Lāl Granthāvalī*, pp. 4–5. A pamphlet written by one of Nand Lal's apparent descendents, Bhai Ram Dyal, the son of Bhai Megh Raj 'Garib' mentioned earlier, claims as much. See Ram Dyal, *The Life of Bhai Nand Lal Goya* (Amritsar: Sikh Tract Society, 1923), tract no. 47. This tract is almost a word for word translation of Ram Dyal's father's *Prem Phulwari*.

42. That the first guru's bani provided the motivation behind the works of the subsequent gurus and Bhai Gurdas is a point made most persuasively by Pashaura Singh, *The Guru Granth Sahib: Canon, Meaning and Authority*, pp. 151–76. It seems likely that any writing inspired by the faithful understanding of the first guru's bani would be generally acceptable as 'Sikh'.

43. For example, note the association between the hymns of Guru Nanak and Guru Amar Das mentioned in ibid, pp. 158–9, and those between Bhai Gurdas and the first guru's work in ibid., pp. 245–6.

44. Christopher Shackle, *An Introduction to the Sacred Language of the Sikhs* (London: School of Oriental and African Studies, 1983).

45. This is outlined in both my 'Bhāī Nand Lāl "Goyā" and the Sikh Tradition' and 'Persian Sikh Scripture: the Ghazals of Bhai Nand Lal Goya,' *International Journal of Punjab Studies* 1, 1 (1994), pp. 49–70. Sufi–Sikh affinities are noted in W. H. McLeod, *Gurū Nānak and the Sikh Religion* (Oxford: Clarendon Press, 1968), p. 158, among other works. In the same vein, Uttam Singh Bhatia, *Gurū Bhagat Bhāī Nand Lāl Goyā* (Patiala: Pavitar Pramanik Prakashan, 1987), pp. 36–50 and 88–101, attempts to discuss both the Bhakti and the Sufi elements which infuse Nand Lal's *Zindagī-nāmah*. Rather than actualities, though, Bhatia relies on affinities.

46. I shall therefore consider the first 17 couplets as part 1 and the final 56 couplets as part 2. This text is, as far as I know, the only work attributed to Nand Lal which begins with a shabad from the Guru Granth Sahib:
> The guru is Gobind, the guru is Gopal, the guru is the Perfect Narayana. The guru is merciful and mighty indeed. The guru, O Nanak, is the support of all those who have fallen by the wayside (*patit*).

Guru Arjan, *Jaitsarī dī Vār* 19, Adi Granth, p. 710. This hymn by the fifth Sikh Master is particularly apt as it includes the names of both the initial and terminal human gurus (at the beginning and end respectively), thus in a sense condensing the entire content of the *Ganj-nāmah* in the same way that the *Māl Mantar*, which begins the Adi Granth, condenses the nature of Akal Purakh and by extension the content of the Sikh scripture (Pashaura Singh, *The Guru Granth Sahib*, p. 84). The hymn appears in Perso-Arabic script in the *Kulliyāt*, p. 109.

47. *Sultanat Dahamm* 2:1–3, 56 of the *Ganj-nāmah*. See *Kulliyāt*, pp. 122–3. The *Ganj-nāmah* includes a brief introduction as well as 10 further chapters, each of which is broken up into two further parts (perhaps in an attempt to mimic the format of Sa'di's *Būstān?*). Each of the 10 deals with one of the Sikh gurus in the traditional sequence of their guruship. In the *Sultanat Dahamm* portion, the first 17 baits glorify both God and Guru Gobind Singh and then proceed to allude to the Guru's qualities based on the Persian letters of his name [G-O-B-N-D-S-N-G-H]. And so, for example,
> The Persian letter 'G' (here, *kāf-i fārsī*) [stands for] the name of the ultimate truth of the universe while the letter 'o' (*vāv*) is the beginning of the cause of the movements of both earth and time.

Sultanat Dahamm 1:6, *Kulliyāt*, pp. 121–2.

48. According to Robert Canfield, '[Persian] Poetry has often been a powerful idiom of popular protest,' *Turko-Persia*, p. 4. The specific challenge to which I allude above may be discerned through *ihām* or ambiguity. Such we discover in the phrase *shah-i shahanshah*. Of course my reading simply translates the honourific *shahanshah* as 'king of kings', a statement one could easily imagine a disciple attributing to his spiritual master in seventeenth-century northern India. But as this honourific often appears as an epithet of the Mughal emperors, the poet may here be attempting to proclaim Guru Gobind Singh the greater of the two. Indeed, in light of Nand Lal's traditional history, such an allusion may not

be far from the mark. The subtitle of this work, moreover—'the Tenth [Lord's] Kingdom' of the 'Treasure Book'—certainly seems to imply that our poet thought of the Guru as a great king, the tenth of 10 'true' treasures if you will, all of whom rivalled the Mughal emperors. A discussion of such interpretations of spiritual masters by their followers in the Sufi tradition specifically appears in Simon Digby, 'The Sufi Shaikh as a Source of Authority in Mediaeval India', in *Purushārtha*, Marc Gaborieau (ed.), *Islam et société en Aise du sud* 9, (Paris: Ecole des Hautes Études en Sciences Sociales, 1986). For dissension in South Asian ghazal poetry (both Persian and Urdu, despite the title), see Harbans Mukhia, 'The Celebration of Failure as Dissent in Urdu Ghazal', in *Modern Asian Studies* 33, 4 (1999), pp. 861–81.

49. Henry Beveridge (trans.), *The Akbar Nama of Abu-L-Fazl* 1, 2 (New Delhi: Low Price Publications, 1998) pp. 50–68. N. Elias and E. Denison Ross (trans.), *The Tarikh-i Rashidi of Mirza Muhammad Haidar Dughlat: A History of the Moghuls of Central Asia* (Patna: Academia Asiatica, 1973), p. 5, describes the pre-Akbar version of the myth of Alankuva. I am not convinced by the suggestion that Abu'l-Fazl's situation was markedly different from that of other poets who praised their patrons because he was a member of the Dīn-i-illahī or Akbar's so-called Divine/Imperial Religion. For background, see Peter Hardy, 'Abul Fazl's Portrait of the Perfect Padshah: A Political Philosophy for Mughal India—or a Personal Puff for a Pal?', Christian Troll (ed.), *Islam in India, Studies and Commentaries* 2: *Religion and Religious Education* (New Delhi: Vikas Publishing House, 1985), pp. 114–37. Interestingly there is a hint in the structure of the lesser-known works of Goya (which I shall try and examine elsewhere) that our poet may have tried to model himself along the same lines as Abu'l-Fazl. This may however be Sikh tradition attempting to portray Nand Lal as the tenth guru's Abu'l Fazl.

50. Muhammad Abdul Ghani, *A History of Persian Language and Literature at the Mughal Court: Part III—Akbar the Great*, pp. 160–71.

51. Kurnish was a practice of the Turco Mongolians which literally means 'interview' and became a ritual during the time of Amir Timur, while under the Mughals it became the formal ritual of obeisance before the emperor. For the kurnīsh under the Mughals, see H. Blochmann (ed. and trans.), *The A-in-i Akbari* I (Delhi: Low Price Publications, 1997), pp. 166–7; Douglas. E Streusand, *The Formation of the Mughal Empire*, p. 124; and Wheeler Thackston (trans. and ed.), *The Baburnama: Memoirs of Babur, Prince and Emperor* (New York: The Modern Library, 2002), pp. 432 and 509. As well, there could be a hint of Guru Nanak's hymns here, though let us note that symbolically offering the head was a common phrase signifying the need for humility.

52. Rueben Levy, *An Introduction to Persian Literature* (New York: Columbia Univ. Press, 1969), p. 26.

53. One such scholar is Haribhajan Singh (trans.), *Sāchī Prīti: Ghazalān Bhāī Nand Lāl jī 'Goyā' ate 'Ganj-nāmā' chon 'Salatanati Dahamm' Satīk* (Amritsar: Singh

Bros., 1989), p. 22. The author here refers to Nand Lal as 'Bhai Nand Lal Singh'. It seems unlikely in the extreme that the Mughal emperor would have allowed Nand Lal to serve if he were a Khalsa Sikh, complete with beard and turban.

54. Ganda Singh (ed.), *Kavī Saināpati Rachit Srī Gur-Sobhā* (Patiala: Punjabi University Press, 1987), chapter 6, especially pp. 88–90.

55. Grewal and Habib, *Sikh History from Persian Sources*, pp. 104–5. Tradition claims that the guru's possession of such symbols is what ultimately triggered the enmity between the tenth master and Raja Bhim Chand, the most powerful of the local hill rajas. That Guru Gobind Singh possessed what Abu'l-Fazl refers to as the military 'ensigns of royalty' (that is, kettledrums, flags/pennants/standards, umbrellas, tents, and, of course, elephants) is clear from his many *hukam-namas*. See Ganda Singh (ed.), *Hukam-nāme: Gurū Sāhibān, Mātā Sāhibān, Bandā Singh ate Khālsā jī de* (Patiala: Punjabi University Press, 1985), especially nos 34 and 35, pp. 128–31. For the 'ensigns', see H. Blochmann (ed. and trans.), *The A-in-i Akbari* I, pp. 52 ff. Many of the works attributed to the Guru that we discover in the Dasam Granth, moreover, demonstrate a clear familiarity with the symbols noted above as well as with rituals of legitimacy, both Hindu and Islamic respectively. Many appear, for example, in the *Bachitar Natak* 2:32, 3:32, 8:18; also *Chandī Charitr Ukti Bilās* 125. Of course Guru Nanak likewise demonstrates an awareness of such symbols. See Guru Nanak, *Rāg Mārū Chaupade* 1, Adi Granth, p. 989. For symbols of courtly legitimacy under the Central Asian Timurids, particularly poetry as one such, see Maria Eva Subtelny, 'Art and Politics in Early 16th Century Central Asia', *Central Asiatic Journal* 27 (1983), pp. 121–48, especially p. 130. Here she notes that:

'In Central Asian Islamic history, every ruler, particularly the petty parvenu, sought to make his court a cultural showplace through patronage, especially of literary activity.'

56. Maria Subtelny, 'Art and Politics', p. 129. Let us be wary of exaggerating the guru's adoption of such dynastic ideals, however. Certainly the task of copying and illuminating manuscripts of the Adi Granth was a highly respected one and may have been one of the principal functions of what we may assume was the guru's equivalent to the Timurid *kitāb-khānah* or atelier. Indeed, many such manuscripts are extant (see Pashaura Singh, *The Guru Granth Sahib*, pp. 60 and 72–3, for example). But it seems certain that artistic productions such as painting and architecture and numismatics, all significant indicators of authority, prestige, and legitimacy amongst the Timurids, were not particularly prized by the Guru's court. This may indicate that the Guru had no interest in challenging the claims of Aurangzeb or the hill rajas to rulership and was content with his possession of Anandpur alone. The importance of the Timurid, atelier is outlined in Thomas W. Lentz and Glenn D. Lowry, *Timur and the Princely Vision: Persian Art and Culture in the Fifteenth Century* (Los Angeles: Los Angeles County Museum of Art, 1989), pp. 63 ff.

57. J. S. Grewal and S. S. Bal, *Guru Gobind Singh* (Chandigarh: Panjab University Press, 1967), pp. 38–9. Also Dharmpal Ashta, *The Poetry of the Dasam Granth* (New Delhi: Arun Prakashan, 1959), pp. 32–3.

58. Lists of such Hindu poets in Mughal and earlier courts may be found in both Muhammad Firishta's *Gulshān-i Ibrāhimī* (*Tarīkh-i Firishta*) and Abu'l Fazl's *Ā'īn-i Akbārī*. See Aziz Ahmad, *Studies in Islamic Culture in the Indian Environment*, pp. 234–8, and Blochmann, *The A-in-i Akbari*, pp. 606–80, especially 608 and 611.

59. Renben Levy, *An Introduction to Persian Literature*, p. 26. Hari Ram Gupta (among others) claims that a draft of a letter to the Shah of Iran penned by Nand Lal pleased the Emperor Aurangzeb. Evidence to support this claim is not forthcoming. H.R. Gupta, *History of the Sikhs* I, p. 380.

60. Uttam Singh Bhatia, *Gurū Bhagat Bhāī Nand Lāl Goyā*, pp. 15 and 17 suggests that Nand Lal went to Agra to be with Prince Mu'azzam after 1695, implying that after this year he shared his time between the two courts. This is a plausible conclusion as the prince was that year released from the confinement in which his father placed him in February 1687 and did indeed make his way to Agra immediately upon his release. Background on the alleged treason and imprisonment of Prince Mu'azzam during his siege of Golconda appears in Jadunath Sarkar, *History of Aurangzeb* 4, 430–3. Also Jadunath Sarkar, *History of Aurangzeb* 5 (Calcutta: M.C. Sarkar & Sons, 1924), p. 302. There is, moreover, a reference to Nand Lal in the employ of the said prince in 1696, which we will note in the gur-bilas text attributed to Sukha Singh. See below, n. 78.

61. In Ratan Singh Bhangu's *Gur-panth Prakāsh* (1841 CE), Nand Lal is in the employ of Farrukh Siyar while in Gian Singh's *Tavarikh Guru Khalsa* he appears as the munshi and messenger of Bahadar Shah. Jit Singh Sital (ed.), *Srī Gur-panth Prakāsh krit Bhāī Ratan Singh Bhangū Shahīd* (Amritsar: SGPC, 1994), pp. 185–92. Gian Singh, *Tavarikh Guru Khalsa* 1, pp. 1133–4. See also Piara Singh Padam, *Kalām-i Bhāī Nand Lāl* (Patiala: self-published, 1985), pp. 9–10. Padam here relies on the evidence of the *Amar-nāmah*, which claims that Nand Lal was the travelling companion of the Emperor just before the death of Guru Gobind Singh in 1708. Ganda Singh (ed. and trans.), *Amar-nāmā: Fārsī mūl, Panjābī Utārā te Arath* (Amritsar-Patiala: Sikh History Society, 1975), pp. 23–4. There are no Sikh sources that claim Nand Lal had relations with Jahandar Shah, which is somewhat surprising as Jahandar Shah was the governor of Multan (apparently Nand Lal's ancestral town) at one point in his career. Perhaps this is because Jahandar Shah was on the throne for less than a year.

62. Jan Rypka's statements to this effect appear in his *A History of Iranian Literature* (Dordrecht: D. Reidel, 1968), p. 85. Annemarie Schimmel voices the same caution in attempting to read 'real experience' into the ghazals as opposed to concepts. Annemarie Schimmel, *As Through a Veil* (New York: Columbia University Press, 1982), pp. 230, n. 33. It is worth noting, however, that in rare cases such 'real experience' can indeed be extracted from the poetry. A case in

point is the Persian baits one discovers in the autobiography of Zahiruddin Babur. See Stephen Dale, 'The Poetry and Autobiography of the *Bâbur-nâma*', *Journal of Asian Studies* 55, 3 (1996), pp. 635–64.

63. One should note that although there are indeed many Nand Lal manuscripts, I have not yet seen an illuminated one. This absence may suggest that the scribes of the eighteenth and nineteenth centuries who prepared such works allocated the works of Nand Lal to a status below that of the Adi Granth, of which there are many such beautifully decorated manuscripts. For manuscripts of the Adi Granth, consult Pashaura Singh, *The Guru Granth Sahib*, pp. 28–82.

64. Although there are critical editions of the three rahit-namas attributed to Nand Lal, it is worth pointing out that there are different versions of each one, in particular the *Prashan-uttar*, which enjoys a number of manuscript editions. See W. H. McLeod, *The Sikhs of the Khalsa* (New Delhi: Oxford University Press, 2003). The earliest manuscript I have seen in which Nand Lal figures is a version of the *Tankhāh-nāmā*, MS 770, Guru Nanak Dev University, Amritsar, which bears a date of Sambat 1775 (1719 CE) and the title *Nasīhat-nāmā* ('letter of advice'). During the Mughal period, *nasāhat-nāmahs* were commonplace and dealt primarily with 'commonsensical' economic advice. See Stephen Dale, *Indian Merchants*, pp. 31–2.

65. MS 1060(s), Guru Nanak Dev University, Amritsar, folios 46b–52a.

66. Among others are *Shardhā Puran*, MS 1097, Guru Nanak Dev University, Amritsar, ff. 20a–36a; *Shardhā Purak*, MS 973, Reference Library, Punjabi Sahitya Academy, Ludhiana, ff. 1b–24b. Clearly these manuscripts may be tentatively dated to the late nineteenth or early twentieth centuries, as the 'akhand path' became a matter of importance under the Singh Sabhas and Chief Khalsa Diwan at that time.

67. MS 684, Punjab State Archives, Patiala, ff. 215a–29a, is a version of the *Prashan-uttar* in which such a discussion takes place (ff. 215a–18b).

68. MS 115373 and 115620, Punjabi University, Patiala, which are versions of the *Sikhān dī Bagatmālā*. Also Tarlochan Singh Bedi (ed.), *Sikhān dī Bagatmālā*, pp. 145–8, 152–5, and 155–7. In sakhi 155 (especially pp. 146–7), Guru Gobind Singh sends along with our poet the *Khālsā Mahīmā* (Svaiya 1–4, Dasam Granth, p. 716), which was written for the occasion and which Bhai Nand Lal recites to the Brahmans who are worried that the creation of the Khalsa will exclude them from the offerings they were previously given. See also Gian Singh, *Tavarikh Guru Khalsa* 1, p. 877.

69. Among many are MS 752 and 764, Central Public Library, Patiala; MS 90272, Punjabi University, Patiala; MS. 104, Bhasha Vibhag Punjab, Patiala; MS 464, 1059(b), 177(a, c), 790, 609(s), and 439(b), Guru Nanak Dev University, Amritsar.

70. GS/MSS 332121, Punjabi University, Patiala, and the incomplete MS 2311 Sikh Reference Library, Khalsa College, Amritsar. The former is dated to Sambat

1906 sammat (1849 CE). I was unable to check for Nand Lal manuscripts in Pakistan in 2002 because of the political standoff between India and Pakistan.

71. MS 115123, Punjabi University, Patiala. In this manuscript (c. late eighteenth or early nineteenth century), it is often individual words or sentences which are translated rather than entire ghazals. Other features of this manuscript merit consideration: it may have been consulted by numerous scribes as there are many different hands at work in the translations, some on the same folio (on a number of individual folios, for example, both Devanagri and Gurmukhi appear). The production of this text in Gurmukhi along with its sporadic translations suggests that there were indeed Sikhs who were not only aware of Nand Lal's *Divān* but used it to recite his hymns, perhaps according to it a revered place among the compositions of the gurus, thus foreshadowing its eventual incorporation into the Sikh canon. Some may, moreover, have used the occasional bait as an augury in the same way that cultured Muslims used the ghazals of Hafez and Rumi. For the Emperor Jahangir's use of such, see Wheeler M. Thackston (ed. and trans.), *The Jahangirnama: Memoirs of Jahangir, Emperor of India* (Washington, D.C.: Smithsonian, 1999), pp. 132 and 222.

72. By way of illustration, consult MS 764, Central Public Library, Patiala. Many Sikh scholars hold that the small size of such manuscripts was essential at a time when Sikhs (particularly Khalsa Sikhs) were hounded by the authorities.

73. For this emphasis on oral transmission of ghazals and hymns within the broader Islamicate, see Robert Canfield, *Turko-Persia*, p. 30. Winand M. Callewaert, 'Singers Repertoires in Western India,' R.S. McGregor (ed.), *Devotional Literature in South Asia: Current Research 1985–1988* (Cambridge: Cambridge University Press, 1992), pp. 29–35, deals with this type of communication within India itself. As Nand Lal's bani is, according to the *Sikh Rahit Maryada*, today accepted for recitation in gurdwaras along with the hymns of the gurus and those of Bhai Gurdas, it is clear that it is still orally transmitted.

74. Although this seems obvious, one may consult for background Pashaura Singh, *The Guru Granth Sahib*, pp. 270–1, and Winand Callewaert, 'Singers Repertoires'.

75. *Encyclopaedia of Sikhism* 2, p. 460. Also Winand Callewaert, 'Singers' Repertoires', p. 29.

76. Bhai Gurdas also authored 675 kabitts in Braj Bhasha. These all appear along with commentary, text, concordance, and an explanation of difficult words in Onkar Singh, *Kabitt Savaiye Bhāī Gurdās: Pāth, Tuk-tatkarā, Anukramnikā ate Kosh* (Patiala: Punjabi University Publication Bureau, 1993).

77. *Bachitar Natak* 13, *Sri Dasam Granth Sahib ji* (Amritsar: Bhai Chatar Singh Jivan Singh, 1988), pp. 71–3. Also Jadunath Sarkar, *History of Aurangzeb* 5, p. 11.

78. Sukha Singh, *Gur-bilās Pātishāhī* 10 16:171–2 [ed. Gursharan Kaur Jaggi] (Patiala: Bhasha Vibhag Punjab, 1989), p. 248. Indubhusan Bannerjee claims that

such intercession was provided not by Nand Lal but by Nand Chand. See Indubhushan Bannerjee, *Evolution of the Khalsa* II (Calcutta: AMC, 3rd edn, 1972), p. 91.

79. Surjit Hans, *A Reconstruction of Sikh History from Sikh Literature* (Jalandhar: ABS, 1988), pp. 250–3.

80. Once again, Uttam Singh Bhatia, *Gurū Bhagat Bhāī Nand Lāl Goyā*, pp. 15 and 17.

81. Piara Singh Padam (ed.), *Bhāī Kesar Singh Chhibbar krit Bansāvalīnāmā Dasān Pātshāhīān kā* (Amritsar: Singh Brothers, 1997), 12:11, p. 204; Ganda Singh (ed. and trans.), *Amar-nāmā: Fārsī māl, Panjābī Utārā te Arath*, pp. 23–4. Prince Mu'azzam's affection for Nand Lal will be further developed in Santokh Singh's *Gur-pratāp Sūraj Granth*. See Vir Singh (ed.), *Santokh Singh*, 12, *ritu 3, ansu 25*, lines 29–31, pp. 5081 and 5082. As we will note, it was this affection which prompted the prince to warn Nand Lal about his father's intention to forcibly convert him to Islam.

82. Indu Banga, *Agrarian System of the Sikhs* (Delhi: Manohar, 1978). For Sikh coins, see Hans Herrli, *The Coins of the Sikhs* (New Delhi: Indian Coin Society, 1993).

83. This couplet was first cast on a coin issued during the period of Banda Bahadar, circa 1710. A variation of the Gobindshahi verse is given immediately below.

Abundance, might, victory, and instant support are the bequest of [Guru] Nanak and Guru Gobind Singh.

Hans Herrli, *The Coins of The Sikhs*, pp. 35–6 and 81–5.

84. Piara Singh Padam (ed.), *Gurā kīān Sākhīān krit Bhāī Svarūp Singh Kaushish* (Amritsar: Singh Bros., 2nd edn., 1991), p. 91. According to tradition, this text was completed in 1790 CE, though a later date is more likely based on internal evidence. See also 'Gurū kīān Sakhīān', in Encyclopaedia of Sikhism 2, p. 210.

85. See sakhi 62 in Gurbachan Singh Naiar (ed.), *Guru Ratan Māl: Sau Sākhī* (Patiala: Punjabi University Publication Bureau, 3rd edn, 1995), p. 71.

86. The actual word used here is *akhārā*—a 'wrestling pit' literally, but also the name used to designate Nirmala as well as Udasi Sikh centres.

87. Sakhi 65 of the *Sau Sākhī* places the following words in the mouth of Guru Gobind Singh:

I will give nothing to the Sikh who commits adultery or learns Persian. I will take nothing from this person. Never drink water [from the hands of this Sikh]. Never accept anything from the house of the person who reads Persian. Trust him at no time. Do not touch his food [as it is polluted] since he has strayed from the path of *dharam*.

Gurbachan Singh Naiar (ed.), *Gur Ratan Māll: Sau Sākhī*, p. 79. What is probably closer to the truth is that such inconsistency underscores the composite nature of the *Sau Sākhīān*.

88. For example, the biography which appears in the introduction to Vir Singh (ed.), *Ganj-nāmah*, pp. 4–17. Santokh Singh's work, however, says very little about Nand Lal's life prior to his engagement with Prince Mu'azzam. For this we rely on ancestral claims found in the work of Bhai Megh Raj 'Garib'. Megh Raj supplies a family narrative which traces the history of Nand Lal's father in Afghanistan and details Nand Lal's life in Multan. It is on this that Vir Singh and Ganda Singh in their various writings on Bhai Nand Lal partially rely. See Bhai Megh Raj 'Garib', *Prem Phulvarā*, pp. 5–27.

89. Jit Singh Sital (ed.), *Srī Gur-panth Prakāsh*, pp. 185–92. This is a re-issued version in clearer print and with the additional notes of the Vir Singh edition published in the early twentieth century.

90. According to Bhangu, Farrukh Siyar is unwilling to follow the advice of his Turks, who wish him to ultimately jail Mata ji in order to force Banda to cease and desist. He replies to their request as follows:

This course of action which you advise is not at all a good one. I owe my crown to that very family; [it was the line of Sikh gurus who] blessed us [and my family] with the royal title.

Ibid., p. 186.

91. Ibid., p. 186. Gian Singh's version of this story excludes Mata ji and deals directly with Guru Gobind Singh, Nand Lal, and Bahadar Shah. Gian Singh, *Tavarikh Guru Khalsa* 1, pp. 1133–4.

92. Jit Singh Sital (ed.), *Srī Gur-panth Prakāsh*, p. 188.

93. Vir Singh (ed.), *Santokh Singh* 12, pp. 5075–6. Santokh Singh's account is closely modelled along the narrative of Nand Lal, we discover in Sarup Das Bhalla's *Mahimā Prakāsh*. Sarup Das Bhalla, *Mahimā Prakāsh* 2 volumes [ed. Gobind Singh Lamba and Khazan Singh] (Patiala: Bhasha Vibhag, Punjab, 1971), II 11:2–9, pp. 768–9.

94. This sakhi appears in the *Miharban janam sakhi* and the *Mahimā Prakāsh Vārtak*. See W. H. McLeod, *Guru Nanak and the Sikh Religion*, p. 52, and his *Early Sikh Tradition: A Study of the Janam-sākhīs* (Oxford: Clarendon Press, 1980), p. 283. The narrative itself is found in M. A. Macauliffe, *The Sikh Religion* I, p. 16.

95. Mahinder Singh Randhawa (ed.), *Pūran Singh Jīvanī te Kavitā* (New Delhi: Sahit Akadami, 1965), pp. 363–6.

96. Vir Singh (ed.), *Santokh Singh* 12, p. 5082. Here one Ghiyasuddin, a superintendent (*darogha*) of the Mughals and a Muslim friend of Nand Lal who accompanies Nand Lal to Anandpur, states:

[Nand Lal,] I acknowledge you as my *murshid*. [Thanks to your teachings] I cleanse my mind of evil day and night (*dinprati*); [Thanks to your teachings] I meditate on the [glories of] the Lord day and night (*nit*, always). I consider you to be the one who will help [me] at the end [of my life].

Later in the narrative Guru Gobind Singh asks Ghiyasuddin whom he calls guru:

The Sayyid heard this and said immediately, 'It is Nand Lal [who is] my guru. I became a Sikh [after having heard] the teachings of Nand Lal. Through him my pain was utterly destroyed.' Vir Singh (ed.), *Santokh Singh* 12, p. 5083.

97. Whom Santokh Singh mistakenly refers to by his later title Bahadar Shah. See Vir Singh (ed.), *Santokh Singh* 12, p. 5077.

98. Macauliffe's references to Nand Lal are clearly based on Santokh Singh. See M. A. Macauliffe, *The Sikh Religion* 5, pp. 79, 102–4, and 230.

99. See again Jit Singh Sital (ed.), *Srī Gur-panth Prakāsh*, p. 186, and M. A. Macauliffe, *The Sikh Religion* 4, p. 379. Richard Eaton discusses the 'connection between political fortune and spiritual blessing' in regard to the Chishti Sufi order and the sultans of Bengal in his *The Rise of Islam and the Bengal Frontier: 1204–1760* (Delhi: Oxford University Press, 1994), p. 84.

100. I base this 'acceptance' on statements found in both the *Bachitar Natak* and the *Zafar-nāmah*, both attributed to Guru Gobind Singh. See *Bachitar Natak* 13:9 and *Zafar-nāmah* 89–94, Dasam Granth, pp. 71, 1393.

101. Louis E. Fenech, *Martrydom in the Sikh Tradition: Playing the 'Game of Love'* (New Delhi: Oxford University Press, 2000), p. 150.

102. Vir Singh (ed.), *Santokh Singh* 12, p. 5076–7.

103. I doubt very much that the 'ilm' here refers to knowledge generically, but consider rather that it refers to those knowledges which would make one learned in a traditional Islamic culture. The claim that he acquired this knowledge in a maktab or traditional Islamic school generally attached to a mosque makes this point.

104. Vir Singh (ed.), *Santokh Singh* 12, p. 5079–82. Another version of this tale is Gian Singh, *Tavarikh Guru Khalsa* 1, pp. 865–6.

105. W. H. McLeod, *Early Sikh Tradition*, p. 142.

106. According to Badauni, Abu'l-Fazl presented the Emperor Akbar with a commentary on the *āyat-ul-kursī* (the 'sign of the throne', Qur'an 2:255) of the *Surat al-Baqarah* (the longest Sura of the Qur'an) which was praised by the emperor. See Muhammad Abdul Ghani, *A History of Persian Language and Literature at the Mughal Court: Part 3—Akbar the Great*, p. 236.

107. Macauliffe will supplement this narrative with one in which Nand Lal demonstrates his erudition through a letter sent to the Shah of Iran. He claims that this is based on oral tradition, a contention which is most likely accurate as I have not found a nineteenth-century source to support this story. M. A. Macauliffe, *The Sikh Religion* 5, p. 103.

108. Vir Singh (ed.), *Santokh Singh* 12, p. 5080:

On hearing [the meaning the prince] became blissful. He exalted [Nand Lal] morning, noon, and night [and proclaimed that Nand Lal's] profound wisdom could understand all things. In great joy he gave Nand Lal a splendid robe of honour.

109. Vir Singh (ed.), *Santokh Singh* 12, p. 5080:

When Aurangzeb heard [Nand Lal's] interpretation from his son he was amazed through and through. [He exclaimed,] 'There is nothing more intelligent than this!'

110. Vir Singh (ed.), *Santokh Singh* 12, p. 5081.

111. Vir Singh (ed.), *Santokh Singh* 12, pp. 5081 and 5082. Santokh Singh also strongly implies that Nand Lal had been aware of Aurangzeb's reputation for cruelty well before his disciple's comment. Before knowing the reason for the prince's unease, he asks:

What has your father asked you to say?

Vir Singh (ed.), Santokh Singh 12, p. 5080.

112. The story of Babur and Guru Nanak's meeting may be found in M. A. Macauliffe, *The Sikh Religion* 1, pp. 113–15. Though this meeting is most likely apocryphal, Babur's penchant for holy men and mystics is well known.

Sikhs and Caste

W. H. McLeod

It all started at a cinema in Dunedin where we had gone to see the film *Monsoon Wedding*. This film (a comedy) does not concern Sikhs, but it does concern Khatris and the extravagant way of life lived by a section of Khatris in New Delhi. How do we know that they are Khatris? We know their identity because the family of the bridegroom are called Varmas and at least anyone brought up in the Punjab will at once know that they are Khatris. We already know that Khatris typically marry other Khatris, and what we have presented to us in the film is more than a picture of wealthy, upper-class Indians. It is a film about wealthy, upper-class Khatris and as such it provides a useful commentary on this particular segment of Delhi society. Would foreigners have known this? It is certain that apart from the tiniest of minorities they would not have known.

Or consider the film *Bend it like Beckham*, one which certainly concerns a Sikh family and which effectively portrays certain aspects of Ramgarhia society in Hounslow. We know that they are Sikhs and we know from references to East Africa that they are probably Ramgarhia Sikhs. But how do we know for certain? The gurdwara that was the site of the wedding in the film is not labelled a Ramgarhia one, but once again the family name of the chief participants gives the show away. The name is Bamrah and every Sikh who lives in England will at once identify them as Ramgarhia Sikhs. But will the ordinary English person? For that person it does not matter, but for any English person concerned with Sikh studies, it should certainly be of interest. Part of the attraction of *Bend it like Beckham* is that it presents the life of Ramgarhia Sikhs lived in England. For those interested in Sikh studies, that illuminates an aspect of the film.

These are trivial examples, but they indicate something of the problem of the foreigner in coping with caste in the Punjab. A person brought up in the Punjab or in Sikh society overseas will absorb many features that are denied to those of us who are foreigners, one of which is the characteristic terminology of caste. He or she will know that a person bearing Bal as a final name will be a Jat whereas someone called Anand is a Khatri. These are perhaps obvious caste names that many foreigners will be able to recognize, but there are many that are much more obscure.[1]

Marital practices can also puzzle foreigners. These arise from the endogamous *jati* and exogamous *gotr* of the caste pattern of this society. Native Punjabis will also take this for granted, whereas those of us who are foreigners will frequently struggle. Most foreigners have the vague idea that Indians all go in for 'arranged marriages', but beyond this erroneous feature, their knowledge often does not extend very far. That this has not bothered us much in the past is in part a measure of the gendered nature of Sikh history. Sikh history is the history of men and the fact that a man belongs to a particular jati and gotr is all that matters.[2] Whom he may have married is of no consequence. In future, though, it will matter more and more, as Sikhs and others interested in Sikh history and Sikh sociology follow Doris Jakobsh's example and books such as *Relocating Gender in Sikh History* (OUP, 2002) become more common.

Who marries who, and how is the marriage planned and conducted? For those who are native Punjabis, questions such as these amount to asking for the most obvious of explanations. Those of us who are foreigners, however, need detailed explanations. Why did the gurus who were married all wed wives of the same jati but of different gotrs? We all know that they belonged to the Khatri jati, but what were their various gotrs? Did their gotrs matter? And what about the various wives that Maharaja Ranjit Singh had? Were they all married in accordance with correct Jat prescription? Why is Sikh history so silent about the place and the role of Sikh women? Does this in any way reflect the caste pattern of Punjabi society? Some of these questions may seem patently obvious to a person brought up in the Punjab, but they are far from obvious to the outsider. Pity the poor foreigner—but pity also the Sikhs. Certain features of what is called the caste system also elude them.

Who Studies Caste among the Sikhs?

When I began preparing this chapter, I was under the misapprehension that Sikh studies suffer from a particular weakness, one that has obstructed our understanding in the past and which, if unchanged, must continue to obstruct it in the future. The proportion of those working on Sikh studies was, I believed, far too heavily weighted in favour of specialists in history or in religion, with not nearly enough trained in sociology or social anthropology. Certain prime areas of Sikh studies are simply not being analysed, or if they are being analysed, the task is being performed by researchers who do not possess the necessary skills.

Reviewing the literature, however, I was bound to admit that I had been altogether too hasty. There are indeed social scientists working on Sikh society and some of their contributions add considerably to our knowledge. If there is a problem, it is that most of these social scientists have produced only one book each. There are various reasons for this. They may be at the beginning of their life's work or they may be relaxing after having achieved the academic rank that they sought. They may have moved to some other employment, died before they could develop a promising career, found the field-work too demanding, been overwhelmed by other demands, or aimed at results which take many years to derive.[3] A few of them had actually produced more than one book or had put their effort more into the production of articles.[4] My mistake had arisen from the fact that as a historian, I was better acquainted with works dealing with Sikh history and religion, a false impression which was further aggravated by the uneven attendance at Sikh studies conferences.

This error does not excuse those of us who work in the Humanities from ignoring the contribution made by social scientists. The boundaries between the various disciplines are indistinguishable and the historian who knows little sociology or anthropology is certainly a very poor one. To understand Sikh history and religion adequately, one must first grasp the true nature of Sikh society. It is here that caste becomes significant. To understand Sikh society, one must comprehend the nature of caste as it affects the Panth. An understanding of the future development of the Sikh religion makes an understanding of caste as practised by Sikhs absolutely imperative. Social scientists already recognize this, although some of their books or articles may skate round it or omit all mention completely. For those of us who are historians, it is likewise imperative. Without it our understanding of both the Panth and its religion must inevitably be flawed.

Defining caste

What is known as the caste system is, needless to say, confusing and disputed. A fundamental problem arises from the fact that the English word 'caste' itself bears two distinct meanings and the attempt to understand the caste system would be greatly aided by having in English two different words for what are, after all, two different concepts. Attention was drawn to the problem by the British historian A. L. Basham. Writing at the very end of the British period, Basham clearly distinguished the varan pattern from caste. According to Basham the varan were classes, not castes. In other words, Brahman, Kshatriya, Vaishya, and Shudra were all classes, with the outcastes forming a fifth class. Relations between the four-fold varan or 'classes' in later Hindu society were governed by rules of endogamy, commensality, and craft-exclusiveness. These varan, he maintained, were not the same as the immense number of hierarchical groups in Hindu society which were governed by the same pattern of exclusiveness. When at the end of the fifteenth century the Portuguese arrived in a world of curious social groups, they gave that social institution which they observed the name *casta*, a Spanish or Portuguese term meaning lineage, tribe, or family.

In attempting to account for the proliferation of castes in eighteenth- and nineteenth-century India, authorities credulously accepted the traditional view that by a process of intermarriage and subdivision, the 3000 or more castes of modern India had evolved from the four primitive classes, and the term 'caste' was applied indiscriminately to both varna or class, and jati or caste proper.[5] This word stuck and caste became the accepted term for what was properly called jati.

Although the argument is not fully proven, it nevertheless warrants a significant measure of acceptance. This primary difference which Basham claims is represented by 'class' as opposed to 'caste' is evident, for example, in the early Punjabi rahit-namas of the eighteenth and nineteenth centuries. My reason for not accepting the argument in its entirety is the name that Basham fastens on the four varan. They are not 'classes', a word that connotes an economic division in a society. Their meaning is much wider than this, extending into a broad social sense with fixed boundaries.[6] Moreover, the nature of those fixed boundaries varies very considerably in different parts of India and with different levels of society. Brahmans are certainly not accepted as the superior varan by all Indians everywhere. This exclusive social sense does, however, exist and it is actually much closer to the meaning of 'caste'. For that reason 'caste' has been used both for the varan and for the jati orders of society.

There is, however, a clear difference in meaning. Varan designates the theoretical model based on Sanskrit texts, with the Brahman at the top in terms of status and the Dalit at the very bottom. In actual practice the model is a highly unstable pyramid.

Jati has only a partial connection with varan. As with the varan model, it is governed by rules of strict endogamy and it demonstrates a limited commensality and sometimes a craft-exclusiveness which is now fading. It covers the many social groups with the same claims to status, but with a variety of origins (commonly economic) and with the opportunity for particular groups to move up or down the status ladder. These are the endogamous groups into which people are born and which they remain in till life's end. We would perhaps be justified in importing into English usage 'varan' for what has been regarded as the classical hierarchy. This would then reserve 'caste' for the pattern of endogamous social groups to which virtually everyone in India belongs. It would mean, though, introducing into English usage a term which would be difficult to sustain and which as a result is most unlikely to take root. It seems that we are condemned to use the same English word for two different concepts, one indicated by varan and the other by jati.

The Sikh System of Caste

Generations of scholars have been brought up on the firm belief that the varan concept of caste was accurate and many still believe it to be true. Today, however, the theoretical schema of the Brahman at the top of the hierarchy and the Dalit at the bottom is under serious attack. The Brahmanical notion of caste may hold for some members of upper-caste India, but for many more, it certainly cannot be sustained. In the Punjab, the Brahman is not seen as particularly high in status (particularly in rural Punjab) and in this regard the Punjabi view is far from being exceptional. Caste may produce a pattern of hierarchies, but those hierarchies are rarely models of the classical varan pattern and the Brahman is by no means always at the top.[7]

This fundamental feature of caste must be clearly understood before any analysis of the Sikh view of caste is undertaken. Caste relates to a number of issues, particularly to those that are economic. This feature does much to explain the meaning of caste in the Sikh Panth and must be firmly grasped before we begin our list of those aspects of Sikh history which need reinterpretation in the light of caste. We must take care, however, not to throw the baby out with the bath-water. The concept of the varan pattern may be dismissed or significantly modified in *contemporary* analysis, yet neither the Adi Granth usage nor that of the eighteenth-century rahit-namas should be overlooked. In both, varan is present, and both were concerned to overthrow the varan or char varan (the four castes). In early Sikh literature, the two concepts of varan and jati are present and both terms require close attention.

The word for varan in Punjabi is actually baran. In the Adi Granth, varan is more frequently employed, but in the works which follow (notably the rahit-namas) baran is more commonly used. Guru Nanak uses 'baran' only once, but its meaning is unmistakable. So too is his meaning of 'jati' which is placed in immediate proximity to 'baran'.

Thus does the bride meet Hari, her husband, gaining the blessing of his love. All [concern for] jati, baran and kul[8] are abandoned as she contemplates the Word [revealed in] the guru's teachings.[9]

Clearly jati means the endogamous social group into which a person has been born, and equally clearly baran signifies the classical four-fold pattern of Hindu society. In other words, baran indicates the division of society into Brahman, Kshatriya, Vaishya, and Shudra.

Guru Nanak, in common with the other gurus recorded in the Adi Granth, shows a marked preference for the varan spelling, but the meaning is the same.

Whenever anyone is exalted [Akal Purakh] does not prefer one caste above another (*varana varan*).
All greatness comes from his hand and is bestowed on whom he approves.
By the exercise of the *Hukam* he confers it and that without delay.[10]

The message is repeated by the other gurus, as is made clear in a line by Guru Ram Das.

Regardless of the four castes (*char baran*) to which he belongs, or which of the four stages of life (*char ashram*) he occupies, if he follows the guru, says Nanak, he crosses [life's ocean] and carries with him all his family.[11]

For Guru Ram Das too, this is the only reference to 'baran', yet there can be no mistaking its meaning. Normally he too used 'varan'. Only with Guru Arjan is 'baran' employed with greater frequency.[12] There seems to be no doubt that the gurus composed in a society which accepted the classical Hindu mode, but they were concerned to show that this mode could have no influence on a person's all-important liberation. That came only from meditation on the Divine Name. They accepted caste both in terms of varan and of jati, but never as systems of high and low status. In other words, they accepted caste in horizontal terms, but never in vertical. All were equal.

The same applies to the eighteenth-century rahit-namas. The first instance of an eighteenth-century rahit-nama's use of 'baran' occurs in 1718–19. This is in the *Tanakhah-nama* attributed to Nand Lal where the author has Guru Gobind Singh declare, 'I shall merge the four castes into one'.[13] The term translated is char baran, a form that cannot possibly carry the same meaning as the social organization of the Punjab. This social organization comprises the hierarchies formed by the range of jatis. Then in the mid-eighteenth century, the author of the Chaupa Singh rahit-nama uses the term 'baran' and this I have again translated as 'caste'.[14] Chaupa Singh (or whoever wrote this section of the rahit-nama) uses it in conjunction with ashram, implying that it is something different from the numerous castes that populate Punjabi society. This usage becomes clearer still when the author of the Desa Singh rahit-nama employs 'baran' as in *bipr baran*, contrasting it with *nich jāti* in the preceding stanza.

Do not permit barbers (*nai*) and Jhivars—those who shave heads—weavers (*kori*), potters (*kunabi*), [those tribals] who are called Gonds, and others of low caste to participate [in your langar].[15]

Here nich jati has been translated as 'low caste', or it could designate what for earlier English writers was known as outcastes (in other words Dalits). This is followed in the next stanza by bipr baran, translated as 'the Brahman caste'.[16]

The author of the Daya Singh rahit-nama provides further evidence. He uses the word 'baran' on four occasions, each time making it clear that it is the classical Hindu mode which he has in mind. On one such occasion he indicates that the Dalits are outside the classical mode:

[If any member of] the four castes takes *amrit* [that person] will achieve spiritual liberation, and likewise those whose status is lowly.[17]

The 'four castes' is a translation of 'char baran' and 'those whose status is lowly' presumably indicates the Dalits. On another occasion, Daya Singh acknowledges that the bearing of weapons and the consumption of *karah prasad* is indeed the *dharam* of Khatris, but adds the following supplement:

To adopt the forms of caste is not to our taste. It is our way of living which we like.[18]

Here also the word used is 'baran'. The two remaining occasions occur in sections 22 (*chatur baran*) and 66 (char baran). Elsewhere he designates the duties required of particular members of the char baran.[19]

In the nineteenth century, the *Mukati-nama*, one of the two rahit-namas incorporated in the *Sau Sakhian*, offers both nich jati and char varan. In stanza 7 it advises a good Sikh to keep his distance from a person of 'low caste' (nich jati).[20] Stanza 19, however, commands those who are Sikhs to treat all four castes as brothers in the faith and here the term is 'char varan'. It will be noted that there is no concern to overthrow the latter. *Mukati-nama* is a Sanatan Sikh composition and the Sanatan Sikhs were certainly not in the business of upsetting treasured social distinctions.

The term 'varan' (or 'baran') is accordingly a viable one, at least until we are into the twentieth century, and plainly it designates the four-fold pyramid of the classical varan mode which the gurus were concerned to flatten but not demolish. In Sikh history, this mode should be accepted, regardless of what the contemporary view of the twenty-first century may display. It is safe to assume that this notion of caste was at least held into the twentieth century and that the theoretical varan model still held sway. In 1898 Kahn Singh Nabha certainly held it up for attack in *Ham Hindu Nahin*.[21] Caste is certainly a very complicated issue and it is imperative that historians who choose to work with it clarify their understanding before venturing too far.

Approximately 30 castes have Sikh members, though many of these rate only 1 per cent or a little more of the Panth's constituency.[22] They even include a tiny Brahman segment. Although one feature of the Singh Sabha movement was an effort to persuade Sikhs to abandon their gotr names, many families have continued to use them. Amongst Jat gotrs, Gil, Grewal, Man, Sidhu, and many more are widely known. All the gurus were Khatris, with the result that the four gotrs to which they belonged have acquired a special sanctity.[23]

All this is well known and there is much more that can be said about caste in a general sense as it relates to the Sikh Panth. A large majority of Sikhs, for example, follow jati and gotr regulations when marriages are arranged, and in some instances commensal restrictions are also observed. Information of this sort is easily acquired, even if it does not figure in reports and analyses as frequently as one might like. The following major differences, however, should be noted.

The first is that the Sikh notion of caste (in theory at least) requires the elimination of the varan differences. Note that this is not saying that Sikhs reject the jati concept, only the varan. The varan concept remains, but it is shorn of all differences of status. Doctrinally, the Sikh faith rejects the Vedas; it lacks the theoretical schema of Brahman, Kshatriya, Vaishya, and Shudra; it is hostile to any claims of Brahman superiority; it dismisses theories of status or power based on sacred claims; and in theory it is against notions of purity as opposed to pollution. The Sikh concept of caste is certainly hierarchical, but it structures hierarchy in terms of economic power and (to a much lesser extent) the size of the individual jati. As an ideal, the Sikh concept of caste excludes the varan theory. It is true that in practice Sikh behaviour may fall short of this ideal, but as an ideal it still stands.

Second, it should be noted that on the sacred ground of some gurdwaras (notably Darbar Sahib in Amritsar) there is no place for caste discrimination on the basis of purity and pollution. Offerings of karah prasad by members of the various jatis are mingled at presentation and those who receive it do not know the origin of what they have been given.[24] Similarly the langar routine requires all to sit in the same line for accepting and eating food without questioning its origin. Note, however, that this practice only applies to some gurdwaras. At this point there is a difference between Sikhs that is based on caste consideration. Although the Jats do not usually display possession by overtly labelling their buildings 'Jat gurdwara', there are many such places of worship where Jats are in complete control. Ramgarhias are less inhibited, particularly in the United Kingdom, which has many Ramgarhia Sikhs who were forced out of East Africa or found it otherwise advantageous to leave. Some United Kingdom gurdwaras bear the name 'Ramgarhia gurdwara', indicating the nature of their sangats. Likewise the Dalits have their own gurdwaras, commonly bearing the name 'Ravidasi gurdwara' after the Bhagat of the Adi Granth who was a Chamar. In the case of Mazhabi places of worship, they may be known as 'Balmiki gurdwaras'.

Third, it must be acknowledged that even if caste is widely practised in the Panth, many Sikhs genuinely believe that caste observance has no place in the Sikh faith. This is an inheritance of the Tat Khalsa view, which was that caste must be wrong because caste was practised by Hindus. Kahn Singh Nabha published his *Ham Hindu Nahin* in 1898 and this small booklet became the rallying cry for the Sikh reformation, with the booklet's title as an insistent slogan: 'We are not Hindus!' Because caste lay at the heart of Hindu society, it must be discarded by all who called themselves Sikh. In actual practice, however, few embraced the new doctrine, at least in a complete sense. It might well be a feature of orthodox Tat Khalsa theology and, as we have already noted, many Sikhs gave up the practice of using their gotr name as a surname, preferring instead the use simply of Singh. By their deeds, however, a substantial majority of Sikhs indicated that at least a significant remnant of their caste background remained. This was their marriage practice, weddings being carried out with due concern for jati and gotr prescription.

Those who followed Tat Khalsa principles and abandoned caste in its entirety may be a small minority, but commonly they make their views very public indeed. Because these Sikhs are normally well educated, these are the views which Westerners often hear, just as the marriages which do not observe traditional regulation are amongst those Sikhs whom Westerners are likely to meet. They are most unlikely to encounter the Sikhs who live in Punjab villages where caste is accepted and traditions are observed. As a result Gurmat is widely if erroneously believed to be free of caste amongst Westerners.[25]

A version of caste is, therefore, generally accepted by a large majority of the Sikh Panth and widely practised by them. The general features have been duly noted, and although the works dealing with Sikh society and caste may be few, they are at least accessible for any who seek an understanding of them. This, though, carries us only some distance towards complete understanding. More needs to be done, and one of the purposes of this essay is to identify some areas where that understanding is faulty, inadequate, or plainly absent. Until these areas are firmly comprehended, our knowledge of the Sikh view of caste must necessarily be deficient.[26] First, though, the caste composition of the Panth should be briefly sketched.

Sikh Castes

(a) Jats

Through the works mentioned earlier and by our own observation, we soon gather that the Jats constitute approximately 66 per cent of the total Panth's membership, and that in spite of their low ranking on the varan scale, they are unquestionably the dominant caste in rural Punjab. Politically, they are dominant over the Punjab as a whole and if they could maintain something resembling unity, they would remain in control of the political process. As it is, a Sikh has usually been Chief Minister since

Independence and all but two of them have been Jats. One of the exceptions, Gurmukh Singh Mussafir, was Chief Minister for only a short period. The other, Giani Zail Singh, who was a Ramgarhia, was said to be entirely acceptable to the Jats when he was first appointed.

The appeal of the gurus' message to the Jats seems to have been that it served to raise their caste status. The gurus preached that one's caste situation had no bearing on access to spiritual liberation. According to the varan concept of caste, the Jats (as Shudras) were certainly not outcastes, but they rated low on the traditional scale because they dirtied their hands in following their traditional rural occupation. Also they permitted widow remarriage. This did not matter according to the message of Gurmat and many of the Jats adopted it because it granted them the benefits of their economic status without the attendant disadvantage of the varan tradition. Many of the Jats remained Muslims and others Hindus. In central Punjab, however, the movement to become Sikhs was powerful, and in the modern Punjab virtually all the Jats are followers of the gurus. This also explains why the Panth, although not comprising a single caste, is strongly Jat in membership.[27]

(b) Ramgarhias

Jats are the dominant caste in rural Punjab because (as we all know) they own most village land and thereby exercise an economic power that no other caste can possibly rival. The Ramgarhias (the Sikh caste drawn largely from the Tarkhan or carpenter caste) were the servants of the land-owning Jats and as servants they remain for as long as they live in the villages. The same can be said of such members of other artisan castes that entered the Panth, merging with the Tarkhans to form the composite Ramgarhia caste (the Lohar, the Raj, and the Nai castes). They too were *sepidar* or traditional servants of the Jats, performing specified services and in return usually receiving payment in grain at the annual harvest. Many Ramgarhias may have escaped from *sepi* through settlement overseas, but they have not necessarily escaped the difference in status.

(c) Dalits and other low-status castes

What can be said of the difference in status of Jat and Ramgarhia must be stated with even greater emphasis of the status of the Sikh Dalits or outcaste Sikhs. Sikh Dalits, like the Hindu Dalits from whom they have come, are distinguished by the different names adopted when they became Sikhs. Member of the Chuhra or sweeper caste became the Mazhabi Sikhs, while those from the Chamar or leather-workers are known as the Ravidasi or Ramdasi Sikhs. Apart from their change of name, however, the condition of the Sikh Dalits is essentially the same as their Hindu counterparts. In most Sikh villages the Dalits live apart from the remainder of the inhabitants, and in many they have their own wells and cremation grounds. They are commonly prohibited from entering their patrons' houses (particularly the kitchen area) and they receive food in their own utensils.[28]

Amongst Ravidasis, the influence of the rahit is very weak. Attendance at a gurdwara (frequently a Ravidasi one) is the practice of some and most marry according to Anand rites, but they also regard Ravidas as their guru. In all respects, he ranks in their eyes as the equal of Guru Nanak or Guru Gobind Singh. A picture of Ravidas is generally displayed in their gurdwaras and homes, they raise *jaikaras* in his honour, they cut their hair, and in general they regard their Ravidasi caste as the marker of their identity, treating it primarily as neither Sikh nor Hindu. In the Doaba they commonly call themselves Ad Dharmi, followers of the 'Original Faith'.[29]

Just when the Dalits entered the Panth is not known for certain, though a reasonable guess places the main incursion at the end of the nineteenth century or early in the twentieth. This was the period of the Christian mass movement, when many Chuhra Dalits converted to Christianity as caste groups in the expectation that they would escape the tribulation of the Hindu caste system.

All this is well known, although frequently it is not mentioned in terms that are quite so clear. Other small groups within the Panth are likewise stationed in locations that correspond to their Hindu, Muslim, or Christian counterparts (the third of these being practically all Dalits). Only one conspicuous exception deserves to be noted, that of the Sikh Kalals or distilling caste. Originally on the Dalit border, the Sikh members adopted the name of an eighteenth-century *misldar*, Jassa Singh Ahluvalia, and as the Ahluvalia Sikhs adopted practices and patterns which conformed to those of higher castes. The device proved successful, unlike the same technique attempted by the Ramgarhia, Sikhs who adopted the name of another misldar of their caste, Jassa Singh Ramgarhia. It has also proved unsuccessful in the case of the Sikh Chhimbas, who have adopted the name Tank Kshatriyas.

(d) Khatris and Aroras

In contrast to the numerically strong rural population of Sikhs, the number of urban Sikhs is small. Two castes stand out. These are the Khatris and the Aroras, each representing less than 2.5 per cent of the total Sikh population. Unlike the Jats, only a small proportion of both castes have become Sikh. In the case of the Khatris, this has often been through initiating the eldest son of a family, leaving the remainder of the family to be raised as Hindus. The occupations of the two castes are similar, but their status differs. This reflects the higher mercantile occupations of many of the Khatris as opposed to the smaller shopkeeping of the Aroras. Although their proportions within the Panth are tiny, their contribution to the Panthic intellectual leadership is impressive. A substantial majority of both Khatris and Aroras remain Hindu, but inter-communal marriages are arranged, providing only that the marriages are in accordance with jati traditions. Khatris commonly claim that they are Kshatriyas. This, however, seems highly improbable. Their strong mercantile traditions make it much more likely that they are Vaishya, their current cognate name being another case of upward mobility by claiming Kshatriya status.[30]

Areas of Sikh Society which Require Further Analysis

We turn now to identifying those areas in which further research is required. Ten such areas will be briefly examined.

(a) Guru Nanak's view of caste

The gurus were all Khatris and those who had children married them in accordance with caste prescription. This simple fact is rarely noted in the literature, yet fact it is. Not only is it a fact, it is also a defensible fact. Guru Nanak was not against the caste structure of Indian society. What he opposed was the hierarchical structure of Indian society and the belief that one's caste status conferred special privilege or special condemnation. Other gurus also accepted this belief. They were certainly opposed to the vertical distinctions of caste, by which I mean that there should be no notion of inequality based on caste and that in terms of access to liberation all people were in the same situation. They did, however, believe in the horizontal application of caste that gave Indian society its stability.[31]

This was the teaching of Nanak, followed by those gurus who have left evidence of their attitude. What hope, though, had it of being accepted? The answer must surely be that it had none. What Guru Nanak taught and what was accepted by his successors was an ideal, namely that all are equal. But in practice, no society has ever accepted this and none ever will.

There will be those who accept it as an ideal, and a few select individuals will endeavour to put the ideal into practice. Societies, however, will by their actions ignore it. The same applies to Sikh society as to any other. To expect that it would be otherwise would be like viewing all Christians as earnestly applying the Sermon on the Mount in every respect. A few do so. A large majority ignore it in whole or in significant part.

To describe the situation as baldly as this will surely cause indignation on the part of those who view it as an assault on the truth. This being so, it is doubtless wise to handle the matter gently. Arousing the faithful to passionate rage will scarcely serve the purposes of serious scholarship. We cannot maintain a total silence, though. Whether baldly or with consummate gentleness, this message needs to be communicated, at least to those who are concerned to reach understanding.

(b) Caste observance in the early Sikh Panth

Marriage in accordance with jati and gotr regulations conferred on Indian society a structure which others have been unable to emulate. A comparison of traditional Indian expectations with the more chaotic Western pattern makes this clear. Instead of parents choosing the most suitable partner for offspring who have been educated to accept their choice, we leave the decision to young people at that point in time when they are least likely to make a sensible decision. The Indian model is, needless to say, an ideal pattern that sometimes goes sadly astray, but then the Western model is much more likely to flounder. Constructing the pattern on the basis of caste regulation keeps it under control and the society that maintains this pattern is fortunate indeed.

This much the gurus were prepared to accept. In medieval India, however, caste meant more than this. It meant hierarchy (as it still does) and access to liberation was believed to be dependent on one's place within that hierarchy, whether Brahman (or any other group) at one extreme or Dalit at the other. This aspect was implacably opposed by the Sikh gurus, but that is not the same as saying that they opposed caste in all respects. Until this is recognized and built into our reconstruction of early Sikh society, we shall continue to record a social structure that is at best only partially understood.

Bhai Gurdas clearly accepted this concept of caste. How else does one explain his use of gotr titles in the lengthy list of loyal followers of the gurus that he provides in Var 11? But some will claim that the determinative change came with the founding of the Khalsa at the end of the seventeenth century. In the course of the amrit ceremony, the rahit is expounded in terms which include the following:

> Because you are all children of the same father you are spiritual brothers, one with another and with all others who have received the *amrit* initiation. You must renounce your former lineage (*kul*), occupation, works, and religious affiliation. This means that you should put aside all concern for caste status (*jāt-pāt*), birth (*janam*), country, and religion, for you are now exclusively a member of the sublime Khalsa.[32]

This, however, merely reinforces the message that had descended from Guru Nanak. The term *jat-pat* designates concern for caste status, not caste as such, and is characteristically used as a term of opprobrium by those who maintain caste as a social order.[33]

And so the attitude continues down through the eighteenth century and for most of the nineteenth. Exposure to British ideals, the conviction that the Sikhs were not Hindus, and the abundant evidence of caste as a vehicle for differential status led the Tat Khalsa to regard all caste differences as contrary to Gurmat. *Ham Hindu Nahin*, declared Kahn Singh Nabha, and because caste was believed to be characteristic of Hindu society, there could be no place for it as far as the Sikhs were concerned. No longer were caste names to be employed by devout Sikhs. The Tat Khalsa had, however, misread the teaching of the gurus. In vertical terms, caste was properly spurned. In its horizontal expression, however, it should be retained.

This awareness needs to be built into our treatment of Sikh society from earliest times until the present day. There is no point in blindly pretending that Sikhs do not accept caste. The evidence against it is overwhelming.

(c) The entry of the Jats into the Panth

The overwhelming preponderance of Jats in the Sikh Panth has already been noted, a figure which is approximately 66 per cent of the total. Just when the Jats entered the Panth cannot be accurately determined, but it can be safely assumed that although they were not yet dominant in Guru Nanak's time, there were certainly Jats among his followers. Khushwant Singh believes that it was under Guru Arjan that they flocked into the Panth,[34] though Bhai Gurdas testifies that the leadership at that time was still largely Khatri.[35]

But come they certainly did, and in so doing they raise a number of questions. One concerns the popularity of the Panth as far as the Jats were concerned. Why did they enter the Panth? Earlier I said that the appeal of the gurus' message to the Jats seems to have been that it served to raise their status significantly. The gurus preached that one's caste situation had no bearing on access to spiritual liberation and the Jats were attracted by this message because it indicated that their growing economic power in Punjab could be matched by a high-status position in rural society. They may have tilled the soil and they may have permitted widow remarriage, but they had the power. The status accorded them must recognize this. In rural Punjab, they steadily increased their power and with this economic advancement went an unrivalled place in the rural hierarchy.

Is this thesis correct? It may appear entirely reasonable, but so far it has not been diligently researched. The thesis seems convincing, yet we may be sure that not everyone will agree with it.

A second question concerns the impact of this Jat predominance on the nature of the Sikh faith. Some would argue that it has had very little influence. As the next section will indicate, much greater influence seems to have been exercised by the tiny minority of Khatris. This, however, is interpreting the Sikh faith too narrowly. The warrior character of the Panth and the warfare which occupies much of Sikh history since the time of Guru Gobind Singh owes little to its Khatri section. It owes an enormous amount to those Sikhs who were Jats.

Third, is the intensely political nature of the Panth and the manner in which political activity is pursued the result of its Jat constituency? We may be ready to volunteer an answer, yet we should nevertheless hesitate to give it. Hesitation is in order because here too the subject has not been properly researched.

And so the questioning continues and at once answers are proffered. The proffering of answers may well be a ready response. The tendering of properly researched responses will, however, be a much smaller one.

(d) Singh Sabha leaders

Kahn Singh Nabha brings us to the period of the Singh Sabha. The castes of the leaders in that period of critical importance that produced the Singh Sabha movement (particularly the Tat Khalsa sector) were of major importance. Two of the prominent members of the Tat Khalsa were Kahn Singh himself and Giani Dit Singh. Kahn Singh was a Jat, and although he did not make a display of his gotr name, he was a Dhillon. Dit Singh was a Ramdasi Sikh and much has been made of his Dalit origins. In this regard, however, he was very much of an exception, for Dalits were exceedingly few as members of the Singh Sabha and Dalit leaders were almost non-existent. The same cannot be said of Kahn Singh, but Jat leadership in the Singh Sabha or in the Tat Khalsa appears to have been much less prominent than their numbers within the Panth would seem to justify. Leadership seems to be conspicuously in the hands of Khatris and Aroras. Vir Singh was a Chugh Arora and Principal Teja Singh was a Khatri. Other Khatris and Aroras included Jawahir Singh Kapur, Mohan Singh Vaid, Bhai Jodh Singh, Bhagat Lakshman Singh, Professor Sahib Singh, Principal Niranjan Singh, Hira Singh Dard, and Master Tara Singh. The incidence of these castes, particularly men from the Rawalpindi area, seems to indicate that leadership within the Tat Khalsa was marked by a prominence of these two castes. There were certainly Jats involved, such as Gurmukh Singh, but their numbers were substantially fewer than their proportion within the Panth as a whole.

But is this a legitimate conclusion to draw? Without adequate research it only seems possible, and if it is indeed a correct conclusion, this dominance of Khatris and Aroras at the upper level is significant. It means that the direction of the movement will have been determined in considerable measure by those whom others call the Bhapas. But perhaps it was not the case. Beyond this, it seems impossible to proceed without further research into the caste constituency of the Tat Khalsa. What this indicates is that in the area of the Singh Sabha, more attention should be paid to the issue of caste. This research will not necessarily reveal marked differences between Khatri and Arora on the one hand and Jat on the other. It should, however, be undertaken. A limited amount has been done, but not enough. If it is not carried out, we may continue to misjudge an important aspect of the movement.

(e) Urban Sikhs

As we have already noted, a certain amount of work has already been done on caste in the village situation. More may well be needed, but I am not competent to say what that should be. The village situation is, however, much better than that of urban Sikh society. How is caste manifested in such places as Amritsar, Jalandhar, or Delhi? Oral information abounds and those who are native Punjabis know many of the answers to the questions which one raises concerning caste in the urban context. Yet how reliable is this oral information? I have been insistently informed that Aroras constitute the majority of Sikhs in Amritsar. Is this correct? It may be, but equally it may be true that they are only the largest caste in the city. Are the Aroras there predominantly shopkeepers? Again I have been told that this is the case, but what is the proof? What influence have the Aroras wielded in Amritsar over the centuries?

And other questions arise. What is the role of Khatris in urban situations? Are they predominantly highly placed in commerce and industry? Is the rate of Jat urban residence increasing and what occupations do they discharge in an urban situation? Are there Ramgarhias to be found in appreciable numbers (apart from Phagwara) or have they chosen emigration over urban settlement? What of the Dalits who live in cities, if in fact they are there in appreciable numbers? What difference has Partition made to this situation, particularly in Patiala? And so the questions continue, but without authoritative answers.

(f) Jats and Bhapas

Bhapa is a word from the Pothohari dialect spoken around Rawalpindi, which means 'elder brother'. Sikhs from this district are known as Bhapas, and as most of these Sikhs are Khatris or Aroras, the term Bhapa has come to mean a Khatri or Arora Sikh whose ancestors derive from the Rawalpindi area. This at least is its strict meaning. In practice, Khatris and Arora Sikhs from Pakistan as a whole are termed Bhapas and increasingly the word has been applied to Khatris and Aroras from the Indian side of the border.

When I first became acquainted with the word more than 40 years ago, it was not one that could be spoken in polite usage—at best uncouth and to many genteel ears hovering on the border of a swear word. Today, however, it is much more freely used, though certainly it has not lost its insulting connotation. It now means a cunning Khatri or Arora as perceived by a sturdy Jat.

To my knowledge the term has not been seriously analysed in print. This is unfortunate, for a word which carries with it these strong emotions is altogether too important to be neglected. The meaning and the connotations which lie behind its usage deserve a thorough analysis.

(g) Female infanticide

Caste points to the key element in an area where research is particularly difficult. This area is the history of female infanticide, a practice in which some Sikhs were as deeply involved as certain high-caste Hindu and Muslim jatis in the Punjab.[36] Some British settlement officers became aware that in a few Sikh gotrs the ratio of male births to female favoured the former, a difference that could only be explicable in terms of deaths amongst newly born female babies. This conviction tallied with the forthright condemnation of female infanticide that was prominently written into four of the seven rahit-namas of the eighteenth century.[37] The first such gotr to be noted were the Bedis of Dera Baba Nanak. The Bedis were not one of the four superior Khatri gotrs in the *char-barah-bavanjah* order, but the fact that Guru Nanak had been born a Bedi gave them a particularly distinguished reputation, so distinguished that no other Khatri gotr could rank as its superior. The problem which thus confronted the Bedis was what other gotr could thereby (in accordance with the conventions of hypergamy) provide them with husbands for their daughters. In medieval Europe, high-born families faced a similar problem, but for them there was a solution. There was always a convent into which the unmarriageable daughters could conveniently be deposited. No such solution was available to the Bedis, however, and all too often they solved the difficulty by killing the female child at birth.

Female infanticide was characteristic of some of those jatis which possessed a high status. This meant that for the Sikhs, they were chiefly to be found amongst the Khatris and, to a lesser extent, the Aroras. There were, however, instances that pointed to Jat participation in the custom. Eastern Doaba was characterized by a small number of *bara pind* villages as opposed to a larger number of the *chhota pind* variety. The bara pind villages were typically larger, but the title also reflected status claims and an effective marriage network. It was the bara pind villages that had a serious sex imbalance as a result of female infanticide that was carried out by their Jat proprietors.[38] Female births were reported as being lower than male births, a situation contrary to the normal proportion of female and male births.[39]

This, it will be appreciated, does not provide an easy area for the conduct of research. No one likes the ancestral village to be declared a site where female infanticide was practised, nor to have one's gotr investigated with this objective in mind. This is particularly so when female infanticide was forthrightly condemned in the rahit-namas. Even so, however, the research needs to be done and it is research that necessarily involves a consideration of caste.

(h) Caste constituency of various sects

Another issue is the distinctive caste constituency of various sects. These include the Nirankaris, the Namdharis, the Nanaksar Sikhs, the Akhand Kirtani Jatha, and the Balmikis.

The Nirankari sect was formed in Rawalpindi in the latter years of Maharaja Ranjit Singh's and because of its Pothohar location, a predominance of the trading castes was entirely natural. This predominance has continued and the line of gurus extending from Baba Dayal are Khatris. The Namdhari or Kuka movement was likewise founded in northwest Punjab, but under its second guru, Ram Singh, it moved its centre to Bhaini Sahib in Ludhiana district. Ram Singh was a Tarkhan and the sect that he led was favoured by other Tarkhans and by poorer Jats. The Tarkhans increasingly fastened their hold on the Namdhari movement and today its members are substantially drawn from the Ramgarhia section of the Panth. The same applies to the Nanaksar sect, most of whose followers are Ramgarhias.

In the case of the Akhand Kirtani Jatha, the leadership is primarily Khatri. Randhir Singh, from whom the sect originated, was a Jat, but after his death, influence passed increasingly to the Khatri and Arora members.

Balmikis are a Dalit sect and proclaim their presence with Balmiki gurdwaras. In their case, separation is enforced as their presence is not welcome in Singh Sabha gurdwaras, as those controlled by Jats are sometimes known.[40]

Not all sects have a distinctive caste basis. As far as I can judge, caste is not important in the Radhasoami Satsang. I am, however, open to correction of this statement. Caste may also be significant amongst the Nihangs. For the remainder, the caste component is certainly present and must surely produce an effect on the form and the teachings of the sect as a whole. But what is that effect? We are told little or nothing about them and to that extent our understanding of them must be diminished.

(i) Caste in the diaspora

Then there is the relationship which caste bears to the Sikh diaspora. The most conspicuous of these migrant groups is surely the Ramgarhia Sikhs who were transported by the British to build the East African railway system. These Ramgarhia Sikhs subsequently transferred to the United Kingdom, beginning with granting of political independence to East African states and significantly hastened by the actions of Idi Amin of Uganda. The British rulers believed that the Ramgarhias would not make good soldiers and army recruitment officers were advised to ignore them in preference to Jats. They did, however, see them as appropriate workers in mechanical trades and there were none more favoured when labour was needed for the East African railways. Their transfer to the United

Kingdom caused some concern on the part of the British, but eventually permission was given and Ramgarhia communities were established in Britain. The account of this transfer is narrated in Parminder Bhachu's *Twice Migrants*, a work that provides a useful analysis of the Ramgarhias.[41] This identity has been maintained and, as we have already noted, it has led to the establishment of distinctively Ramgarhia gurdwaras and a significant maintenance of orthodoxy.[42] Ramgarhias have also been prominent in South-East Asia, with a large number having settled particularly in Thailand.[43]

It is in the United Kingdom, as we have noted, that the greatest effort to understand the caste constituency of the Panth has been made, though even here the effort has been little enough. In his essay in *Desh Pardesh*, Roger Ballard does, however, have a section headed 'The continuing significance of caste' and in it he briefly treats the rivalry amongst the three predominant jatis.[44] As would be expected, one of these three jatis is that of the Jats, the relationship being only partly the same as existed in the Punjab. The status of the Ramgarhias is regarded as low by the Jats, but in England the Ramgarhias are in no way dependent on the Jats for employment as they are in the villages of the Punjab. Moreover, the attention to orthodox observation followed by the Ramgarhias tends to reverse the status order of the two jatis.[45]

The third jati treated by Ballard is the tiny Bhat caste, the oldest of all the Sikh castes in the United Kingdom.[46] The Bhats comprise a caste of pedlars and astrologers, mainly from Sialkot and Hoshiarpur districts, several of who were in England in the early 1920s selling trinkets and foodstuffs door to door out of suitcases or offering to tell fortunes. Although both the Jats and the Ramgarhias regard the Bhats as their social inferiors,[47] they are the most conservative group of Sikhs in the United Kingdom as far as their religion is concerned. Poverty is not a problem for the jati, yet they have not ventured into large-scale business, preferring instead to continue with their small enterprises. They are also behind both the Jats and the Ramgarhias as far as educational achievement is concerned.[48]

Ballard's book was followed by a clutch of essays dealing with the Sikhs of the United Kingdom in the work edited by Pashaura Singh and N. G. Barrier, entitled *Sikh Identity: Continuity and Change*.[49] One of these directly concerns the question of caste in the British community. This is Sewa Singh Kalsi's 'The Sikhs and Caste: the Development of Ramgarhia Identity in Britain'.[50] The United Kingdom situation has been followed up by Kathleen Hall's recent book *Lives in Translation*, which treats the situation in greater detail.[51]

The situation in Canada or the United States is not nearly as clear as that in the United Kingdom. One can recognize some caste names amongst the big earners in both countries, but there is a considerable distance to be travelled before we can identify the jatis and analyse them in anything resembling the imperfect clarity of the United Kingdom. The answer may be that caste does not matter to Sikhs, yet we can see that indeed it does matter. A failure to carry out research in this area must assuredly mean that individual skills and hidden networks must remain concealed. This in turn must mean that the nature of Sikh diasporic society must remain to that extent obscure. What, for example, are we to make of Dalit Sikhs who have emigrated? In New Zealand, they worked in separate gangs of scrub-cutters and today they are still treated as Dalits by most of the other Sikhs.

(j) Recruitment in the Indian Army

The final issue concerns the Indian Army, particularly during British times. During the period of the Raj, the British formulated the myth of the martial races of India, and within this myth Jat Sikhs enjoyed a particular prominence.[52] A famous expositor of the martial races theory was Lieutenant-General Sir George MacMunn, who early in the twentieth century identified the Jat as a 'great muscular, hardworking, rather stupid yeoman farmer' and concluded on these grounds that he made an excellent soldier.[53] Falcon is at once more complimentary to the Jats and even clearer in his statement of the suitability of Jat Sikhs as soldiers:

The [Jat] Sikh is a fighting man and his fine qualities are best shown in the army, which is his natural profession. Hardy, brave, and of intelligence; too slow to understand when he is beaten; obedient to discipline; attached to his officers; and careless of caste prohibitions, he is unsurpassed as a soldier in the East, and takes the first place as a thoroughly reliable, useful soldier. The [Jat] Sikh is always the same, ever genial, good-tempered and uncomplaining; as steady under fire as he is eager for a charge; he possesses a keen knowledge of the value of money, and a love of saving: when well and sufficiently led he is the equal of any troops in the world, and superior to any with whom he is likely to come into contact.[54]

Falcon is guilty of the misunderstanding that results from his notion of the anthropology of the Sikhs, as in his ranking of the Malwa Sikhs above those of the Manjha and the superiority of both to the 'softer' kind who inhabit Doaba. This leads him to brand certain *tahsils* as 'very good' for recruitment purposes, as opposed to others that are 'very bad'.[55] Even so, however, this theory of the martial races has had a considerable impact, confirming Jat Sikhs in their belief that they are indeed the true warriors of India. An attractive statement of this belief is found in Amandeep Singh Madra and Parmjit Singh's *Warrior Saints: Three Centuries of the Sikh Military Tradition*.[56]

This is not to say, of course, that the Jat Sikh's belief in his military tradition is mistaken. Unquestionably this is not the case, as the battles of the eighteenth century and later bear abundant testimony. The point is rather that the issue requires careful research when it is being investigated, partly because it is bound up with this question of caste. Certain castes were treated favourably by the British and others were unfairly treated with disdain. Why, for example, does Falcon believe that Mazhabi Sikhs make good pioneers?[57] The answer surely is that they are traditionally suited to sweeping. Or why are the Aroras written off as 'quite unsuited in character'?[58] They are quite unsuited because the British saw them as mean moneylenders. This contrasts with the General Aurora who in Independent Indian days took the Pakistan surrender following the war that resulted in the creation of Bangladesh.

Independent India saw a marked reduction in Sikh numbers in the armed forces, though it certainly did nothing to diminish the Sikh belief in their military tradition. Quotas were allocated to different states in accordance with their size rather than recruiting on the basis of a martial races belief. This of course led to a steep decline in the number of Sikh soldiers. There were, though, other changes. Khatris and Aroras, treated with scant respect by their British officers, began to return to a career in the armed forces. They did not return, however, in the manner favoured by the British recruitment officers. Whereas Jat Sikhs were particularly valued by the British as non-commissioned officers and other ranks, the Khatri or the Arora was unlikely to take up an army career unless he could be guaranteed the rank of an officer. The Jats were still enlisted as ordinary soldiers, with some still finding a commissioned rank open to them. It was not so for the Khatri or Arora. For them enlistment meant the promise of a commission.[59]

Such factors need to be taken into account when writing about the Sikhs in the armed forces. The Indian Army is not a caste-free area of study, and the same may also apply to the Navy and the Air Force. It may not be a serious issue, but it does exist.

Conclusion

These 10 areas need to taken into account as we press onwards in our attempt to write a comprehensive history of the Sikhs. They should also be taken into account (or at least some of them should be) in our quest for an understanding of Sikh society. Do Sikhs believe in caste? The answer must be that by their actions a large majority certainly do. Is the caste system which they uphold the same as other versions upheld by other varieties of Punjabi society or the society of India at large? It may be very similar to the caste system as applied in the Punjab as a whole, but beyond its own region, all manner of practice can be found. And if we step aside from our academic concerns and express an opinion concerning the value of such a belief, what is that belief likely to be? Confident in the assurance that I belong to no more than a small minority of academics, I would certainly support the system. Whether we support it or reject it, the time has arrived when this system of caste must be analysed and the analysis applied wherever it affects our research.

Notes

1. It is of course one thing to identify the problem. It is quite another finding a solution. Sometimes a reference to H. A. Rose's *A Glossary of the Tribes and Castes of the Punjab and North-west Frontier Province* will provide an answer. In other instances *Gurushabad Ratanakar Mahan Kosh* will specify both *gotr* and jati for a particular individual. Neither, however, is adequate in coverage. More useful is Falcon, who in his *Handbook on Sikhs for the Use of Regimental Officers* (Allahabad: Pioneer Press, 1896) lists Jat gotrs. This list can certainly be of assistance as far as Jats are concerned, though one should be warned about taking his descriptions of the various gotrs as accurate. It is, however, a useful inventory, all the more so in that it provides a reasonably accurate geographical spread for each of them. At least native Punjabis should be aware of the problem faced by foreigners and whenever dealing with a particular gotr, determine whether or not the jati also deserves to be mentioned.

2. The Punjabi terms are *zat* and *got*.

3. Tom G. Kessinger, *Vilayatpur 1848–1968* (Berkeley: University of California Press, 1974), is an example of the author of an excellent work having thereafter changed his employment. Paul Hershman, author of *Punjabi Kinship and Marriage*

(Delhi: Hindustan Publishing Corporation, 1981), died before his similarly excellent work could be completed. It was edited by Hilary Standing. Other authors who merit attention include Joyce Pettigrew, Satish Saberwal, Harjinder Singh, Art Helweg, Harry Izmirlian, Parminder Bhachu, Roger Ballard, Kathleen Hall, and Anshu Malhotra.

4. I. B. Singh could be an example of the article writer.

5. A. L. Basham, *The Wonder That Was India* (London: Sidgwick and Jackson, 3rd ed., 1954), pp. 147–8.

6. Arguably a better term would be 'mode'. This though lacks the connotations of status and hierarchy that 'caste' so insistently bears.

7. An interesting observation is communicated by Gerald D. Berreman:

In the relatively isolated, traditional, mountain village in which I did my initial Indian field research, I recounted to low caste people an explanation of caste almost identical to that which Dumont has since conveyed in this book (for it is a common one). They laughed, and one of them said, 'You have been talking with Brahmins.' And so I had. And so, it seems, has Professor Dumont.

Gerald D. Berreman, 'The Brahamanical View of Caste', *Contributions to Indian Sociology* (n.s.) 5, in *Social Stratification*, Dipankar Gupta (ed.) (Delhi: Oxford University Press, 1992), p. 92.

8. Lineage, loosely translatable as 'family'.

9. M1, *Sārang 3*, Adi Granth (henceforth *AG*), p. 1198.

10. M1, *Sirī Rāgu Asht 1, AG*, p. 53.

11. M4, *Kānaṛa 11, AG*, p. 1297.

12. M5, *Āsā 132, Devagandārī 4, Bilāvalu 61*, and *Sārang 138, AG*, pp. 404, 529, 816, and 1231.

13. W. H. McLeod, *Sikhs of the Khalsa* (New Delhi: Oxford University Press, 2003), p. 285.

14. W. H. McLeod, *The Chaupa Singh Rahit-nama* (Dunedin: University of Otago Press, 1987), items 11 and 121, pp. 59, 72, 150, and 160.

15. W. H. McLeod, *Sikhs of the Khalsa*, p. 306.

16. Ibid.

17. Ibid., p. 311. The reference of 'those whose status is lowly' is evidently to the Dalits.

18. Ibid., p. 321.

19. Ibid., items 73 and 75, p. 320. 'Khatri' is apparently treated here as 'Kshatriya'.

20. Ibid., p. 330.

21. Kanh Singh Nabha, *Ham Hindū Nahīn*, (Amritsar: Kendari Sri Guru Singh Sabha Shatabadi Kameti, 2nd edn, 1978), pp. 69–73.

22. A survey is provided in Hew McLeod, 'Caste and the Sikhs', in Kamlesh Mohan (ed.), *Making of Caste: Myth or Reality* (New Delhi: ICHR, forthcoming).

23. The four are the Bedi, Trehan, Bhalla, and Sodhi gotrs.

24. It is, however, possible for individuals to keep karah prasad free from what they imagine to be pollution by receiving back a portion of what they have exclusively offered.

25. Gurmat or 'the teachings of the guru' is the term which Western usage calls 'Sikhism'.

26. Two important papers which should be considered in this regard are by Surinder S. Jodhka. They are 'Caste and Untouchability in Rural Punjab', *Economic and Political Weekly*, 11 May 2002, pp. 1813–23; and 'Sikhism and the Caste Question: Ideology, Anthropology and the Empirical', read at a Sikh Studies conference held in Birmingham, United Kingdom, in October 2003.

27. A useful article is Ravinder Kaur, 'Jat Sikhs: a Question of Identity', *Contributions to Indian Sociology* (n.s.) 20, 2 (1986), pp. 221–39.

28. Sewa Singh Kalsi, 'The Sikhs and Caste: the Development of Ramgarhia Identity in Britain', *Sikh Identity: Continuity and Change*, Pashaura Singh and N. G. Barrier (eds) (New Delhi: Manohar, 1999), p. 256.

29. Message from Harish Puri. For an interesting and informative article, see his 'Scheduled Castes in Sikh Community: a Historical Perspective', *Economic and Political Weekly* 38, 26 (28 June 2003), pp. 2693–713.

30. For a useful synopsis of Sikh castes, see chapter 2 of Joginder Singh, *The Sikh Resurgence* (New Delhi: National Book Organisation, 1997).

31. I deal with this question in W. H. McLeod, *The Evolution of the Sikh Community* (Oxford University Press, 1976), pp. 84–90.

32. W. H. McLeod, *Sikhs of the Khalsa*, p. 399 (with Punjabi terms added in parantheses).

33. This was the term also used by Gian Singh in the translation that appears in ibid., p. 47.

34. Khushwant Singh, *A History of the Sikhs*, Vol. 1 (Princeton: Princeton University Press, 1963), p. 57.

35. This is clear from the listing in Var 11.

36. A recent contribution to this difficult research is Anshu Malhotra, 'Infanticide, Hypergamy and Marriage Expenses', *Gender, Caste, and Religious Identities: Restructuring Class in Colonial Punjab* (New Delhi: Oxford University Press, 2002), pp. 49–61. Andrea Major is also currently conducting research in this area.

37. W. H. McLeod, *Sikhs of the Khalsa*, p. 233.

38. W. H. McLeod, *Punjabis in New Zealand* (Amritsar: Guru Nanak Dev University, 1986), pp. 25–26.

39. *Jullundur District and Kapurthala State, 1904* 14A (Lahore: Punjab District Gazetteers, 1908), pp. 59–60. In 1892 W. E. Purser, the Settlement Officer, had named Jamsher, Pharala, Kuleta, Dosanj Kalan, Rurka Kalan, Bundala, Jandiala, Samrae, and Bilga as 'Jat villages suspected of female infanticide'. *Final Report*

of the Revised Settlement of the Jullundur District in the Punjab (Lahore, 1892), p. 74.

40. For a brief survey of most of these groups, see W. H. McLeod, *Sikhism* (London: Penguin, 1997), chapter 9. A weakness of the chapter is that it omits the Balmikis or any other Dalit sect.

41. Parminder Bhachu, *Twice Migrants: East African Sikh Settlers in Britain* (London and New York: Tavistock, 1985), chapter 2.

42. Roger Ballard, 'Differentiation and Disjunction among the Sikhs', Roger Ballard (ed.), *Desh Pardesh: the South Asian Presence in Britain* (London: Hurst, 1994), p. 111.

43. Himadri Banerjee has discovered Jats and Ramgarhias in Assam, with the Ramgarhias maintaining a separate gurdwara in Jorhat. 'Sikh-Diaspora' 24 August 2003. *The Tribune* for 30 August 2003 reports a Sikh community in Argentina which, in view of the work for which they were originally taken there by the British, may also be Ramgarhia.

'Recalling history of the Sikh diaspora in Latin America, Mr Tarlochan Singh [Chairman of the National Commission for Minorities] said it was about 100 years ago that Sikhs from Punjab were taken to Argentina by the British for the construction of a railway line between Argentina and Bolivia. They settled in the province of Salta in northern Argentina and engaged themselves in agriculture. They have moved from farming to business and are now considered as a highly respected community in that area. During the past 50 years, the community got itself assimilated in Argentina's culture by marrying local women. Its members now speak Spanish. After the visit of Giani Zail Singh, the then President of India to Salta, Sikhs built a gurdwara in Rosario de la Frontera, where they offer "langar" (community kitchen). The community has recently engaged a Punjabi-knowing granthi.'

44. Roger Ballard, 'Differentiation', pp. 109–12.

45. See for example the interview recorded by Kathleen Hall in *Lives in Translation: Sikh Youth as British Citizens* (Philadelphia: University of Pennsylvania Press, 2002), pp. 160–1.

46. Hitherto the jati has been generally known as the Bhatra caste. Members of the caste now regard Bhatra as a demeaning term. I owe this information to Kanta Kaur Marriot.

47. Kathleen Hall, *Lives in Translation*, p. 161.

48. Roger Ballard, 'Differentiation', pp. 111–12. D. A. T. Thomas and P. A. S. Ghuman, *A Survey of Social and Religious Attitudes among Sikhs in Cardiff* (Cardiff: Open University in Wales, n.d.), deal with the Bhat community. Kanta Kaur Marriot is currently working on an Oxford DPhil thesis concerning the Bhats.

49. N. G. Barrier and Pashaura Singh, *Sikh Identity*, pp. 255–73 and 315–63. Vishva B. L. Sharma also contributes an essay on the Sikhs in East Africa. Ibid., pp. 217–30.

50. Ibid., pp. 255–73.

51. See footnote 45.

52. The word 'myth' is not used here as a synonym for legend. It is used as an interpretation of reality, not reality itself. See W. H. McLeod, *Early Sikh Tradition* (Oxford: Clarendon Press, 1980), pp. 8–12.

53. George MacMunn, *The Martial Races of India* (London: Sampson Low, Marston, 1933), p. 252. The first edition was published by Adam & Charles Black of London in 1911. See also idem, 'The Martial Races of India' in *Army Review* 1: 2, reprinted in *The Panjab Past and Present* 4, Part 1 (April 1970), pp. 75–7 and 82.

54. Falcon, *Handbook on Sikhs*, pp. 65–6.

55. Ibid., pp. 69–71.

56. London and New York: I. B. Tauris, 1999.

57. Falcon, pp. 78–9.

58. Ibid., p. 80.

59. For example, it is no surprise to note the case of Air Marshal (Ret'd) A. S. Bedi. Bedi is a Khatri gotr (the gotr of Guru Nanak).

The Dalit Sikhs: A History?

John C. B. Webster

I n 1992, I wrote a book entitled *The Dalit Christians: A History*[1] in response to a perceived need among Dalit Christians to understand their own history and heritage. The standard histories of Christianity in India could hardly meet that need since they confined treatment of Dalit Christians to their chapters on the mass conversion movements from the last quarter of the nineteenth century to the outbreak of World War II, as if the Dalit Christians had no history besides and beyond their conversion and their Dalitness had nothing to do with their own or the Church's history. Moreover, it became apparent that the history of Dalit Christians did not follow the same trajectory as did the stories of the missionaries and Christian elites which dominated the history books. So, rather than follow a 'Christian history approach' to this subject, I adopted a 'Dalit history approach' to it by setting the history of the Dalit Christians within the context of the history of the modern Dalit movement instead of the history of the Christian church. I saw the modern Dalit movement passing through three stages, marked off by important Constitutional developments affecting Dalits, and arranged my chapters accordingly.

The question posed by this chapter is whether a similar rationale would warrant, even require, such a writing of Dalit Sikh history. Perhaps the strongest argument against such a project would be that whereas the majority of Christians in India are Dalits, the majority of Sikhs are not and thus relegating Dalit Sikhs to a minor role in Sikh history is quite justified. Certainly that is the role that they are assigned in the standard histories of the Sikhs.[2] These histories assume not only that all Sikhs are on the same historical trajectory but also that the social differences and conflicts between them are of far less significance than are the religious beliefs, practices, and interests they have in common as Sikhs. That may be true, but it also might not be. It might therefore be worth testing the validity for Dalit Sikh history of this 'Sikh history approach', which both absorbs and downplays by using an alternative 'Dalit history approach' to see what it produces. It is entirely possible, perhaps even likely, that what is true of Dalit Christian history is also true of Dalit Sikh history: Dalit identity may be of as much historical significance to Dalit Sikhs as the religious identity they share with other Sikhs.

What this chapter proposes to do therefore is to begin by examining the resources available for such a project in some important works, employing first a Sikh history and then a Dalit history approach. It will then utilize some Christian missionary source materials on the Chuhras and Mazhabis, discovered in the process of writing a history of Christianity in north-west India, both to critique and to supplement what has already been said in the monographs under review. This section of my chapter will of necessity be sketchy, but it should add something to our understanding of late nineteenth- and early twentieth-century Mazhabi Sikh history. I will conclude by referring to some recent studies of caste and caste conflict among Sikhs in the Punjab. The aim throughout is merely to indicate whether or not a Dalit Sikh history is worth pursuing and, if so, what its contours might look like; I am not in a position to offer a well-grounded alternative to the histories already in print.

I

The most influential of the recent general histories of the Sikhs are those written by Khushwant Singh and J. S. Grewal. In the view of the former, 'The story of the Sikhs is the story of the rise, fulfillment, and collapse of Punjabi nationalism.'[3] The theme of his first volume (1469–1839) was 'the rise of Punjabi consciousness and the establishment of an independent Punjabi state under Sikh auspices', while that of the second volume (1839–1964) was 'the Sikh struggle for survival as a separate community'.[4] In neither of these did the Dalit Sikhs play a significant role. The first volume makes no mention at all of Dalit Sikhs, but does state that the Sikh social order of the first 100 years was to:

embrace all the people; no class was to be beyond the pale, and even though the caste system continued to count when it came to matrimonial alliances, it was abolished in matters of social intercourse. The doors of Sikh temples were thrown open to everyone and in the Guru's *langar* the Brahmin and the untouchable broke their bread as members of the same family.[5]

This social ideal, Khushwant Singh believes, was undermined by the Punjab Land Alienation Act of 1900, which divided the Sikhs into three distinct caste groupings—Jat, non-Jat, and untouchables—for each of whom caste ties proved to be stronger than religious ties.[6] In between, Dalits make their first appearance in this history as thugs in the chaos immediately following the British annexation of the Punjab, then as labourers, and soon thereafter as recruits for the British army, as marginal beneficiaries of land distribution in the canal colonies, and as a significant portion of the Namdhari or Kuka sect. He also makes the point that employment in the army and 'a sprinkling' of Dalit landowners in the canal colonies did contribute to a measure of social mobility among them.[7]

J. S. Grewal's *The Sikhs of the Punjab* tells the story of the Sikh Panth as a distinct entity in Punjab history. While emphasizing the same social ideal that Khushwant Singh mentioned in much the same way,[8] Grewal, unlike Khushwant Singh, describes the caste structure and social composition of the Sikh Panth at several points in its history, including its formative years. In referring to the writings of Guru Ram Das, the fourth guru, Grewal said that:

The low caste also figure prominently in the compositions of Guru Ram Das. While Khatris and Brahmans were ignored by God, Namdev was drawn close. There were other low-caste devotees of God who attained to salvation through their devotion, like Kabir, Jaidev, Tarlochan, Ravidas, Dhanna, and Sen. Appreciation for the low-caste Sants and Bhaktas may be treated as an indication of the presence of the low caste among the Sikhs.[9]

Grewal also mentions Dalit Sikhs as members of the army not of the British but of Maharaja Ranjit Singh (in this case just the Mazhabis), as contributors to the growth of the Sikh Panth in the early twentieth-century census reports, and as recipients of Scheduled Caste benefits in 1956.[10]

In the closing chapter of *The Evolution of the Sikh Community*, Hew McLeod addresses the issue of caste in the Sikh Panth head on. Two questions concern him: attitudes towards caste within the Sikh Panth and the caste constituency of the Panth itself. The teachings and institutions of the gurus themselves show that for them caste and caste ranking were irrelevant to one's salvation. 'The way of salvation is open to all regardless of caste.'[11] However, the gurus did marry within their own castes, a seeming contradiction which McLeod resolves by pointing out that the gurus were 'opposed to the discriminatory aspects of the vertical relationship [to God] while continuing to accept the socially beneficial pattern of horizontal connections'.[12] In his description of the caste constituency of the Sikh Panth, he refers to the Mazhabis, the Raidasias, and the Ranghreta (who trace their family ancestry to those Mazhabis who delivered the head of Guru Tegh Bahadur to his son, Guru Gobind Singh). He then goes on to say that:

A substantial portion of both Mazhabis and Ramdasias represent the result of an influx into the Panth during the early decades of the present [20th] century, a movement paralleled by similar conversions to Christianity or to a new grouping designated Ad Dharmi. There can be no doubt that the impulse behind this movement was a desire to purge the traditional taint of the outcaste status and that a majority of the converts regarded the egalitarian traditions of the Khalsa as the best hope of achieving this end. It would be false to claim that the hope has been fulfilled. Equally false, however, would be the claim that there has been no gain in status whatsoever.[13]

In his historical treatment of Sikh identity, *Who is a Sikh?*, McLeod further clarifies his earlier position and provides important new information of relevance to a history of the Dalit Sikhs. With regard to the gurus' normative teachings, he says that:

The anti-caste thrust of the Gurus' teachings must thus be seen as a doctrine which referred to spiritual deliverance and to the assemblies which helped individuals to achieve that objective. It is also legitimate to deduce a firm rejection of injustice or hurtful discrimination based on caste status. What is not implied is a total obliteration of caste identity.[14]

It is for this reason that at the end of the book he answers the question 'Can a rejection of caste be included in our definition of Sikh identity?' with a yes and a no.[15] In between he points out that caste traditions, seen most obviously in the case of Jat tradition, were one of the three major sources of Sikh rahit and makes reference to the discrimination against Dalits even in the gurdwaras, which the Singh Sabha reformers protested against (especially the Dalit Giani Ditt Singh, who sought 'a return to the casteless ideal of the Khalsa')[16] as well as to the competition between the Singh Sabha and the Arya Samaj for Dalit support.[17] His recent history of

Khalsa rahit indicates that several of the eighteenth- and nineteenth-century rahit-namas were explicitly discriminatory against Dalits, but despite this McLeod felt that, in balance, 'Sikh attitudes concerning caste were relatively enlightened during this period'.[18]

Harjot Oberoi's study of religious boundaries in the Sikh tradition sheds further light on the nineteenth-century Dalit Sikh situation and on the views of the Singh Sabhas in particular. He distinguishes between the Sanatan Sikhs, whose views and practices had prevailed throughout most of the century, and the Tat Khalsa Sikhs whose paradigm came, in a remarkably short time, to replace the Sanatan paradigm. The Sanatan Sikhs both accepted the caste system as an integral part of Sikh faith and enforced it.[19] The Tat Khalsa Sikhs publicly opposed the caste system, but were more ambivalent about it in private.[20] He describes the clash between the two in terms which are quite revealing in the light of McLeod's analysis:

Similarly, while the Tat Khalsa leadership pleaded with the Sikh public to abolish the caste system, Sanatan Sikhs came to its defence. When neo-Sikhs claimed that the Sikh gurus wanted to eradicate the caste system, Sanatan writers countered that none of the Sikh gurus had married outside his caste, that their marriage arrangements had been strictly governed by caste rules. This fact was used to buttress the claim that the founders of the Sikh faith were not against the caste system. In recognition of the purity-pollution dichotomy, Sanatan manuals of conduct listed ritual procedures for cleansing those individuals who had been accidentally polluted. As part of Sanatan caste regulations untouchable Sikhs, commonly known as Mazhabis, were forbidden to enter the inner precincts of the Golden Temple and bathe in the sacred tank.[21]

However, it is apparent from Oberoi's reading of the situation that caste reform was a relatively low-priority item on the Tat Khalsa cultural agenda; other matters were far more important to them in redefining Sikh identity religiously and in the public arena.

Perhaps the fullest treatment of Dalit Sikhs is to be found in the chapter on 'The Menial and Untouchable Castes of the Sikhs from 1881–1947' in Ethne K. Marenco's *The Transformation of Sikh Society*.[22] This chapter, based exclusively as well as rather tediously and uncritically upon census reports, focused upon ethnographic trends between 1881 and 1931 in numerical growth, migration (to the canal colonies or urban areas), occupational mobility (from 'traditional occupations' to agriculture or industry as skilled or unskilled labour), as well as literacy and education among members of this category of castes in the Punjab. Where possible, Dalit Sikhs were compared with their Hindu and Muslim counterparts, and different Sikh castes (most frequently the Chuhra Sikhs and Chamar Sikhs) were compared with each other. The chapter ends by summing up the indicators of both 'corporate caste change' and individual social mobility. On most of these indicators, Dalit Sikhs did slightly better than did Dalit Hindus or Muslims.

Finally, Harnik Deol's recent history is worth mentioning not only because it concentrates primarily upon the post-Independence period but also because it raises conceptual issues of considerable importance to this discussion. A political scientist interested in nationalisms, Deol used the historical method to analyse what she calls the Sikh ethno-nationalist movement or struggle. She sought to trace the transition of the Sikhs from a religious congregation into an ethnic community and then from that into a nation,[23] as well as the concurrent rise and development of Sikh ethno-nationalism as an ideology. Of the three markers of ethnic identity assertion she mentions at the outset, she makes considerable use of only religion and language, while confining 'tribe' (by extension kinship, lineage, and hence caste) mostly to references to the dominant Jat Sikhs. She does acknowledge caste diversity among the Sikhs,[24] thus begging the question of whether the Sikhs could legitimately be called an 'ethnic community' instead of a religious community embracing several ethnic communities. Moreover, when discussing caste among the Sikhs, she makes the point that at the local level (which is the only level at which caste operates concretely), 'the economically dominant group, particularly the group that owns the land, is also the highest caste'.[25] This allows her in her chapter on the impact of the Green Revolution to subsume rural caste conflicts within the categories of agrarian class analysis (for example, landlord, peasant, small farmer, tenant, labourer, etc.) and, in so doing, to rob the Dalit Sikhs of their own 'ethnicity as tribe'. I found only one reference to them as role players in this history: it was in a table on the castes of the Sikh activists during the Sikh 'ethno-regional movement' of the 1980s.[26]

This brief review of some of the secondary literature on Sikh history is more suggestive than comprehensive. Nonetheless, it does indicate that there may be something of a scholarly consensus about how caste and its importance have been understood as well as how and where it operates within the Sikh Panth. Our review also indicates that Dalit Sikhs do suffer from quite serious neglect in the histories of the Sikhs and

Sikhism. While those scholars who have used this 'Sikh history' approach have provided some useful insights, information, and puzzles[27] which warrant further and deeper investigation, this approach has not, and probably cannot, give the Dalit Sikhs their due. We therefore turn to the 'Dalit history' approach.

II

The Dalit history approach is based on two important assumptions. The first is that of Dalit agency. In this case, Dalit Sikhs move to centrestage to become the chief actors in and shapers of their own history; the historian will therefore focus upon them, their views, their struggles, their actions. The second is that a conflict model of society, with caste as not the only but the most important contradiction in Indian society, provides the most appropriate paradigm for understanding their history. In addition to these two general assumptions, a further clarification about the caste system is required in order to make sense of Dalit Sikh history in particular. Susan Bayly in her recent history of caste in India since the eighteenth century makes an important distinction between two traditions about caste. One is the priestly Brahmanic tradition which places emphasis upon the ritual purity/pollution criteria for the caste hierarchy; the other is the lordly Kshatriya tradition which emphasizes patronage, deference, and service,[28] or, to borrow a most eloquent phrase from J. S. Grewal, 'the time honoured institution of vassalage',[29] which penetrated all the way down to the village level, where it shaped landlord–menial relationships. While the former is by no means absent in the Punjab, the latter tradition is very prominent and influential there.

The pioneer work on the Punjab employing the Dalit history approach is Mark Juergensmeyer's *Religion as Social Vision*.[30] Although it focuses upon Ad Dharm as well as some other primarily Dalit anti-untouchability movements and does not deal with the Dalit Sikhs at all, this work nevertheless provides a potential model for the study of their recent history. Juergensmeyer refers to the efforts of the Chief Khalsa Diwan to create its own 'depressed classes movement' as well as to the strong Sikh opposition to Mangoo Ram and Ad Dharm at the time of the 1931 census. He also points out that Ad Dharm, while appropriating elements of Sikhism, saw itself as a distinct religious tradition and in so doing clears up some confusion between Ravidasis and Ramdasia Sikhs.[31] However, apart from modelling a Dalit history approach, perhaps Juergensmeyer's most useful contribution to a history of the Dalit Sikhs is contained in this statement which appears at the outset of his chapter on 'The Religion of Village Untouchables':

The labels of the major communities—Hindu, Muslim, and Sikh—have been applied to Untouchables by upper caste people very loosely. In the Punjab, those terms are appellations for members of the upper castes, whereas the Untouchables are described as that, Untouchables, or as Chuhra-Chamar, or as members of special categories of upper caste religions reserved for the low, such as Mazhabi Sikh or Achut Hindu. Untouchables seldom describe themselves as Hindu, Muslim, or Sikh, except when political or social reasons make it expeditious to do so. In areas dominated by Sikhs, for instance, all the Untouchables in those areas will affect Sikh signs and habits. Some lower caste people use different names on different occasions; in the presence of Hindus a person may identify himself as Ram Chand, among Sikhs as Ram Singh, and with Christians, John Samuel. The British census-takers, in noting this phenomenon, spoke of the lower castes' 'fickleness' with regard to religion, and the determination of the correct apportionment of lower caste followers among Hinduism, Sikhism, and the other major religions was one of their knottier problems. The numbers would shift peculiarly from one census to another, to the embarrassment of the statisticians. During politically active periods, such as the 1920s and later, post-independence, members of upper castes would vie with one another over the right to claim Untouchables within their religion.[32]

Harish K. Puri's article in the *Economic and Political Weekly*, 'Scheduled Castes in Sikh Community: A Historical Perspective', which he describes as an exploration of 'the trade-off between the doctrinal principles of Sikh religion and the ruling social and political interests in the context of the changes in society and economy of Punjab',[33] is more a history of how those in power have treated Dalit Sikhs than a history of the Dalit Sikhs themselves. Nonetheless, it not only is based on a caste-conflict model of Punjabi society but also shows quite clearly how appropriate the Kshatriya tradition of caste is to the Sikh case when concluding that 'Interactions with the dalits in Punjab ... reveal a pervasive tendency to view the interests of economic and political domination as the force behind caste-based humiliation, rather than [Sikh] ideology as the primary reality'.[34]

Puri covers much the same ground—the teaching and practice of the Sikh gurus, occupational and social mobility under the British, the Singh Sabha movement—as the writers already described. However, he goes on to show how the Akali movement ignored the untouchability issue, opposed Ambedkar's conversion to Sikhism because it threatened their position within the Shiromani Gurdwara Parbandhak Committee (SGPC), but worked for and gained Scheduled Caste benefits for all Dalit Sikhs. He concludes with a summary of the findings of recent field studies which reveal a broad pattern of Jat–Dalit conflict over discrimination in gurdwaras (with the result that separate Dalit gurdwaras are rapidly multiplying) and the rising incidence of atrocities against Dalits.

There have been some histories in Punjabi written or sponsored by Dalit Sikhs, but I am not in a position to analyse them to see whether they fit more easily into the 'Sikh history' or the 'Dalit history' paradigm. I also do not know what additional information they have to offer concerning the history of the Dalit Sikhs. Certainly a Dalit history approach poses challenges for the historian, especially when seeking to recover the Dalit 'voice'. In most traditional sources that voice is either silent or so heavily filtered by the interests of the dominant that it is difficult to discern, while Dalit Sikh writings, biographies, or histories are relatively rare and inaccessible. Nonetheless, where viable, this approach has great potential.

III

Denzil Ibbetson in the 1881 census described the Chuhra as 'the sweeper and scavenger *par excellence* of the Punjab', but also indicated that in the central Punjab, which was 'the centre of Sikhism' and where most of the Chuhra conversions to Christianity as well as to Sikhism occurred, they did most of the actual agricultural labour.[35] Sikh Chuhras or Mazhabis, he said,

take the *pahul*, wear their hair long, and abstain from tobacco, and they apparently refuse to touch night-soil, though performing all the other offices hereditary to the Chuhra caste... But though good Sikhs so far as religious observance is concerned, the taint of hereditary pollution is upon them; and Sikhs of other castes refuse to associate with them even in religious ceremonies.[36]

The census and other official publications refer to Mazhabi traditions and service in the armies of both Maharaja Ranjit Singh and the British as well as testifying to a desire among Chuhras to improve their social standing by becoming Sikhs.[37] In addition, they also include some amusing errors, like listing the Mazhabis among the Sikh sects,[38] and gross exaggerations, of which the following says more about British views on 'martial races' than about the Mazhabis:

One of the highest qualities of Sikhism is its power to improve the social condition of its adherents, by removing the trammels of caste. As a Mazhabi Sikh, the despised Chuhra or sweeper *at once* becomes a valiant and valued soldier, and imbued with the spirit of his martial faith, loses all memory of his former degraded calling.[39]

Thus, according to these sources, a Chuhra who becomes a Mazhabi Sikh has taken at best a limited step upward, as the effects of 'the trammels of caste' remain ambiguous.

There are at least three points at which Christian missionary source materials are particularly helpful in filling out the history of that and subsequent decades. The first is that they supply eyewitness accounts which simply reinforce our current understanding of the status of Mazhabi Sikhs as both separate and subordinate within Sikh society at the end of the nineteenth century. To cite but one example, Miss E. G. Gordon, writing from Sialkot in 1875, described the Mazhabis as a distinct social group 'received from the low caste Hindoos' with whom other Sikhs refrain from eating, 'although the Sikh religion ignores caste'. Thus the Mazhabis, 'although somewhat elevated above the lowest, yet really have no caste [standing]', and, instead of living in the Sikh wards of Sialkot, 'they live in separate wards of the city', in one of which Miss Gordon's mission had recently opened up a girls' school.[40]

A second and more significant point at which mission sources are of assistance concerns social mobility. By referring to the Chuhra as 'the sweeper and scavenger *par excellence* of the Panjab', Ibbetson created problems for historians like Marenco, who use census data to measure occupational mobility. As suggested by Ibbetson himself and as pointed out by contemporary missionary observers who were more interested in understanding and winning than in classifying rural Chuhras, this statement was far more true of Chuhras living in towns, cities, and military cantonments than of the vast majority who lived in villages, where their primary work was agricultural labour. Missionaries used such terms for them as 'serfs' or 'slaves of the village in which they live',[41] and even described the various kinds of arrangements under which they worked for the village landlords.[42] They were almost literally the backbone of the rural economy in central and western Punjab. Thus to see a shift from 'traditional occupation' to 'agricultural labour' as an indication of occupational and hence upward social mobility is to misunderstand the rural Chuhra/Mazhabi situation: even though agricultural labour was not their defining caste occupation, it was what they really did. No mobility occurred at all. The same is true of migration to the canal colonies. Christian missionaries tried to keep track of Chuhra converts who migrated to the canal colonies in search primarily of high wages and better working conditions. Their reports confirm what Imran Ali has written about poor rural migrants in general:

The landless rural population of the Punjab did not receive land grants, nor did it possess the resources to purchase land at the competitive prices bid at auctions... Landless workers, whether agricultural labourers, sub-tenants, or caste servitors, did migrate to the canal colonies to meet the new demands for labour. But they still fulfilled roles similar to the ones they had been confined to in their home villages. With the availability of new lands, many took on subtenancies where they had previously been simple labourers. A favourable land/labour ratio also promised improved wages for them, and some relief from the harsher forms of exploitation they might have previously endured. In status, however, they were still *kamins* or 'menials,' the term officially used for them. They remained as the lowest stratum of Punjabi society.[43]

Thus, while a few Mazhabi military families may have benefitted from some allocation of land, the vast majority made little or no progress at all. The 1900 Land Alienation Act, by denying them agricultural caste status even though they did most of the actual agricultural work, made it very difficult for Chuhras and Mazhabis to own agricultural land until after Independence.[44] The agrarian social structure thus remained intact and, according to Imran Ali, the British were determined to keep that way.[45]

The third point in Mazhabi Sikh history on which mission sources shed important light is in the interpretation of census data concerning the numerical growth of the Mazhabi Sikh population between 1881 and 1931. The census totals for Mazhabi Sikhs and/or Sikh Chuhras are shown in Table 6.1.[46]

Table 6.1: Mazhabi Sikhs and Sikh Chuhras, 1881–1931

1881	45,834
1891	94,872
1901	30,478
1911	57,522
1921	106,709
1931	169,247

These figures suggest that the Mazhabi Sikh population was probably stable between 1881 and 1911, with the unusual high in 1891 and the unusual low in 1901 due in all likelihood to problems within the census operation itself rather than to major shifts back and forth among the Mazhabi Sikhs. However, between 1911 and 1931, there is a steady and significant rise in the Mazhabi Sikh population which would increase greatly in subsequent decades.

In 1921, the Census Commissioner attributed the near doubling of the Mazhabi Sikh population to two things. One was the efforts of the Sikh preachers, an obvious acknowledgment of the work of the Singh Sabhas. The other was the recruitment policies of the military during World War I, which greatly favoured Mazhabi Sikhs over Hindu Chuhras.[47] What was omitted from this analysis was a reference to the grant of separate electorates to the Sikhs in the 1919 Constitution. While the 1921 census would have had no bearing on the existing allocation of seats in the Punjab Legislative Assembly, the fact remains that communal electorates had politicized the conversion process, as numerical size would affect a community's share of political power.

This becomes most apparent in the decade between the 1921 and 1931 census. This time the Census Commissioner attributed the increase in the Sikh population to the influence of the Akali movement. The increase, he said, was notable among the 'members of the depressed classes, agriculturalists and artisans in rural areas, who obviously consider that they gain in status as soon as they cease to be Hindus and become Sikhs.'[48] Missionaries certainly noticed that Sikhs were more active than previously in spreading their faith.[49] However, it was not quite as simple as that. As Mark Juergensmeyer noted, there was a considerable rivalry between Sikhs and Ad Dharmis over how Dalits should record their religion in the 1931 census. Moreover, as this observation by a missionary in Ferozepore district indicates, coercion was also involved:

The Sikh farmers of the Punjab tried to force their low-caste servants to declare themselves Sikhs, even though it were only for the time being. Many of our Christians permitted themselves to be written down as Sikhs to please their landlords. Others refused, and were persecuted for Christ's sake. They were discharged, and the means of living shut off, and no opportunity was given them to earn during the harvest. For six months now the persecution has continued in some localities.[50]

In fact, as an earlier rural missionary account from Gojra indicates, the Akali movement had a very ambivalent attitude towards Mazhabi aspirations:

During the Akali agitation many thousands of Sikhs had been thrown into prison for their lawless behaviour, and in order to fill the ranks of the Akali *Shahidi Jatthas* or Bands of Martyrs, the Sikh leaders welcomed warmly any one and every one who would help their cause in any way. Many thousands of *Chuhras*, the outcaste farm labourers of the province, joined them and, adopting all outward marks of Sikhism, were enrolled as the *Mazhabi* Sikhs. But when the Akalis had attained their object they had no further use for the *Mazhabis*, and the latter returned to their villages, disappointed and disillusioned, to find themselves still treated as outcastes, forbidden to draw water from the village wells, or to enter the Sikh temples, or to take any part in the social life of the Sikhs.[51]

The Census Commissioners were consistently right in pinpointing Chuhra/Mazhabi aspirations for improved status as the chief reason for their interest in Sikhism; what they were almost equally consistent in omitting was how frustrated and disappointed Chuhras/Mazhabis became in seeking to realize those aspirations through the adoption of Sikhism. Some organized large protest meetings at which representatives of other religions were invited to speak. As a result of some meetings in Gujranwala and Jhang Bar districts, some Mazhabis became Ahmadiyya Muslims and others became Christians.[52] In 1927 C. H. Loehlin reported from Moga about another public meeting which made Mazhabi aspirations quite clear:

Last spring the missionary was sent a notice printed in Gurumukhi, from 6000 Mazhabi Sikhs who had organized themselves into the 'Central Maulva Khalsa Kaum Sudar Committee', to the effect that they were tired of being treated like animals and denied real fellowship by the Sikhs, and were looking to either the Muhammadans, Aryas or Christians for real social and religious fellowship. The immediate cause of this dissatisfaction seems to be the refusal of the Hindu Sikhs to eat with their Mazhabi brethren at the conference in Panjgraian.[53]

Such protests may explain why the increase of the Mazhabi Sikh population was not larger than it was, just as the earlier examples of coercion may explain why it was as large as it was. The point is that there is evidence here of some serious caste cleavages and conflicts within Sikh society which deserve far more attention than they have received so far. While perhaps not in itself definitive, the evidence mentioned here is sufficient to suggest that official interpretations of Mazhabi progress under the aegis of the Singh Sabha and Akali movements do not stand up very well. A more thoroughgoing Dalit history approach is clearly required for understanding this period of Dalit Sikh history.

IV

The anthropological and sociological field studies published since Independence are more akin in spirit to the Sikh history than to the Dalit history approach in that they tend to focus on either the village as a whole or Sikhs in general rather than upon the Dalit Sikhs in particular. Invariably in these descriptions or analyses, the dominant dominate. However, in the sections on inter-caste behaviour and on religion, where actual Sikh practice is compared to normative Sikh belief, Dalit Sikhs come more into their own. A brief survey of some of this field research indicates that there have been both continuities with the past and significant changes in the lives of Dalit Sikhs since 1947. These can perhaps best be highlighted by examining some of the data first on inter-caste relations and then on religion in chronological order.

Indera P. Singh's early work on Daleke, a Sikh village in Amritsar district, provides a useful base point because it includes quite a bit of information about the Mazhabis who worked as labourers and made up about half of the village population. The Sikhs of Daleke took great pride in the fact that Sikhism taught the equality of all castes. The Mazhabis there lived separately and had their own well. They had used the other village well on occasion and had entered the homes of upper-caste Sikhs. 'There is no feeling of pollution attached to their [the Mazhabis'] touch, person or clothing.'[54] Both categories of Sikhs shared and sat intermixed in the same gurdwara. Mazhabi marriage parties were even allowed to stay overnight in the gurdwara, provided they did not desecrate it by smoking or using opium. Both groups attended fairs together, ate and drank from the same utensils, and together drank country wine (which the Mazhabis made). The same *granthi* performed all marriages in the village and a Mazhabi was usually one of the *pathis* when an Akhand Path was conducted.[55]

Writing two decades later about a village near Ludhiana, Harry Izmirlian presented a picture at odds with that given by Singh. Izmirlian reported that there was 'little joint activity ... performed by members of caste-groups with the exception of ceremonial activities performed by Ramgharias and Harijans' and that 'members of all castes are circumspect in their relations with Harijans',[56] who were 'virtually excluded from social intercourse with other villagers'.[57] Nonetheless, he found open caste conflict to have been rare. He could cite a case in which Jat Sikhs sought to punish the Dalits for having voted for the Congress Party in the 1962 elections[58] and an earlier dispute over the ownership of a tree. Writing another decade after Izmirlian, Clarence McMullen found Mazhabi respondents to his survey more likely than other Sikhs to feel that there was a caste system among Sikhs.[59] When taken with Singh's study, this data would suggest either that caste relations had grown more distant over time or that they varied from village to village.

In 2002, Surinder S. Jodhka completed 683 individual interviews in 51 Punjabi villages concerning prevailing caste relations and the practice of untouchability. While Dalit Sikhs were not singled out as a special category of respondent in the report of his findings, they are obviously covered by it since, as he points out, about 90 per cent of the rural population in the Punjab are Sikhs.[60] He found the practice of untouchability, as measured by most customary indicators,[61] virtually gone in the 'private sphere', the sphere of traditional *jajmani* relations, the sphere of everyday social and economic life, and in the sphere of modern institutions which had not been a part of village life. Much of this was, in his view, related to processes of dissociation, distancing, and autonomy rather than to changes in moral or religious values.[62] The exceptions, where untouchability and caste prejudice continued on, were few but noteworthy. One was the continued practice of separate cremation grounds; another was village festivals where Dalits were served food last and in some villages had to use separate utensils. However, it was in the village *panchayats* that traditional patterns of domination are most obvious and 'caste continues to be an important player in the rural power structure', even if a Dalit becomes *sarpanch*.[63]

Turning now to religion, Indera P. Singh's early findings on Mazhabi Sikhism in Daleke reveal considerable continuity with the past. Those who profess to be Sikhs still pay respect to Valmiki, to the village and ancestral gods, as well as to the devis.[64] Singh also notes that those Mazhabis who were most regular in Sikh prayers and in going to the gurdwara were those who served in the army![65] Perhaps most important, Singh found that those Mazhabis who were dependent upon Sikh farmers for their livelihood had found it advantageous to become Sikhs as well[66] and that Sikhism had helped to raise their own sense of social status:

Some of [the Mazhabis] even said that permission to enter [the] gurdwara and eat with all others in the Guru's Kitchen are distinct advantages of being Sikhs. Their social status is raised if not in their own village, at least outside the village, where they are considered at par with other Sikhs. 'You are always addressed as a Sardar outside the village,' added another.[67]

These observations have been largely confirmed by subsequent reports, including that of Juergensmeyer already referred to.[68] The 1981 census indicated that the Mazhabi population had risen dramatically to 1,221,131 (up from 169,247 in the undivided Punjab of 1931), so that they constituted 77 per cent of the Chuhra population, as compared to a mere 4.25 per cent back in 1881.[69] McMullen in his survey concluded that among his informants, the Mazhabis were lowest in religious participation, deviated most from normative Sikh beliefs, and were very liberal with regard to the ritual and communal requirements of Sikhism. This, however, he said, may have been linked more with education than with caste.[70] Thus in religion there appears to have been considerable continuity, at least well into the 1980s.[71]

Jodhka in his 2002 study did not examine the religious beliefs and practices of Dalit Sikhs so much as their treatment in village gurdwaras. About 76 per cent of his Dalit respondents said that they faced no discrimination in entering an upper-caste gurdwara, but those who had experienced it cited examples of being served langar only after others had finished eating, of being asked to sit in separate queues, of not even being informed of special functions at the gurdwara, and of not being allowed to join in the preparation and distribution of langar food. However, his most significant finding was that the most common way in which Dalit Sikhs resisted such humiliations was to marshal their resources and build their own separate gurdwaras, as had happened in 41 of the 51 villages involved in his study! He did not go into details about these gurdwaras, but the one Mazhabi gurdwara he refers to seems to have been quite orthodox, while the Chamar gurdwaras referred to would include pictures of Guru Ravidas, and one had a picture of Sant Balmiki as well.[72] Another source puts this figure as high as 10,000 Dalit gurdwaras in 12,780 Punjabi villages.[73]

On 5 June 2003 there was a violent conflict between Dalits and Jats over the control of a religious site in the village of Talhan near Jullundur that received considerable attention from members of both the press and the academic community. The site was Gurdwara Shahidian, built on the samadhs (graves) of Harnam Singh Granthi and Baba Nihal Singh in 1962–3. However, as Paramjit S. Judge has pointed out, while the gurdwara has continued to function within the Sikh tradition, the samadhs on which it was constructed are part of the composite, not the exclusively Sikh, religious tradition of the Punjab.[74] Since it brings into the village annual offerings of up to 60 million rupees, management of the gurdwara in this

Dalit majority village is really more of a political than a religious struggle, although it has been given a religious veneer.[75] Not only did the violence in Talhan spread beyond the village, but Talhan became a symbol of broader Jat–Dalit conflicts in rural Punjab as well as of a widespread Dalit assertiveness as they gained greater economic independence and wealth.[76]

As with the historical monographs cited earlier, these studies have not focused upon the Dalit Sikhs *per se*. They do nonetheless provide important information about and insights into some continuities and changes in Dalit Sikh life, perhaps the most striking features of which are the increases in the number of Dalit Sikhs and Dalit Sikh gurdwaras, as well as a more generalized Dalit assertiveness among them. It is this assertiveness, its forms, and arenas, including SGPC and Punjab politics above the local level, which would be the central subject of a post-Independence history of them which employs a Dalit history approach.

V

This chapter began by raising the question of whether a history of the Dalit Sikhs is a project worth pursuing. Our brief survey indicates that the Dalit Sikhs have been badly neglected by historians and social scientists alike. That alone provides ample justification for such a project, assuming that the ultimate aim is to create a truly inclusive and comprehensive history of the Sikhs. Moreover, this examination of the reigning 'Sikh history' paradigm from a vantage point informed by a 'Dalit history approach', in which caste is brought constantly to the forefront and questions are raised about where the Dalit Sikhs fit into the larger picture and what their experience has been, has perhaps accomplished two other things as well. It has uncovered enough evidence to suggest, as a working hypothesis, what the broad contours of Dalit Sikh history might look like; that same evidence has also cast enough suspicion on the subordinating, marginalizing, and 'covering-up' tendencies of the 'Sikh history approach' to warrant consideration of an alternative more informed by the 'Dalit history' paradigm. A brief, concluding word will be said about each of these in turn.

From the preceding analysis of historical and social-science literature, it seems clear that caste has been and remains a meaningful social unit among Sikhs. The Sikh gurus did not set out to annihilate caste with what McLeod has called its 'horizontal connections'. Whether they sought to annihilate caste *hierarchy* has been, as Oberoi has shown, a more debatable point. Certainly the gurus, through their teachings and the institutions they developed, did much to undermine the validity of the Brahmanical purity/pollution criterion according to which castes had been hierarchically ranked. By delegitimizing Brahmin ascendancy in this manner, they opened up the way for a Khatri, Arora, and especially a Jat ascendancy within the Panth, based not upon ascribed status at birth, but upon piety, devotion, and power. This has not eliminated caste hierarchy within Sikhism, but it has drastically altered the positions of specific castes within the still-pervasive hierarchy. It is no wonder, then, that social scientists attribute the peculiar nature of the caste system in the Punjab (which follows Bayly's Kshatriya rather than Brahmin model and puts the Jats at the top) in good part to the influence of Sikhism.[77]

The working hypothesis suggested by the evidence gathered here is that Dalits have sought, perhaps more unconsciously than intentionally, to emulate the Jats by using those channels of caste mobility which Sikhism has opened up to move to positions of increasing status and respect within the broader Punjabi caste hierarchy. Of course, Dalit Sikhs have had far fewer resources at their command to do this than had the Jat Sikhs, and not all Dalits have gone about this in the same way, as the diverse paths of the Mazhabis, Ravidasis, and Ramdasias would suggest. Nonetheless, all have encountered many forms of opposition and non-recognition from Sikhs of 'higher' castes who remain attached to caste hierarchy, to their privileged positions within that hierarchy, and thus to keeping Dalit Sikhs 'in their place'. For Dalit Sikhs, as for other Dalits, the struggle has been to free themselves from caste oppression and degradation. The attraction of Sikhism has been that it has offered them, at least in theory, greater possibilities of achieving that goal than have other perceived religious options open to them. Sikhism's problematic has been that the main opposition to the realization of Dalit aspirations for an alternative, more just, religiously sanctioned social order has come from within the Sikh panth, and at times even in the name of Sikhism. For Dalits, therefore, the history of Sikhism has been one of inevitable, persistent, and multi-faceted caste conflict. This is a history which needs to be 'fleshed out' in some detail.

This experience and perception of Sikh history is at odds with the perceptions found in the 'Sikh history' books. It could be dismissed, therefore, as that of a minority which is, unfortunately, outside the 'mainstream'. Historians such as McLeod, Grewal, and Oberoi, who take social history seriously, certainly have taken note of caste differences and divisions within Sikhism. However, caste conflict, which has been a central reality for Dalit Sikhs, has not been the primary, or even a secondary, 'interpretative lens' through which they have viewed the history of either the Sikh people themselves or of the changing definitions Sikhs have used to interpret the very nature of their religion. Clearly it would be a gross form of reductionism to use the social roots of the Sikh religion or Panth (or of any other religion and religious community, for that matter) as a total explanation of its history. Its depth of experience of ultimate reality and the ways in which it expresses that through words, rituals, religious disciplines, and customs are central. That is what the 'Sikh history' approach recognizes and that is its main strength. However, having said that, it is also important to recognize that different social groups within any religious community (in this case, caste groups within the Sikh Panth) are apt to having differing views, differing interests, and even differing 'little traditions' which are going to clash with one another and thus, in those conflicts, shape both the changing interpretations of the tradition and the ways in which the community itself changes over time. Those who are dominant will get their views and experiences enshrined in the history books; others often get ignored or downplayed to the point where conflict is, in effect, covered up. The 'Dalit history' approach, a particularly germane form of social history 'from below', seeks to bring caste conflict out into the open by making it a central theme in the writing of Sikh history. It thus provides a rather different, potentially stimulating, and realistic lens through which to take a closer look at Sikh history as a whole.

Notes

1. John C. B. Webster, *The Dalit Christians: A History*, Delhi: ISPCK, 1992; second edition 1994.

2. See, for example, Khushwant Singh, *A History of the Sikhs: 1: 1469–1839* (Princeton: Princeton University Press, 1963) and *Volume 2: 1839–1964* (Princeton: Princeton University Press, 1966) as well as J. S. Grewal, *The Sikhs of the Punjab: The New Cambridge History of India* 2 and 3 (Cambridge: Cambridge University Press, 1990).

3. Khushwant Singh, *A History of the Sikhs* 1, p. vii.

4. Ibid., 2, p. vii.

5. Ibid., 1, p. 97.

6. Ibid., 2, pp. 155–6.

7. Ibid., 2, pp. 95, 110, 112, 113, 118, 120, 129, and 134.

8. J. S. Grewal, *The Sikhs of the Punjab*, pp. 30 and 60. He provides much fuller treatments of this subject, albeit in different contexts, in *Guru Nanak in History* (Chandigarh: Panjab University, 1969), pp. 186–92, and in *Contesting Interpretations of the Sikh Tradition* (Delhi: Manohar, 1998), pp. 195–212.

9. Ibid., p. 52. Other references may be found on pp. 95, 98, and 118.

10. Ibid., pp. 116, 139, and 183.

11. W. H. McLeod, *The Evolution of the Sikh Community: Five Essays* (Delhi: Oxford University Press, 1975), p. 88.

12. Ibid., pp. 90–1.

13. Ibid., p. 103.

14. W. H. McLeod, *Who is a Sikh? The Problem of Sikh Identity* (Oxford: Clarendon Press, 1989), p. 21.

15. Ibid., pp. 109–10.

16. Ibid., pp. 69 and 71.

17. Ibid., 82.

18. W. H. McLeod, *Sikhs of the Khalsa: A History of the Khalsa Rahit* (New Delhi: Oxford University Press, 2003), p. 215. See also pp. 119, 130, and 216.

19. Harjot Oberoi, *The Construction of Religious Boundaries: Culture, Identity and Diversity in the Sikh Tradition* (Delhi: Oxford University Press, 1994), pp. 106–7 and 242.

20. Ibid., p. 288–9.

21. Ibid., p. 385.

22. Ethne K. Marenco, *The Transformation of Sikh Society* (Portland: HaPi Press, 1974), pp. 247–93. A much more lucid account of religious and occupational change among Mazhabi Sikhs, as revealed primarily in census reports, is that provided by Nisha Sharma in her M. Phil. thesis at Guru Nanak Dev University (1985) and later published in summary form. 'Mazhabi Sikhs of the Upper Bari Doab, 1881–1941', Nisha Sharma, J. S. Grewal, and Indu Banga (eds), *The Khalsa over 300 Years* (New Delhi: Tulika, 1999), pp. 145–50.

23. Harnik Deol, *Religion and Nationalism in India: The Case of the Punjab* (London: Routledge, 2000), pp. 4 and 125.

24. Ibid., pp. 10, 31, and 61.

25. Ibid., pp. 60–1. See also p. 132.

26. Ibid., p. 141.

27. The most obvious one is Giani Ditt Singh's views on caste in which a quotation in Oberoi, *The Construction of Religious Boundaries*, p. 308, contradicts McLeod's assertion above. Another, perhaps more important one, concerns Dalits in the canal colonies, about which more will be said later.

28. See Susan Bayly, *Caste, Society and Politics in India from the Eighteenth Century to the Modern Age*, The New Cambridge History of India (Cambridge: Cambridge University Press, 1999).

29. Ibid., p. 104.

30. Mark Juergensmeyer, *Religion as Social Vision: The Movement Against Untouchability in 20th-Century Punjab* (Berkeley: University of California Press, 1982), pp. 28 and 66–7.

31. Ibid., 89–90. A Ramdasia Sikh belong to the Chamar caste and has converted

to Sikhism, whereas a Ravidasi is a (generally Chamar) follower of Ravidas (sometimes called Raidas), who was a Chamar Sant. Although he was not a Sikh, his writings nevertheless appear in the Guru Granth Sahib.

32. Ibid., 92–3.

33. Harish K. Puri, 'Scheduled Castes in Sikh Community: A Historical Perspective', *Economic and Political Weekly* (28 June 2003), p. 2693.

34. Ibid., p. 2701.

35. *Punjab Census 1881* 1, p. 318.

36. Ibid., 1, p. 319.

37. These are pretty well brought together in H. A. Rose, *A Glossary of the Tribes and Castes of the Punjab and North West Frontier Province* 3 (Languages Department, Punjab, 1970), p. 75–6.

38. *Punjab Census 1931* 1, p. 309.

39. Italics mine. A. H. Bingley, *Sikhs* (Simla, 1899), p. 93. This truism was later repeated *verbatim* in Major A. B. Barstow's *The Sikhs: An Ethnology. Revised at the Request of the Govt. of India* (Delhi: B. R. Publishing Corporation, 1985), p. 155. This is a reprint of the 1928 edition.

40. E. G. Gordon, 'Foreign Missions', *The United Presbyterian* (25 May 1875), p. 2.

41. *The Twenty-Sixth Annual Report of the Board of Foreign Missions of the United Presbyterian Church of North America Presented to the General Assembly in May 1885*, p. 26.

42. For example, John F. W Youngson, *Forty Years of the Panjab Mission of the Church of Scotland 1855–1895* (Edinburgh: R. & R. Clark, 1896), p. 14. See also: W. P. Hares, 'The Chuhras of the Punjab', *The Church Missionary Review* (June 1920), pp. 119–20. H. J. Strickler, 'The Religion and Customs of the Chuhra in the Punjab Province, India' (unpublished MA thesis, University of Kansas, 1926), pp. 5–7. Hervey DeWitt Griswold, *Insights into Modern Hinduism* (New York: Henry Holt and Company, 1934), pp. 229–30.

43. Imran Ali, *The Punjab Under Imperialism, 1885–1947* (Princeton: Princeton University Press, 1988), pp. 92–3. For example, one missionary report describes 'the fluctuating Christian population (some of them tenants at will, but mostly labourers)' in the canal colonies. 'The Mission Field', *Church Missionary Intelligencer* (July 1901), p. 549. Another states that 'The remaining 3,000 baptized Christians are scattered about the district in villages often twelve or fifteen miles apart... Ignorant and poor, employed generally by unsympathetic non-Christian masters, their lives have little of sunshine in them. They are subjected to petty persecutions. Not unseldom, after clearing and preparing the land for cultivation, they are turned adrift by their employers on paltry grounds without a farthing of compensation.' T. Holden, 'The C. M. S. Jhang Bar Mission', ibid. (April 1904), p. 267.

44. Barstow in 1928 stated that Mazhabis had been declared a separate agricultural tribe in Gujranwala and Lyallpur districts. Imran Ali, *The Punjab Under Imperialism*, p. 97.

45. Imran Ali, *The Punjab Under Imperialism*, pp. 92–8.

46. *Punjab Census 1881* 2: Table VIIIA, p. 4; *Punjab Census 1891* 2, p. 272; *Punjab Census 1901* 2, Table XIII, pp. viii and xx; *Punjab Census 1911* 2, pp. 244 and 272; *Punjab Census 1921* 1, p. 178; *Punjab Census 1931* 1, p. 308.

47. *Punjab Census 1921* 2, pp. 179 and 184.

48. *Punjab Census, 1931*, p. 293.

49. See, for example, the report of a missionary in Taran Tarn in *The Vision of the Hands, being the Story of the Year 1923 in the Work of the Church of England Zenana Missionary Society*, p. 56.

50. *The 97th Annual Report of the Panjab Mission of the Presbyterian Church in the U.S.A., Cooperating with the United Church of Northern India for the Year 1930–31*, p. 10. In Ludhiana district, rural Dalit Christians were harassed at census time not only by landlords but even by Ad Dharmis and Mazhabi Sikhs, so keen was the competition for numbers. Ibid., pp. 27–8. See also *Eighth Annual Session of the Indus River Annual Conference of the Methodist Episcopal Church Held at Lahore Oct. 21–26th 1931*, p. 36.

51. W. P. Hares, 'Among the Mazhabi Sikhs of the Punjab', *Church Missionary Outlook* (December 1926), p. 249. This view of Akali ambivalence was reinforced by Professor Joginder Singh of Guru Nanak Dev University, who informed me that in going over the Akali publications from this period, he found no references to the Mazhabis or Dalits in general. The issue simply did not concern the Akalis as it had the Singh Sabhas. Interview, 24 October 2003.

52. W. P. Hares, 'Among the Mazhabi Sikhs', pp. 249–50.

53. *The 93rd Annual Report of the Punjab Mission of the Presbyterian Church in the U.S.A. in connection with the Presbyterian Church in India for the Year 1927*, pp. 83–4.

54. Indera P. Singh, 'A Sikh Village', Milton Singer (ed.), *Traditional India: Structure and Change* (Philadelphia: The American Folklore Society, 1959), p. 279.

55. Ibid., pp. 279–81.

56. Harry Izmirlian Jr, *Structure and Strategy in Sikh Society: The Politics of Passion* (New Delhi: Manohar, 1979), p. 113.

57. Ibid., p. 114.

58. Joyce Pettigrew in her earlier study of Jat Sikhs had noted that the only segment of the Sikh population which she found to be consistently anti-Akali was the non land-owning Dalits (Mazhabis). Joyee Pettigrew, *Robber Noblemen: A Study of the Political System of the Jat Sikhs* (London: Routledge & Kegan Paul, 1975), p. 91.

59. Clarence Osmond McMullen, *Religious Beliefs and Practices of the Sikhs in Rural Punjab* (New Delhi: Manohar, 1989), p. 109.

60. Surinder S. Jodhka, 'Caste and Untouchability in Rural Punjab', *Economic and Political Weekly* (May 11, 2002), p. 1814.

61. Residential segregation, unclean occupations, entry into higher-caste homes, use of drinking-water sources, provision of such services as that of the barber, and access to village streets.

62. Surinder S. Jodhka, 'Caste and Untouchability in Rural Punjab', p. 1822. For example, Dalits were making themselves increasingly economically independent of the Jat landlords in their own villages and upper caste families were withdrawing their children from village schools, so that they became *de facto* Dalit schools and thus of little public interest.

63. Ibid., p. 1821.

64. Indera P. Singh, 'Religion in Daleke: A Sikh Village', L. P. Vidyarthi (ed.), *Aspects of Religion in Indian Society* (Meerut: Kedar Nath Ram Nath, n.d.), pp. 192–3. This was probably published in 1961.

65. Ibid., pp. 205 and 219.

66. Ibid., pp. 218–19.

67. Ibid., p. 219. Pettigrew also noted that some Mazhabis had adopted Jat clan names in order to raise their status in the eyes of others. Joyce Pettigrew, *Robber Noblemen*, p. 41.

68. *Infra.*, 141.

69. *Punjab Census 1981, Paper I of 1984: Household Population by Religion of Head of Household*, p. 738.

70. Ibid., p. 110.

71. A dissenting voice would be that of Parkash Singh Jammu, who noted in 1974 that Sikhism was losing force as a religion but not as a political movement 'because Sikhism which is the major religion in the new Panjab was as good or perhaps better as a political ideology than as a religious ideology'. This, however, refers to Sikhs in general and not just to Dalit Sikhs. Prakash Singh Jammu, *Changing Social Structure in Rural Punjab* (New Delhi: Sterling Publishers, 1974), p. 107.

72. Surinder S. Jodhka, 'Caste and Untouchability in Rural Punjab', p. 1818.

73. The original source is an article in *The Spokesman* of July 2003 cited in Gurnam Singh Muktsar, 'Sikhs Divided into 3 Warring Camps: Upper Castes, Jats and Dalits', *Dalit Voice* (1–15 August 2003), pp. 21–2. I am grateful to Dr Ronki Ram of Panjab University, Chandigarh, for this reference.

74. Paramjit S. Judge, 'Recent Caste Clash in Talhan in Punjab', *Dalit International Newsletter* (February 2004), p. 11.

75. Praveen Swami, 'Dalits' Battle in a Punjab Village', *Frontline* (9 May 2003), p. 94. For a narrative of some of the Sikh identity issues which the conflict and its settlement raised, see Praveen Swami, 'The States: Unquiet Peace in Talhan', *Frontline* (5–18 July 2003).

76. See Surinder S. Jodhka and Prakash Louis, 'Caste Tensions in Punjab: Talhan and Beyond', *Economic and Political Weekly* (12 July 2003), pp. 2923–6. Ronki Ram, 'Making Sense of Caste Violence in Talhan: A View from Within' (unpublished paper, Panjab University, Chandigarh, 2003).

77. For example, Harish K. Puri, 'Scheduled Castes in Sikh Community', pp. 2697–8; Surinder S. Jodhka, 'Caste and Untouchability in Rural Punjab', pp. 1814–15.

British Rule, Technological Change, and the Revolution in Transportation and Communication: Punjab in the Later Nineteenth Century

Ian J. Kerr

The woodcut reproduced in Figure 7.1 can be found in the J. Lockwood Kipling collection in the Victoria and Albert Museum, London, England.[1] Its creation is attributed to an unknown Punjabi artist *c.* 1870. The woodcut appears in a number of publications, but likely the first and most striking use was by W. G. Archer in his *Paintings of the Sikhs*.[2] Archer noted that the Sikhs had been 'vanquished' in 1849. Their 'national ideal had collapsed' yet perhaps was capable of resuscitation through co-operation with their modernizing conquerors, the British. This possibility, Archer suggests, was hinted at in the woodcut of the train, 'a woodcut of a starkly different kind'.[3] Archer continued:

Symbolic of the new Punjab, it shows a railway train in two sections standing at a station. The upper section is by a platform, the lower section has an engine about to start. Railways had reached the Punjab in the early 1860s and the Sikhs had been confronted by a new machine as powerful in its way as the British government which had subdued them. At first, all trains were run and controlled by British drivers, but presently Sikhs were actively associated with them. In the woodcut, the passengers include both men and women, both Sikhs and British; and the same collaboration appears elsewhere. The driver and fireman are British or Anglo-Indian but the stationmaster holding the vital tally, the clerk in the ticket office, and the guard waving a flag and setting points are all Sikhs. If we interpret the train as the Punjab, the meaning of the parable is only too clear.

The woodcut and Archer's commentary command our attention and demand further discussion. Both the woodcut and the commentary

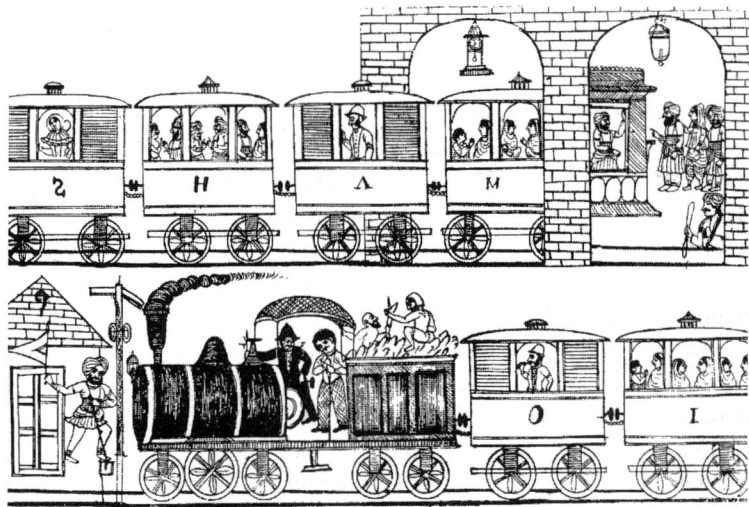

Figure 7.1: Sikh Woodcut, c.1870

provide an entry point into little-studied aspects of Punjab history. At the level of representation, we note a Punjabi artist some twenty years after the Punjab was annexed to British India in 1849 using an established medium for popular art, the woodcut, to create an image of a train, its personnel, and its passengers. This secular treatment stands in sharp distinction to the more common religious images—most typically, in the case of Sikh woodcuts, stylized portraits of Guru Nanak, Guru Gobind Singh, or collective portraits, conclaves, of all ten gurus—present in most popular woodcuts. Produced as letterpress reproductions, with print runs of 1000–2000 not uncommon, woodcuts were sold cheaply in the bazaars and at religious fairs. Thus, we can infer that trains had become a significant presence in the Punjab by 1870, entered the popular world of the woodcuts, and had become a marketable commodity within a representational medium dominated by images of the gurus or of great Sikh leaders such as Ranjit Singh or the martyred warrior Baba Dip Singh.[4] Certainly Archer suggests that this was so. The secular image of the train was marketed alongside inspirational woodcuts that conveyed the ideals of Sikhism through depictions of defining places (such as the Golden Temple) and central personages of the Sikh tradition.

To continue with the representational aspects, we can leap ahead to the 1960s and find a Western scholar, W.G. Archer, with a keen and well-informed interest in Sikh art seeking to counter 'the charge that the Sikhs were a non-artistic people'.[5] The Sikhs, Archer argued, were pioneers in later nineteenth-century India in the popular patronage of art. The train woodcut plays an important role in Archer's argument precisely because it could be read as 'symbolic of the new Punjab' and representative of a dynamic Sikh response to the new, British-driven changes. Archer interpreted the woodcut and its content as evidence of a fruitful Anglo– Sikh collaboration and as a representation of a new reality that had begun to emerge in the Punjab by 1870.

All of the above is interesting and, insofar as it goes, quite possibly correct. However, like many studies of representational phenomena, it takes appearance for reality. Simulacra become reified and the representations of change are studied rather than the socio-economic and techno-developmental processes within which men, women, and children make their own histories, albeit always constrained by 'circumstances directly encountered, given, and transmitted from the past'.[6] What needs to be examined is the assertion that a new Punjab began to take shape after 1849, made (at least in part) by technological innovations introduced by the British; made by potent new machines, among which steam locomotion may have been the most striking but certainly was not the only innovation. Were the new technologies powerful agents of change? If so, how and why were they powerful? In short, did technology drive the history of the Punjab in the period extending from 1849 to roughly 1870 and beyond, as Archer's gloss suggests?[7]

There are no quick, easy answers to the questions posed above. There never is for the historian whose attempts at explanation usually involve expansive constructs within which a great deal of temporally and spatially variegated information is brought to bear. Four ideas, however, provide points of departure. First, machines—technology—never have agency in and of themselves, although their invention, refinement, and application can drive history–albeit in ways that are socially determined. Technology, in short, never exists outside its social context; technology (and technological change) is not an autonomous historical force.[8] I might add, parenthetically, that colonial contexts with their imposed technologies— as in railways in India—are good examples of cases where technological change was clearly driven by something other than an inherent momentum energized by an inner technological or scientific logic.

Second, it is not the technological artifact—the tool or machine—that is crucial and potentially society-shaping but the large-scale assembly of productive processes such as those we label railways. Railways are consequential because they are large-scale technical systems: 'complex and heterogeneous systems of physical structures and complex machineries' that provide 'material integration or coupling over large spans of space and time which support or sustain the functioning of very large number of other technical systems, whose organizations they thereby link'.[9] The steam locomotive depicted in the woodcut was only socially and economically consequential as part of a railway system, a railway network comprised of the permanent way, stations, workshops, rolling stock, signals (all of which are based on capital formation and expenditure), personnel, administrative structures, and so on. The importance of any particular component of a railway system comes from its interactive and relation function within the system.[10] Furthermore, the railway had to have passengers and goods to transport to be effectual, although there is something of the chicken and egg conundrum present in the relationship between a railway and its source of traffic: railways tapped markets and helped to create markets.

Third, especially in the case of the Punjab after 1849, we need to return to colonialism, to the imposition of British rule. Archer describes the railway 'as powerful in its way as the British government which had subdued' the Sikhs. This is not a useful description. Rather, we need to see the development of railways in the Punjab as an integral part of the colonial project to master the Punjab and Punjabis—although, of course, the intent to master never resulted in full mastery.[11] A constant and largely unintended consequence of British induced changes in South Asia was to open space for Indian resistance. Regardless, the railways and related innovations helped to ensure the security of British rule in the Punjab, to integrate the Punjab into the British Indian Empire, and to develop the commercial potential of the Punjab.[12] We need to view the railway as a technology of power deployed as one element within a spectrum of such technologies utilized by the colonial regime to maintain control and to develop the commercial resources of the Punjab.[13] Another technology, namely canal irrigation, played a similar role. David Gilmartin has written about irrigation as a problematic application of imperial science and technology to agricultural development in the Indus basin. Gilmartin analyses 'the impact of the interlocking, yet conflicting, discourses of "scientific empire" and "imperial science" on the colonial politics of technological and agricultural transformation'.[14]

Resource development, in turn, was driven partly by the ever-present British concern to rule cheaply, to enable the colonies to contribute to the costs of colonial administration, and to benefit some British commercial, industrial, and financial interests.[15] Railways were a particularly good example of the latter. British marketing firms benefited from Punjabi exports, British locomotive manufacturers made engines for the Sind, Punjab, and Delhi Railway Company (hereafter SP&DR), and British interests purchased SP&DR stock with a 5 per cent rate of return guaranteed by the revenues of the Government of India.

The fourth point of departure takes us into railways and the making of colonial space. Here it is fruitful to place the railways within a context populated by other large-scale transportation and communication systems introduced or expanded by the British in the Punjab: most notably roads, the electric telegraph, and the post office. My inclusion of roads and the post office may seem out of place alongside the dramatic technological advances represented by steam locomotion and the electric telegraph but they, too, were large-scale transportation systems with significant institutional components (for example, the Public Works Department charged with building and maintaining roads and bridges and constructing and staffing dak-bungalows or the postal service with its network of offices, clerks, and routes). Moreover, both the road system and the post office utilized new forms of technology—simple forms to be sure, but no less surely representing technological advance, for example, stamps and better vehicles for conveying the mail or new ways to 'metallize' road surfaces.

Equally important is the fact that the roads, telegraph, post office, and railways all interacted with one another and, indeed, were interdependent. Roads and rails carried mail. Roads facilitated the movement of people and goods to and from railway stations, and linked towns well away from the railway lines. Indeed, where roads were good, distances short, and traffic substantial, road transport could compete with railed transport. Some 70 ekkas (one-horse carriages), each carrying three to four passengers, plied the 32-mile road between Amritsar and Lahore in the late 1860s. Each passenger paid about one-half of the third-class railway fare—a difference more than big enough to maintain a customer base among the many for whom the financial saving was more important than the saving in time train travel provided.[16] The electric telegraph made the safer operation of the railways possible, linked buyers and sellers, and placed many colonial officials in faster communication with their superiors.

Collectively the roads, telegraph, post office, and railways formed a mega structure, a very large network of routes and flows that began to revolutionize the structure of transportation and communication within the Punjab and between the Punjab, the rest of India, and increasingly the entire world. Throughout this chapter, I use the phrase 'transportation and communication revolution' because I consider them closely related but separate developments. Transportation involves the physical movement through space of someone or something and the infrastructure that makes transport possible: roads, carriages, railway lines, locomotives, and telegraph lines, etc. Communication requires the physical transportation of the thing communicated (in the case of the telegraph via an electric impulse along the wire), but it deals primarily with social exchange: the exchange of commodities, of information, and of ideas. The latter two could be transported in a letter, in a newspaper, or face to face—when, for example, a Sikh reformer from Amritsar was transported to Tarn Taran, where he orally advocated (in discussion or in lecture) the Tat Khalsa version of Sikhism. My emphasis is on the physical and institutional components of transportation that fostered communication. Transport precedes communication.

By 1871, the road mileage in the Punjab totalled 19,895: a number that increased to 25,053 in 1876.[17] The first 32 miles of railway, Lahore to Amritsar, opened in 1862, and by 1871, 554 miles of line were in operation. Figure 7.2 provides a railway and road map of the Punjab in the early 1870s. Figure 7.3 depicts the roads and railway lines in the central Punjab district of Lahore circa 1870. Post offices numbered 120 in 1868, when 10,215,976 letters were delivered, increasing to 528 offices in 1875 and the delivery of 14,141,972 letters.

In 1869, the Punjab had 14 telegraph offices serviced by 761 miles of line. Telegraph service vastly expanded between 1870 and 1875 with the offices increasing to 30 and the line mileage to 2,374. The road network in 1849 was, according to most accounts, rudimentary and poorly maintained—perhaps more so than some years earlier, thanks to the disturbed state of affairs following Maharaja Ranjit Singh's death in 1839. There were, of course, no railways and telegraph lines in 1849. However, the rivers of the Punjab, even in their less navigable upper reaches, carried more boat traffic than they did after the British-imposed changes began to take hold. Boat transportation, however, always had two limitations in the Punjab: limitations based on low water levels during many months,

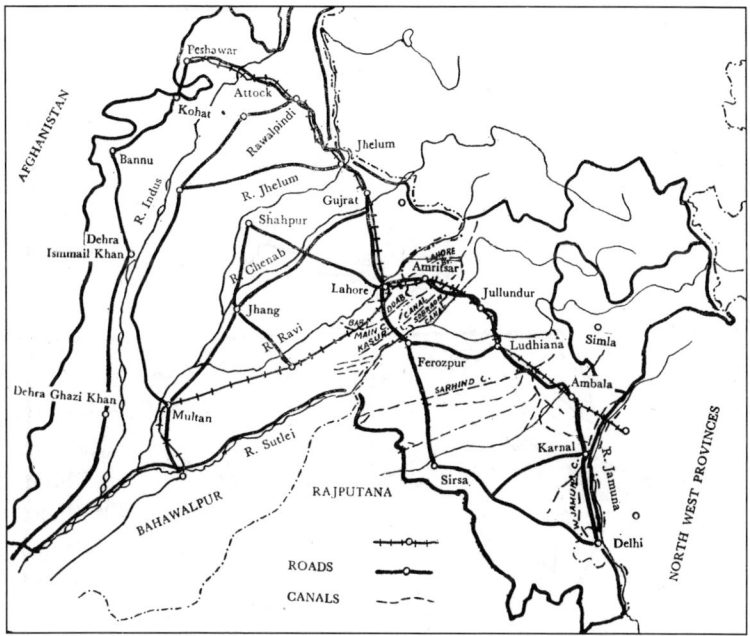

Fig. 7.2: Major Roads, Railways, and Canals in the Punjab c. 1870
(Courtesy Y. B. Mathur, *British Administration of the Punjab*)

especially on the Rivers Jhelum, Chenab, Ravi, Beas, and Sutlej; and
the north-to-south drainage of the rivers that precluded east–west
transportation by water (see Figure 7.2).

Technological change contributed significantly to the making of the
Punjab's colonial space. An enhanced understanding of the post-annexation
decades and the consequences of the transportation and communication
revolution then begun can, I suggest, be found by using ideas drawn from
a number of spatial theorists. Regardless of their differences, nuances,
elaborated and at times elaborate (and opaque) vocabulary, the fundamental
insight of the spatial theorists is simple but powerful. Space is not a fixed
entity nor is it simply the container within which, along with time,
phenomena exist and interact. On the contrary, space(s) is relative, multiple,
and malleable. Humans manipulate—produce—space(s) and are
manipulated by the space(s) they and others produce. In short, to follow
David Harvey, 'time and space are both social and objective...'.[18]

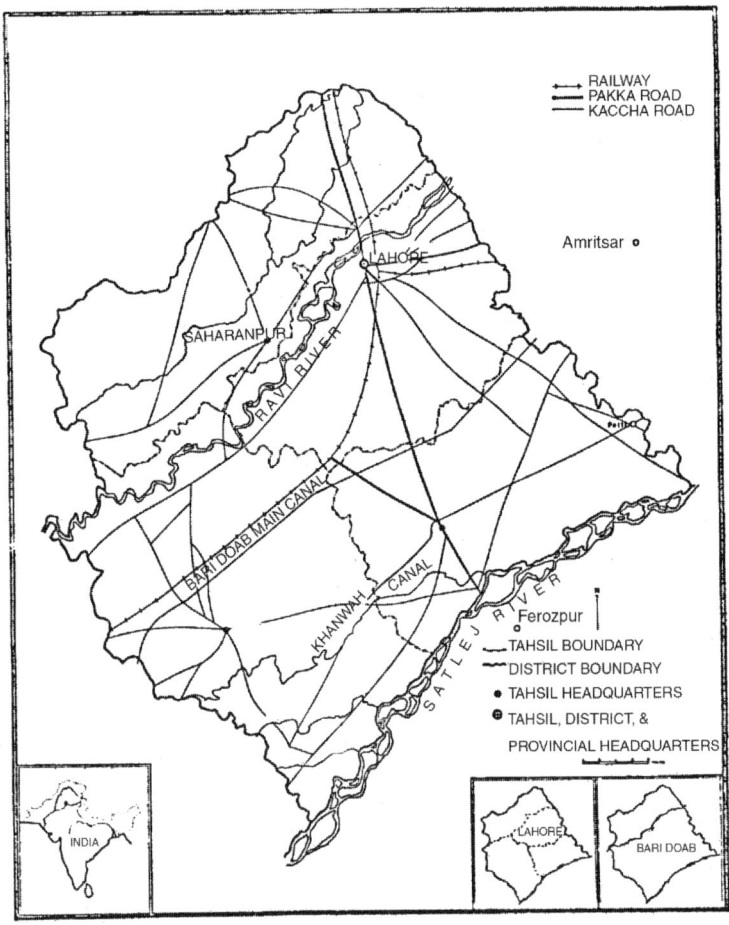

Fig 7.3: Lahore District c. 1870: Roads and Railways

A temporal window of accelerated change, of the enhanced making
of history, is opened at moments of 'revolutionary' technological change.[19]
One such moment throughout the world in the nineteenth century was
the introduction of railways powered by steam locomotion. In the case
of the Punjab post-1849, it was a package of changes capped by railway
development: changes imposed quickly from above by the Punjab's new
colonial masters. It was, however, a short-lived moment, for in their
production and domination of space, the railways imbedded themselves

into the socio-economic and physical, landscape as a powerful source of inertia that could prevent, retard, channel, or constrain subsequent processes of societal change.[20]

The concept of 'dominant space' provides a powerful point of entry into the workings of the 'socio-spatial dialectic' and the resultant 'socially-based spatiality', 'the created space of social organization and production', that emerged in colonial India in the railway age.[21] Henri Lefebvre, for whom and for many influenced by him, '(Social) space is a (social) product', distinguished between 'dominated' spaces and 'appropriated' spaces.[22] Dominated spaces, 'closed, sterilized, emptied out' spaces, can only be fully comprehended when contrasted with their dialectically related opposite: appropriated spaces, spaces that meet the possibilities and needs of humankind. Dominated and dominant space for Lefebvre is 'a space transformed—and mediated—by technology...'. 'Thanks to technology,' Lefebvre writes, 'the domination of space is becoming, as it were, completely dominant.' There is more than a little of Lefebvre's value preferences in his daunting and at times dense reflections on the production of space. Nonetheless, he gives us a stimulating outline of what a theory of the social production of space might contain and a vocabulary through which such a theory can be articulated.

At first approach, colonial contexts appear to provide clear, straight-forward examples of the production of dominated spaces. New concepts of space and time were imposed on subject areas and subject peoples through the imposition and maintenance of colonial authority.[23] Railways and other advances in transportation produced or reproduced spaces of communication and exchange, in short refashioned or created networks, and thus facilitated the maintenance of colonial rule and the inaugura-tion of colonially determined processes of socio-economic change.

'Dominant space,' writes Lefebvre, 'is invariably the realization of a master's project.'[24] Colonialism with its assumption of foreign sovereignty through conquest or other mechanisms reduced the agency of the colonized—power and authority was in the hands of the delegates of the metropolitan power—and gave the colonial authorities a freer hand to impose projects such as roads and railways on colonial territories. High on the list of instructions Governor-General (1848–56) Dalhousie, as imperious a colonial master as ever held that position and a committed modernizer, provided to the newly constituted Punjab Board of Administration (Henry Lawrence, C. G. Mansel, and John Lawrence) in 1849 was to develop the resources of the Punjab. The Board was expected to encourage agriculture and to develop roads, canals, railways, and post offices.[25]

The Board took their developmental responsibilities in the area of transport and communication seriously. The first Punjab Administration Report extolling the accomplishments of British rule during the first three years (1849–51, inclusive), contained a lengthy section detailing the progress of public works. Roads were classified as to their importance, urgency, and imperial as opposed to more local purposes. First-class trunk roads, initially just the continuation of the Grand Trunk Road through the Punjab and onwards to Peshawar, were designed to provide all-weather routes 'raised above all inundations, completely bridged and metalled...'. Work on the Grand Trunk Road had been pursued vigorously. Second-class roads were intended 'to connect the principal towns and military stations with each other and with the North-West Provinces, Bahawulpore and Scinde'. Six routes had been largely surveyed and traced and some, in as yet a rudimentary state, were in heavy use, but raising and bridging all the roads was yet to be actively undertaken. Thus the Multan to Lahore road was only fair-weather passable but it did enable the mail cart to cover the distance in 30 hours for much of the year and a government bullock train to operate. However, repair of the road was constantly needed and metalling required, especially given the demands of an increasing commerce with Bombay.[26]

First- and second-class roads were to be funded from general revenues. Third-class district roads were paid for from a local road fund of 1 per cent of the land revenue. These roads were intended for internal communication within the Punjab: to connect the main administrative centres and towns of 'neighbouring districts with each other or with military stations', 'to connect the subordinate police and revenue stations', and more generally 'to open out the interior of the country'. The third-class roads were, in turn, prioritized into those of greatest importance 'or liable to the marching of troops', those of 'lesser importance not subject to the marching of troops', and the least important roads, namely those across hilly or otherwise difficult terrain or in poor districts where the road tax could not pay for wider roads and where the traffic was small and unlikely to increase any time soon.[27]

Not surprisingly, what is immediately apparent in this schema is the close connection between the emerging improved network of roads and the administrative and military needs of the colonial regime. This is an expected finding but one that deserves elaboration, given the close connection in the Punjab between the security concerns of the colonial authorities and the development of transportation and communication in the newly conquered Province. The British wanted to secure the Punjab, beyond whose boundaries lay the instabilities of the North West Frontier and Afghanistan, and beyond that the threats, real or imagined, of an expansive imperial Russia. Moreover, post 1857–8 the British increasingly needed to ensure the loyalty of Punjabis (or at least their acquiescence to British rule) because the Punjab increasingly became the most important recruiting area for the British Indian Army—a process Rajit Mazumder labels the 'Punjabisation of the Indian Army'.[28]

Clive Dewey and Rajit Mazumder, among others, have explored the connections between the security concerns of the British, the development of the transportation infrastructure in the Punjab post-1849, and the stimulation of the economy of the Punjab.[29] Dewey's detailed account of the major effects military expenditure had on the economy and society of the Upper Sind Sagar Doab includes a telling section on the improvement of communication. Dewey notes that the initial railway line into the Punjab linked towns and major cantonments with one another— Meerut, Ambala, Jullundur, Amritsar, and Lahore—and that the main line to the frontier (opened 1878–82) went through seven more cantonment towns, of which four were located in the Upper Sind Sagar Doab. In an observation that presages some of the arguments made in this chapter Dewey states that important as the railways were for communications along their 'narrow corridors', road transportation was required to penetrate the many areas rail transport left 'as impassable as ever'.[30] He then details how a 'whole network of military roads soon converged on Rawalpindi' thus giving the 'Pothwar plain one of the densest and best-maintained road systems in the sub-continent'.[31] Cart traffic on these roads quickly grew and was followed in the twentieth century by motor cars, buses, and lorries. Mazumder, meanwhile, takes the entire Punjab as his arena and outlines how military imperatives led to the development of roads, railways, and telegraphic and postal services that provided the infrastructure for the Province's economic development.

The work of Dewey and Mazumder reinforces the position taken in this paper, namely the need to think in terms of an emergent mega structure of transportation and communication closely tied to the needs and concerns of colonial rule. Archer, to repeat, did not get it quite right: the railway and the British Raj were not separate phenomena; the railway was an integral component of the mastery pursued by the colonial authorities. The space of the Punjab was made and remade. The emergent road network of the immediate post-annexation years provided the initial lineaments of a new space that was in the process of becoming dominant; a space transformed and mediated by technological advance; the more so when the telegraph, the post office, and the railways became full parts of the emergent megastructure of networked communication.

The transportation routes—the lines of road, the railway lines, the telegraph lines—were the new or improved arteries and veins that channelled and focused communication along corridors connecting places primarily of importance (at least initially) to the colonial regime. David Harvey's observation fully applies: 'those who command space can always control the politics of place even though, and it is a vital corollary, it takes control of some place to command space in the first instance.'[32] The same corridors were corridors of power for the colonial regime and their security important to the security of the Raj.[33] Thus, first-class and second-class roads had well-developed policing arrangements, while few structures better symbolized the importance of the railways to the Raj than Lahore's fortified railway station, opened in 1862.

Of course, many of the places deemed important to the British were significant locations within the Punjab long before the British took over. There is usually a good deal of inertia present in most spatial relationships. Amritsar, Lahore, Multan, and Peshawar became nodal locations for the British precisely because they were already important. Big urban areas became bigger and better connected with one another. Towns and cities maintained or increased long-standing trading connections although the specific routing of the connections could and did change.[34] Thus, what became more important after 1849 were the new (or improved) connecting corridors that channelled, quickened, and intensified transportation and hence also communication. Gone were the days when, as in Nadir Shah's advance through the Punjab towards Delhi, the front of his advancing army was probably three miles wide.[35] Increasingly gone, albeit by no means overnight (we are talking about processes of change extending over decades), were Banjaras whose pack animals could not easily be confined to a small corridor represented by a road or a cart track. The Punjab rivers other than the Indus, especially in the less navigable stretches north of Multan and Bahawalpur, became increasingly less used for river-borne transportation. The completion in 1878 (albeit with a ferry link across the Indus between Sukkur and Rohri until the Lansdowne Bridge opened in 1889) of the rail link between Karachi and the central Punjab heralded the end of the rivers as a significant part of the Punjab's transportation network.[36]

Arguably, therefore, what was most important to the communication revolution begun in 1849 was the improved or new spatial corridors between established places coupled with the increased intensity of communication (be it the bulk transportation of commodities, the rapid movement of a body of police, or the terse, almost instantaneous passage of a telegram) transported along those corridors.[37] The long-established nodal locations did, of course, benefit from all of this, but so did intermediate points, many hitherto insignificant and poorly connected, if at all, to the networks of transportation. One thinks of some district headquarter towns or even tahsil headquarters.

None of this is meant to suggest that the Punjab before British rule—or any part of India for that matter—was a static, immobile world with little trading or other connections between its various inhabited locations. It was not. Circulating groups of merchants, peddlers, and itinerant artisans unceasingly, albeit with a seasonal rhythm, crossed the countryside and made regular trips to the greater trading marts within a nexus of interconnections that stretched from Central Asia to the Gangetic valley and deep into the Deccan and south India. Hundis were issued at one location, transported, and cashed at another location many hundreds of miles distant. Banjaras transported a variety of commodities throughout the Subcontinent. Ordinary men, women, and children in considerable numbers attended melas and tirthas.[38]

Nonetheless, something did change because of British-imposed transportation and communication innovations. For the Punjab, the beginnings of those changes—cumulatively revolutionary in effect although implemented over many decades—date from the period 1849–70. By 1870, the outlines of the new space can be discerned; by the 1880s, some of the revolutionary consequences of what began primarily as a British effort to dominate space in the interests of securing and maintaining colonial rule had ramified out into many areas of Punjabi economic and cultural life. Print capitalism—with all that it meant for Hindu, Sikh, and Muslim movements of religious reform or revitalization, for literary movements in the many languages of the Punjab, and for communal disputes over languages—came formidably onto the scene and began to reconfigure the cultural space of Punjabis.[39] The 419 presses in business between 1880 and 1905 enumerated by Barrier and Wallace published newspapers (and other materials) in Urdu, English, Punjabi, Hindi, Persian, Arabic, and Sindi (Urdu predominating).[40] They existed because the transportation revolution made wider markets for printed materials possible. Some of these materials would have been transported via the postal mail—the same mail that enabled some Punjabis to stay in touch with one another whether they resided in the Punjab, elsewhere in India, or (increasingly) overseas.

The complexities of the transportation and communication revolution and the synergies that became available are well illustrated by a service introduced by the post office in 1877 and refined over the next decade.[41] This was Value Payable Post or VPP (known in Britain and North America as 'cash on delivery', i.e., COD) where the post office, for a small commission, collected the value of a shipment from its recipient and transmitted the payment to the sender, usually a commercial individual or firm. By the mid-1880s, after lengthy negotiations with the railway companies, large parcels could be sent by train with the invoice going by postal mail and the value of the train shipment collected by the post office on delivery of the invoice as VPP. 'The facility of receiving the published matter at the door-steps under the value payable system encouraged the people to purchase the published matter and newspapers'.[42] None of this required any new technology but it did require institutional innovation within the post office (with European practice as the model) and eventually cooperation between two institutionally separate components of the transportation megastructure: the railways and the postal service. The result of this small innovation was enhanced commerce and the increased circulation of information and ideas. In their manipulation of space, their compression of space, the British created space in which contestation and resistance could be nurtured. The presses enumerated by Barrier and Wallace had a better opportunity to succeed commercially and to make their various messages more accessible to more people. This happened primarily after 1870; but the basic elements, the railways and the post office, were in play by the early 1870s.

Swift and sure mail deliveries were, in turn, dependent on improvements in road and rail transport.[43] Symbolic of the recursive relationship was the fact that the crack express trains were often mail trains. Moreover, by 1864, specially designed mail sorting vans were in use, in which the mail was sorted while in transit by rail. A similarly recursive development occurred in 1883, when post offices began to be utilized as combined postal and telegraph offices, thus making telegraph facilities available in many smaller places where free-standing telegraph offices were not economically viable.[44]

At the same time and in quite a different dimension, by the early 1880s, the Punjab had become an important exporter of wheat to world markets. In 1881–2 the Punjab exported 2,262,425 cwt. of wheat (ten-fold greater than in 1877–8).[45] This 'great change in the rural economy' of the Punjab was a direct result of railway development and particularly the through connection to Karachi. The railways 'assured an easy access to previously inaccessible areas; from Pathankot to Peshawar or from Karnal to Kotri, all important fertile tracts were directly or indirectly brought into closer contact with Karachi, offering traders newer avenues of export of various agricultural commodities to the outside world'.[46] The electric telegraph was an important part of this process. It made price information quickly available and facilitated buying and selling, thus reducing transaction costs.

Thus arguably the most consequential of the new communication innovations was that which is represented in the woodcut, Archer's new machine, the railway. When Jean Deloche published in 1980 his magisterial two-volume study *La circulation en Inde avant la revolution des transport: I La voie de terre; II La voie d'eau*, he hinted at a subsequent transport revolution which became clear in the English translations (with added materials), titled respectively *Transport and Communications in India Prior to Steam Locomotion, 1: Land Transport* and *2: Water Transport*.[47] In his introduction to the first volume (p. 1), Deloche notes that despite the importance of roads in Mauryan and Mughal times, South Asia's transport revolution did not arrive until the mid-nineteenth century:

Previous to that time, natural agents were employed, the energy of man and animal on land, the motive force of wind on water; *afterwards*, steam power was implemented. The pace of transport means had remained unchanged since antiquity; then, within half a century, it was to increase to an unimaginable rate [emphasis in the original].

Although, as we have argued earlier, the railway must be placed within an emerging infrastructure of networked railways, roads, telegraph lines, and post offices, it did represent a technological breakthrough into a potentially new world (and again, to be tiresome, I must insist that this was a development that occurred over many decades) of exponentially improved transportation and communication: faster, more sure, and with much greater carrying capacity. The electric telegraph, for all of its importance (including its contribution to the safe running of the trains), did not have the same impact, although coupled with railway development, the telegraph was a vital part of the ongoing communication revolution that, among other consequences, helped to safeguard the Raj.[48] Moreover, from the late 1850s through World War I, railways received the most support from the colonial authorities. The assumption that railways were most important 'led to the cessation of any new road construction, and even to the abandonment of some of those already in existence...'.[49] W. S. Dorman states that after the railway from Delhi to Rohtak was completed, 'sections of the parallel road were deliberately dug up and rendered unfit for wheeled traffic'.[50] Hugh Trevaskis was more blunt. He wrote about the 'perverted political economy' of the early railway decades when roads were considered harmful when they 'competed with a wealth-producing railway, only such advantages as had a money value being then recognized as wealth...'.[51] The comparative neglect of roads until the demands for transportation generated by World War I changed official thinking emphasizes again how the emerging network of transportation routes was shaped by the assessments and perceptions of the colonial authorities.

What some call space–time compression and what Marx called the annihilation of space through time is captured in MacGeorge's late nineteenth-century estimate that the railway had reduced the subcontinent to one-twentieth of its former size. Places 400 miles apart in the 1840s had effectively become 20 miles apart c. 1900, as the railway sped a traveller or a shipment of commodities (possibly books or newspapers) across space in hours rather than days.[52] The 505 miles from Agra to Lahore requiring some 20 days of road travel in the pre-railway age required less than two days in the early years (1870s) of continuous rail service. Even the postal *dak* of the East India Company, with a continuous journey via successive relays, would have taken some five days to cover the same route in fair weather in the early 1850s.[53] Within the Punjab, in November of 1866 one could leave Multan by train at 7:30 a.m. and arrive at Lahore at 5:30 p.m.[54]

The effects of the space–time compression were experienced by many on all sides of the colonial situation. One of South Asia's long-standing popular cultural practices, pilgrimage, was affected. Sikhs, Hindus, and Muslims could attend a religious fair or reach a place of pilgrimage more easily and more quickly—day trips to sites that were more distant became possible. The SP&DR carried about one quarter of a million pilgrims during the 18 days of the Hardwar mela in April 1879.[55] Meanwhile,

Christian missionaries in the Punjab also found their lives significantly affected by the railways. They could travel faster and more frequently, and take furloughs to distant Britain, Canada, or the United States. Concurrently, the same railways made it easier to consult more frequently with church authorities, thus reducing the autonomy of the missionary in the field. Like British civil and military officials, the missionaries discovered that improved communication meant more control for their superiors.

The railway, therefore, was a symbol, a cause, and an instrument of the communication revolution.[56] It was also, crucially, an instrument of colonial control and of colonially inspired projects of progressive (as the British saw it) modernization.[57] Where the railway lines and workshops went, what equipment they used, and how they were staffed (for instance, European locomotive drivers as in the woodcut) were decided by the colonial authorities and by an SP&D Railway Company board of directors in London. The space produced in the Punjab after 1849 through a variety of colonial initiatives—and certainly not only in the realm of transportation and communication—was a space of colonial mastery and colonial masters. However, and crucially, other forces began to bubble up in the same space. Lefebvre reminds us that the rational techniques, plans, and programmes of the state provoke opposition. 'The violence of power is answered by the violence of subversion.'[58] The space of improved communication began to create spaces of engagement, contestation, and resistance to colonial authority or spaces of manoeuvre for those jockeying for position or advantage within communities (as between different visions of Sikhism) or between communities (as in expressions of Hindu–Muslim discord).[59]

As early as 1856, the *Lahore Chronicle* noted how the Grand Trunk Road, the electric telegraph, and 'rapid postal communication with the most important centres of intelligence' benefited the newspaper.[60] Jump ahead to 1880 and the printed output of the 419 presses identified by Barrier and Wallace included material, increasingly well-circulated, that advanced contestatory positions. However, following Chrish Bayly, we need to recognize that print capitalism 'was midwife to intellectual change, not in itself the essence of that change'.[61] We must also recognize the presence of accommodation within the new space: accommodation or the emergence of innovative hybrid cultural forms and practices were as much a part of emerging world as the fraught contestations driven by binary oppositions.

A new Punjab did begin to take shape after 1849 and that shaping was strongly influenced by the technological innovations introduced by the British. Those innovations, least of all at the level of artifact and machine, were not independent agents of change but, as part of systemically interrelated networks of transportation and communication driven by colonial interests and concerns, they did begin to change the Punjab. The outlines and effects of the new space produced in the Punjab—a space of colonial mastery mastered in considerable part by the new technologies of transportation and communication—were becoming evident around 1870 when the woodcut was created.

The unknown artist would have been well aware of those changes, of the new spatiality in which Punjabis lived. If he (most likely it was a male artist) lived in Lahore, he would have seen the ways in which British rule had begun to alter the cityscape. He would have seen the effects of the SP&DR and its workshops on land-use patterns as a colonial Lahore with its civil lines and cantonment grew up around the old walled city.[62] The railway was both a magnet and a divider: the tracks divided while the station and workshops at Naulakha (the workshops were moved to Moghulpura during 1910–14) were strong magnets that attracted not only railway workers and their families—many of whom, especially Europeans and Eurasians, lived in railway colonies adjacent to the lines and the workshops, but also some small businesses whose customers included the railway company, railway travellers, and railway workers. It was, in fact, the railway workshops and the station, along with the cantonment and the civil lines, which represented the nodal points around which colonial Lahore grew.[63] As early as 1866, a Lahore newspaper commented on the filling in of the hitherto largely empty area between Anarkuli and Mian Mir and stated: 'The Railway, an entirely new and separate Department, with its large staff, and bringing with it an enormous following of workmen and their families, filled up another great gap in the new site.'[64]

Possibly, the artist travelled by train. About 284,806 passengers, not including infants, reportedly travelled between Lahore and Amritsar between the line opening in early 1862 and late January 1863.[65] Perhaps the artist had been in one of the carriages already 'brimful of their human freight' waiting at the Lahore station at around 3:40 p.m. in June of 1862 for the 4:00 p.m. departure to Amritsar. The crowded carriages 20 minutes before departure time led a writer in the English-language newspaper the *Lahore Chronicle* to observe: 'people are learning punctuality, that time and tide in the shape of that grim monster, the locomotive—aptly called "John Lawrence"—waits for no man, leastways for Rambuksh stopping to take a whiff of his hookah.'[66] Or perhaps the woodcut's creator had been among the Sikhs who took the train from Lahore to Amritsar in early 1862? Robert Cust, a British administrator wrote: 'our railway is now in full force, and Amritsar is only one hour and a half distant. 1300 Sikhs went off to bathe in the sacred tank on one day last week: the people thoroughly enjoy it. I may yet see Lahore and Calcutta 1200 miles connected: only 250 miles are unprovided for.'[67] A little over a year later the SP&DR ran special trains from Amritsar to carry people to the Bhaddarkal mela at Niazbeg, some seven miles southeast of Lahore.[68]

Yet again the artist might have been one of those who took in the sights at the Amritsar or the Lahore station simply to see the fascinating new machines or to witness a ceremony at the station involving the coming or going of some dignitary. Perhaps he was at the Lahore station among the 'myriad of natives of all kinds, eager to witness the novel spectacle' that marked the official inauguration of the Lahore–Amritsar section of the Punjab Railway on 1 March 1862?[69] Or perhaps he witnessed, or was told about, the princes, chiefs, and British officials of the Punjab gathered in all their finery (including the young Raja of Patiala, 'blazing in diamonds') to welcome John Lawrence, by then Governor-General of India, at the Lahore station on 14 October 1864.[70] The railway station had become a public space of considerable importance both in the ordinary and extraordinary lives of Punjabis. It was a liminal space of arrival or departure for dignitaries and for common folk alike. The station, its interior, and its forecourt was a brand new space, simultaneously lived, perceived, and conceived.

Meanwhile, our woodcut artist might well have been reading (or have read to him) one of the vernacular newspapers—perhaps the *Panjab-i-Akhbar* or the *Koh-i-Nur*—whose pages in the later 1860s and early 1870s often contained reports about the railways.[71] The newspaper stories detailed accidents, incidents of corruption, poor conditions at stations or in the carriages, lack of separate accommodations for female travellers, mistreatment of Indians by railway officials, the failure to provide signs and time-tables in Urdu or Hindi, and on through various other blameworthy acts, committed or omitted. Complaints about the operation of the railways far outweighed praise but, complaints or not, they represented a significant engagement on the part of opinion-making Punjabi society with the new form of transportation. By 1870, people were riding the rails in considerable number; railways had a significant presence in their lives—directly experienced for a growing number and vicariously by many more.

The railway station was an easily identifiable example of a new space created in the Punjab after 1849. It was a highly visible, concrete representation of the new Punjab that was in the process of becoming. What we need to recognize was the emerging presence of a new space of communication and transportation throughout the Punjab, indeed throughout India and even globally.[72] Part of this new space had a physical presence—the roads, rails, telegraph lines, and so on that provided the technological infrastructure of the new space discussed in this chapter— but its power came from its spatially transforming use, from the flows of ideas, people, and commodities along the new or improved transport corridors. It was a produced space that initially strengthened colonial authority and subsequently enabled contestation and subversion. Spatial practice, representations of space, and representational spaces changed, but at the heart of the new Punjab was a quantitative and qualitative change in the volume, intensity, speed, and extent of communication and circulation: be it of ideas (often conveyed physically in newspapers or letters, by the post office, using road and railed transportation), commodities, or people, with the latter being everything from soldiers and police securing the Raj to those Punjabis who opposed the British and/or other Punjabis.

The woodcut hints at some of this, as do Archer's comments. Sometimes a representation can provide a historian with the beginnings of a way in or a way to a new destination, an improved understanding. The train in the woodcut waits to depart from its station just as the various contributions to this volume represent new departures and new destinations for future scholarship.

This volume is a collection of chapters contributed in honour of Hew McLeod in the way we knew best, namely considering new directions in Sikh and Punjab studies and to look at the Punjab and at the Sikhs in fresh and more illuminating ways. The departing train can be read as symbolic of the goal of this volume. We need to explore further the departures, the new directions, presented in this volume. However, I am convinced that revolutionary changes in transportation and communication from the mid-nineteenth century forward should be understood as a necessary precondition, a necessary if not sufficient cause, for many of the other momentous changes the Punjab has experienced in the last 150 years. Perhaps some future historian will add land-line telephones, radio,

movies, television, the internet, and wireless telephones to the production
and reproduction of Punjabi space: space which, as some contributions in
this volume make clear, is now worldwide and within which the processes
of contestation, appropriation, and accommodation continue on a wider
and more rapid basis among Punjabis and between Punjabis and their
adopted countrymen and countrywomen.

Notes

Acknowledgements: I am indebted to the sponsors and organizers of the
'New Directions in Sikh Studies/Punjab Studies' symposium for inviting me to
participate and for the splendid local arrangements they provided. I am
particularly indebted to Tony Ballantyne for his exemplary coordination of the
symposium and to Professor W. H. McLeod, without whom there would have
been no symposium and for whom, and for Margaret McLeod, I travelled to New
Zealand. My transportation costs from distant Canada were generously supported
by a University of Manitoba/Social Science and Humanities Research Council
(SSHRC) Travel Grant augmented by funds kindly provided by the Faculty of
Arts and the Department of History at the University of Manitoba. Research
for this chapter was supported by a SSHRC Research Grant. This revised version
of my paper benefitted from comments provided by symposium participants.

1. The woodcut, 305 × 460 mm black and white, is held as Item 93 in the
J. Lockwood Kipling Collection at the Victoria and Albert Museum (V&A),
London. I am indebted to W. H. McLeod for informing me about the Lockwood
Kipling Collection. The Collection was assembled by Kipling during his tenure
in Lahore as Principal of the Mayo School of Art and Curator of the Central
Museum (1875–93) and donated to the V&A by Kipling's famous son Rudyard
in 1917. Thirty-one of the roughly 230 items in the collection are discussed in
W. H. McLeod, *Popular Sikh Art* (Delhi: Oxford University Press, 1991), pp. 20–
24 and *passim*. The woodcut is reproduced by permission of the V&A.

2. W. G. Archer, *Paintings of the Sikhs* (London: HMSO, 1966). The woodcut
appears on p. 274. Other reproductions appear in Michael Satow and Ray
Desmond, *Railways of the Raj* (New York and London: New York University
Press, 1980), pp. 38–9, in an elongated, single-level format—the V&A version is
bi-level as above—and in Ian J. Kerr, 'Representation and Representations of the
Railways of Colonial and Post-Colonial South Asia', *Modern Asian Studies* 37, 2
(May 2003), p. 318.

3. W. G. Archer, *Paintings of the Sikhs*, pp. 69–70.

4. There is an alternative explanation for the production of this woodcut. It
could have been a limited production for a British patron or patrons. European
examples and British preferences and demands became a part of the production
and marketing of a range of artistic objects across north India in the nineteenth

century. See W. H. McLeod, *Popular Sikh Art*, pp. 16–18, and Mildred and W.G. Archer, *Indian Painting for the British 1770–1880* (Oxford: Oxford University Press, 1955). However, Archer treats the train woodcut as a production for the Indian market. As I argue later in this chapter, there are good reasons to believe a train in a station would have been popular with Punjabis and Punjabi artists circa 1870.

5. W. G. Archer, *Paintings of the Sikhs*, p. 70.

6. I partially quote Marx's epigrammatic summary of the problem of structure and agency: 'Men make their own history, but they do not make it just as they please; they do not make it under circumstances chosen by themselves, but under circumstances directly encountered, given, and transmitted from the past'. Karl Marx, *The Eighteenth Brumaire* (1852), partially reprinted in Robert C. Tucker (ed.), *The Marx-Engels Reader*, (New York: W. W. Norton & Co., second edition, 1978), p. 595. The statement goes on with the famous and metaphorically powerful: 'The tradition of all the dead generations weighs like a nightmare on the brain of the living.'

7. For a stimulating set of papers discussing the pros and cons of the more general issue of technological determinism, see the contributions in Merritt Roe Smith and Leo Marx (eds), *Does Technology Drive History? The Dilemma of Technological Determinism* (Cambridge: Massachusetts Institute of Technology (MIT) Press, 1994).

8. This sentence identifies me as an adherent of the social constructionist approach to technology: an approach that has variant forms and among whose practitioners are many, including myself, who accept that in many historical instances we can read technology as recursively socially constructed and society shaping. Two edited volumes usefully explore, with case studies, the social constructionist approaches to technology: Wiebe E. Bijker, Thomas P. Hughes, and Trevor Pinch (eds), *The Social Construction of Technological Systems: New Directions in the Sociology and History of Technology* (Cambridge: MIT Press, hardback, 1987; paperback edition, 1989) and Wiebe E. Bijker and John Law (eds), *Shaping Technology/Building Society: Studies in Sociotechnical Change* (Cambridge: MIT Press, hardback, 1992; paperback edition, 1994).

9. Bernward Joerges, 'Large Technical Systems: Concepts and Issues', Renate Mayntz and Thomas P. Hughes (eds), *The Development of Large Technical Systems* (Frankfurt am Main: Campus Verlag, 1988), p. 24.

10. A major contributor among historians to the literature on technological systems is Thomas Hughes. See Thomas Hughes, 'The Evolution of Large Technological Systems', Bijker, Hughes, and Pinch (eds), *The Social Construction of Technological Systems*, pp. 51–82.

11. British efforts to police Punjabis after 1849 were attempts at mastery that overlap in some ways with this chapter. Policing illustrates well British successes and limitations as colonial masters. Particularly where mobile segments

of Punjabi society were the issue—often represented by the British as dangerous criminal elements—the British techniques of surveillance and control involved the manipulation of space. The British wanted to constrict and observe better the space within which the 'dangerous' groups circulated. Read Andrew J. Major, 'State and Criminal Tribes in Colonial Punjab: Surveillance, Control and Reclamation of the "Dangerous Classes"', *Modern Asian Studies* 31, 3 (July 1999), pp. 657–88; and Arnaud Sauli, 'Circulation and Authority: Police, Public Space and Territorial Control in Punjab 1861–1920', Claude Markovits, Jacques Pouchepadass, and Sanjay Subrahmanyam (eds), *Society and Circulation: Mobile People and Itinerant Cultures in South Asia 1750–1950* (Delhi: Permanent Black, 2003), pp. 215–39.

12. '...the period of British rule in the Punjab was dominated by three major themes: political entrenchment, revenue extraction, and military requirements.' Imran Ali, *The Punjab under Imperialism, 1885–1947* (Princeton: Princeton University Press, 1988), p. 5.

13. I borrow the phrase 'technologies of power' from Bernard S. Cohn and Nicholas B. Dirks, 'Beyond the Fringe: The Nation State, Colonialism, and The Technologies of Power', *Journal of Historical Sociology* 1, 2 (June 1988), pp. 224–9. Their concern is primarily with cultural forms of power, although it seems to me that more material forms deserve equal if not greater attention in colonial settings. I am sometimes moved to quote a pungent observation of the young Alfred Lyall—an observation he made in 1863 when he was stationed near Agra, not all that far from the Punjab. Lyall wrote to his mother on 30 July 1863: 'there is nothing real in our system but the British bayonet.' OIOC, MSS. Eur. F/132/4.

14. David Gilmartin, 'Scientific Empire and Imperial Science: Colonialism and Irrigation Technology in the Indus Basin', *Journal of Asian Studies* 53, 4 (November 1994), p. 1129.

15. The more extensive British embrace of a developmental strategy in the Punjab began with the creation of canal colonies in western Punjab starting in the 1880s. See Imran Ali, *The Punjab under Imperialism*. The railways were a necessary precondition for the commercial success of the canal colonies. Without railways, the massive agricultural production of the colonies could not have been marketed effectively.

16. OIOC, Government of India, Home Department Progs, Public, December 1867, 'Minute by the Hon'ble G. N. Taylor, relating to a tour from Simla through the Kangra Valley to Umritsur and Lahore', dated 10 December 1867.

17. The following information regarding roads, railways, post offices, and telegraph comes from Y. B. Mathur, *British Administration of the Punjab 1849–1875* (Delhi: Surjeet Book Depot, n.d., c. 1973), pp. 112, 124, and 128–9.

18. David Harvey, 'Between Space and Time: Reflections on the Geographical

Imagination', reprinted in Trevor Barnes and Derek Gregory (eds), *Reading Human Geography: The Poetics and Politics of Inquiry* (London: Arnold, 1997), pp. 256–79.

19. The revolutionary potential (realization is a more complex issue) of some technological change is accepted by theorists of different ideological persuasions although rarely in a uni-causal, deterministic way. Joseph Schumpeter and Ernest Mandel, for example, acknowledged the revolutionary potential of technology under certain socio-economic conditions.

20. Imbedded capital (as in railways) as a source of inertia is discussed in Robert A. Dodgshon, *Society in Time and Space: A Geographical Perspective on Change* (Cambridge: Cambridge University Press, 1998), especially pp. 14–6 and chapter 5.

21. Other theorists have similar formulations but here I draw upon the vocabulary and concepts of Edward Soja, *Postmodern Geographies. The Reassertion of Space in Critical Social Theory* (London: Verso, 1989), p. 79 *et passim*.

22. Henri Lefebvre, *The Production of Space*, Donald Nicholson-Smith (trans.) (Oxford: Blackwell, 1991), pp. 26 and 164–8. Lefebvre also writes, p. 266: 'Social space is multifaceted: abstract and practical, immediate and mediated.' Central to Lefebvre's analysis of social space (which he distinguishes from mental space and physical space) is his conceptual triad comprised of spatial practices (perceived spaces), representations of space (conceived spaces), and representational spaces (lived spaces). See *Production of Space*, p. 33 *et passim*.

23. David Harvey, 'Between Space and Time', p. 258.

24. Henri Lefebvre, *Production of Space*, p. 165.

25. Y. B. Mathur, *British Administration of the Punjab*, p. 14.

26. All material in this paragraph comes from *General Report Upon the Administration of the Punjab Proper, for the Years 1849–50 and 1850–51; Being the Two First Years after Annexation* (Calcutta: 1853), pp. 131 and 138–40. Hereafter I cite this item as *PAR 1849–51*.

27. *PAR 1849–51*, p. 131.

28. Rajit K. Mazumder, *The Indian Army and the Making of the Punjab* (Delhi: Permanent Black, 2003), chapter 1.

29. Clive Dewey, 'Some Consequences of Military Expenditure in British India. The Case of the Upper Sind Sagar Doab, 1849–1947', Clive J. Dewey (ed.), *Arrested Development in India* (Riverdale, Maryland: The Riverdale Company, 1988), pp. 93–169. The development and populating of the canal colonies in ways designed to consolidate the loyalties of those Punjabi groups from whom soldiers were most actively recruited is a theme explored in Imran Ali, *The Punjab under Imperialism*.

30. Clive Dewey, Arrested Development, p. 139.

31. Ibid., p. 140.

32. David Harvey, *The Condition of Postmodernity: An Enquiry into the Origins of Cultural Change* (Oxford: Blackwell, 1990), p. 234.

33. O'Dwyer, a later Lieutenant-Governor (1912–19) of the Punjab understood this well. Sir Michael O'Dwyer, *India As I Knew It 1885–1925* (London: Constable and Company, 1925), p. 295 *et passim* makes mention of the attacks on railway lines and railway stations in 1919. O'Dwyer believed that 'the persistent attempts on the railway and telegraph lines through the whole length of the Punjab from Delhi to Attock, showed more than anything else a prearranged design to immobilise our troops and isolate the main centres of rebellion'.

34. W. S. Dorman. 'Highways in the Punjab, Past and Future', *Minutes of Proceedings of the Punjab Engineering Congress, 1919*, 2 (Lahore: 1919), pp. 7–12.

35. K. Mitchell, 'Development of Communications in the Punjab', *Proceedings*, (Punjab Educational Conference, 1926), p. 303.

36. Himadri Banerjee, *Agrarian Society of the Punjab 1849–1901* (New Delhi: Manohar, 1982), p. 48.

37. Let me emphasize again that this was a slow process of improvement. Most roads in the Punjab at the end of the 1850s were still in miserable condition. Only a few miles of road, almost all of it the Grand Trunk Road, were metalled. Telegraph lines, however, were developed quickly and entirely through government financing and management, driven by a clear appreciation of their political and military value to the Raj. See Saroj Ghose, 'Commercial Needs and Military Necessities: The Telegraph in India', Roy MacLeod and Deepak Kumar (eds), *Technology and the Raj: Western Technology and Technical Transfers to India, 1700–1947* (New Delhi: Sage Publications, 1995), pp. 153–76. Ghose makes a firmer distinction between transportation systems for colonial India (e.g., railways) and communication systems (e.g., telegraphs) than I do.

38. Recent efforts to emphasize the mobile, socially and economically circulating dimensions of South Asia—and to show how some older patterns persisted into the later nineteenth century and beyond—are to be found in the contributions in Claude Markovits, Jacques Pouchepadass, and Sanjay Subrahmanyam (eds), *Society and Circulation*. Particularly relevant to this paragraph is the contribution by Neeladri Bhattacharya, 'Predicaments of Mobility: Peddlers and Itinerants in Nineteenth-Century Northwestern India', pp. 163–214.

39. A perceptive statement of the impact of the technology of printing on Muslims—and the limits of that impact—is to be found in Francis Robinson, 'Technology and Religious Change: Islam and the Impact of Print', *Modern Asian Studies* 27, 1 (1993), pp. 229–51.

40. N. Gerald Barrier and Paul Wallace, *The Punjab Press 1880–1905* (East Lansing: Research Committee on the Punjab and Asian Studies Center, Michigan State University, 1970).

41. Mohini Lal Mazumdar, *The Imperial Post Offices of British India (1837–1914)*, 1 (Calcutta: Phila Publications, 1990), pp. 293–9.

42. H. Noor Ahmed, *India Post Through Ages: A Saga of Communications* (Alur/Kurnool: Postal History Society India, 1996), p. 64.

43. It should be noted that the application of new technologies to improved transportation in South Asia resulted in large numbers of people losing their jobs. In the Punjab, A. Latifi tells us: 'The builder of boats was important before the railways killed river-navigation, and his trade with it.' A. Latifi, *The Industrial Punjab: A Survey of Facts, Conditions and Possibilities* (Bombay and Calcutta: Longmans, Green & Co. for the Punjab Government, 1911), p. 217. Postal runners, for example, were let go as rail or improved road transport took over their functions. Banjaras were increasingly squeezed out. Ironically, we find that many of the porters at the railway stations in and around Mumbai are Banjaras (or Vanjaris). Read Dennis Weitering, 'Carrying the Load Together: Mumbai Railway Coolies and their Quest for Labour, Income and Social Security' (MA thesis in cultural anthropology, University of Nijmegen, 2003).

44. Krishnalal Shridharani, *Story of Indian Telegraphs: A Century of Progress* (New Delhi: Posts and Telegraphs Department, 1953), pp. 55–6. The complete administrative amalgamation of the two departments took place in 1912. The Imperial Post Office began to experiment with rudimentary telephone service in the early 1880s.

45. Himadri Banerjee, *Agrarian Society of the Punjab*, p. 50. A similar if more broad-brush assessment of the effects of railways on the economic development of the Punjab is to be found in H. Calvert, *The Wealth and Welfare of the Punjab* (Lahore: Civil and Military Gazette Press, second edition, 1936), especially chapter 6.

46. Himadri Banerjee, *Agrarian Society of the Punjab*, p. 50.

47. Translated from the French by John Walker (New Delhi: Oxford University Press, 1993–4).

48. The role telegraph messages from Ambala and Delhi played in helping to secure the Punjab for the British in 1857 is well known. Dalhousie's reference to the telegraph as 'such an engine of power' proved to be on the mark. See Krishnalal Shridharani, *Story of Indian Telegraphs*, pp. 19–23. See also Mohini Lal Mazumder, *The Imperial Post Offices*, p. 59.

49. W. S. Dorman, 'Highways in the Punjab, Past and Future', p. 13.

50. Ibid.

51. Hugh Kennedy Trevaskis, *The Land of the Five Rivers* (Oxford: Oxford University Press, 1928), p. 225.

52. G. W. MacGeorge, *Ways and Works in India: Being an Account of Public Works in that Country from the Earliest Times, up to the Present Day* (Westminster: Archibald Constable and Company, 1894), p. 221.

53. Or so I infer from the fascinating set of tables in Jean Deloche, *Transport and Communications* 1, pp. 280–6 and accompanying text.

54. 'Punjab Railway Time Table', *Lahore Chronicle*, 3 November 1866, p. 751.

55. David Ross, *Military Transport by Indian Railways* (Lahore: Sind, Punjab and Delhi Railway Company's Press, 1883), p. 102.

56. Apart from some discussion in more general works, we have very little writing specifically about railway development in the Punjab, although many are the works—some cited in these footnotes—that briefly highlight the importance of the railways to the modern history of the Punjab. There is the semi-popular P. S. A. Berridge, *Couplings to the Khyber: The Story of the North Western Railway* (New York: Augustus M. Kelley, 1969) and two brief notices: G. S. Khosla, 'The Growth of the Railway System in the Punjab', Harbans Singh and N. Gerald Barrier (eds), *Punjab Past and Present. Essay in Honour of Dr. Ganda Singh* (Patiala: Punjabi University, 1976), pp. 283–90, and Narjeet Kaur, 'Railways in Punjab 1849–1947', *Punjab Past and Present* 24, 2 (October 1990), pp. 309–18.

57. Ian J. Kerr, 'Representation and Representations' for a discussion of railways, progress, and the British 'civilizing mission' in later nineteenth-century India.

58. Henri Lefebvre, *Production of Space*, p. 23. I understand 'violence' in this context to encompass physical and non-physical forms of subversion. The nineteenth and twentieth century histories of the Punjab provide ample evidence of both.

59. N. Gerald Barrier, *Banned: Controversial Literature and Political Control in British India 1907–1947* (Columbia: University of Missouri Press, 1974) provides a careful examination of the British attempts to control material deemed to be seditious.

60. *Lahore Chronicle*, 30 August 1856, p. 557.

61. C. A. Bayly, *Empire and Information: Intelligence Gathering and Social Communication in India, 1780–1870* (Cambridge: Cambridge University Press, 1960), p. 374. Because I am most interested in the material underpinnings, the infrastructural components of the communication revolution, I simplify other dimensions of these complex phenomena. See C. A. Bayly, *Empire and Information*, especially chapter 10 and his 'Conclusion'.

62. This paragraph borrows from Ian J. Kerr, 'The Railway Workshops of Lahore and Their Employees: 1863–1930', Surjit Dulai and Arthur Helweg, *Punjab in Perspective: Proceedings of the Research Committee on Punjab Conference, 1987* (East Lansing: Asian Studies Center, Michigan State University, 1991), especially pp. 68–9.

63. Grenfell Rudduck, *Towns and Villages of Pakistan: A Study* (Karachi: Manager of Publications, 1964), pp. 117–20. M. Mushtaq, 'Lahore: Major Urban Regions', *Pakistan Geographical Review* 22, 1 (January 1967), pp. 24 and 32–3. This argument is supported by the cartographic record—for example, a comparison of the 'Plan of the City and Environs of Lahore showing the Civil Station of Anarkulee and the Cantonment of Meean Meer', c. 1869, with 'Lahore and Surrounding Country', c. 1912, which are to be found in the map collection of OIOC.

64. *Lahore Chronicle*, 21 March 1866, p. 180.

65. *Lahore Chronicle*, 31 January 1863, p. 68.

66. *Lahore Chronicle*, 18 June 1862, p. 388.

67. R.N. Cust to his mother, dated Lahore 6 April 1862, Cust Papers 1828–66. Royal Commonwealth Society Collection, University Library, Cambridge.

68. *Lahore Chronicle*, 28 May 1863, p. 340. The *Gazetteer of the Lahore District 1883–4* (Calcutta: Punjab Government, c. 1884), p. 60, describes Bhaddarkal as a festival held in June to honour the Devi. Some 60,000 people from Lahore, Amritsar, and neighbouring villages attended. Pilgrims became an important part of railway traffic from the inception of the railways in the Subcontinent. For more on railways and pilgrims, read Ian J. Kerr, 'Reworking a Popular Religious Practice: The Effects of Railways on Pilgrimage in 19th and 20th Century South Asia', Ian J. Kerr (ed.), *Railways in Modern India* (New Delhi: Oxford University Press, 2001), pp. 304–27.

69. *Lahore Chronicle*, 5 March 1862, p. 149.

70. 'The Durbar at Lahore', *The Intelligencer*, Vol. I new series (February 1865), p. 38.

71. For example the *Koh-i-Nur* of 13 May 1865, 18 March 1871, and 15 July 1871 and the *Panjab-i-Akhbar* of 27 September 1867, 17 September 1869, and 5 August 1871. These items plus a good many others can be found in the government's weekly translations from the vernacular newspapers designed to 'inform' the colonial government about Indian opinion. My extracts come from the series *Native News Reports*, Punjab, located in the National Archives of India, New Delhi, although OIOC has some of the same of records.

72. One can propose a variety of metaphors to capture the 'shape' of the new space. See Tony Ballantyne, 'Rereading the Archive and Opening up the Nation-State: Colonial Knowledge in South Asia (and Beyond)', Antoinette Burton (ed.), *After the Imperial Turn: Thinking with and through the Nation* (Durham: Duke University Press, 2003), pp. 102–21. Ballantyne's preference is for the 'complex web'.

Punjab and the Sikhs
through the Prism of Plague

Ian Catanach

Punjab is not my special field of academic interest. I have spent little time there; I lack the long and direct experience of landscape and people which so often makes for the writing of good history. And I do not know Punjabi; I am therefore unable to participate in the important debates about religious texts that have characterized so much of the very best recent scholarship on the homeland of that language. My contribution to this volume is that of an 'outsider'. It came about largely as a result of a long association with Hew McLeod, as a friend and as a fellow New Zealander, but also as a fellow historian of South Asia.

It is in that last capacity that I attempt here—while remaining, perforce, an 'outsider'—to make some contribution to what is now a very strongly developed (though perhaps slightly inward-looking) regional academic discourse.[1]

It will be evident that, as a historian of South Asia, I am by no means averse to the introduction of methods, and a little 'theory', from other disciplines. As an outsider, I sometimes think that historical study of the Punjab could be more concerned than it has been of recent years with social and economic questions, and, perhaps, with what has been called the 'subaltern' element. But these are largely matters of degree, of emphasis. Ultimately, I remain, with Hew McLeod, essentially an 'old-fashioned historian',[2] concerned very much with 'what actually happened'. Here and there in this chapter, I suggest a few directions that the study of the Punjab might take. But I do so quite tentatively, conscious continually of my 'outsider' status and conscious also, very often, that the directions suggested are, in fact, not entirely 'new' and certainly not, in the broad spectrum of historical study, especially radical.

The hunch that led to this chapter was the notion that the late nineteenth- and early twentieth-century history of plague in the Punjab could present us with a prism. Through this prism, we could view a society—and particularly the Sikh element within that society—at a significant time in its evolution. I began by considering the possibility, indeed the probability, that the considerable mortality caused by plague gave a severe social, economic, and psychological wrench to the Punjab at this time. This wrench might well have exposed to the historian's gaze the already existing, but normally not especially visible, tendencies and stresses in a past society. And the wrench could also have itself created new tendencies and stresses. Perhaps, I thought, some of the important developments in the religious and political realms that took place in the Punjab at this time could be linked, in ways hitherto unnoticed, with the phenomenon of the plague.

I had, in fact, used a similar approach in the study of Indian plague on several earlier occasions. One use of such an approach involved an examination of South Asian Muslims—including, to some extent, Punjabi Muslims—under the impact of the disease.[3] A corpus of work, largely French, on the plague in medieval and early modern times and on the European cholera epidemic of the nineteenth century, was available as a model.[4] It was true that a historian of sleeping sickness in the northern Congo in the earlier twentieth century had sounded a note of caution about such an approach. Crises provoked by epidemics, she warned early in her study, are essentially aberrations, and aberrations may not readily provide indications of the norm. Nevertheless, Maryinez Lyons still found that the study of a society in a situation of crisis caused by epidemic disease was, in the end, an extremely useful exercise.[5] I was also encouraged by the discovery that, in the course of a very valuable essay, Ian Kerr had suggested that the influenza of 1918–19 could well have had a 'psychological' effect on rural Sikhs. This, in turn, could have been part of the reason for the rise of the Akalis in the 1920s.[6] If that were so, I thought, surely there was reason to look more closely at the plague of earlier years. According to official statistics, influenza killed somewhat under a million Punjabis, mainly in about three months in 1918. Again, according to official statistics, in 1907, the year of the greatest mortality from plague, that disease took the lives of under seven hundred thousand in the province, also mainly in about three months. The ghoulish totals are different, but they are not incomparable. A more important difference is probably to be found in the fact that 1907 was preceded by a decade of bitter experience of the plague, whereas the influenza of 1918 was a sudden and apparently new phenomenon.

I have to admit that my investigations into the effects of plague on Punjabis—and particularly on Sikhs as distinct from Punjabis in general—have not yielded quite all that I had hoped for. Nevertheless, it is, I think, worth detailing here the path and the results of at least some of those investigations. Our students and our students' students may be able to take some matters further, possibly much further.

* * *

Especially in the early days of the plague in the Punjab, there were problems about identifying the disease. On occasion, furthermore, members of the lowest levels of the official statistics gathering apparatus—the *patwaris*, the *lambardars*, and, in particular, the village *chaukidars*—who kept the 'dirty tattered affair[s]'[7] that were the village registers of deaths were themselves among the victims of the disease. Nevertheless, there seems to be at present no good reason to doubt that in a period of slightly over twenty years—from the province's two earliest cases in April 1897 (as it happened, in a Jullundur village in which a large proportion of the population was Jat Sikh)[8] to the end of World War I in 1918—plague killed about three million Punjabis. In terms of absolute numbers of deaths from plague and in terms of numbers of deaths per unit of its population, Punjab, at this time, was the hardest hit of all the Indian provinces.

As we have seen, the disease peaked in the Punjab in 1907. In other words, it peaked (though the fact is often hardly noticed) in a year of considerable political agitation. This was the time when many of the British in the province convinced themselves that there was an urban-based conspiracy against them of considerable proportions, with tentacles stretching out into the countryside. They were then forced to beat something of a retreat in the face of growing scepticism in the highest ranks of the Government of India and the British government at home.[9] Plague also happened to peak at a time when, mainly under the impact of the Tat Khalsa elements within the Singh Sabhas, the beliefs and the practice of many who could call themselves 'Sikh' were (so, at least, it is frequently supposed) undergoing strenuous change. One of the tasks of a later section of this chapter will be to consider whether there were, possibly, significant links—provided especially, perhaps, by members of the Sikh community—between two phenomena: the plague and the rural elements of the unrest of 1907. But 1907 cannot be seen in isolation from what had taken place in, at the least, the decade or so before. In a plague-oriented perspective on Sikhism in those years, the pressures towards uniformity and distinctiveness that were generated at this time by elements within the Singh Sabhas remain as an important part of the picture, but, it will be argued here, certainly not the only part.

In the Punjab, the plague tended to concentrate much of its wrath on the central districts and the adjacent submontane and Canal Colony areas. Peculiarities of temperature and humidity have long been recognized as a large part of the explanation for this state of affairs.[10] But they do not provide a total explanation for the fact that within the plague-stricken areas of the province, and as distinct from all of the rest of India, the disease was primarily a rural, rather than an urban, phenomenon.[11] It is possible that another part of the explanation for this state of affairs is to be found in the vigorous expansion of irrigation that had been occurring over several decades in many parts of the rural Punjab. On the whole it can be said that it was such parts of the Punjab—which were, of course, much wider in extent than the so-called Canal Colonies—that suffered most from plague.

Rodents that move about underground and have much to do with the spread of the zootic plague—and, ultimately, the human plague—are attracted by water. A gradual rise in the water table in an area may well have had some bearing on the spread of the plague in southern Russia in the late eighteenth and early nineteenth centuries.[12] Certainly, recent work in Rajasthan has indicated how the advent of large-scale irrigation and the consequent appearance of lush green crops can bring about immense changes in rodent ecology. Plague-affected wild rodents and domestic rodents not hitherto affected by the plague can be brought into contact. Rodent mothers can have litters of fifteen instead of five.[13] Matters such as these are normally quite unfamiliar to the historian, of whatever stripe. There may be some need for change.

But human beings must undoubtedly remain the historian's chief concern. In the Punjab of the late nineteenth century and early twentieth century, the plague-prone areas happened to be, to quite a large extent as a result of the population movements and the conquests of earlier times, the zones of greatest Sikh concentration. Within those zones, furthermore, the plague was found more especially in larger villages with compact populations,[14] and Sikh-dominated villages were quite commonly of this variety.[15] More than that, on the purely statistical front, we cannot easily say. We simply have no way of telling with precision how many of those who died from plague were 'Sikh'—however that community is defined. At the time when the plague was at its height, Census officials and others, under pressure from the Tat Khalsa members of the Singh Sabhas, were beginning to give Sikhs a separate official identity.[16] But in death, Sikhs were still, more often than not, listed in the statistics as 'Hindu'. Amongst all communities, the plague attacked the healthy as much as it attacked the unhealthy, the rich virtually as much as the poor. And it struck particularly at adults in the prime of life.

There is one further observation about the Punjab plague that must be made here. To a greater extent than in all of the rest of India except the United Provinces, the plague in the Punjab was more a disease of females than of males. In the Punjab, 12 women died of the plague for every 10 men dying of the disease.[17] But at the commencement of the plague era in the Punjab, there were already markedly fewer females than males in the total population. Indeed, for reasons that we need not go into here, the proportion was lower in the Punjab—especially, quite possibly, amongst Sikhs—than in most of the remainder of the country.[18] The predominance of women in the province's plague mortality figures is, therefore, all the more striking. But it is also striking that in those verbal accounts of the impact of the disease in the Punjab that survive, while women are not entirely absent, they figure almost incidentally. From the vivid detail of one exceptional document, we learn of a married woman who goes to see her family in another village. The second village happens to be hit by the plague. 'As is the custom amongst natives', she returns with presents of clothes, and these, in 1898, are thought to be the carriers of plague to the woman's home village.[19] We learn, too—but only in passing—that Thalu has nursed Devi Chand;[20] that a victim, Attri, has visited Mehtab Kaur and washed her clothes for her;[21] that the female neighbours of a woman suffering from the plague—a Muslim, as it happens—have visited her to 'touch the wound with the "hem of their garment" so as to diffuse the pain over several persons';[22] that a Chamar woman has 'act[ed] as hakim';[23] that a leechwoman has drawn blood from an affected person.[24] A similar report dating from the following year refers to the visit of an Arain woman to another village in order to 'take part in the weeping' for a plague victim.[25] There is no further inquiry into such matters; it is simply taken for granted that women should visit the sick, nurse them, perhaps attempt to cure them, and, very often, mourn them publicly when they die.

Women rarely appear in the narrative record, even in passing, as what they were most often: victims—although a fairly early official report does note that 'women were almost always the first persons affected'.[26] They certainly do not appear in the Punjab as moulding, or even helping to mould, people's public responses to plague in the fields of 'religion' or 'politics', at least as those fields are conventionally envisaged by present-day historians. Somewhat surprisingly, perhaps, matters were rather different in some other parts of India: one thinks of the role in plague politics of Pandita Ramabhai in Maharashtra and the participation of Sister Nivedita (Margaret Noble) in the evolution of elite Indian attitudes to the plague in Calcutta. Of course, the 'silences' of Punjab's European rulers about women as well as the 'silences' of Punjabis themselves tell us a good deal about both rulers and ruled at this time. To say this is to advert to a theme that has shown signs of emerging elsewhere: in the future, gender matters must surely find a greater place in historical studies of the Punjab. But we are compelled to note that it may be difficult to always discover appropriate sources for such a shift of intellectual concentration.[27]

* * *

In its first two seasons in the Punjab, 1897–8 and 1898–9, plague largely confined its attention to villages in the Garhshankar tehsil of Hoshiarpur district and the Nawashahr tehsil of Jullundur. A comparatively small number of villages—about eighty—were affected in the first year, fewer in the second. In the third 'season', 1899–1900, a somewhat greater area was affected, but the disease was still relatively confined and urban areas remained very largely exempt. Most British officials (both civil and medical) were at first inclined to believe that in the rural areas, amidst what H. J. Maynard described as 'an ignorant and prejudiced population',[28] the disease could and should be tackled with very considerable vigour. So, house-to-house searches—admittedly somewhat haphazard—were made for plague cases. People and their belongings were sometimes emptied onto the streets and alleys while houses were deluged with disinfectant. Some, but by no means all, rural victims were thrown into makeshift 'hospitals' (often in spite of the entreaties of husbands, wives, and relatives);

Punjab's most widely read vernacular newspaper called such places mere 'sheds in jungles'.[29] (The comparison with the dread 'famine sheds' was implicit.) Virtually from the beginning in the Punjab, there were some inoculations of the willing and the semi-willing with Haffkine's not always especially efficacious[30] plague vaccine. This had been first produced at the end of 1896.

All this seemingly confident activity disguised—in fact, to some extent, proceeded from—a basic ignorance at this time amongst officialdom, both civil and medical, about the nature of the plague. Until about 1905, most of the British persisted in rubbishing the 'rat-flea' theory of plague's origins that had been put forward in 1898 by the Frenchman Paul-Louis Simond.[31] The role of rodents other than rats was even more slowly understood—indeed, we are still learning about such matters today. Those in charge of plague work in the Punjab in the early days professed themselves to be convinced that the 'germs of infection' were 'generally, if not always, imported by human agency',[32] in other words, through human movement. Such a view led to the most characteristic early administrative response to plague in the Punjab: the large-scale imposition of 'cordons'—at first mainly made up of policemen—around affected villages. These villages were, in theory, watched around the clock. At the beginning of May 1898, staff employed in such matters included— besides a deputy commissioner, four assistant commissioners and sundry tehsildars on special 'plague duty'—one district superintendent of police, four assistant superintendents, four inspectors, 27 deputy inspectors, 272 sergeants, and no fewer than 2,564 constables.[33] Such a concentration of authority was possible only while the plague was confined to relatively few villages.

Late in April 1898, as the Punjab heat grew more intense, overt resistance to such measures broke out in an area surrounding the town of Garhshankar. At a village named Bhangal, some lambardars were arrested, but were 'rescued by a mob numbering about one thousand partly collected from other villages'.[34] Garhshankar tehsil was 'inhabited largely by Sikh Jats';[35] it is highly likely that their supra-village connections came into play here. Over the years I have become convinced of the importance in rural politics in other parts of India of what is often called in the anthropological literature the 'marriage circle': the informal collection of villages from which brides are normally drawn.[36] Such marriage and kinship connections are almost certainly not the only supra-village connections of real importance in the Punjab.[37] But I find it somewhat surprising that, apart from the writings of Joyce Pettigrew on very recent times,[38] there seems to be little devoted to the 'political' importance of supra-village connections of any variety in the rural Punjab. It would be fascinating—and that not simply from the point of view of the historian of epidemics—to be able to analyse something that was apparently compiled in 1898 with the idea that the movement of plague could be tracked by a detailed tracing of the movements of people. This was a 'complete village record of all the inhabitants of Garhshankar and Nawashahr tehsils and of the Phagwara Ilaka of the Kapurthala State, with notes on the localities in which their marriage connections reside'.[39] It is just possible that this presumably massive document, or series of documents, is lying forgotten in some record room in India or Pakistan; our successors in research should keep a weather eye open.[40]

The Bhangal affair of 1898 has about it all the marks of a rural revolt of a variety which in 1857, though rare in the sternly disciplined Punjab, was common amongst Jats in the North-Western Provinces.[41] In 1898 it may have been Muslim Rajputs rather than Jat Sikhs who, a few days after the Bhangal-centred disturbance, were mainly involved in a plague-connected émeute in the town of Garhshankar; they were certainly dominant in that town's population.[42] Nevertheless, there was official talk of an 'organized conspiracy' in Garhshankar tehsil, involving both town and country.[43] Nervous police in Garhshankar town opened fire without orders to do so.[44] Nine men were killed and 35 wounded.[45] Significantly, those who survived to be brought before the courts were given generally light sentences.[46] However there appears to have been a feeling in some official circles that 'the incident, regrettable though it was, had a marvelously [sic] salutary effect... It was the great turning point in the plague operations'.[47] Unhappily, there were to be echoes of such sentiments after the rifles had been emptied at Amritsar in 1919.

The chief architect of much of the earliest plague policy in the Punjab—policy that can be said to have led to the Garhshankar shootings—was an official to whom we have already referred, H. J. (later Sir John) Maynard, then a junior secretary in the Punjab government. In his later years, Maynard acquired a reputation as 'an officer accessible to the people and one who was believed to be sympathetic to Indian aspirations'.[48] One sometimes wonders whether an Australian scholar was altogether correct when some years ago he portrayed Maynard consistently as an outstanding but singular counterfoil to the supposedly dominant paternalistic tendency in the Punjab of his time.[49] It is true, however, that in 1907 (by which time, it must be said, he had the security provided by a divisional commissionership) Maynard was able to write:

As I was myself largely responsible for most of what was done in the era of compulsion, I feel free to criticise the work in the light of my own later experience. The error that was made in the first epoch of plague (1897–1901) lay not so much in the recourse to compulsory measures as in the character of the agency which was employed to enforce them. The proper course would have been to call into existence some sort of authority in the village itself, with power to coerce the waverer and recalcitrant minority... There should have been no chaprasis or constables, hustling and plundering headmen, village proprietors and kamins alike, but gazetted officers advising and dealing direct with the village authorities, and supporting the latter in such compulsory measures as it might be necessary to take with their own people.[50]

Actually, as early as mid-1898, the Government of India had begun to permit, even to encourage, what was in some respects a *de facto* relaxation of plague policy. But in many ways the Punjab government persisted in the policy of 'compulsion' in plague matters. In 1901, the plague extended its grip well beyond the tehsils of Nawashahr and Garhshankar into the districts of Sialkot and Gurdaspur. There was oppressive behaviour, allegedly directed especially at women, by a Hindu Naib teshsildar on plague duty at a place called Sankhatra in Zafarwal tehsil, Sialkot. A crowd bore down on the official, killed him, and burnt his body. But, as the Government of India pointed out,[51] the misdeeds of a single official could not have been the only reason for the disturbances that occurred shortly afterwards—in late April—in Shahzada, also in Zafarwal tehsil. In this case, there is no doubt about Sikh involvement; there is no doubt, either, of the importance of traditional links between villages. By this stage, the British, as a matter of administrative and financial necessity, were replacing police cordons in plague areas with 'cordon levies', raised partly from 'pensioners' and 'reservists' but partly, it would appear, from amongst 'villagers.' The documents do not tell us who exactly these 'villagers' were;[52] one suspects that they are unlikely to have been Sikh. Certainly at Shahzada, one of these cordon levies was 'furiously attacked by a crowd composed largely of Jat Sikhs, armed with sticks and in some cases gandasas, chavis and even swords.'[53] These people were said to be from 'several villages in the neighbourhood'—about twenty-five villages, according to the *Pioneer*[54] of Allahabad. It was 'confidently stated', furthermore, that 'the Sikh Jats of the large village of Barra Dulla in Shakargarh [in Gurdaspur

District] had promised... assistance in case of need'.[55] As in the Bhangal case in 1898, this was autonomous, one might say essentially 'traditional', rural revolt; leadership, such as it was, came from within.

The Deputy Commissioner of Sialkot, H. P. Tollinton, concluded that 'deep-rooted hatred of all plague medical officers and cordons constitutes in my opinion a serious political danger. To allay popular feeling I would recommend a reduction of staff and a change in the nature of that staff from an Executive to an Advisory body'.[56] The Government of India, while quite strongly criticizing several of Tollinton's actions, in effect agreed with this part of his analysis.[57] Under strong pressure from that government— but also, it may be argued, under pressure from Jat Sikhs and their supra-village links—the Government of the Punjab finally gave way. The plague cordons were completely lifted.

In 1902, in the face of a still greater extension of plague, the government of Sir Charles Rivaz turned to a policy of, basically, mass inoculation with Haffkine's vaccine. Inoculation, it will be remembered, had been part of the armoury against plague in the Punjab almost from the beginning; its use had increased as the century had turned. In 1902–3, almost half a million Punjabis were inoculated with Haffkine's vaccine, and that, as I have remarked elsewhere, was 'a considerable bureaucratic and medical achievement'.[58] But the plague was certainly not stopped in its tracks. And a nemesis soon came—probably in the shape of a dirty needle used by a careless British doctor who was part of a hastily recruited team sent out for inoculation work. (But the Punjab and the Indian governments made strenuous, lengthy, and, it may well be concluded, shameful efforts to turn the blame on Haffkine, the man responsible for providing the 'fluid' used in the inoculations.)[59] At the end of October 1902, 19 of those inoculated in a small village in Gujrat district, named Malkowal, died from tetanus.

Soon, to a large extent as the result of the 'Malkowal, incident', 'in the larger towns and centres' of the Punjab, and amongst the 'higher and educated classes',[60] the grand inoculation campaign virtually ground to a halt. The Government of the Punjab felt that it could no longer continue using brews of vaccine that (officially, anyway) it believed to be suspect. However, rather interestingly, it appears that in the rural and semi-rural areas of Amritsar district—areas where Sikhs were important numerically and in other ways—rumours about the Malkowal incident did not immediately lead to a complete cessation of willingness on the part of some people to be inoculated. Indeed, the Amritsar District Plague Officer claimed that in late 1902, villagers told him that they had 'heard of' the 'accident', but 'that they had seen for themselves the good effect of inoculation, and that the sooner I stopped talking and began operating the better they would be pleased'.[61] The existence of such attitudes at this time in Amritsar district would seem to be confirmed by a report from the same time in the *Tribune*, the province's leading English-language nationalist newspaper; it came from the Sikh stronghold of Majitha.[62]

After the troubles of 1901 in Sialkot, how do we explain this apparent willingness of rural Sikhs in the very next year to ignore Malkowal? It is worth recalling that Gujrat district, where Malkowal lay, was not really part of what the 1892–93 *Gujrat Gazetteer* called the 'Sikh tract';[63] events there may not have appeared to be especially or immediately relevant in powerful Sikh-dominated villages in, say, rural Amritsar. Furthermore, Malkowal was merely a hamlet, a 'poor little Pind',[64] inhabited by a mixed group of only about thirty families. It would appear that none of the 19 who died at Malkowal—all male, incidentally—were Sikh.[65] Then there is the fact that in 1902, the plague had quite suddenly greatly extended its reach in the Punjab. For many in a district such as Amritsar, the year 1902 had provided a first experience of the disease. In that situation, people may well have been more prepared to give inoculation a trial than they otherwise might have been. But probably most important was the fact that, in 1902, the element of compulsion had in fact still not been completely banished from the Punjab government's practice in plague matters. Indeed, the New Zealand-born W. S. Marris, then rising in Government of India circles, claimed that it was an 'open secret that inoculation measures in the Punjab were far from being entirely voluntary'.[66] What appears to have happened in the earlier months of 1902 was that *zaildars* and especially lambardars were told that their continuing good standing in the eyes of government to some extent depended, first, on their allowing inoculation of themselves and their families and, second, on their seeing to the provision of large musters of takers at the village inoculation sessions.[67] (There may well be, in fact, some similarity between the inoculation campaign in the rural Punjab in 1902 and the recruitment campaigns in the province during World War I.) Some zaildars and the like seem to have kept up the pressure for inoculation for some time after the virtual collapse of the urban campaign. But gradually it dawned on those people that now, 'whether they assisted or stood aloof, mattered little'.[68]

We would do well to take note of a stern reminder in the *Tribune* in late 1902. That paper was replying to the *Pioneer*—staple reading of many

British officials throughout northern India—which had apparently asserted that the seemingly mild reaction to the Malkowal incident in the Punjab showed that province to be possessed of a basically good 'temper'. 'Has the Garhshankar *fracas* between the citizens and the police been forgotten?', asked the *Tribune*. 'The Zaffarwal [sic] affair, too, must still be fresh in the *Pioneer*'s memory.'[69] We must not forget that in both the Garhshankar and the Zafarwal tehsils Jat Sikhs and Jat Sikh methods of organization were to the fore.

* * *

That said, it may still be true that if at this stage we concentrate overmuch on trying to discern a distinctively Sikh reaction to the plague and plague measures, we run the risk ultimately of narrowing rather than extending our understanding.

To elaborate, Sikhs are specifically mentioned sometimes, but only sometimes, in those of the detailed official examinations of people's movements in the plague-affected areas made in 1897–9 that have presently been uncovered. In Khatkar Khurd, a small village in Jullundur district, the majority of the population are at first said to be simply 'Hindus, chiefly Jats', although a little later there is talk of 'Chamars and Rahtia Sikhs'. But when the village is supposedly 'reinfected', all those previously attacked by the disease are said to be 'Jat Sikh'.[70] Such variations in the inflection of official description are typical of the time. Elsewhere, we are told of a Sikh who breaks the cordon in order to conduct a 'solemn reading of the Granth to avert the evil' in a neighbouring village that is affected by the plague. He brings back the cloth which he had been given 'for performing the ceremonies', thus (it is alleged) quite possibly introducing the plague into his own village.[71] But in most such reports, as in the statistics that we have discussed earlier, if the fact that the central characters are Sikh is mentioned at all, it is not treated as particularly noteworthy.

It can be argued that in some ways, in the late nineteenth century and very early twentieth century, such an approach to the Sikhs was not inappropriate—or, at the least, understandable. One strongly suspects that the position of Sikhs in many villages in these early days of the plague—more accurately, perhaps, what the French social historians would call their *mentalité*—is reasonably well illustrated in this piece from John Maynard:

When an outbreak [of plague] is apprehended there are signs of religious revival. A Granthi is installed under a canopy in the village rest-house to recite the Scriptures; 'Havan' is freely practised; public prayers are offered in the village mosque; hard work is done on the excavation of the tank; the poor of the neighbourhood are collected and fed. The lower deities or demons are also not forgotten; fakirs are summoned and highly fed for the performance of their charms; the village site is surrounded with a circle of stakes... to serve as supernatural guardians.[72]

Maynard wields his pen in his usual vivid but ultimately somewhat patronizing way: the immediate source of his notions is, again, the possibly rather untypical Ambala; his 'village' is probably generalized rather than a single village. But the implications of Maynard's words are fairly clear: at this stage, the way of the Sikhs, insofar as it was a separate way, was one of several that were on offer in the village. Perhaps especially at times of crisis, people might resort to several ways or aspects of those ways, at once or in quick succession. In many respects, this is in fact the picture of life in the villages that was drawn at this time by the Tat Khalsa Sikhs. It was, of course, a picture of a situation of which they disapproved, but the picture was, surely, not too far from reality.

On the face of it, then, it would seem unlikely that at least in their early reactions to the plague, rural Sikhs at this time differed greatly from their neighbours. In the days before antibiotics, most people who came down with plague died within a few days, but often not before passing through a period of delirium that was frightening to behold. So the vernacular newspaper *Akhbar-i-Am* described the first appearance of plague in the village of Pharalla, very near Jullundur city, in May 1898 in these terms: 'The people were thrown into a state of indescribable excitement, and panic. The villagers took no food at night and began to pack their goods. The air was rent with the piteous cries of women and children.'[73] A commentator on an assessment report, looking back on the coming of the plague after some years, thought that 'the people must have thought that God and man had conspired against them'.[74]

There is, however, one discussion of the effect of epidemics in India in the early twentieth century that could lead us to a rather different picture of the impact of plague both on Sikhs and on the various other communities of the Punjab. It comes from a European member of the Indian Medical Service, Clifford Gill. Gill's first introduction to the plague seems to have been as a young surgeon-lieutenant in the Punjab in or about 1906. In later years, he came to be regarded as something of an expert on the scientific aspects of plague and other epidemic diseases. In 1931, he contributed a wide-ranging article on 'Epidemics' to the *Encyclopaedia of the Social Sciences*[75]—largely, it would appear, on the basis of his Punjab experience. In it, he wrote:

The onslaught of epidemics is marked by extreme humility and patience. In affected households, an uncanny silence, only broken by the ceremonial wailing of women, the beating of breasts, is often the only outward sign of the prevailing misery. Life goes on as usual in the neighborhood and funeral processions wending their way almost unnoticed to the burial ground and the burning ghat may be the only indication of the tragedies of the epidemic... Even the most virulent epidemic is short-lived and these ill effects disappear with astonishing rapidity and with them all memory of the epidemic. Nor are epidemics often the proximate or remote cause of civil strife.

A later section of this chapter will be devoted, explicitly or implicitly, to an examination of Gill's last sentence—'Nor are epidemics often the proximate or remote cause of civil strife'—particularly so far as the year 1907 is concerned. But first a few remarks on the relevance of Gill's remarks to the problem of the overall social impact of the plague on the Punjab.

In several respects, he must be pronounced to be misguided. We know that Gill did not himself experience the initial impact of plague on the Punjab countryside. It is not unlikely that, outwardly at least, there was not quite so much alarm when the plague struck in, say, some of the middle years of the first decade of the twentieth century as there had been in 1897 or 1898. But outward equanimity need not necessarily betoken inner calm. In any case, the plague—as we have seen, greatly dependent on the vagaries of the movements of rodents under the ground—had a scattershot effect in its attack in the rural areas. As early as 1904, there are reports from normally sober-headed officials such as W. M. Hailey of Punjab villages losing 50 or even 70 per cent of their population.[76] But even in 1907, it was only a minority of villages that were so cruelly affected. Normally, in a single season the plague left the majority of villages alone, or almost alone. As an epidemiologist, Gill was, or at least gradually became, well aware of this phenomenon. But as a social observer, he seems to have failed to have realized that epidemiological fact could, at least to some extent, explain why in many villages human activity could appear, at least superficially, to be occurring more or less 'as usual' even while the plague raged elsewhere.

A further point that must be made about Gill's assertions is that it is very unlikely that the plague of the early twentieth century vanished rapidly from the memories of at least a significant number of Punjabis. For one thing, in most years until the 1950s, the plague still had a presence in the province, although that presence was never again of the variety found in, say, 1907. Malcolm Darling could still write in 1930 of the 'terror' that plague could inspire.[77] And in 1946–7, when Darling was making the last of his rural rides, he found that the plague era of the early years of the twentieth century was still firmly entrenched in memory—certainly in the memory of a tehsildar who had been brought up in Ambala district.[78] If the plague has now largely disappeared from popular memory in the Punjab—and of that I, for one, cannot be sure[79]—it may be because it has become overlain by the immensity of the tragedy of Partition. It is likely that even in the 1930s, many European readers were inclined to accept Gill's assertion that in the face of calamities such as epidemics, Indians in general (and, indeed, a good many other non-Europeans) reacted passively, even 'fatalistically'. After all, such a cry was common amongst European empire builders and 'muscular Christians'; it is, in fact, one of the basic tenets of 'Orientalism'. Not so many years ago, I still felt obliged to deal in print with the notion.[80] Here I need say only that generally speaking, it simply cannot be argued that even in the later years of plague, the inhabitants of the Punjab—Hindus, Muslims, Sikhs, and Christians—made no strenuous efforts to rid themselves of the disease. It is true, however, that very often their efforts were rooted in their own traditions; very often those methods included the 'other-worldly' methods of religion—of the variety that, for example, Maynard described in 1902. The title of Susan Wadley's excellent anthropological study of a modern Uttar Pradesh village, *Struggling with Destiny in Karimpur*,[81] is of considerable relevance here. On the whole, Destiny in India is not, and was not, something to be accepted blindly; it is and was something with which at times one struggled. In the course of this struggle, Indians were on occasion prepared to experiment with European methods of coping with disease, such as inoculation. But they would do so only if they had heard of those methods, if they could afford them, and, perhaps above all, if they worked.

It is quite likely that there is sometimes a distinct and indeed separate place for Sikhs in this picture of the *mentalité* of the rural Punjab in the plague years. But at present we quite often cannot make even informed guesses as to the nature of such differentiation as there may have been.

That is not only because of a seeming lack of relevant records. While there is some superb anthropological work from the scholar–officials of the Punjab in the era of the Raj—fully utilized by, for example, Harjot Oberoi—there is not, at least to my knowledge, a great deal of published anthropological work on the Punjab from the decades that have followed Independence. Doubtless, conditions in more recent years have at times been too disturbed to allow a great deal of such work. But more of it might well have given us vital clues to the answers to rarely asked questions about the past: I have certainly found that to be the case with Maharashtra and Gujarat.

The questions we, as historians, wish to ask the anthropologists are sometimes rather different from those asked a hundred years ago. For example, a reading of Clarence McMullen's suggestive but incomplete little book, *Religious Beliefs and Practices of the Sikhs in Rural Punjab*, might well confirm in some of us a feeling that the Sikh response to the plague, even as compared with the response of some other Punjab communities, must have been basically 'positive', 'world-affirming'.[82] But we would probably find it difficult to elaborate on that notion. This 'outsider' knows of no modern investigation of, for instance, Sikh attitudes to death, and in particular the relatively sudden death that was very often a mark of the plague. The work of T. N. Madan and a number of others tells us that for 'Hindus', such a death could rarely be a 'good' or a 'natural' death: there had been insufficient time to prepare for it.[83] But we would appear to have little or no evidence as to whether people who described themselves as Sikhs thought in this way at the time of the plague. Similarly, there would appear to be no real evidence as to what such people made of the fact that, as one report put it, 'the sturdy Sikh died as easily as the weakly Brahmin'.[84] Were there questions about whether such a situation was 'natural'? Did notions of something like 'justice' or 'fairness' come into the matter, as the work of some of the Subaltern historians might lead us to suspect? What did Sikhs think about the fact that in the villages, those the British sometimes called 'sturdy agriculturalists' were hit just as hard by the plague as the 'menials' who in the past had born the brunt of so many other diseases? Punjab may have possessed a relatively 'flat' social structure, but as Piet van den Dungen pointed out a good many years ago, in that province 'the lowest levels of society (menials and artisans) were universally recognised as such'.[85] Or perhaps the fact that menials were not, on this occasion, providing a considerable proportion of the victims of epidemic disease was not immediately obvious at the time? The annual season and crop reports (a somewhat neglected source) make it reasonably clear that Sikh and other landholders in the Canal Colonies and elsewhere in the first decade of the twentieth century were very ready to blame the ravages of the plague for the prevalent shortage of agricultural labour.[86]

* * *

In a situation in which it is difficult to say a great deal on some aspects of the outlook of Sikhs on the plague, it is tempting to retreat to a framework that sees the problem of the plague to a very large extent in terms of the impact of the external factor of 'colonialism'. In my time, I have criticized such an approach in connection with the impact of the plague on other groups in South Asia.[87] I note, too, that recently Tony Ballantyne, while criticizing what he has called the 'internalist' approach to Sikh history, has cautioned against 'privileging the prescriptive power of the colonial state'.[88] Yet the more one investigates the plague question in the Punjab, the more one is conscious of the intermeshing of what we may call, simply, in the remainder of this chapter, the 'internal' and the 'external'—with the 'external' being, by and large, the 'colonial'.[89]

An example of this intermeshing is to be found in a paper—at first sight not especially relevant to our purposes—by Harbans Singh. Harbans Singh tells us that the supporters of the Singh Sabhas were initially met, in some quarters of the Punjab, with scorn. That view may be somewhat inconvenient to those who wish to portray, in somewhat triumphalist terms, a steady and often unimpeded rise of the Singh Sabhas. But the way Harbans Singh illustrates his point is interesting. He tells us of 'a villager's deliberate corruption of the name of the movement from Singh Sabha to Singh Safa, the word "safa" signifying widespread destruction caused by the plague epidemic of 1902'.[90] The word *safa* apparently has about it, in this context, notions of a thorough 'clean-out'—of the variety that was not infrequently inflicted on Punjabis by the agents of colonialism in the cause of plague control.[91] A development that is often portrayed in largely 'internal' Sikh terms, the rise of the Singh Sabhas, is thus seen at this point to be intimately linked in the imagination of some Sikhs with the 'external', the activities of the colonial state in connection with the plague.

We may mention another example. Bhai Randhir Singh was to become the founder of the strict Sikh 'sect' that takes his name, the Bhai Randhir da Jatha, now commonly called the Akhand Kirtani Jatha. Basant

Singh (to use the name that he was originally given by his family) was for some years a student at, interestingly, Forman Christian College, Lahore. Even then he was seemingly somewhat immersed in religious matters, though he was at that stage, in his own estimation, 'only a candidate for Sikhism, not a Sikh'.[92] The great extension of the plague in 1902 provided him both with a position in government service and, he said later, with an opportunity for serving both 'humanity' and God. (It may be worth noting that Bhai Randhir wrote of serving 'humanity' rather than the Panth.)[93] He was appointed as personal assistant, with Naib Tehsildar rank, to one of the doctors, R. W. Fisher, who had been newly recruited from Great Britain for inoculation work.[94] Dr Fisher appears to have been 'very fond of religious discussions'. Indeed, if Bhai Randhir's autobiography provides any indication, as they travelled about the countryside, the two spent a good deal of time debating whether worship of the Guru Granth Sahib was 'idolatry'.[95] Randhir Singh was, in fact, setting out on the path that was to lead to the Bhai Randhir da Jatha.

Somewhat earlier, in 1898, Mirza Ghulam Ahmad of Qadian, the founder of another Punjabi 'sect', had begun prophesying in Islamic circles and beyond about the plague. He had produced a 'revealed cure for the bubonic plague', Marham-i-Isa, the ointment of Jesus.[96] Fears provoked by the coming of the plague were undoubtedly an important part of the background to the growth of the Ahmadiyya movement in the Punjab.[97] In a possibly less powerful (but still very tangible) way, the plague was part of the background to the developments within Sikhism which are associated with Bhai Randhir Singh's name. Bhai Randhir's participation in the 'external', the British-sponsored plague administration, played a significant part in what is generally seen—when it is noticed at all—as very much an 'internal' development in Sikhism. It is worth underlining a point about the Bhai Randhir da Jatha that is made by Hew McLeod. Because very little of its literature is in English, its story is not nearly as well known as the activities of the Singh Sabhas.[98] In fact, Bhai Randhir and his followers represent a notable if somewhat contrapuntal theme in modern Sikh history, both in the earlier twentieth century (when the Singh Sabhas have quite often seemed to dominate historians' perceptions) and again in the 1980s.

It must be added that Bhai Randhir was not just a 'religious' leader. While he was with the plague administration in 1902, he experienced a good deal of petty corruption. For example, minor officials on tour received funds for buying food, but at the same time, in time-honoured fashion, squeezed rations from villagers. There can be no doubt that, at least in part, it was Bhai Randhir's experiences of the operation of bureaucracy at this time that led him to decline an offer of permanent government employment as a tehsildar and, in fact, to begin to see British imperialism as something that 'swindle[d] the people', that was lacking in justice. To join such a regime, he claimed to have told a British deputy commissioner who tried to persuade him to throw in his lot with the Raj, would be to 'lose all my character and spiritual future'.[99] Within little more than a decade, Bhai Randhir was beginning a 17-year period of imprisonment for plotting armed revolt against the British.

* * *

The intermeshing of the 'external' and the 'internal' is again quite strongly visible when we come to examine, with some of the preoccupations of the earlier sections of this paper in mind, the events of 1907 in the Punjab.

After the failure of the inoculation scheme at Malkowal in 1902, elements within European officialdom in north India had gradually come to display signs of an attitude towards the plague which, with some justice, could be described as one of apathy. (Indeed, one might even use here the dread word 'fatalism'.) Certainly little was done by government for the plague cause in the Punjab during two years of quite considerable mortality, 1904 and 1905; even less was done in 1906. In April 1907, as the plague mortality statistics rose to unprecedented heights, an Amritsar newspaper asserted that the British-dominated government was 'wholly indifferent' to the plague and 'thinks only of collecting taxes'.[100] The Private Secretary to the Viceroy, J. R. Dunlop Smith (an old Punjab hand), wrote frankly to his chief in June 1907: 'The vast majority of both Administrative and Medical officers feel that all efforts to cope successfully with the disease have failed and there is nothing to be done.'[101]

I have done a small amount of archival work on the 1907 troubles; Jerry Barrier has done a great deal more. There is little doubt that, at least in theory, there is more that could be done, especially in district and departmental record offices in India and Pakistan.[102] But even easily obtainable published official documents on economic matters lead us to conclude that in the earlier months of 1907, the vastly increased presence of plague was a cause for very considerable concern amongst many Punjabi landholders. In the countryside, there was a strong belief that it was plague—supposedly the reason for the shortage of labour referred to earlier—that led to crops not being watered or weeded at the proper time. Sometimes, indeed, the crops were not harvested or were only partially harvested.[103]

There were, of course, other causes for concern. There had been boll-worm in the cotton in 1905–6.[104] In 1906–7 there was rust in the wheat crop and a plague of locusts.[105] And the inhabitants of the Canal Colonies had a number of genuine and frequently voiced complaints relating to the British insistence in these 'model' settlements on the observance of a multitude of rules—and the opportunities for corruption that such a situation gave to minor officials. Plague administration, of course, as we have seen, had provided similar opportunities in past years.

For all that, it must probably be admitted that neither the plague of the present or the past, nor the other factors that we have mentioned were sufficient, either individually or even collectively, to precipitate disturbances of the nature and the scale of those of 1907. Almost certainly, in other words, earlier students of the subject have been right to see the 'proximate' causes of the disturbances of 1907 (to use Gill's terminology) as the Punjab Colonization of Land Bill of October 1906 and the virtually contemporaneous increase in the rates charged for Bari Doab waters. These moves, of course, were 'external' factors, associated with British colonialism. Crucially, the British succeeded in alienating at the same time both the Canal Colonists and their relatives in the old central Punjab districts from which they had come.

But to me it seems likely that as the agitation of 1907 got under way in the rural Punjab, more 'remote' causes, associated with plague and with Sikhs, came fairly strongly into play. The case for such a proposition is by no means complete, but it deserves to be set down.

The rural agitation against the Colonization Bill appears to have come into being in the Canal Colonies by mid to late January 1907. This, admittedly, was before anyone had realized that the plague of 1907 was going to be worse than the plague of any preceding year. There was a mass meeting of 3,000 peasants at Sangla, in Lyallpur district, at the end of January 1907; a few days later, Lyallpur city witnessed a similar gathering of 10,000.[106] Such meetings certainly seem at first sight to be rather different from the somewhat violent supra-village assemblages of 1898 and 1901. For one thing, they generally give the appearance of concluding peacefully, with the passing of 'resolutions'. At least some of the British in 1907 kept a very wary eye on these meetings: Maynard told his wife that the Deputy Commissioner of Lyallpur, Q. Q. Henriques, was 'expecting a riot'.[107] But a good many amongst officialdom persisted in thinking that the troubles were essentially the result of the machinations of 'urban politicians'; colonists in the canal areas, such officials believed, generally would not turn of their own volition against the regime that had given them so much.[108] Even thirty-five years ago, Jerry Barrier was clear that urban politicians were not responsible for the beginnings of the agitation in the Canal Colonies. Barrier also believed, however, that leadership in the early Canal Colony agitation did not come from ordinary colonists; it came, rather, from 'ex-government servants or educated Punjabis living in the colony'.[109] I have to say that I have some doubts—partly inspired by my reading of the 'Subaltern' historians, but partly inspired by my understanding of the rural plague protests of 1898 and 1901—about the notion that, in the Colonies, organization from 'above' was an essential part of the 1907 disturbances.

Let me elaborate on this point by looking first at two apparently influential reports on the Canal Colonies agitation made in June 1907 by Frank Popham Young and Muhammad Shafi. Popham Young was then acting as provincial settlement commissioner, but somewhat earlier he had been a powerful and very greatly respected colonization officer in the Chenab Canal area. He was undoubtedly taken aback by the turn of events in 1907. Muhammad Shafi was at this time a Lahore lawyer, but he was to go on, of course, to play a prominent part in Indian Muslim politics in the era of the Montagu–Chelmsford Reforms. Popham Young implied that leadership in the Colonies agitation had come from such people as 'retired Munsifs, Postal officials, Subedar-Majors, and Police Inspectors'. Such people, in the Colonies, were 'all located together, and each found that he was no one in particular in the eyes of his neighbours'. (Here, perhaps, is one of the points of origin for Barrier's ideas about leadership in the Colonies in 1907.) Popham Young believed that in the sentiments they uttered, 'many agriculturists' in the Colonies, 'mostly Jat Sikhs, in close connection with the Native Army, were amongst the most violent and disloyal'. He admitted that he had not been to the Samundri tehsil of Lyallpur district. But he had been told that that area was 'the centre of the most openly-avowed hostility to British rule, so far as the agricultural community is concerned'. Popham Young admitted, again, that he did not personally know the 'settlers in that neighbourhood'. But they were 'mostly Jat Sikhs of the Amritsar District'.[110]

Muhammad Shafi, in his memorandum, pointed out that there was 'very naturally a constant personal and postal intercourse' between the settlers and their 'relations and friends residing in the villages and towns where they had their original homes.'[111] These connections were undoubtedly significant in the development of the agitation both in the Colonies and in the 'old' districts. But there was something that Shafi and Popham Young appear to have missed in their analyses. While the Colonies were being created, there had often been an emphasis on placing together in each new area of settlement people drawn from various social groups in a single area in the 'old' districts. The aim had been, so far as possible, to replicate in the Colonies the social system—indeed, the very social relationships—that people had known in the places from which they had come.[112] 'Menials' were encouraged to accompany to the Colonies those for whom they had worked hitherto. And, more important for our purposes (even if the fact appears to be unnoticed by Imran Ali in his otherwise very perceptive study),[113] landholders in the new colonies would often have as their neighbours people they had known in the 'old' districts. Even Popham Young may not have fully realized—certainly he did not seek to explicate—the possible consequences of this last factor in a situation of unrest. It seems likely that in the Canal Colonies, a good number of the supra-village relationships that had been found in the 'old' districts continued to function, or in 1907 began to function again, in the new setting. It is very possible that such continuing links allowed—indeed, to some extent, led to—the coming together of so many people at, for example, Sangla and Lyallpur. And it is very possible that some of the violence that Popham Young detected in the sentiments expressed in the Colonies in 1907 was not altogether different from that which had been displayed in Jat Sikh protests against plague measures in 1898 and 1901. With the material at my disposal on the Colonies I cannot say more than that.

It is notable that there is nothing at all, in either the Popham Young or the Shafi reports, on the impact of the plague in the Canal Colonies. It may well be significant, however, that in the papers of John Morley, Secretary of State for India at the time, copies of Popham Young's and Muhammad Shafi's reports are to be found virtually next door to a letter from Lord Minto, the Viceroy, in which the plague is discussed at some length. The fact is that both Viceroy and Secretary of State fastened on the plague as a reason for what Minto called 'all the curious unrest'.[114] As early as March 1907, Minto had publicly expressed surprise that so little attention was given in public debate in India to the 'perennial harvest of the plague'.[115] Morley mentioned the plague in parliament in his Indian budget speech of 6 June[116] as he thrashed about in an effort to explain the troubles in the Punjab and elsewhere in India. It is, in fact, just possible that Morley and Minto between them found in the plague an all too convenient explanation for unexpected agitation.[117] What is notable—at least in the papers I have seen—is that such an explanation does not appear to have been suggested to either of them directly, in writing by officials. This may have been the result of either lack of imagination or, more likely, lack of interest in the whole matter of the plague on the part of those who were at the top in the Government of India and the India Office.

The picture of the 1907 agitation becomes a good deal clearer when we come to consider the disturbances in the 'old' districts and, in particular, the part played in those areas by a man with a good Sikh name, Ajit Singh. According to Professor Barrier, while Ajit Singh had little to do with the Canal Colony agitation, he 'engineer[ed] the demonstrations against the Bari Doab assessments'[118] that occurred from early April 1907—at a time, that is, when the plague was at its height. Along with Lajpat Rai, he was deported to Mandalay in June, only to be released in November as a result of the Viceroy's direct intervention in Punjab affairs. At first sight, anyway, Ajit Singh stands out as seemingly uniting in his words and his actions the rural agitation of 1907, popular unease about the plague, and at least some of the concerns of a good many Jat Sikhs. He certainly provides a pointer to the resolution of some of the problems we have raised about leadership in the agitation.

We may look first at Ajit Singh's words. Minto admitted to Morley: 'We cannot get correct reports of the speeches in the absence of shorthand reporting of vernaculars, and must trust to oral reports from informers.'[119] Nevertheless, there is considerable consistency between key passages in reports of speeches which Ajit Singh gave in two places in April 1907. (It is, of course, entirely possible that he was shadowed by the same informer in both places.) Here, at least according to report, is Ajit Singh at Rawalpindi on 21 April: 'Plague is working havoc among you, and it is better to die the more honourable death of the martyr for your country.'[120] Here he is at Batala exactly a week later:

God had sent plague into the country solely to teach the people to use the power they possess. Lakhs of people were dying of plague,[121] many more would die. It was better to die for their country than to die of plague. He implored the people to use their power and to consider what could be done with their power.[122]

Here, too, is Ajit Singh in a 'widely circulated' pamphlet:

The English have treacherously robbed the Sikhs of their King and have reduced them to live the lives of slaves in their own land. The best part of their lives, of their property and honour has been confiscated by the English... If you are brave enough, expel the English from your land.[123]

In Ajit Singh's speeches, there are references to the plague that point clearly to its provoking very considerable fears in 1907, if not before. And in the Rawalpindi and Batala utterances, there is surely a direct appeal to Sikhs—in particular, to the Sikh notion of martyrdom—about which Lou Fenech has recently enlightened us.[124] Here, too, in the pamphlet from which we have quoted, is an appeal to past Sikh greatness. It appears, in fact, that Ajit Singh, probably more instinctively than in a calculated way, was adept at playing to the sentiments and the prejudices of the Jat Sikhs. He spoke their language. He could talk of *zulum* and *izzat*; he could condemn Englishmen as licentious and unclean. The meetings with which he was associated, says the Australian scholar, Max Harcourt, were 'colourful affairs, preceded by music and utilising poetry in the traditional "Mushaira" style'.[125]

Ajit Singh had been born a Jat Sikh. His father, originally from Jullundur District, had taken up two squares of land in the Chenab colony.[126] Ajit was sent to the Dayanand Anglo-Vedic College in Lahore, where he imbibed Arya Samaj ideas. In his time, he was one of the very few Jat Sikhs to have had a college education. Work amongst Europeans as a teacher of Indian languages gave him a highly unfavourable view of the Raj and of European life generally. In this, though not in other ways, he had some similarities to Bhai Randhir Singh. Ajit Singh became known first as an Arya Samajist (as did, of course, amongst others, Bhagat Lakshman Singh). In fact, Fenech has found a note in the *Khalsa Advocate*, apparently dating from as early as 1904, in which it is asserted vehemently, 'The man [Ajit Singh] is not a Sikh but the reverse of that... an Arya Samajist.'[127] It is said that in later life, at least, Ajit Singh declared himself to be an atheist.[128] But in 1907, he was perfectly capable of bringing the Divine into his oratory. And in a poem that circulated in Canada in 1914, he is described as a 'son of the Tenth Guru'.[129]

So much for what Ajit Singh said. However, when it comes to Ajit Singh the man of action, the man attempting to be a 'leader', he has been seen as having some 'deficiencies'. These supposed deficiencies are, in fact, central to our argument. Ajit Singh, says Max Harcourt, was both 'brilliant' and 'baffling'.[130] He was subject to fits of depression. It was in one of those periods that, early in June 1907, he gave himself up to the authorities. He claimed to have been in contact with at least one Russian anarchist. It seems probable that, in reality, at least some of his feeling for justice and equality, even for 'revolution' of a quasi-socialist variety,[131] came from his understanding of the religion into which he had been born. Here, perhaps, we come to another contrapuntal element in Sikhism. It seems difficult to deny that, on occasion, some such qualities as those that are denoted by the English words 'justice' and 'equality' were enjoined by the gurus. Interestingly, after World War II, there seem to have been, for a time, quite a number of 'Sikh communists'.[132] But generally speaking, in practice, 'economic egalitarianism' has not been seen by Sikhs as 'part of the egalitarian legacy of the Sikh past'.[133] That was perhaps one reason why, after Ajit Singh had seemingly captured the mind of a mass meeting held under formal Singh Sabha auspices in Lahore on 6 April 1907, the Singh Sabhas on the whole increasingly dissociated themselves from him and began stressing their 'loyalty' to the British.[134] It would seem that it was not just some of the British who feared the possibility of the rural agitation in the Punjab in 1907 turning violent. The urban elites who dominated many of the Singh Sabhas could not but feel a certain lack of sympathy towards aspects of the appeal to 'traditional' Jat Sikh mores that was so much a part of Ajit Singh's rhetoric. They may well have understood, in fact, the capacity of rural Sikhs to look after their own affairs in their own way. And those town-dwellers from the Singh Sabhas may well have not altogether liked what they saw.

It should probably be added that the urban/rural divide in the Punjab was not entirely unbridged. People from the countryside and people from the towns certainly had something in common. 'I have observed (principally in connection with measures of plague prevention)', wrote Maynard in 1904, 'that the zamindar takes his opinions mainly from the place where he does his marketing, and the larger the town, the more notably does it affect the ideas of the neighbourhood.'[135] As always, Maynard's opinions deserve to be mulled over. But in 1898, it will be remembered, Maynard had characterized Punjabi peasants as 'ignorant and prejudiced': in this respect at least, he remained, ultimately, a man of his time. Ignorant peasants, Maynard and other officials thought, obtained their ideas from townspeople, were led by them—indeed, they were at times, so it was claimed, misled by them.

Ajit Singh and his career may have conformed to this paradigm on occasion. But there was, it would seem, too much spirit, too much independence, too much intelligence, and, perhaps, too much violence amongst rural Sikhs, especially Jat Sikhs, for them normally to have allowed themselves to be organized by townspeople. A study of the rhetoric of Ajit Singh undoubtedly tells us a good deal about the fears of ordinary rural Punjabis so far as the plague was concerned. But even so, Ajit Singh does not appear to have had quite the hold over those rural Punjabis that some have thought that he had. In other words, in 1907, in at least some parts of the Punjab, the supra-village links that had been so important in the plague-related disturbances of 1898 and 1901 may well have come into their own again. And, it may be added, it is likely that such links were to continue to be important in the Punjab, including the Canal Colonies. In 1919, for example, there was official talk—not all of it necessarily to be taken at face value, of course—of the activities of a 'gang of villagers, mostly Jat Sikh colonists' in Lyallpur district.[136]

* * *

In this chapter I have tried, amongst other things, to establish some sort of case for a link (though certainly not an exclusive link) between plague and the agitation of 1907. At present the link seems often to have been provided by Sikhs, particularly Jat Sikhs. More archival work needs to be done if the case is to be more firmly established. Historians of the modern Punjab—especially of the Sikhs—seem to have been, doubtless for various good reasons, perhaps not quite as diligent in their use of archives as have been historians of some other parts of India.[137] An 'outsider' might suggest, amongst other things, that one of the 'new directions' for Sikh historical studies in the future could be an increased use of archives of various sorts. Archives can surely be made to yield more—and not just about such relatively neglected topics as popular organization at the supra-village level, economic matters, women's lives, as well as (of course) plague and other diseases.

But the burden of this chapter is not mainly a plea for an extension of the gathering of information. It is, rather, a plea for new, or (very often) simply more unusual, ways of thinking about such information. Feminist perspectives would undoubtedly make some difference; so too, on occasion, would a deeper acquaintance with economic matters and even perhaps with aspects of the biological sciences. Historians of the modern Punjab may also need to read as much in the fields of anthropology and sociology as they do at present in the field of religion. If the anthropologists are not, from the historian's point of view, asking the right questions, they may have to be gently prodded. If the sociologists are neglecting the subalterns, they too may have to be gently prodded. And I would say—again, of course, very much as an 'outsider'—that if historians of the Punjab are themselves largely confining their reading of history to the history of the Punjab, they certainly need to be gently prodded. With horizons duly broadened, such historians could then profitably return to such matters as the study of the Punjab at times of crisis. The study of a society in crisis—and it has been argued here that Punjab in the midst of the plague was very much a society in the midst of crisis—can provide us with a most useful way into the inner workings of that society. Often what is revealed is interconnectedness, intermeshing—of 'internal' and 'external' factors, for example. Sometimes hitherto somewhat neglected factors, such as the role of the supra-village networks in social and 'political' life, or, in the field of religion, the rise of the Bhai Randhir Singh da Jatha, come to the fore. At other times, what is revealed may seem to be little more than sheer complexity. But in the final analysis, even a developed awareness of that complexity is no bad thing.

Notes

ABBREVIATIONS USED BELOW:

Census = *Census of India, Punjab*, pt.i, *Report* [followed by relevant year]
NAI = National Archives of India
NNP = Selections from the Vernacular Press, Punjab
OIOC = Oriental and India Office Collections, British Library
Progs = Proceedings
S&C = *Season and Crop Report, Punjab* [followed by relevant year]

1. See Tony Ballantyne, 'Looking Back, Looking Forward: The Historiography of Sikhism', *New Zealand Journal of Asian Studies* 4, 1 (2002), pp. 5–29. A somewhat revised version of this article is to be found in Tony Ballantyne, 'Framing the Sikh Past', *International Journal of Sikh Studies* 10, 1 and 2 (2003), pp. 1–23.

2. W. H. McLeod, *Discovering the Sikhs: Autobiography of a Historian* (Delhi: Permanent Black, 2004), p. 40.

3. Ian Catanach, 'South Asian Muslims and the Plague 1896–c.1914', *South Asia*, 22, Special Issue (1999), pp. 87–107.

4. Elisabeth Carpentier, *Une ville devant la Peste: Orvieto et la Peste noire de 1348* (Paris: SEVPEN, 1962); Louis Chevalier (ed.), *Le choléra: La premiere épidémie du xixe siècle* (La Roche-sur-Yonne, 1958); Rene Baehrel, 'La haine de classe en temps d'épidémie', *Annales: Economies, Sociétés, Civilisations* 8, 2 (1952); Asa Briggs, 'Cholera and Society in the Nineteenth Century', *Past and Present* 19 (April 1961). For more on these matters, see Ian J. Catanach, 'Rats, Lice and Indian History',

in John McGuire, Meredith Borthwick, and Brij V. Lal (eds), *Problems and Methods of Enquiry in South Asian History* (Nedlands: Centre for South and Southeast Asian Studies, University of Western Australia, 1984), pp. 55–70.

5. Maryinez Lyons, *The Colonial Disease: A Social History of Sleeping Sickness in Northern Zaire 1900–1940* (Cambridge: Cambridge University Press, 1992), pp. 52 and 219.

6. Ian J. Kerr, 'Fox and the Lions: The Akali Movement Revisited', in Joseph T. O'Connell, Milton Israel, and Willard G. Oxtoby, with visiting editors W. H. McLeod and J. S. Grewal, *Sikh History and Religion in the Twentieth Century* (Toronto: University of Toronto Press, 1988), p. 224.

7. Malcolm Lyall Darling, *Rusticus Loquitor, or The Old Light and the New in the Punjab Village* (London: Oxford University Press, 1930), p. 71.

8. C. H. James, *Report on the Outbreak of Plague in the Jullundur and Hoshiarpur Districts of the Punjab, 1897–98* (Government of Punjab, 1899), p. 1 (available in printed form, National Documentation Centre, Pakistan; microfilm copy, OIOC, Pos. 5548.)

9. See the classic article by N. G. Barrier, 'The Punjab Disturbances of 1907: the Response of the British Government in India to Agrarian Unrest', *Modern Asian Studies* 1, 4 (1967), pp. 353–83; also his regrettably unpublished Ph.D. dissertation, 'Punjab Politics and the Disturbances of 1907', Duke University, 1966. I must here acknowledge the loan, years ago, from a very helpful Jerry Barrier, of microfilm of some relevant Government of India Proceedings.

10. F. Norman White, 'Twenty Years of Plague in India with Special Reference to the Outbreak of 1917–18', *Indian Journal of Medical Research* 6, 2 (1918), pp. 195–7.

11. Ibid., p. 197.

12. John Norris, 'Geographical Origin of the Black Death: Response', *Bulletin of the History of Medicine* 52, 1 (1978), p. 120.

13. Anamitra Choudhury, 'Tiny Terrors', *Down to Earth: Science and Environment Fortnightly* [New Delhi], 30 November 1995, p. 34. A possible counter-argument to the latter part of this paragraph might be that in the Punjab some irrigation canals flowed quite near urban areas—Lahore, for example—which, however, were comparatively free of plague. But these canals were, on the whole, the older ones.

14. Clifford Allchin Gill, *The Genesis of Epidemics and the Natural History of Disease: An Introduction to the Science of Epidemiology Based upon the Study of Epidemics of Malaria, Influenza, & Plague* (London: Baillière, Tindall and Cox, 1928), p. 375. Gill based his conclusion on much earlier work by E. H. Hankin and by the Plague Research Commission.

15. If the plague managed to get into a small village with a concentrated population, it could actually be more vicious than in a larger village. For reasons for this phenomenon, see O. J. Benedictow, 'Morbidity in Historical Plague Epidemics', *Population Studies* 41, 3 (1987), pp. 420–28.

16. See Census, 1911, pp. 153 and 156.

17. F. Norman White, 'Twenty Years', p. 211; 13 women died in UP for every 10 men.

18. See, for example, Census, 1911, pp. 230–60, esp. p. 259.

19. C. H. James, *Report, 1897–98*, p. 25.

20. Ibid., p. 52.

21. Ibid., p. 65.

22. Ibid., p. 80.

23. Ibid., p. 78.

24. Ibid., p. 85.

25. C. H. James, *Report on the Outbreak of Plague in the Jullundur and Hoshiarpur Districts of the Punjab during the Year 1898–99* (Government of Punjab, 1902), p. 35 (available in printed form, National Documentation Centre, Pakistan; microfilm copy, OIOC, Pos. 5548.)

26. Ibid., p. 6.

27. I have dealt with some of these matters more fully in '"The Gendered Terrain of Disaster": India and the Plague, 1896–1918', *South Asia*, forthcoming. Also see Doris R. Jakobsh, *Relocating Gender in Sikh History: Transformation, Meaning and Identity* (New Delhi: Oxford University Press, 2002).

28. Maynard, Junr Sec., Punjab, to Commissioner, Jullundur, No. 276S of 17 June 1898: J&P 1372 of 1898, L/PJ/6/484, OIOC.

29. *Paisa Akhbar*, 15 March 1898, NNP.

30. Clive Dewey probably underestimates the usefulness of the Haffkine vaccine—*The Mind of the Indian Civil Service* (London: Hambledon Press, 1993), p. 75, but it certainly did not always safeguard those to whom it was given and the reaction to it was not always mild.

31. See Ian Catanach, 'Plague and the Tensions of Empire: India 1896–1918', in David Arnold (ed.), *Imperial Medicine and Indigenous Societies* (Manchester: Manchester University Press, 1988), pp. 158 and 162–4.

32. H. J. Maynard, Remarks, Punjab Home (Medical & Sanitary) No. 1479 of 17 December 1898 (printed with C. H. James, *Report... 1897–98*), p. 6.

33. Ibid., p. 3.

34. Telegram, Punjab to India Home, No. 387 of 25 April 1898: Enclosure No. 79 with Sanitary Letter from India No.11 of 12, May 1898, OIOC.

35. Malcom Lyall Darling, *Rusticus Loquitor*, p. 27; *Hoshiarpur Gazetteer* (1905), p. 72, points particularly to Mahilpur thana within the Garhshankar tehsil as 'almost entirely composed of villages owned by Jat Sikhs'.

36. See Ian Catanach, 'Agrarian Disturbances in Nineteenth Century India', *Indian Economic and Social History Review* 3, 1 (1966), p. 73, reprinted in David Hardiman (ed.), *Peasant Resistance in India* (Delhi: Oxford University Press, 1992), p. 196.

37. See Tom G. Kessinger, *Vilyatpur 1848–1968: Social and Economic Change in a North Indian Village* (Berkeley: University of California Press, 1974), pp. 40 and 78.

38. Joyce Pettigrew, *Robber Noblemen: A Study of the Political System of the Sikh Jats* (London: Routledge and Kegan Paul, 1975), pp. 35, 48–9, and 186; 'Martyrdom and Guerilla Organization in the Punjab', *Journal of Commonwealth and Comparative Politics* 3, 3 (1992), p. 395.

39. H. J. Maynard to all Commissioners in the Punjab, Punjab Home (Medical and Sanitary) No. 554 of 4 April 1898: Enclosure No. 78 with Sanitary Letter No.11, 1898, OIOC.

40. Future researchers might also keep a weather eye open for official 'diaries' dating from this time.

41. See M. C. Pradhan, *The Political System of the Jats of Northern India* (Bombay: Oxford University Press, 1966), pp. 107–9. Eric Stokes, *The Peasant and the Raj: Studies in Agrarian Society and Peasant Rebellion in Colonial India* (Cambridge: Cambridge University Press, 1978), pp. 131, 193–5, and 197.

42. Ian Catanach, 'South Asian Muslims and the Plague', p. 90.

43. Major E. Inglis, Deputy Commissioner on Special Plague Duty, to Commissioner, Jullundur, No. 321 of 30 April 1898, L/PJ/6/484, OIOC. The *Civil and Military Gazette* of Lahore, 1 May 1898, went so far as to say that 'the townsmen of Garhshankar merely headed a combination of malcontents from neighbouring villages, who encouraged them to resist'. This is certainly not a case of townsmen 'organizing' revolt in the countryside.

44. Telegram cited in n.34 above.

45. C. H. James, *Report, 1897–98*, p. 9.

46. Punjab Home (Medical & Sanitary) Progs, December 1898, 47, OIOC.

47. C. H. James, *Report, 1897–98*, p. 9.

48. Bhagat Lakshman Singh, *An Autobiography*, ed. Ganda Singh (Calcutta: The Sikh Cultural Centre, 1965), p. 255.

49. See P. H. M. van den Dungen, *The Punjab Tradition: Influence and Authority in Nineteenth-Century India* (London: Allen & Unwin, 1972), especially pp. 297–8. In retirement, Maynard became a Labour parliamentary candidate and published a book on the changes the Russian peasant was undergoing under communism.

50. H. J. Maynard, Commissioner Multan, to Govt., No. 755 of 13 August 1907, Punjab Home (Medical and Sanitary) Progs, November 1907, 31, OIOC.

51. J. P. Hewett, Sec. India Home, to Punjab Judicial and General, Home Sanitary (Plague) No.1353 of 19 July 1901, with Sanitary Letter No. 11 of 11 July 1901, OIOC.

52. On the 'cordon levies', see *The History of Plague in the Punjab, with a Memo. of the Measures Adopted for Dealing with it and Instructions regarding the Measures to be Adopted in 1902–03 (Punjab Plague Manual, 1902)*, (Government of Punjab, 1902), p. 5.

53. H. P. Tollinton, Deputy Commissioner, Sialkot, to Commissioner, Rawalpindi, No.159 (Confidential) of 30 April/1 May 1901, part of Enclosure No. 22 with Sanitary Letter No. 11 of 27 June 1901, OIOC.

54. *Pioneer*, 5 May 1901.

55. G. C. Walker, Commissioner, Rawalpindi, to Secretary Punjab Judicial and General, No. 1707 of 10 May 1901, Enclosure No. 11 to Sanitary Letter cited.

56. H. P. Tollinton to Commissioner, Rawalpindi, letter cited. I have corrected several spelling and punctuation errors in the printed version of this letter.

57. J. P. Hewett to Punjab, letter cited above, in n.51.

58. Ian Catanach, 'Plague and the Tensions of Empire', p. 160.

59. Ibid., pp. 160–61.

60. Browning Smith, 'Report', p. 212.

61. Ibid.

62. *Tribune*, 22 November 1902.

63. *Gujrat Gazetteer* (1892–93), p. 64.

64. *Tribune*, 11 December 1902.

65. Ibid.

66. W. S. Marris, demi-official note, 9 August 1903, on India Home Sanitary (Plague) Deposit Progs, October 1903, 2–4, NAI.

67. Browning Smith, 'Report', p. 212; *Tribune*, 18 and 20 November 1902.

68. Browning Smith, 'Report', p. 212.

69. *Tribune*, 11 December 1907.

70. C. H. James, *Report, 1897–98*, pp. 24–5.

71. Ibid., p. 73

72. H. J. Maynard, Deputy Commissioner, Ambala, quoted E. Wilkinson, *Report on Plague in the Punjab from October 1st 1901 to September 30th 1902* (Government of Punjab, 1904), p. 23.

73. *Akhbar-i-Am*, 13 May 1898, NNP.

74. E. R. Abbott on Assessment Report, Certain Estates of the Chenab Circle of the Behra Tehsil, Shahpur District, Punjab Revenue and Agriculture Progs, February 1909, 32, OIOC.

75. I have used the 1937 edition of this work.

76. W. M. Hailey (later Sir Willam Hailey, still later Lord Hailey), Report on the Jhelum Canal for the year ending 30 September 1904, *Annual Report for the Chenab, Jhelum, and Chunian Colonies for the Year Ending 30 September 1904* (Government of Punjab, 1905), p. 34. Hailey himself almost died from plague at this time.

77. Malcolm Lyall Darling, *Rusticus Loquitor*, p. 71.

78. Malcolm Lyall Darling, *At Freedom's Door* (London: Oxford University Press, 1949), p. 137.

79. Andrew Major has pointed out to me that the *Tribune* quite recently (9 March 2002) had a 'main feature' on the history of the plague in India. Much similar material appeared, of course, when the plague made a (mercifully brief) return in 1994.

80. Ian Catanach, '"Fatalism"? Indian Responses to Plague and other Crises', *Asian Profile* 12, 2 (1984), pp. 183–92.

81. Susan S. Wadley, *Struggling with Destiny in Karimpur, 1925–1984* (Berkeley: University of California Press, 1994).

82. See Clarence Osmond McMullen, *Religious Beliefs and Practices of the Sikhs in Rural Punjab* (New Delhi: Manohar, 1989), pp. 63–5.

83. T. N. Madan, *Non-Renunciation: Themes and Interpretations of Hindu Culture* (Delhi: Oxford University Press, 1987), Chap. 5. See also the essays in Brendan Quayle (ed.), *Hindu Death and the Ritual Journey*, University of Durham, Working Papers in Social Anthropology, No.4. 1980, especially Peter Phillimore, 'Disposing of the Soul: Examples of Ritual Journey in Death Ceremonies in Himachal Pradesh', pp. 114–15.

84. C. H. James, *Report, 1897–98*, p. 146.

85. P. H. M. van den Dungen, 'Changes in Status and Occupation in Nineteenth Century Punjab', in D. A. Low (ed.), *Soundings in Modern South Asian History*, (London: Weidenfeld & Nicolson, 1968), p. 63.

86. S&C, 1905–6, p. 3; S&C, 1906–7, p. 7; S&C 1907–8, p. 8. F. W. Kennaway had this to say in his Assessment Report of the Thanesar Tahsil of the Karnal District (1908), p. 14: 'As far as I am aware, chamars are not usually more subject to the [plague] epidemic than any other caste, but certainly in Thanesar it has always been represented to me that the chief damage to any village has been caused by mortality among chamars.' Punjab Revenue and Agriculture Progs, June 1909, 8, OIOC. See the interesting assertion in the 1911 Census, p. 100, that a reduction in the numbers of Chamars in the Punjab was in part the result of conversions to Sikhism. In the Colonies, the supposed shortage of 'menials' was to quite a large extent the result of a failure to pay wages sufficient to compensate for the inconveniences of removal either from the 'old' districts or from the hills and Kashmir. To some extent, too, it was the result of the increasing tendency of some groups (not, on the whole, Sikhs) to see work in the fields as beneath their dignity.

87. Ian Catanach, review of David Arnold, *Colonizing the Body: State Medicine and Epidemic Disease in Nineteenth-Century India*, in *South Asia* n.s.17, 1 (1994), 122–4.

88. Tony Ballantyne, 'Looking Back, Looking Forward', pp. 18–19; Ballantyne, 'Framing the Sikh Past', p. 10.

89. Ballantyne's approach, it should be noted, is a good deal more finely tuned than the one adopted here.

90. Harbans Singh, 'Origins of the Singh Sabha', Ganda Singh (ed.), *The Singh Sabha and other Socio-Religious Movements in the Punjab 1850–1925*, third edition, (Patiala, 1997), p. 29. The original source is given as Giani Nahor Singh, Singh Sabha Gujarwal, in Grewal, Itihas (1970), p. 114.

91. Here I must acknowledge the very kind assistance of Professor Pashaura Singh.

92. Trilochan Singh (ed.), *Autobiography of Bhai Sahib Randhir Singh* (Ludhiana:

Bhai Sahib Randhir Singh Trust, 1993), pp. 11–12. I must thank Louis E. Fenech for sending me a photocopy of the relevant pages of this book.

93. Ibid., p. 10.

94. Harbans Singh (editor-in-chief), *Encyclopaedia of Sikhism* 3 (Patiala: 1996), p. 476.

95. *Autobiography of Bhai Sahib Randhir Singh*, pp. 14–15. Bhai Randhir Singh mentions that he later published a book which was based on these conversations with Dr Fisher about the Guru Granth Sahib. Pashaura Singh, who very kindly alerted me to the existence and contents of this book, tells me that it was first published anonymously in 1910, under the title *Ki Sri Guru Granth Sahib ji di Puja But Prasti Hai?*. In 1923 (when Bhai Randhir Singh was in jail), it was republished under Bhai Randhir Singh's name by Giani Nahar Singh of Narangwal. A revised edition was published in 1940; and the ninth edition of the book appeared in Ludhiana in 1990, published by the Bhai Randhir Singh Trust. It is obviously a 'text' of some importance in the development of Sikhism in the twentieth century.

96. See Kadiyani Ghulam Ahmad, *A Revealed Cure for the Bubonic Plague* (Lahore, 1898). In the past, this pamphlet could be seen in the Oriental Printed Books section, British Library, and it is presumably now in OIOC.

97. See Ian Catanach, 'South Asian Muslims and the Plague', p. 100.

98. W. H. McLeod, *Sikhism* (London: Penguin, 1997), pp. 199–200.

99. *Autobiography of Bhai Sahib Randhir Singh*, pp. 16–7.

100. *Hitkari*, 19 April 1907, NNP.

101. J. R. Dunlop Smith, Note on Plague, 24 June 1907, Morley Papers, MSS Eur. D573/12, f. 25, OIOC.

102. It may be countered that some years ago it was reported that in Pakistan at least any 'academic request' for access to district records from the days of the Raj would probably be 'met by official scepticism or even outright rejection, unless powerfully supported'. Martin and Zawahir Moir, 'Old District Records in Pakistan', *Modern Asian Studies* 24, 1 (1990), p. 201.

103. W. M. Hailey, Jhelum Report, 1904. S&C, 1906–7, p. 2.

104. S&C, 1905–6, p. 2.

105. S&C, 1906–7, p. 2.

106. N. G. Barrier, 'The Punjab Disturbances', pp. 364–5.

107. 'Really,' Maynard continued, 'Government goes mad now and then.' H. J. Maynard to his wife, 4 March 1907 (continuation of letter begun on 22 February), Maynard Papers, MSS Eur. F224/3, OIOC.

108. N. G. Barrier, 'The Punjab Disturbances', pp. 364 and 369.

109. Ibid., p. 365.

110. F. Popham Young, (Confidential) Note on the Administration of the Chenab Canal Colony, 11 June 1907, Morley Papers, MSS Eur. D573/12, ff. 40–43(b), OIOC.

111. Muhammad Shafi, 'The Punjab Colonies. A Memorandum', 29 June 1907, ibid., f. 37.

112. See *Chenab Colony Gazetteer* (1904), p. 50. Sometimes newly founded villages were given the same names as the villages from which most of their inhabitants had come. (I owe my earliest understanding of the Canal Colonies to Basil Poff, Massey University, Palmerston North, who delved deeply into Punjab history under the late Eric Stokes).

113. Imran Ali, *The Punjab under Imperialism, 1885–1947* (Princeton: Princeton University Press, 1988).

114. Minto to Morley (Private), 10 July 1907, MSS Eur. D573 / 12, f. 47(a), OIOC.

115. Minto's summing-up in the budget debate in Imperial Legislative Council, 28 March 1907, *Financial Statement of Government of India, 1907—08*, p. 238. Great Britain, Parliamentary Papers, 1907 (140) lviii.

116. Great Britain, House of Commons, *Debates*, 4th ser., clxxv, 876.

117. Something like this was suggested to me years ago by Bepin Chandra.

118. N. G. Barrier, 'The Punjab Disturbances', p. 367.

119. Viceroy to Secretary of State, Private Telegram, 7 May 1907, J&P 1461 of 1907, L/PJ/6/810, OIOC.

120. Speech of Ajit Singh at Rawlpindi, 21 April 1907, Appendix No. 6 to Note on Ajit Singh, Jat, Jullundur District, enclosed with E. D. Maclagan, Chief Secretary, Punjab to Secretary, India Home, No. 695 of 3 May 1907, J&P 1461 of 1907, OIOC.

121. These words are underlined in red pencil in the India Office copy of the speech. Here, conceivably, is the origin of Morley's linking of plague and unrest in his speech in June.

122. Speech of Ajit Singh at Batala, Gurdaspur, 28 April 1907, enclosed with Maclagan letter cited in n. 120 above. See also *Pioneer Mail*, 10 May 1907.

123. Daily Report of Director of Criminal Intelligence, 10 July 1907, India Home Political B Progs, Nos. 5–90, August 1907, quoted in Rajiv A. Kapur, *Sikh Separatism: The Politics of Faith* (London: Allen & Unwin, 1986), pp. 49–50.

124. Louis E. Fenech, *Martyrdom in the Sikh Tradition: Playing the 'Game of Love'* (New Delhi: Oxford University Press, 2000). One would like to know what Indian word is translated by 'country' in the reports of Ajit Singh's speeches.

125. M. V. Harcourt, 'Revolutionary Networks in Northern Indian Politics 1907–1935: A Case Study of the "Terrorist" Movement in Delhi, the Punjab, the United Provinces, and Adjacent Princely States', (D.Phil. thesis, University of Sussex, 1973), p. 66.

126. See note on Ajit Singh cited in n. 120 above.

127. Louis E. Fenech, *Martyrdom in the Sikh Tradition*, p. 277, n. 23. A letter to the *Civil and Military Gazette*, 15 May 1907, from 'A Loyal Sikh' certainly makes that claim.

128. See Fauja Singh, 'Ajit Singh (Sardar)', S. P. Sen (ed.), *Dictionary of National Biography* 1 (Calcutta: Institute of Historical Studies, 1972).

129. N. G. Barrier, *The Sikhs and their Literature (A Guide to Tracts, Books and Periodicals, 1849–1919)* (Delhi: Manohar Book Service, 1970), p. 110 and n. 2.

130. M. V. Harcourt, 'Revolutionary Networks', p. 60.

131. See Jagjit Singh, *The Sikh Revolution: A Perspective View* (New Delhi: Kendri Singh Sabha, 1986).

132. Malcolm Lyall Darling, *At Freedom's Door*, p. 123. Darling indicates that Mahilpur, in Hoshiarpur, was an area with a considerable communist presence at this time. He puts communist influence there down to the fact that 'many Sikh emigrants' had returned 'with new wine in their heads'. Mahilpur thana is part of Garhshankar tehsil, the scene of the plague troubles in 1898 referred to above. Darling might perhaps have looked further back in time for some of the antecedents of the phenomenon he was describing.

133. J. S. Grewal, 'Legacies of the Sikh Past for the Twentieth Century', O'Connell et al. (eds) *Sikh History and Religion*, p. 28. Grewal continues, with special reference to the present: 'If socio-economic inequalities are increasing or decreasing within the Sikh community due to State policies, the process is looked upon with indifference. Possibly, the gain of the few is equated with the gain of the community.'

134. See N. G. Barrier, 'Sikh Politics in British Punjab', pp. 180–1.

135. H. J. Maynard, Commissioner of Excise, No. 23 of 24 March 1904, Punjab Financial Commissioner's files 441/104A, quoted in P. H. M. van den Dungen, *The Punjab Tradition*, p. 292. There is a relevant literature on rural–urban relations in pre-modern European history. One work that comes to mind—and it has been used by Harjot Oberoi—is Carlo Ginzburg, *The Cheese and the Worms: The Cosmos of a Sixteenth-Century Miller* (Harmondsworth: Penguin, 1992). This book, it should be noted, gives us a salutary warning against assuming too rigid a divide between 'rural' and 'urban' ways of life.

136. *Disorders Inquiry Committee, 1919–20, Report* (New Delhi: 1976, reprint), p. 88.

137. Jerry Barrier and Andrew Major are, of course, exceptions to this generalization so far as the Sikhs are concerned.

Sikhism in Orissa: From the World of the Nanakpanthis to the Domain of the Khalsa

Himadri Banerjee

Political messages hidden in the language of religion have become a part of contemporary Indian politics, with the projection of Hindutva as a distinct political faith being an obvious manifestation of this trend. Hindutva has been accused of spreading a message of militancy among a sizeable number of Hindus in the Jamuna–Ganga belt. Its political rhetoric has captured the imagination of many among the minorities who are keen to redefine the boundaries of their communities and protect their ethnic identities. Thus, the mercury of India politics continues to rise as important public arenas of the country are communalized. The apprehended long-term impact of communalism on our plural cultural traditions has prompted critics to examine its roots within our wider historical framework. Some of them raise serious doubts as to whether the Indian polity, with its multi-ethnic roots, will survive in the coming years. Others worry that communal tensions will hasten the process of a Balkanization of India along linguistic and communal lines. In this sense, any attempt to locate some of these important issues in the context of the wider Indian religious traditions may provide a critical perspective of the problem.

We may begin with the debate on whether our social life is generally guided by a uniform code of religious discipline and behaviour. Our grass-roots-level experience often conveys a different impression, pointing to areas of our shared religious beliefs and social practices which connect neighbouring communities. One may therefore question the recent projection of Hinduism as a monolithic faith, rigid in its dogma, inflexible in its regulations, and conservative in its worldview. Is it a valid historical assertion cemented by adequate literary, archaeological, or other evidence? Are not its laws of purity and commensality, birthrights and death rituals, dress code and food habit, modes of worship and rules regarding sacred space, and so on, extremely varied, if not sometimes conflicting, in different parts of the country? Recent studies reviewing the 'Great Traditions' of Hinduism have also been redefining the significance of different regional traditions. The latter often serve, it is argued, as 'the true melting pot of the local and the all-India tradition'.[1]

Anthropologists also draw attention to some of these interesting issues. While reconstructing the history of local Islam in global contexts, they refer to 'a wide variety of beliefs and actions labelled Islamic by the people themselves' which are generally propelled by 'internal pluralism, ethnic diversity and multiple discourse'. The scholars travel beyond the 'culture core' of Islam 'defined by its place of origin, Arabia, and by Arabic language and culture only' and seek to review 'the peripheral Islam' residing in dissimilar parts of the globe. The Muslim world not only 'interacts' there 'with other civilizations', but also gives rise to a 'variety of localized adaptations and responses'. 'In a world of overlapping social networks with cross-cutting boundaries and flows of meaning', anthropologists of Islam find 'a multiplicity of voices coming from common Muslims, diversified as they are in age, gender, class, ethnicity, education and so on'.[2]

Richard Eaton's pioneering research on the history of Muslims in the Bengal delta similarly point outs that it is incorrect to view Islam as a monolithic essence that 'simply' developed across space, time and social class and assimilated great numbers of people into a single framework of piety. On the contrary, he has tried to emphasize how different groups, 'by situating them in their unique historical contexts', tried to construct 'the religion [Islam] in the particular way they did'. 'It is testimony to the vitality of Islam—and one of the secrets to its success as a world religion— that its adherents in Bengal were so creative in accommodating local socio-cultural realities with the norms of the religion.'[3]

I

Against this background, here I intend to refer to Sikhism and its evolution in a region beyond its 'culture core', that is, Punjab. Any reconstruction of the history of the Sikhs residing outside Punjab is significant because it not only represents a less-explored area of Sikh studies, but is also likely to offer a profile of Sikhism which may appear to some critics as 'unorthodox', while others may just label it a form of 'syncretism' and see it is as nothing unknown or unusual as far as the wider Indian religious traditions are concerned. But given the 'explosiveness' of terms such as 'syncretism' and 'unorthodox' within Sikh studies, one needs to be very cautious and critical in introducing these phrases and idioms in reconstructing any 'advance' of Sikhism from its 'heartland' (i.e., Punjab) to a 'periphery' (for instance, coastal Orissa).

This study is relevant perhaps from another point of view. Even today, the attention of scholars engaged in Sikh studies either revolves around Punjab or the Sikh diaspora. The wider Indian panorama beyond Punjab is often missed or ignored in many of these works. The Sikh Panth's intimate relationship with the plural Indian religious traditions began in the days of the gurus. According to one estimate, one out of every five Sikhs lives beyond Punjab, within the wider Indian traditions. In many cases, they have been in these places since the sixteenth century. In this context, an outline of their four hundred years of experiences in some of the coastal districts of Orissa is likely to add a new dimension to Sikh studies. Recent scholarship on Sikhism in relation to Orissa primarily concentrates on a very small area of the 'early Sikh tradition', that is, Guru Nanak's *udasi* (travel) to Puri. Here the significance of the dominant regional Jagannath cult has not been adequately explored. In Sikh studies, one thus comes across a space awaiting serious historical investigation. We need to locate its significance in the wider framework of Sikh studies because this may help us understand how two distinct and distant regional traditions find time and space for a meaningful dialogue along the pilgrims' road to Puri in Orissa.

Generally speaking, this local history of the Sikhs is largely unknown beyond the coastal region of Orissa. Intensive fieldwork in Puri, Cuttack, and Bhadrak (all in Orissa) may bring us near a few Oriya folk images of Nanak. Perhaps these portrayals refer directly to those Nanakpanthis and Udasis (many of them were possibly Khatris) visiting the tract for pilgrimage, long-distance trade, soldiering, and many other reasons. Interacting in a mixed language with a north Indian accent, these visitors occasionally set up sangats on their way to Puri. They not only remind us of the activities of the Gosain traders pointed out by Bernard Cohn nearly four decades ago,[4] but also keep us guessing about their likely role in bringing the two *pada*s of the poet Jaidev from coastal Orissa to Punjab.[5] Their proficiency in running religious congregations cum hospices (locally called *mathas*) for travellers and pilgrims was renowned, as was their expertise in administration, the creation of trade 'linkages' and 'banking and credit networks'.[6] The elaborate matha network exposed them to the 'complexities of local life' and stimulated incorporation of many traces of the regional historical realities. These not only brought wealth and power to the Nanakpanthis and Udasis, but also stimulated tension and dissent. We therefore need to know more about their secular activities, which were deeply interlinked with Puri and beyond, because these have so far hardly figured in Sikh studies.

The coastal Orissan Sikh experiences were not restricted only to the activities of the Nanakpanthi fakirs and Udasi sadhus. By the closing year of seventeenth century, Himmat Rai's journey from Puri to Anandpur was mentioned in a few Punjabi sources. He was hailed as one of the first *panj piyare* ('five beloveds'). The Oriya vernacular materials as well as the British records generally maintain silence on the early Khalsa presence until the first quarter of twentieth century. Does it indirectly underline the entrenched position of the Nanakpanthi or Udasi mathas in Puri with their intimate link with the Jagannath temple rituals and economy at the local level?

One may also be interested to know whether this explains the absence of conflict in Orissa that had been going on between the two traditions of Sikhism (Sanatani Sikh and Tat Khalsa) in Punjab since the days of the Singh Sabha resurgence (1873) or the Akali movement of the 1920s. And following on from this, was there any other significant reason prompting the Khalsa to take a back seat in the local Oriya milieu until the first three decades of the twentieth century? Did the latter ever strike back to these mathas? Under what conditions and in which direction? Who then came to their support and on what consideration? What were the reactions in the local Sikh world? Did it precipitate the breakdown of the Nanakpanthi–Udasi matha network or lead to some significant realignment at the local level, thereby widening the gulf between the Nanakpanthis and the Khalsa?

These questions suggest that Sikhism's interactions with the Orissa coast has a long story beyond Guru Nanak's single udasi to Puri or the visit of Himmat Rai to Anandpur. In this context, the local Sikh past perhaps cannot be reconstructed with the help of the Punjabi literary evidence that dominates mainstream Sikh studies alone. Here the historian needs to use 'stouter boots', because he would be going beyond the limits of archives to review such sources and objects, many of which lie beyond the central record rooms or private collections available at the local level.

A sizeable part of this 'vast wealth of unused and under-used historical data' is available in Oriya vernacular writings and a few others still stand as an 'untapped pool of source materials' in regional oral traditions. Nearly thirty years ago, two editors of the Research Committee on the Punjab encouraged their colleagues to go beyond the 'heavily tied... government records and publications' and review other sources for reconstructing the Sikh past.[7] One must remember their pioneering efforts while scrutinizing a few non-archival sources in the present study. These are likely to provide an interesting profile of Sikhs in the context of the wider Oriya popular culture engaged in an uninterrupted dialogue with the Jagannath tradition over the centuries. This may also refer to the Sikh Panth's earlier links with the distant Indian regional traditions as well as their relevance in reconstructing the Sikh past of our times.

II

It would be perhaps convenient to begin with some of the well-known Sikh points of view. According to *janam sakhi* sources, the first Sikh guru came to Puri in 1509 or thereabouts. It is widely believed that he came with Bhai Mardana, one of his close disciples, and composed the famous '*sabad Gagan moi thal*' in Rag Dhansari recorded in the Adi Granth. It is also claimed that it subsequently led to the foundation of the Nanak Baoli (locally known as the 'Derasura-Bhaisuro Kua') near the Swargadwar area in Puri.[8] After a gap of nearly two centuries, we come across another reference (see above) regarding Himmat Rai and his becoming one of the first panj piyare of the Khalsa. Finally, we have the third citation relating to one of the deathbed wishes of Maharaja Ranjit Singh (1839). It is thus recorded in a contemporary source:

Bhai Gobind Ram said that the Sarkar [the Maharaja] had very often said that Kohinoor had been left by the old kings and none of the Sultans had taken it along with himself... So he decided to make over the piece of diamond for Sri Jagannathji, according to the custom of his predecessors. He further added that the Sarkar had said that the time and that hour had come unexpectedly... By a sign the Sarkar pointed out that soon its Sankalp [promise] should be made and it should be sent over to Sri Jagannathji.[9]

The Lahore darbar, however, refused to execute the order. The Kohinoor remained in Lahore until it was transferred to London after the annexation of Punjab in 1849.

One may pose the following questions here: What do these three isolated pieces of Punjabi sources with Jagannath Puri in the background signify, since nearly three centuries separate them? Do they merely imply imagined or real points of contact between two distant regional traditions separated by more than thousands of miles? Or were these just watermarks of the relationships between them, places linked by motives of pilgrimage, long-distance trade, soldiery, and other things? Did these have any reflection in the contemporary Oriya writings?

We will, however, try to answer these questions in reverse order for a cohesive presentation of the local Sikh past. Perhaps the earliest Oriya response to Guru Nanak's presence in Puri is recorded in Iswardas' *Sri Chaitanya Bhagabata*. It refers to Guru Nanak's meeting with Sri Chaitanya in Puri in the early sixteenth century, though the text was completed only by the end of the next century. In this sense, it can hardly be regarded as a contemporary evidence of the suggested meeting between Guru Nanak and Sri Chaitanya. However, it continues to remain a topic of debate among scholars.[10] In recent years, there has been an attempt to suggest that the contemporary *Madala Panji*, the Puri Temple chronicles, also refer to Guru Nanak's presence in Puri.[11] But many historians and archaeologists have questioned the authenticity of information available in the *Madala Panji* on sixteenth-century Orissa.[12]

Apart from these sources, there are a few significant oral traditions coming from other parts of the state. These were in wide circulation along the pilgrimage route in the coastal districts from Bhadrak to Puri. One may conveniently begin from Bhadrak, an important seat of Mughal administration since the late seventeenth century. It was situated near the ancient pilgrimage road and served as a resting place. 'As the gateway to neighbouring Bengal, Bhadrak has traditionally served as the cradle of a rich composite culture'[13] which was enriched by the Afghan, Mughal, and Maratha ways of life until the early years of the nineteenth century. There is a village named Sangat and it is believed that the Sikh Guru visited the place on his way to Puri. It also refers to an oral tradition about the Nanakpanthi/Udasi presence in the region.

Oriya playwright Bansiballav Goswami's well-known folk drama *Mogal Tamsa*, completed around the middle of eighteenth century, offers an intimate profile of the situation.[14] We are not certain whether it was inspired by the contemporary Maharashtrian Tamasha tradition, but it became very popular during the Maratha rule in Orissa (1751–1803).[15] It is likely that Goswami's play was circulated in different manuscript versions and exchanged hands over a long period till it was finally available in print in the second half of the last century. Prior to its present published form, it was perhaps annually staged in different adjoining villages around Bhadrak, Gadarpur, Santhia, Purana Bazaar, Sankarpur, Mirzapur, Januganj, and Banka Bazaar during the last few days of the month of Chaitra (March–April).[16]

Such regular performances in a short span of time, within a small radius of roughly thirty miles, perhaps not only stimulated a sense of competition and specialization, but also encouraged meaningful involvement and participation regarding stagecraft, preparation of musical instruments, costumes, and performance at the village level. The venue of the *Tamsa* was generally 'a sort of open-air theatre', with its main character, Mirza Sahib, a Mughal official, often speaking in Persian and sitting on a special platform, always occupying centre stage. Torches were used for lighting the stage and the audience sat around it all night to enjoy the performance. The entire story was 'developed through acting as well as singing'. 'It uses many languages and registers, prose and poetry, the idioms of the court as well as that of the country, appropriate to characters and situations.' A good number of minor characters representing different social occupational groups appeared one by one, often talking in mixed Hindi, Urdu, Oriya, and Bengali.[17] As one may construe from the title itself, the *Tamsa* was primarily a socio-political charade, articulating fun and satire at the subaltern level about some corrupt local Mughal officials. It also refers to other layers of the social framework not directly related to the local bureaucracy. It leaves enough room for popular participation—from the selection of the date and place of the performance to local funding, to rigorous scanning and screening of the actual performers at different levels. A significant part of the folk play therefore stemmed from the everyday life of the region and there was sufficient fun, lampoon, and caricature that the viewers could identify with. The larger part of the audience no doubt came from the local peasant world, many of whom would return home after some direct interaction with the dramatic personages.[18] It perhaps once more brought them back to the world of *Mogal Tamsa*, with its fun and excitement that continued to remain as an integral part of the popular culture along the pilgrims' road to Puri.

The world of the *Mogal Tamsa* did not end here. It offered also a space to a group of Nanakpanthis, perhaps on their routine pilgrimage to Puri. Like many commoners on their way to Lord Jagannath, they briefly appeared on the stage and presented a chorus in a mixed language, though its tune was very earthy and the lyrics easily understandable. Here we find them as a group of peripatetic saints, exhausted after a long journey from 'a distant land' and seeking just 'a handful of rice' and a paisa in the name of Ram (i.e., God). They also pray for the well-being of everyone and advise 'not to make any differentiation between Ram and Rahiman'.[19] Thus their song goes:

Ek paisa dene babu jhuth baat nein bolne Ram.
Bal bachcha sab anand rahega, achchha ji Bhandari Ram.
Ek muthi dene babu, achchha ji Bhandari Ram.
Bahu durse aaye babu, achchha ji Bhandari Ram.
Goru bachhara sab bhala rahega, achchha ji Bhandari Ram.
Muthi bharke dene babu, achchha ji Bhandari Ram...
Ram Rahiman juda na karo dil ko sachcha rakho ji...

A 'syncretic plurality of names for the Supreme Deity' may constitute a part of their self-representation, but there is reference to no other esoteric experience in the song. They also do not suggest anything like *nam, dan,* and *ishan,* which were generally held as the model code of conduct for any Nanakpanthi of that period. Instead of underlining the significance of the sharing of an individual's income (*bhand-chhakna*) or the dignity of individual labour (*kirat-karna*), they simply prayed for the welfare of all in the local world, particularly of the cattle that constituted a valuable section of the agrarian economy. The message was one of universal welfare and it was based on common sense and local reality. Finally, there was nothing abusive in the Nanakpanthis' attitude towards the local Muslim officials who provided such an undercurrent of fun in the play. On the contrary, they looked forward to their support, though it had been universally prohibited in some of the rahits of the early eighteenth century.

Now, of course Guru Nanak had universally denounced pilgrimage while the third guru, Amardas, urged the Sikhs to have their 'new pilgrimage' of Goindval situated on the right bank of the Beas. Besides, there was hardly any room for begging for food and money in the teachings of the Sikh gurus. Thus one may debate why these Nanakpanthis were still coming to Lord Jagannath in Puri, at odds with the long-established norms spelt out by the gurus, or seeking material support from a Mughal official, which is directly opposed to the principles of the contemporary rahits. Do these Nanakpanthis of the *Mogal Tamsa* here represent an opposite role to that modelled by their counterparts in Punjab at the same period? Do they lack 'the sophistication of Nanak's own understanding?' Do we therefore 'find ourselves drawn dramatically away from his actual teachings and from the faithful replicas which his successors produced'?[20] The above Nanakpanthi narrative grew out of the realities of the local milieu, which is delineated in the barest outline, and conveys some of the expectations of the rural society around it. In this sense, the medieval world of Sikhism had an Orissan perspective. We shall also see that it had more than one dimension.

III

We have another set of oral evidence from Cuttack city. The first comes from the northern outskirts of Cuttack, from the Kaliaboda area near the Mahanadi river. Situated on the pilgrims' road between Puri and Bhadrak, modern Cuttack is generally known in the wider Sikh world for its historical Datan Sahib Gurdwara. In the post-Independence years, this impressive gurdwara came up almost dominating the entire Kaliaboda area of the town. It underlines how the Sikhs of the Khalsa[21] had increasingly become a significant force in the locality during the last three quarters of the twentieth century. Flanked by two mighty rivers, Mahanadi and Kathajodi, the town had been the most important political centre of medieval Orissa till the last days of the local Ganga and Gajapati rulers. Its commercial importance is corroborated by numerous medieval sources. This might have encouraged the arrival of many northern Indian traders, particularly the Khatris, after the Mughal conquest of Orissa under Akbar (1592).[22]

Long before the recent assertion of the Khalsa Sikh identity around the Datan Sahib Gurdwara, Cuttack was a centre of Nanakpanthi/Udasi activities over centuries. Even today, one may come across there a small Hindu religious place there. It is perhaps a remnant of an old Udasi matha, standing in the backyard of the older Datan Sahib gurdwara building (1935), now converted into a gurdwara school. Much of the valuable lands of the matha have been wrested out of its control and one can hardly estimate its old prestige and power from its present condition.[23] Memory of the Datan Sahib is intimately associated with Guru Nanak's visit to Cuttack. Local legends point out that the Sikh Guru came here with his son Sri Chand, the founder of the Udasi sect. The Guru's presence, however, led to an immediate confrontation with Chaitanya Bharati, a local yogi, which ended in the complete rout of the latter. Then the Sikh Guru advised Sri Chand to remain there as the head of the new matha to look after the sadhus who would frequently pass here on their way to Sri Jagannath. Thus the Cuttack matha continued as an Udasi establishment and its *mohants* were generally *brahmacharis* with close links to the mathas of Puri.[24] A twentieth-century Oriya biographer of Guru Gobind Singh also confirms the past prosperity of the Cuttack matha and the steady erosion of its estate due to the annual flood of the mighty Mahanadi.[25]

With this understanding of the Kaliaboda area, let us move on to the other end of the city, the Jhanjharimangala region situated around the banks of the Kathajodi river. It is generally regarded as another locality with a long history of human settlement under the Cuttack municipal administration.[26] It is also claimed by many that the river served as an old trade link, thereby bringing different language groups together over the years. Perhaps these new settlements gave the locality a plural cultural character.

A single visit to the Jhanjharimangala area, where the goddess Mangala still remains the presiding deity, would in ordinary times hardly offer any ready clue to either its local oral tradition associated with Guru Nanak or the plural cultural heritage of the neighbourhood. Here we need to remember the Ramleela festival, which was widely celebrated in the past during and after the Ramnavami days. It may provide a possible link with the early Sikh tradition as well as evidencing a closeness to the local cultural roots.

It is likely that the legend of Nanak (or the memory of the Nanakpanthi/Udasi sadhus, traders, moneylenders, and pilgrims) did not take long to travel from the Kaliaboda area to the other end of the city in the medieval days. We have already mentioned Cuttack's significance as a busy commercial and political centre. After the Mughal conquest, its interaction with the rest of northern India steadily increased. Todar Mall, a senior northern-Indian Khatri long associated with Emperor Akbar's administration, later came down for a new land revenue settlement of Orissa. Besides, a small section of the Khatris who had already been in Orissa in connection with the Mughal commissariat arrangement did not immediately return to northern India. Finally, there was the new Mughal administration facilitating rapid trade links between Cuttack and the distant northern Indian marts as far as Punjab via Burdwan, Patna, Banaras, and Agra. Following the administrators and traders, one can well imagine the presence of an increasing number of northern Indian pilgrims, yearning for a glimpse of Lord Jagannath, passing along the pilgrimage road through Cuttack, Bhadrak, and Kasijora (in Medinipur district, then in Orissa).

The Mughal rule thus not only forged a closer link between Orissa and the imperial north, but also turned Cuttack town into a more cohesive administrative unit. It perhaps facilitated interaction between the Kaliaboda matha and the Kathajodi–Jhanjharimangala locality too. As an indirect outcome of this emergence of newer channels of communication, many popular religious beliefs and cultural traditions from northern India started pouring into the local world.

The same period witnessed 'a shift' towards 'a more devotional' and 'a more populist form of Rama worship' in northern India. 'As a result of this orientation of the Rama cult', the Ramleela became an increasingly important platform of popular culture and provided many interesting examples of how Rama legends came to be modified by an 'imaginative blending of historical and mythological-religious elements', showing that these could be recycled into a different regional context far away from its place of origin.[27] The northern Indian Ramleela thus steadily reached the coastal Orissa districts. But the local world had had its own Ramayana tradition since the days of Balaram Dasa, one of the five *Bhakta kavis* (Bhakti devotee–poets) who flourished in the first quarter of the sixteenth century.[28] The northern Indian Rama tradition, which arrived through different channels, perhaps had an interesting dialogue with its Oriya counterpart around the Jhanjharimangala area of Cuttack and underwent some modifications. Here also it continued to remain 'a form of open-air drama', but was staged in front of the Mangala (a local mother goddess) temple during the period of the Ramnavami festival. 'The songs of the drama are taken from the works of different lyricists of medieval and modern Orissa. Many of them are being sung from very olden days whose [sic] authors are not known.'[29]

In the Ramleela of the Jhanjharimangala locality, we come across the presence of Nanak in the galaxy of the many saints blessing King Dasharatha on the occasion of Rama's coronation. He does not communicate in Oriya, but in a mixed language, with the northern Indian intonation. In the context of the local Ramkatha festivity, this part of the performance does not seem to be a forcible engrafting affecting the course of the dramatic narrative. One may still question its historical incongruity: the presence of Nanak in the company of other Hindu saints, and many of them not of his time and tradition. But the audience faces very little difficulty in accommodating him because he has also been an integral part of the Oriya Puranic world.[30]

In this sense, the Nanak of Jhanjharimangala is not a duplication of the Sikh Guru Nanak preaching monotheism. The former's legend is based on the Oriya experiences in the locality and therefore significantly differs from what one comes across in Punjab. His name figures in the popular religious invocations and he shares a common space with a few Oriya Hindu deities of the region. Thus, within a radius of barely ten miles of the same city, we have two distinct profiles of Nanak: one projecting the image of an otherworldly sadhu with a distinct Udasi bias (at Kaliaboda) while the other represents an integral part of the local Ramkatha tradition, making his debut through an open-air opera tradition. If the Udasis of the Kaliaboda area, with their ash-smeared bodies and 'sect-marks on the forehead in the fashion of the Dasnamis',[31] were then coming closer to the local Nath–Shaivite tradition, the Nanak of the Jhanjharimangala locality was perhaps steadily looking forward to his Vaishnavite (Ramite) affiliation.[32]

IV

The close connection between the Nanakpanthis/Udasis and the regional popular cultural tradition extended as far as Puri. As already pointed out, there is still no confirmed local evidence of Guru Nanak's visit in the early sixteenth century. In this regard, the records of the Kaliyuga *pandas*, who generally keep records and look after pilgrims from northern India, including Punjab, do not add anything significant or new to our knowledge. Their *bahi*, record books of pilgrims maintained by these priests at the local level, are not very reliable regarding the history of the pre-British times.[33] Second, a late nineteenth-century British inquiry launched in connection with a civil litigation of the most important Nanakpanthi/Udasi matha (Mangu Matha) also categorically denied the possibility of any such visit.[34] The janam sakhis, McLeod points out, which 'provide only glimpses' of the historical Nanak, do not however altogether rule out the possibility of such a visit.[35] In view of this ongoing debate regarding Guru Nanak's visit to Puri, we cannot altogether deny the possibility of the first Sikh guru's presence there. We also need to review a few Oriya sources referring to the journeys made by the Nanakpanthi traders, Udasi sadhus, and other Sikhs to the area in subsequent times.[36] The annexation of Orissa by the Mughals quickened their presence.

Since medieval times, the local rulers of Orissa (the Gangas and the Gajapatis) universally declared themselves as the *sevaka* (servants) of Lord Jagannath with the 'motive of legitimizing their rule over the entire Oriya-speaking tract of the deity'. Such political manoeuvres 'certainly increased the popularity of the Jagannath cult' and the importance of Puri as a 'centre of pilgrimage (tirtha)'.[37] The Mughal general Raja Man Singh, who had come there after the annexation of Orissa, was perhaps aware of the significance of the local Jagannath tradition. He took the necessary steps for the protection of the sacred space of Puri. Thus, by the time of the Mughals, Puri continued to predominate as one of the major centres of pilgrimage in eastern India.[38]

During this same period, newer sangats sprang up in different parts of eastern India. These places witnessed the presence of Sikh traders, bankers, sadhus, and soldiers connecting Punjab with centres as far as Dhaka in the east via Agra, Allahabad, Banaras, Sasaram, Patna, Burdwan, and Murshidabad. The annexation of Orissa facilitated the extension of communication further towards the south-east from Burdwan, Arambag, and Bishnupur to Puri via Bhadrak, Jajpur, and Cuttack.[39] The development of Puri as one of major tirthas also coincided with the augmentation of a large number of mathas for providing food and shelter to pilgrims. The pilgrims came from 'different cultural traditions' with 'highly diverse motives' such as bathing, pradakshina (circumambulation), and prayaschitta (atonement) ceremonies.[40] These mathas started acquiring an important role in the 'ritual calendar' of Lord Jagannath.[41] This was increasingly embellished by the addition of 'a vast number of new festivals'.[42] These were steadily extended throughout the years, thereby inviting greater participation and involvement by a larger number of pilgrims. The pilgrims were specially advised to eat edible offerings (mahaprasad) from the central temple kitchen because of its 'special religious merit and significance'. These mathas gradually expanded their area of operation and set up similar units along the road leading to Puri. This also meant that they earned significantly more.

In the context of these developments in Puri, it was likely that the Nanakpanthis and Udasis strengthened their relationship with the local political authority, the Raja of Khurda (who was also the Raja of Puri), universally respected as the highest sevaka of Lord Jagannath. They would have actively participated in different temple services and rituals. Their relationship with the Jagannath cult would also have grown stronger as they took an active part in the supervision of the traders, mercenaries, sadhus, and others who came there as pilgrims. They also had to look after the cultivation of rent-free lands scattered over different parts of Orissa and beyond. A sizeable part of these lands was given away in the name of god, but left under their management for better utilization of resources. They had to collect rent from those estates and utilize the surplus by investing in different trade ventures, including moneylending.[43] All these needs perhaps prompted them to have an organization of their own, leading to the foundation of a matha near the Dolamandap Shahi area, close to the central gate of the Jagannath temple.

V

The Nanakpanthi–Udasi activity, therefore, had its widest limit in Puri. While this was due to the long and uninterrupted stay of these men over centuries, we do not have any printed documents or evidence specifying the time of their earliest presence in Puri. But the records preserved in the private possession of the present mohant of the Mangu Matha discloses that in 1722, Bir Kishore Dev, the Raja of Khurda and Puri, issued a *chamu citau*[44] for setting up a Nanakpanthi–Udasi matha.[45] Prior to that, the Nanakpanthis were no doubt present in Puri town, and a report of 1873 thus reconstructed the past:

It is very difficult to find the exact time when this mut [matha] was first established. This mut belongs to the Nanak Panthis of Punjab. It does not appear that Nanak Saha [Shah] ever came to Poore [Puri] but his two disciples Gadhar and Mangoo, both of the Punjabi extraction, came one after the other to this town. It appears that Mangoo was inferior in order to Gadhar and hence acknowledged his subordination as long as Gadhar lived. Gadhar had his first residence in Poore near the Singha Doar (Lion's Gate) not in a house but in [an] open space which now lies close to the Chowkiidari Tax Office. Gadhar, like the founder of all other muts, commanded some influence on the then Raja who thought it advisable to make the ascetic settle in the town. The Raja made some endowments and built the mut for him but as Gadhar pretended above all worldly affairs, the monastery was established in the name of his follower Mangoo. Hence the mut is called Mangoo Mut after its founder Mangoo.[46]

If 1722 marks the official year of foundation of the Mangu Matha, the presence of the Nanakpanthis can be traced to a time before that date. The Raja of Khurda must have known the Nanakpanthis even earlier. The latter also took a couple of years to establish the necessary credentials, thereby drawing sympathetic royal attention in their favour. It is likely that before 1722, these men also supported the pilgrims and others coming there. Any material and moral help and assistance provided to the pilgrims, particularly those coming from Punjab, must have strengthened their position. On the other hand, any decline in the regular flow of pilgrims to Puri would affect the royal finance. In this sense, the

Nanakpanthis, by offering their service, were extending significant support not only to the pilgrims but also to the Raja of Puri. This mutual self-interest played an important role in extending royal patronage to the Nanakpanthi and Udasi matha.

The matha still stands in the Dolamandashahi area. Its history over the first hundred and fifty years (1722–1873) was one of steady growth. There were at least eight royal orders issued by the successive rajas of Puri extending different rights and privileges to the matha during the period. It is likely that the first mohant, Mangu Ram Das, was alive until 1750/51. During his three-decade tenure, the matha was established on a solid foundation. In 1740, it was allowed to construct a few more rooms for its own use. The Raja also gave 'Bhikaripada Perganah Rahang' to Mangu Matha by the *lakheraj* (revenue-free) settlement of 1743. It was declared an endowment, which was to be used as *amritamonohi* land.[47] In 1777, two more new areas were 'granted by a Sanad of the same tenure'. It was declared that 'the whole proceeds' from these lands 'must have been spent in getting eatables for dedication to the Lord Jagannatha of the Universe'.[48]

The line of succession to the office of the mohant after Mangu Ram Das is not clear. It is likely that Udasi Gobind Ram Das was raised to the gaddi after the death of Mangu Ram. In a separate royal order addressed to the temple superintendent, the matha was confirmed in all the rights and privileges it had been enjoying under its predecessor:

As per tradition, Mangu Matha will continue to supply *Chhabhoga* (six offerings)... molasses required for the daily offerings of the deities in different festivals of the temple... Further, the pilgrims coming from other places should not be detained, rather they should be provided facilities to visit the deities.[49]

These orders suggest that the Raja of Puri had been playing 'a crucial intermediary function' of 'linking' the local Jagannath temple officials with the pilgrims and the different Puri mathas, each standing at different levels of social relationship. The royal 'protective role' in the 'redistribution of resources' perhaps stimulated the growth of a number of well-demarcated areas of influence where the different interdependent units would function within their limits. Second, these orders were issued with an eye to an easy flow of pilgrims to the Jagannath temple. It added to the prosperity of the 'religious economy' of Puri, connecting the central temple, town, hinterland, and the ancient pilgrim road with the wider Indian networks.[50]

All these developments brought about certain significant changes in the position of the Mangu Matha. It had a well-defined role in different temple rituals such as the Chamar Seva, Mayurpuchchha Seva, Amritamonohibhoga, and Chhabhoga, which brought the matha closer to the local sacred world. It was also intimately integrated with its secular milieu in different areas of the same complex.[51] It received rent-free land grants not only from the Raja of Puri, but also from other secular heads of the adjoining Gadajata areas and pilgrims coming from different parts of the country.

According to an official report of 1848, it controlled land with an annual rent of Rs 5 and its market value was estimated at Rs 20,000. The same report also confirmed that it stood fifth among the 30 richest mathas of Puri.[52] Apart from its income from landed estates, the cash brought in by the pilgrims was considerable and takings generally reached a peak during the time of the Rathajatra (the chariot festival in late June or early July). With the gradual rise in income, the mohant of the matha had to set up its own small administration unit for the regular collection of rent from the lands, extending essential ritual services to the central temple, and building up institutions for 'sheltering and feeding its long-term residents' and 'pilgrims'.[53] Finally, its importance steadily grew in relation to the distant mathas of Cuttack, Bhadrak, and Kasijora. Sometimes these mathas operated in a close circuit, catering to the different needs of the pilgrims, many of them coming from northern India.

VI

The Nanakpanthis and Udasis thus carved out a place of their own in the sacred complex of Puri from the first quarter of the eighteenth century. Their century-long interaction with the dominant regional tradition was stimulating interesting reactions, a few of which are recorded in Oriya sources. They had long 'participated in the shared inheritance of Indic cosmologies and temporalities' of northern India and therefore they could accommodate 'the syncretic plurality of names for the supreme deity' in a place far away from Punjab.[54] On their way to Puri, they had long been passing through many similar places of pilgrimage.[55] In this sense, the Nanakpanthis and the Udasis perhaps did not find the coastal districts of Orissa altogether an alien world.[56] As the areas of interaction with the Jagannath temple expanded over the years, their economic network grew complex and got embedded in the local framework. These experiences also steadily gave them a regional profile.

Interestingly enough, these things were happening in Orissa when the birth of the Khalsa had already heralded many significant changes in the contemporary Sikh world of Punjab. But it could not altogether get rid of many of the linkages of the old Nanakpanthi world. The studies by McLeod, Oberoi, and Deol point out that even in the eighteenth century, many Sikhs in fact did not belong to the Khalsa. There were many and varied categories of Sahajdhari Sikhs such as the Udasis and the Nanakpanthis with forehead mark (*tikka*) and sacred thread (*janeo*). They were permitted to conduct non-Khalsa funeral rites. Many of them neither belonged to the Khalsa nor adopted its martial ways. They regularly visited many Hindu tirthas and shared popular Hindu religious customs which affected the belief of the Sikhs. The Sanatani Sikh world continued to hold an important position in the Sikh Panth of the pre-Singh Sabha days, where the Puranic narrative of the Dasam Granth and the Sahajdhari beliefs and symbols could easily be accommodated within the Khalsa.

With these Punjab experiences in the background, the Nanakpanthis and Udasis found enough space for an interesting dialogue with the popular culture of Puri. Here the Naga dance, closely associated with the local Shahijatra celebrated in the month of Chaitra, provides a glimpse of the extent of the interactions between the two distant and distinct regional cultures. The former has long been an important part of the Oriya folklore. Its relationship with the legendary military tradition of the Jagannath cult finds expression in Oriya sources. Many faithful Oriyas believe that Lord Jagannath had even taken up arms for the protection of the honour of His devotees and defended the liberty of the Oriyas against enemies. The local Kanchi–Kaveri tradition refers to His war against the ruler of Kanchi in His famous Naga dress.[57]

The local militarism was largely coloured by the Kalapahar episode.[58] It was then widely whispered in and around Puri that the Muslims would again try to 'pollute' the 'sacred' image of Lord Jagannath. With an eye to countering this eventuality, a few *jega-ghar* perhaps came up in different parts of Puri. A jega-ghar 'is a club, gymnasium and cultural society rolled into one'.[59] In the wider Indian religious traditions, the Nagas represented a 'religio-commercial sect' of the Shaivite devotees. They visited 'regular places of pilgrimage' and carried on different trade transactions, including the moneylending associated with their mathas.

As suggested earlier, these men generally in close contact with the Udasis sometimes constituted another important group of the same Shaivite 'warrior-ascetic' tradition.[60] Cohn's study points to their 'annual cycle of pilgrimage' being spread over a significant part of northern Indian territories, and they would often 'move down to Puri and the temple of Jagannath'. The same study suggests that many of them settled down in different parts of eastern India. It was therefore not unlikely that a significant number of these Nagas and Udasis would also be among the pilgrims in Puri. They often found accommodation in the local Nanakpanthi–Udasi mathas due to their proximity of religious beliefs.

It seems that the Naga dance had a close connection with other local cultural traditions as well. It also shared a common platform with the local Sathera group of dancers, representing another military tradition in the Puri sacred complex. A local vernacular source refers to the Satheras as 'members of Sikh faith ever ready in protecting and preaching Sikhism in the region'.[61] Like the Nanakpanthis of Bhadrak or the Nanak of the Jhanjharimangala Ramkatha (Cuttack), the Satheras generally interacted with the local people in a mixed Hindi–Oriya version. When local people requested them to disclose their identity, they responded:

Sunle Bhaiya kahanse aya
Lahore hamara dera,
Rikvedse paidya hamne
Nanakji gurudwar,
Pita hamara dharma niranjan
Mata adi kumari
Guruji hamko bhej diyahai
Banaye Brahmachari.
Guru hukamse larki thuke
Bhiksha mangke phira
Ganga Jamuna tirath nahe
Pryagraj Hardwara.[62]

It underlines that these men are from Lahore and they have an intimate link with the Udasi / Sutherasahi tradition.[63] They trace their roots to the Rig Veda though Guru Nanak continues to remain their guru. They are bachelors and claim to have visited different places of pilgrimage such as Prayag and Hardwar. Finally, like the Nanakpanthis of Bhadrak, they find nothing wrong in interacting with the local world in their 'syncretic' narrative. Thus, the Sathera dancers of Shahijatra (Puri) suggest an interesting presence of Sikhism with enough 'fluidity' within it.

Here Sikhism does not represent a closed-door affair restricted to the four walls of Mangu Matha. It is open enough to adjust itself to local social conditions and religious beliefs. We have enough Oriya source materials projecting the Sathera participants with their turbans, beards, and arms in different war-like postures.[64] Simultaneously, they keep on singing and conversing with the people in mixed Hindi, which is not entirely unknown in the neighbourhood. It is not unlikely that mohants of the Mangu Matha of Puri had played an important role in financing such Sathera festivities, thereby conveying a message of Sikhism understandable to the local world. In the midst of such celebrations, the two distant traditions often overlapped, enriching both in the process.[65] The Sathera Sikhs, with a few external symbols of Sikhism, also shared some of the common markers of the 'warrior-ascetic' traditions of the medieval days. Their heroic dance and music staged in connection with the Ramnavami festival in the month of Chaitra did leave behind a deep impact on the popular mind. Local people had an active participation there and a mid-twentieth-century poet thus recapitulates the past with a note of nostalgia:

Nrutya karibaku tahun hela paribesh
Gerua bashan sange muktakachchha hoi
Nanakakang sishyagan ashilek tahun,
Mathare ushnish haste dikathia dhari
Bhajan gaile tahun sumadhur kari.[66]

VII

With the growing popularity of the Satheras as well as the predominant role of the Mangu Matha in some of the temple rituals, the gaddi of the mohant became an important symbol of prestige and power in the locality. Its affluent standing and close links with the local world made it a coveted position among the seniormost inmates of the matha. The incumbent of the gaddi could effectively control dissent and rivalry among disciples as long as he was efficient and tactful. However, the situation might turn hostile in the event of his accidental death, thereby leaving the succession wide open. It was likely to invite fierce rivalry among his disciples. Apart from its inner rivalry for succession, the local Nanakpanthi–Udasi group was also not a homogeneous one on the grounds of religious beliefs and practices. The financial success of the matha might have widened those fissures at the local level. Perhaps the Nanak Baoli situated very close to the Mangu Matha sometimes provided an ideal platform to some of the protestors.[67]

The standing of the Mangu Matha had already been extended to distant corners of Orissa. One such place was Kasijora, more than one hundred and fifty miles from Puri. Its ruler was originally a Punjabi Khatri of the Sarhind region. According to one local tradition, he had come here in connection with a pilgrimage to Puri. Later he settled down in Kasijora, and his descendants continued to maintain close ties with the mohants of Mangu Matha. They established a temple dedicated to Lord Jagannath in the locality and granted a sizeable amount of land to the Mangu Matha.[68] Khasali Ram Das, the eighth mohanta of the Mangu Matha, visited the place in connection with the supervision of the local matha. His sudden death there, away from Puri, brought the simmering conflicts in the matha to the surface. The succession question marked the beginning of a long period of civil litigation and it brought many of the evils of the matha to public attention.

The financial well-being of some of the mathas in Puri and the corrupt practices of their mohants had become a subject of debate at different levels of the provincial bureaucracy. In the early part of the second half of the nineteenth century, Kedar Nath Dutt, headmaster of a Bhadrak school, brought out a monograph highlighting the irregularities associated with the different mathas of the region. He pointed out:

The Mohunts have given up their antiquated hospitality. The Muts are now converted into temples of Bacchus and Belzeebub. Pilgrims and sick men never approach for fear of being rudely expelled from their portals laden with abuse. The Mohunts have yielded to most degrading and grossly carnal pleasure, and their Chellas or pupils emulate their vices and try to surpass their Mohaprovas [i.e. mohants] in sensuality and obscenity. The Muts at midnight regularly become the resort of concubines and harlots.[69]

The prolonged civil litigation proved very costly for the Mangu Matha. It not only exhausted a significant amount of its financial resources, but also paved the way for the gradual weakening of the hold of the mohant over the matha's administrative network.[70] There used to be occasional public criticism against the misuse of funds in some of the major mathas.[71]

These institutions were then projected as symbols of an old order and therefore needed an overhaul in matters of financial irregularities and the gross negligence in ritual services extended to the central temple throughout the year. Taking advantage of the occasional public outcry and bitter infighting among the higher inmates, many peasants, who had so far been cultivating the lands of the Mangu Matha and paying dues to the local agents of the mohants, started showing reluctance in reimbursing the rents.

VIII

The erosion of matha authority was taking place in the background of a new sense of Oriya identity among a section of the Western-educated middle-class since the late nineteenth century. Long separated and scattered within three different provincial administrative units—Bengal, the Central Provinces, and the Madras Presidency—it was striving hard for a greater political unity among the Oriya-speaking people within one governmental framework. Many of its leaders came from the ranks of Oriya Brahmos, who generally subscribed to the message of monotheism and criticized idol worship. Like their Bengali counterparts, they had a deep respect for Guru Nanak's voice of protest against the dominance of the priestly hierarchy, expensive religious rituals, casteism, and superstition. They believed in the politics of loyalty and refused to look forward to many of the contemporary Indian political questions. The Brahmos made their mother tongue the most important vehicle of patriotic expression and gave it a new orientation through their own print media set up in different urban centres such as Cuttack, Puri, and Baleswar. They founded a political platform under the banner of the Utkal Sammelani (1903) and expected moral support from the British in their Oriya unity movement in the early years of the twentieth century.[72]

A section of the Oriya Brahmos deserve all the credit for bringing back the message of monotheism of Guru Nanak to modern Orissa. But they maintained silence on other areas of Sikhism, particularly the fighting tradition of the Khalsa, which had long been an important segment of the Indian nationalist imagination. As the twentieth century rolled on and the movement against colonial rule assumed an increasingly radical character, the history of Sikh militarism started drawing the attention of a larger number of Oriya authors. These writers were neither Brahmos nor did they subscribe to the first Sikh guru's message of monotheism. In their writings, the history of Sikh armed resistance under Guru Gobind Singh, with a distinct Hindu orientation, steadily assumed a greater importance. They had also very little regard for the politics of moderation so long pursued by the Oriya Brahmos.

The new political climate hastened the dawn of a new age in Oriya nationalism. In spite of its early popularity, the moderate politics of the Utkal Sammelani thus suffered a temporary setback after nearly a decade since its inception in the early years of the twentieth century. The void was rapidly filled in by a new Oriya leadership coming from the Satyabadi school.[73] It made the agenda of the popular movement of the Indian National Congress its declared goal. The new leadership not only made the Oriya unity movement an all-India issue and but also opened new frontiers of mass communication. It heralded the arrival in Orissa of many nationalist experiences through newspapers such as *Samaj, Utkal Dipika, Puribasi, Sakti,* and *Parjatantra.*[74]

An immediate outcome of this was the warm reception of the message of the non-violent Akali struggle for the gurdwara reforms in Punjab. It coincided with the tumultuous experiences of the non-cooperation movement in the Orissa coast (1920s). The Oriya nationalists found many things in common with the Akalis, including experiences of police brutalities as well as widespread corruption at different levels of the gurdwara and the matha management. The following paragraph written by Gopabandhu Das, one of the most respected Congress leaders of the period, reflects a part of the sentiment:

Like the temples of the Hindus, the Sikhs of Punjab have many gurudwaras of their own. A few Sikh Babajis [i.e. Mohants] control all these gurudwaras. In Orissa, the Mohants have established their respective rights over the property of the mathas; the Sikh Babajis of Punjab had occupied the assets of the gurudwaras in a similar fashion. These mathas as well as the gurudwaras represent the property of the common people. If dedicated individuals, wise men and sadhus are appointed in these places, income from these properties could be used for the well being of the commoners. But the heads of the mathas and gurudwaras are using these arenas, as if these are their ancestral properties.[75]

Here, the congruence views and interests between the Oriya Congress proponents of non-cooperation and the Akali satyagrahis has been underlined. Incidentally, Gopabandhu Das was from Puri district. He had seen the functioning of the mathas from close quarters over a long time. It was also quite possible that he might have witnessed how the message of Sikhism had undergone a metamorphosis in the sacred complex of Puri. Like a true Gandhite of his times, he did not want complete rejection of the contemporary Puri matha system. On the contrary, he was in favour of its role as one of the trustees of the people. The Akali struggle for gurdwara reforms therefore offered him an opportunity to express his dissatisfaction with the existing mismanagement.[76] The provincial government, on the other hand, feared that any major reshuffling of the existing Puri matha administration would likely strengthen the Congress movement in Orissa.

The news of the Akali struggle thus left behind a significant impact on contemporary Oriya politics. The administration decided to keep a close watch over the local situation so that there was no repetition of the bloody experiences taking place in faraway Punjab. The government was in favour of maintaining the status quo with regard to the existing matha arrangement.[77] In spite of its policy of caution and restraint, the administration was no less keen on extracting some advantage out of it by keeping the Oriya non-cooperators outside the scene. On the other hand, the Congress-led Oriya nationalists of the 1920s restricted their support for the Akali cause to the moral and emotional level. They brought out numerous emotional editorials, reports, and photographs highlighting the sacrifices of the Akalis, but they did not go beyond that limit. During these years, the Datan Sahib was also considered as a matha and conveyed no clear message about its Sikh/Khalsa link at the local level. It was then situated in an isolated corner of the city, away from its present position. Its daily rituals and management were in the hands the mohants, who had some occasional links with their counterpart at the Mangu Math at Puri.

Thus, during the early 1920s, something like the gurdwara takeover of the Akali model could never occur in Orissa. This was partly due to the cautious policy of the provincial administration and a lack of adequate numbers of Sikhs of the Khalsa in Orissa professing the Akali cause. Even the Oriya Congress non-cooperators never dreamt of coming out aggressively in favour of the Sikh struggle. Perhaps they were not aware of the implications of the taking over of the Datan Sahib Gurdwara in the Akali pattern, thereby putting the local administration to some difficulty. In the early 1930s, when Gopabandhu was no longer alive, the Orissa Congress continued to remain a divided house. It was passing through a phase of bitter infighting and acrimony.[78] It offered the provincial administration some breathing time to prepare its own blueprint.

IX

The government took some time to chalk out its plan of action. As the initial enthusiasm about the Akali satyagrahis gradually died down in

Orissa, it was made aware of the significance of the Datan Sahib at Kaliaboda (Cuttack). In the early 1930s, as the call for the Civil Disobedience Movement gathered momentum, a scheme was drawn up that would drive a wedge into the ranks of the Oriya nationalists. It was a game plan where all the participants would be as good as undeclared nominees and the schedule would also be monitored from a safe distance. The wide space lying vacant around the Kaliboda Datan Sahib, long associated with the memory of the first Sikh guru's trip to Puri, was selected for its safe execution. Its historic link with the wider Sikh world had an emotional appeal, which the administration tried to exploit to the best of its advantage. Its stage of operation would also be away from Puri, and so commence without disturbing the existing matha arrangement.

The leading participants were a mixed group of loyalists, but professing the nationalist cause through British support and constitutional means. They were respected citizens of Cuttack and belonged to three distinct faiths: Brahmoism, Sikhism, and Hinduism. Three of them were from the Indian Educational Service (IES) and had never been a part of contemporary politics. Three others directly subscribed to the politics of the Utkal Sammelani and their relationship with the local administration was more or less friendly and warm. It would, however, be incorrect to suggest that the blueprint of the Datan Sahib manoeuvre was entirely envisaged by the government with no room for individual initiative. Bawa Kartar Singh (1886–1960), Professor and Head, Chemistry Department, Ravenshaw College, the most respected educational institution in Cuttack, was very enthusiastic about the plan right from the beginning.[79]

Scion of a respected Sikh family, Bawa had very little connection with the radical politics of the recently founded Shiromani Gurdwara Parbandhak Committee, Amritsar. He was a member of the IES and went to England on a governmental scholarship. He was perhaps first approached by a small section of the local Sikhs and Oriya Brahmos who elaborated to him the significance of the Datan Sahib on the all-India map of gurdwaras. In connection with his profession, he had been for a brief period in Lahore and in Cuttack when the Akali struggle was on in Punjab.[80] As a devout Sikh, he was therefore aware of the possible favourable repercussions of the Datan Sahib takeover in the wider Sikh world. He could convince the government of its significance and underline the advantages the government might possibly derive out of it. The government gradually realized that the plan, if successfully executed, would take much of the wind out of the sails of the Oriya Congress nationalists. One of Bawa's colleagues was Niranjan Niyogi, Professor of English at Ravenshaw College, a Bengali Brahmo widely respected for his intimate family ties with the earlier generation of Oriya Brahmos and his deep commitment to the message of monotheism that had long remained an important part of the twentieth-century Oriya resurgence.

This made it easier for Bawa Kartar Singh to involve Niyogi in his plan. Bawa also received support from three other important members of the contemporary Oriya intelligentsia closely associated with the politics of the Utkal Sammelani.[81] One of them was Chintamani Acharya, a leading lawyer of the Cuttack Bar. The second one was Brajasundar Das, the editor of the famous literary magazine *Mukur*. Next came the well-known literary personality Gopalchandra Praharaja.[82] In the early 1930s, Bawa almost became the one-man army of the Sikhs of the Khalsa in Orissa. In spite of the want of a large number of Sikhs professing the cause of the Akalis, coupled with the lack of an effective Khalsa Sikh organizational support, he carved out with government patronage a wider space for them in the Datan Sahib gurdwara. They agreed to celebrate there the birthday of Guru Nanak in a big way on 10 January 1935. At least two Oriya newspapers carried the news of it.

The meeting ended with an appeal for the immediate construction of a new gurdwara building. It took another three years to complete it, with funds pouring in from different directions, primarily because of the initiative of Bawa Kartar Singh. His colleagues of the IES from different parts of India and two front-ranking rajas of Orissa (who had incidentally been very close to the provincial government and the politics of the Utkal Sammelani) remitted funds generously. A critical analysis of the names in the list of donors, inscribed on the marble plaque on the walls of the gurdwara building, suggests that it was largely the individual success of Bawa. A token sum, however, came from the Shiromani Gurdwara Parbandhak Committee of Nanakana Sahib and the staff of Khalsa College, Amritsar.[83]

Though never a member of the radical Sikh politics of his times, Bawa created an important platform for the Khalsa in Orissa, which it did not have before. The Sikhs of the Khalsa had no public gurdwara of their own so far. Perhaps many of them were not happy with the way the name of Guru Nanak was appropriated by the mohants and their mathas. But they had no organizational support to make their voice of protest heard. The Datan Sahib Gurdwara thus offered those Sikhs of Orissa a significant platform. It also marked a new beginning—from now on, they would look forward to new organizational support from other urban centres of Orissa.

The Sikhs of the Khalsa thus started experiencing a new chapter of their history in coastal Orissa. The Nanakpanthi–Udasi community, based on their matha network, had so long virtually been the entire world of Sikhism in the land of Jagannath. They came steadily closer to the regional Jagannath tradition over centuries and became almost an integral part of it. Since the last quarter of the nineteenth century, the Brahmos did talk about the message of Guru Nanak in terms of monotheism, opposition to idol worship, and criticism of the priestly hierarchy, but it was primarily restricted to the educated middle-class. On the other hand, Oriya popular culture was generally more concerned with the different streams of cultural performances such as the Sathera, Naga, Ramkatha, and *Mogal Tamsa*.

The ancient pilgrims' road to Puri via Bhadrak and Cuttack could create enough space for portraying a living Oriya Nanak of their choice, which was distinctly different from the dominant Sikh tradition of Punjab. It offered an arena where the early Sikh tradition could evolve in its own way alongside the Jagannath cult. It may seem to many either a shocking metamorphosis of the message of Guru Nanak or a mere syncretic face of Indian civilization, but in the domain of Oriya popular culture, it represents an interesting index of its vitality in recreating the religious traditions of the Sikhs of Punjab. It perhaps found an interesting exposure in Puri, where it was offered space for lively popular participation through cross-cultural fertilization. This stimulated the growth of a composite culture, often communicating in a mixed language of its own.[84]

The coastal districts of Orissa, however, in the course of the last eight decades have increasingly been associated with the Sikhs of the Khalsa. It is a comparatively new tradition in the region and its entry to Orissa through the Datan Sahib Gurdwara episode introduces us to an experience, which is distinctly different from that of Punjab. As the Datan Sahib gurdwara was constructed on the land owned by the Udasi mohants of the Kaliaboda Matha through peaceful and legal means, it suggests that one of the many early forms of Akali struggle for gurdwara reforms appeared in Punjab in the 1920s.[85]

The role of the colonial administration, however, needs to be remembered in this connection. It played a crucial part in rallying a few

select Sikh sympathizers very close to the Utkal Sammelani politics for
that particular occasion. Simultaneously, it sought to drive a wedge between
them and the Oriya non-cooperators by not encouraging the participation
of the latter. The British administration learnt many things from its past
Punjab experiences and became adequately shrewd and tactful in selecting
its junior partners in Orissa. Instead of fighting the Oriya Congress directly
or giving the Khalsa Sikhs a blank cheque for the Datan Sahib Gurdwara
reconstruction programme, it prepared a blueprint and allowed a game
on its own terms and conditions. Thus the message of the Khalsa was
given an organizational framework in Orissa, but the Shiromani Gurdwara
Parbandhak Committee (by virtue of the legal disability imposed under
the Gurdwaras Act of 1925) had no power over it. In the construction
of the new gurdwara building (1935) also, the Shiromani Gurdwara
Parbandhak Committee (Amritsar) did not contribute.

After attaining an important foothold on the Orissa coast, the Sikhs of
the Khalsa did not look back. With the independence of the country, a
large number of Sikhs came to settle there and many of them steadily
engaged in different commercial ventures such as transport, mining,
and construction works. (A few others are also found in diverse service
sectors.) Their success story gave the community a distinct identity in the
region. Like in other parts of India, they have already constructed a few
impressive gurdwaras and schools in major urban centres such Cuttack,
Bhubaneswar, and Rourkela. In 1967, they also set up a central body, the
Orissa Sikh Pratinidhi Board, for coordinating community activities in
different parts of the province. The 'decision of this Board' is declared
to be 'binding' on all gurdwaras and Sikhs 'residing in Orissa'.[86] But the
Riots of 1984 and the movement for Khalistan temporarily made them
insecure and self-protective in the 1980s. The Tercentenary Birth
Celebration of the Khalsa (1999), however, generated a new confidence
in the community leadership. Then they also started a *morcha* from the
Nanak Baoli in Puri with expectations of 'getting it back' into their fold in
near future and opened negotiations at different levels, raised funds, and
tried to build a tolerant image of the community in and around Puri.[87]

This has evoked mixed reactions in the sacred complex. The possible
presence of the Khalsa, with its money and muscle power, has caused an
anxiety in both the Puri mathas, which had earlier been associated with
the Nanakpanthi–Udasi domain in the region. Memories of the Datan
Sahib Gurdwara often visit them. The present mohant of the Mangu Matha
(who indirectly controls the administration of the Nanak Baoli) has sought

legal protection from the Udasin Panchayati Akhara, Allahabad, and has declared himself a member of that organization so that the Khalsa cannot claim his matha property.[88] Sikhs of the Khalsa also do not represent a homogenous body at the provincial level. Their bitter rivalry and animosity have made the foundation of a new gurdwara extremely difficult. But they have not turned their eyes away from Puri. With the pressure of the Khalsa steadily increasing over the years, there is hardly any doubt that the older world of Nanakpanthis is feeling insecure and uncertain of its future. It is simultaneously getting ready for a trial of strength against its newer progeny.

Notes

1. A. Eschmann et al. (eds), *The Cult of Jagannath and the Regional Tradition of Orissa* (New Delhi: Manohar Publications, 1986), p. xiv.

2. Leif Manger (ed.), *Muslim Diversity: Local Islam in Global Contexts* (Surrey: Curzon Press, 1999), pp. 2–19.

3. Richard M. Eaton, *Essays on Islam and Indian History* (New Delhi: Oxford University Press, 2002), pp. 5 and 275.

4. Bernard S. Cohn, 'The Role of the Gosains in the Economy of Eighteenth and Nineteenth Century Upper India', *The Indian Economic and Social History Review* (hereafter *IESHR*), 1: 4 (1965), pp. 175–82.

5. Pashaura Singh, *The Bhagats of the Guru Granth Sahib: Self Definition and the Bhagat Bani* (New Delhi: Oxford University Press, 2003), pp. 118–19.

6. For early trading activities among the Nanakpanthi Sikhs, see W. H. McLeod, *The Evolution of the Sikh Community* (Delhi: Oxford University Press, 1975), pp. 92–3; also see his 'Trade and Investment in Sixteenth and Seventeenth Century Punjab: The Testimony of the Sikh Devotional Literature', Harbans Singh and N. G. Barrier (eds), *Essays in Honour of Dr. Ganda Singh* (Patiala: Punjabi University, 1976), pp. 81–91. Dilbagh Singh, 'Presidential Address: Medieval Section, Punjab and the Trading Diaspora of the 17th Century', *Proceedings, Punjab History Conference*, Twentieth Session (Patiala, 1995), Part 1, pp. 238–43.

7. W. Eric Gustafson and Kenneth W. Jones (eds), *Sources on Punjab History* (New Delhi: Manohar Book Service, 1975), pp. 1–3.

8. Bishumohan Das, 'Bauli Matha', *Orissa History Congress Souvenir* (Puri: 1983), pp. 19–20.

9. Lala Sohan Lal Suri, *Umdat-ut-Tawarikh, Daftar III, Part V: Chronicle of the Reign of Maharaja Ranjit Singh, 1831–1839*, V. S. Suri (trans.) (New Delhi: S. Chand & Co., 1961), p. 694.

10. Authorities such as Ganda Singh, W. H. 'Hew' McLeod, and others have expressed serious reservations about it. Ganda Singh is ready to believe that the

Sikh guru was in Puri, but in his opinion, the former had already left the place when the latter came there to preach. Hew McLeod is equally uncertain about the meeting. Anil Chandra Banerjee has gone to another extreme and questioned whether Iswardas' observations should be treated as an authentic contemporary testimony, since he wrote long after the event had taken place. There is a gap of nearly one hundred years between Iswardas' completion of the text and the supposed meeting between Sri Chaitanya and Guru Nanak at Puri. For this, see the author's *The Other Sikhs, 1: A View from Eastern India* (New Delhi: Manohar Publications, 2003), p. 74.

11. H. K. Patnaik, 'Monasteries in Puri', M. N. Das (ed.), *History and Culture of Orissa* (Cuttack: Vidyapuri, 1977), p. 437.

12. Kulke argues that 'the Chronicles of Puri developed from a constant process of *reconstruction of the past* with the purpose of safeguarding or even *renewing the present.*' Hermann Kulke, 'Reflections on the Sources of the Temple Chronicles of the Madala Panji of Puri', Kulke (ed.), *Kings and Cults: State Formation and Legitimation in India and Southeast Asia* (New Delhi: Manohar Publications, 2001), p. 189. Also see Krishnachandra Panigrahi, 'Madlapanjir Janmakal', Hermann Kulke (ed.) *Itihas O Kingbandanti* (Bhubaneswar: Utkal University, 1962), pp. 69–70. Tripathy, however, feels that 'the contents of the Panji cannot be brushed aside as either quite unreliable and baseless', but he shares some of Panigrahi's doubts regarding the early sections of the manuscripts, particularly the way its language was modernized at the time of copying. K. B. Tripathy, 'The Chronicles of the Jagannatha Temple', *Proceedings of the Indian History Congress*, Twentieth Session (Cuttack, 1957), p. 207.

13. Sachidananda Mohanty and Sanatan Mohanty, 'Reviving Bhadrak's Mogal Tamsa', *Seagull Theatre Quarterly*, 17, March 1998, p. 58.

14. Krishnacharan Behera, *Kavi Bansiballab Goswami: Mogal Tamsa* (Cuttack: Bhagabata Press, 1966). There are, however, differences of opinion regarding its date of composition. For a different view, see Sachidananda Mishra, 'Mogal Tamsar Rachanakal', *Jhankar*, January 1974, p. 945.

15. Nearly forty years ago, Balwant Gargi contributed five interesting essays on the regional folk theatres of India. In these essays, he reviewed separately the Maharashtrian Tamasha and the Jatra traditions of eastern India, including Orissa. He did not, however, refer to any interactions between these two distinct and distant popular open-air theatre forms. It is likely that that there was a link between them. It seems that the Maratha rule of more than fifty years over Orissa was largely responsible for it. In *Mogal Tamsa*, like in its Maharashtrian counterparts, one comes across hilarious jokes, witty satire, loud music, and the presence of the milkmaid (*gauduni* in Oriya, *gaulan* in Marathi). For Gargi's discussion on the Maharashtrian Tamasa, see Balwant Gargi 'Aspects of the Indian Heritage: Folk Theatre–4: The Tamasha', *The Illustrated Weekly of India*, 2 May 1965, pp.

35–6. On *Mogal Tamsa*, see Krishnacharan Behera, *Kavi Bansiballab Goswami: Mogal Tamsa*, pp. 38–48. Like Gargi, Sudhi Pradhan also misses the point. Sudhi Pradhan, *Marxist Cultural Movement in India* 2 (Calcutta: Navana, 1982), pp. 80–1.

16. Sanatan Mohanty and Sachidananda Mohanty, 'Lokanatya Mogal Tamsa', *Jhankar*, June 1977, p. 366.

17. Sachidananda Mohanty and Sanatan Mohanty, 'Reviving Bhadrak's Mogal Tamsa', *Seagull Theatre Quarterly* 17, March 1998, pp. 58–62.

18. Dhiren Das, *Orissar Jatara* (Bhubaneswar: Orissa Sangit Natak Akademi, 1981), p. 48.

19. Krishnacharan Behera, *Kavi Bansiballab Goswami: Mogal Tamsa*, pp. 27–8.

20. W. H. McLeod, *Who is a Sikh? The Problem of Sikh Identity* (Oxford: Clarendon Press, 1989), pp. 16–7.

21. Hew McLeod had earlier used this concept. I borrowed it with a view to distinguishing these Sikhs with five Ks from the Nanakpanthis and Udasis who had already been here in Orissa. *Sikhs of the Khalsa: History of the Khalsa Rahit*, New Delhi: Oxford University Press, 2003.

22. Harekrushna Mahatab, *Sadhanar Pathe*, Part 1 (Cuttack: Prajatantra Press, 1949), p. 1.

23. This was my experience when I visited the Kaliaboda area in March 2001, accompanied by one of my local Oriya friends with good knowledge of the region. He drew my attention to the sprawling Datan Sahib Gurdwara complex, steadily growing since 1938, and the corresponding reduction in size of the Udasi matha property during the same period. Later, one of my Sikh friends assured me that the present gurdwara management committee had no intention of completely 'dislodging the matha people from their hereditary property'. I will again be dealing with the new power equation of the locality in a later section of this chapter.

24. Bhaskar Mishra, 'Mangu Mathar Aitijya', *Srimandir: Rathayatra Bisheshanka* (Puri: The Administrator Shri Jagannath Temple, 1999), p. 58.

25. Lakhsminarayan Sahu, *Guru Gobinda Singha* (Cuttack: Satyabadi Press, n.d.), pp. 1–3. During my visit (March 2001) there, one of the priests of the Cuttack matha also drew my attention to the long list of mohants who had been its earlier heads. He also showed me photographs of two of them and confirmed the presence of the Adi Granth there till the early years of the twentieth century.

26. Jasobanta Narayan Dhar, 'Lanes and Localities of Cuttack City', K. S. Behera et al. (eds), *Cuttack—One Thousand Years* 2 (Cuttack: The Cuttack City Millennium Felicitations Committee, 1990), p. 31.

27. I have borrowed this argument from H. T. Bakkar, 'Ayodha as a Place of Pilgrimage', *Indo-Iranian Journal* 24 (1982), pp. 107–8, 117. This does not suggest that the Ramayana tradition was unknown among the contemporary Sikhs. It was a part of the *Rahiras* before the arrival on the scene of the Tat Khalsa. W. H. McLeod, *Sikhs of the Khalsa*, p. 193.

28. Basanta Kumar Mallick, *Paradigms of Dissent and Protest: Social Movements in Eastern India (c. AD 1400–1700)* (New Delhi: Manohar Publishers, 2004), pp. 110–12.

29. Personal communication, Shyam Sundar Misra of the Orissa Educational Service, dated 25 June 2001. Mishra is also an old resident of the Jhanjharimangala area. I had a brief discussion with him on this point during my second visit to Cuttack (October 2002).

30. Shyam Sundar Mishra, 'Jhanjharimangalar Ramleela: Ek Bismrita Lokanatya Kala', *Sriramcharita Kathamrita* (Cuttack: Jhanjharimangala, Cuttack, 1993), p. 21. Incidentally, one of my Oriya friends has handed over to me an old notebook containing a handwritten Oriya poem entitled 'Nanak Bandana'. It mentions Nanak along with references to other Hindu gods and goddesses. This was collected from this same Jhanjharimangala locality of Cuttack.

31. G. S. Ghurya, *Indian Sadhus* (Bombay: The Popular Book Deport, 1953), p. 161. For a detailed discussion on the Dasnami *sadhus*, see Jadunath Sarkar, *A History of Dasnami Naga Sanyais* (Allahabad: Sri Panchayati Akhara, n.d.).

32. For a similar Udasi and Ramaite linkage with the corresponding Shaivite and Vaishnavite beliefs and practices in Bihar, see William Pinch, *Peasants and Monks in British India* (Delhi: Oxford University Press, 1996), pp. 23–47. In Kashi, Surajit Sinha and Baidyanath Saraswati found that the local Udasi and Nanakpanthi organizations had certain common affiliations. Surajit Sinha and Baidyanath Saraswati, *The Ascetics of Kashi* (Varanasi: N. K. Bose Memorial Foundation, 1978), p. 140. In central India also, 'the Nanakpanthi community are known as Udasi'. R. V. Russell and Hira Lal, *Tribes and Castes of the Central Provinces of India* 1 (London: Macmillan and Co., 1916), p. 280. For the local centres of the Nath tradition in Orissa, see Dolagobinda Shastri, *Nathadharmar Kramavikasha* (Cuttack: Prachi Sahitya Pratisthan, 1971), pp. 240–8. Nearly a decade ago, Harjot Oberoi also referred to the 'religious diversity' in the early Sikh tradition. Harjot Oberoi, *The Construction of Religious Boundaries: Culture, Identity and Diversity in the Sikh Tradition* (Delhi: Oxford University Press, 1994), p. 24

33. From the late nineteenth century onwards, many interesting bits of information regarding the visit of a pilgrim from Punjab—his individual name as well as the name of his village/town/district, year and month of visit, caste status as well as father's name—are generally available in these records. These sources are recorded as per the panda's own scheme of work and kept under the close supervision of their family/office staff. I have copies of a few pilgrims' records from Punjab districts such as Ludhiana, Jullundur, Hoshiarpur, Amritsar, Muzaffargarh, Bannu, Dera Ismail Khan, Sialkot, Lahore, Jhelum, Peshawar, Kohat, and Hazara.

34. Kedar Nath Dutt, Deputy Collector, Puri, letter dated 28 April 1870, Orissa State Archives, Bhubaneswar, Index No. 11765.

35. W. H. McLeod, *Guru Nanak and the Sikh Religion* (Delhi: Oxford University Press, 1968), pp. 68–9. Hereafter *GNSR*.

36. W. H. McLeod, *GNSR*, pp. 113–4. Balwant Singh Dhillon, *Pramukh Sikh te Sikh Panth* (Amritsar: Singh Brothers, 1997), pp. 151–2. Jeevan Singh Deol, 'Text and Lineage in Early Sikh History: Issues in the Study of the Adi Granth', *Bulletin of the School of Oriental and African Studies*, 64: 1 (2001), pp. 34–58.

37. N. K. Behura, 'Jagannath of Puri and His Pilgrimage', M. Jha (ed.), *Dimensions of Pilgrimage: An Anthropological Appraisal* (New Delhi: Inter-India Publication, 1985), p. 107.

38. In the eyes of devout Oriya Hindus, the Jagannath cult symbolized a syncretic tradition representing Shaivism, Shaktism and Vaishnavism. Many regard Jagannath as a non-Aryan deity who passed through a long process of Hinduization over the centuries, while some others respect the deity as an incarnation of Lord Buddha. For an excellent discussion on some of these views, see A. Eschmann et al. (eds), *The Cult of Jagannath*. The writings of W. W. Hunter merit special attention. For this, see N. K. Sahu (ed.), *A History of Orissa: By W.W. Hunter, Andrew Stirling, John Beams and N.K. Sahu* (Calcutta: Sushil Gupta, 1956 reprint), p. 7.

39. For the early history of some of these sangats, see Ganda Singh (ed.), *Hukamname* (Patiala: Punjabi University, 1993). Tara Singh, *Sri Guru Tirath Samgraha* (Amritsar: Bhai Buta Singh and Pratap Singh, 1895), pp. 93–6. Giyani Giyan Singh: *Gurdham Samgraha* (Amritsar: Dharam Prachar Committee, n.d.), pp. 30–40 and 117–22. Ved Prakash, 'Sikhs and Sikhism in Bihar', Syed Hassan Askari and Quyamuddin Ahmad (eds), *The Comprehensive History of Bihar*, 2 (Patna: Kashi Prasad Jayaswal Research Institute, 1987), pp. 276–90. Abhoypada Mallik, *History of Bishnupur Raj* (Calcutta: Author, 1921), p. 95. For the significance of the economic resources of medieval Orissa, see Irfan Habib, *An Atlas of Mughal India* (Delhi: Oxford University Press, 1986), pp. 41, 48, and 51.

40. Agehananda Bharati, 'Pilgrimage in the Indian Tradition', *History of Religions 3*, 1, pp. 135–67. Baidyanath Saraswati, *Kashi: Myth and Reality of a Classical Cultural Tradition* (Simla: Indian Institute of Advanced Study, 1975), p. 37.

41. Anonymous, 'Relation of the Mathas of Puri with the Jagannath Temple', *Sri Jagannath*, Special Number, 1985, pp. 50–7. For the history of the local mathas, see: Himanshu S. Patnaik, *Lord Jagannath: His Temples, Cult and Festivals* (New Delhi: Aryan Books International, 1994), pp. 58–71 and 143–8. Bhaskar Mishra, *Purir Matha Sanskriti* (Puri: Satgrantha Niketan, 1999).

42. Arjun Appadurai, 'Kings, Sects and Temples in South India, 1350–1700 AD', *IESHR*, 14: 1 (1977), p. 66.

43. Basudeb Chattopadhyay, *Crime and Control in Early Colonial Bengal, 1770–1860* (Calcutta: K. P. Bagchi, 2000), p. 10.

44. This is a royal order written in Persian, generally addressed to the temple superintendent. There are different categories of chamu citau preserved in the

Orissa State Museum, Bhubaneswar. A team of Indo-German scholars is engaged
in translating these royal orders into English. There have so far been a few interesting
essays on the chamu citau. Kulke's contribution is included in Hermann Kulke
(ed.), *Kings and Cults*, pp. 51–65. Also see S. K. Panda, 'Royal Authority and the
Cult of Jagannatha, the Politico-Ritual Relation between the Kingdom of Khurda
and Sambalpur: A Study Based on Chamu Citaus', *New Perspectives on the History
and Culture of Orissa* (Calcutta: Punthi Pustak, 2000), pp. 90–9.

45. Bhaskar Mishra, Officer on Special Duty, Shri Jagannath Temple
Administration, Puri, claims that he had seen the *sanad*. Mitra, *op. cit.*, p. 49. This
claim by Mishra does not seem unlikely because of his official position as well as
his intimate relationship with the present mohant of the matha. I have subsequently
met both of them and they both agreed on that point. They also kindly allowed
me to see the document.

46. Kedar Nath Dutt, Deputy Collector, Puri, letter dated 28 April 1870,
Orissa State Archives, Bhubaneswar, Index No. 11765.

47. This was a special category of land grant extended to the matha for the
preparation of nectar (sweet food) offered to Lord Jagannath.

48. Sarat Chandra Jena, 'Origin of Mangu Muth and its Management in British
Orissa', *Our Documental Heritage: Some Aspects of Cultural History of Orissa* 4
(Bhubaneswar: Orissa State Archives, 1997), p. 138.

49. The original date of the chamu citau is illegible. It is based on a true copy,
with an endorsement from the Cuttack Court. The date of its endorsement seal
is 29 July 1882. I am grateful to the present mohant of the matha for its copy. A
similar royal order was issued when the next mohant, Udasi Sukhdeb Ram Das,
took over as in-charge of the matha.

50. E. Hein, 'Temple, Town and Hinterland: The Present Network of
"Religious Economy" in Puri', A. Eschmann et al. (eds), *The Cult of Jagannath*, pp.
439–68.

51. Baidyanath Saraswati, *Kashi*, pp. 46–7.

52. Brij Kishore Ghose, *The History of Pooree: With an Account of Juggunnath*
(Cuttack: Orissa Mission Press, 1848), pp. 18–19.

53. Burton Stein, 'Temples in Tamil Country, 1300–1750 AD', *IESHR*, 14: 1
(1977), pp. 26–7.

54. Jeevan Deol, 'Eighteenth Century Khalsa Identity: Discourse, Praxis and
Narrative', Christopher Shackle et al. (eds), *Sikh Religion, Culture and Ethnicity*,
(Richmond: Curzon Press, 2001), p. 30.

55. One such place was the Trilochan temple of Banaras. For a detailed
description of the situation there, see M. A. Sherring, *Benares: The Sacred City of
the Hindus* (New Delhi: Low Price Publications, 1996), pp. 101–2. Similarly, a number
of ceremonies at the Patna Sahib continued to be dominated by many pre-Khalsa
symbols and rituals. The study of Ved Prakash, *The Sikhs in Bihar* (Patna: Janaki
Prakashn, 1981), may be taken into consideration in this connection.

56. In this connection, the following remarks of Rajat Kanta Ray merit special attention: 'In India, the identity of the people was rooted in a mixed, plural culture, and not in political institutions. Identity, moreover, was not merely ethnic, it was also religious: and there were multiple ethnic and religious identities... An overarching cultural unity had invested the land in India with emotional values derived from notions of sacred space.' Rajat Kanta Ray, *The Felt Community: Commonalty and Mentality before the Emergence of Indian Nationalism* (New Delhi: Oxford University Press, 2003), p. 14.

57. For a detailed description of the warlike Naga dress, see Kunjabehari Das, *Palligiti Sanchyan* 3 (Cuttack: Premlata Das, 1974), pp. 16–17.

58. For a detailed discussion on the Kalapahar episode, see G. N. Dash, 'Kalapahar, the Iconoclast: The Making and Message of a Legendary Tradition: Reconversions in Medieval Orissa and Bengal', Hermann Kulke and Burkhard Schnepel (eds), *Jagannath Revisited: Studying Society, Religion and the State in Orissa* (New Delhi: Manohar Publications, 2001), pp. 227–52.

59. In his study, J. P. Das writes of his recent experiences of Naga dance: 'There are *jega-ghars* for the different localities of Puri, where young men gather to play cards, practice wrestling, organize cultural shows or just to while away time. The paintings on the walls of the *jega-ghar* consist of a figure of Jagannatha or of other deities as well as that of a Naga. A Naga is a well-built figure dressed in the regalia of a warrior modelled on the Nagarjuna *vesa* [dress] of Jagannatha and is an appropriate motif on the *jega-ghar* wall. Once a year, on the occasion of the Sahi-Jatra, the youths of Puri dress themselves as Nagas and join in a festival to display their physical prowess.' J. P. *Puri Paintings* (New Jersey: Arnold-Heinemann, 1982), pp. 54–5. Kunjabehari Das however argues that the Naga dance has a close link with the local *paik* tradition. Kunjabehari Das, *Palligiti Sanchyan*, p. 10. The paiks represented an important section of the local militia upto the time that Orissa was under Maratha rule. Many of them were thrown out of employment under the British administration, resulting in a major revolt in 1818. For a list of the names of the different jega-ghars of Puri, see Himanshu S. Patnaik, *Lord Jagannath*, pp. 149–50.

60. I have borrowed the phrase 'warrior ascetics' from David N. Lorenzen, 'Warrior Ascetics in Indian History', *Journal of the American Oriental Society*, 98 (1978), pp. 61–75.

61. Baidyanath Gochhait, 'Sathera', *Srikhetra Hanuman Jayanti Committee Smaranika* (Puri: Hanuman Jayanti Committee, 1983), p. 24.

62. Siddheswar Mohapatra, *Puri Boli* (Bhubaneswar: Orissa Sahitya Akademi, 1996), p. 72. For a slightly different version of the couplet, see Kunjabehari Das, *Palligiti Sanchyan*, pp. 18–19.

63. I also refer to the Suthresahis because in one of the lines of the couplet, there is an interesting reference to the striking of sticks (*larki thuke*) at the time of their begging in the name of the guru (i.e., Guru Nanak). This practice has

252 TEXTURES OF THE SIKH PAST

been associated with them over the centuries. In Bhadrak also, we come across a similar experience in *Mogal Tamsa*. For a detailed description of this, see 'An Account of the Sikhs, 1808: From Ghulam 'Ali Khan, Imadu's Sa'adat', J. S. Grewal and Irfan Habib (trans. and eds), *Sikh History from Persian Sources* (New Delhi: Tulika and Indian History Congress, 2001), p. 214. It is likely that the Oriya word 'Sathera' has a close resemblance with the 'Suthresahis' in Punjabi.

64. R. S. Tak and S. S. Sagar's field survey of early 1974 referred to a similar 'Nanak Sahi dance' with 'wooden sticks' in Midnapur town (now in West Bengal) in the early decades of the twentieth century. See 'Nanak's Visit to Kharagpur, Midnapur and Candrakona (W. Bengal)', *Journal of Sikh Studies* 2, 1, Appendix 4, p. 148. In Tamluk, at present a subdivision town situated in Midnapur district, I have come across a family tracing their roots to medieval Punjab (Pathankot). According to the family tradition, they settled here after a long pilgrimage to Lord Jagannath. They still have a shop in the town and its name is 'Nanakalaya'. Personal communication, Tarak Nath Choudhury, 5 May 2001. Choudhury is the present owner of the shop.

65. We have at least two important vernacular sources referring to the performance of the Satheras. One of them is Baidyanath Gochhait, 'Sathera', *Srikhetra Hanuman Jayanti Committee Smaranika*, p. 24. In another Oriya poem, 'Sahare Sahijatra', *Sachitra Saharee Zaleem* (Puri: Shakti Press, 1929), pp. 48–9, we come across a marginal difference in the formal dress of the Sathera performers. Siddheswar Mohapatra, *Puri Boli*, p. 70, has also drawn our attention to the Sathera performance.

66. Its translation into English follows: 'Thus the time for dancing came there. The disciples of Nanak wearing saffron colour *dhoti* appeared in their joyous mood. They put on headgear with two sticks in their hands and presented devotional music in a deep melodious tune.' Phaturananda, *Shahimahabharata* (Cuttack: Author, 1987), p. 301.

67. I visited the Nanak Baoli in January 2001. I saw a place hidden from the commoners' view. I was told that there the bodies of the earlier mohants had been buried in accordance with their wishes. They were all yogis. I am not sure whether the Mangu Matha had any such place within its limit. But the sharp line of demarcation between the two mathas was not always clearly drawn till the last quarter of the nineteenth century. We do not have any definite documentary evidence of it. I have so far been able to trace only one Bengali printed source of more than one hundred years ago referring to the position of the Nanak Baoli. It underlines the dissatisfaction of an old lady, wife of the then mohant, regarding the 'prevalence of widespread idolatry' in and around the Jagannath temple. Anonymous, 'Satyadasher Sat Prasanga: Nanak Math', *Dharmabandhu*, Phalgun 1294 BS, p. 252. Perhaps the inmates of the Nanak Baoli were more inclined to the message of monotheism and anti-idolatry underlined by Guru Nanak. They were

possibly not very happy with the prevailing atmosphere of the Mangu Matha. In the absence of more definite proofs, our conclusions in this regard would be inconclusive and tentative.

68. Tarapada Santra, 'Kasijora Parganar Itibrittva: Anchalik Itihaser Nana Sutra o Tatwaya', *Aitihasik*, Baisakh-Chaitra 1407 BS, pp. 22–38. That Mangu Matha held a sizeable amount of land there gets an indirect confirmation from Letter No. 1428, 4th July 1787, *Calendar of Persian Correspondence, 1785–7*, vol. 7 (Delhi: Manager of Publications, 1940), 7, pp. 372–3.

69. Kedar Nath Dutt, *A Discourse on the Muts in Orissa* (Calcutta: D'Rozario & Co., 1860), p. 3. There is hardly any doubt that Dutt's observations convey an exaggerated version of the evils linked with the different mathas of Puri. These were partly coloured by his individual sufferings at the hands of one or two mohants. The government enquiry of 1868 pointed out the need for a rearrangement of the numerous irregularities associated with the management of these mathas. The disastrous Mutiny experiences as well as the post-Mutiny 'conservative' reactions perhaps prevented any immediate official intervention in matters of religion.

70. The Deputy Collector of Puri in his report (February 1874) found that 'Santaprosad, one of the rivals [to the gaddi] has now gradually succeeded to obtain possession of the lands and has been collecting revenues by his own Gomastha'. Even the regular sending of bhog (dedicated eatables meant for Lord Jagannath) out of 'the proceeds of the Estates' under the management of the Mangu Matha was almost abandoned during the same period. We do not also have enough information pointing out how the impact of rising prices of living or the money-minded and business-like attitude of the temple functionaries had affected the economic position of the mohants. A study by Nityananda Patnaik on the religious economy of Puri has drawn our attention to the impact of some of these forces in recent years. Nityananda Patnaik, 'Impact of Socio Economic Changes on a Religious Complex', *The Economic Weekly* 15 (1963), pp. 1361–2.

71. In one of his short stories, Fakir Mohan Senapati (1913) caricatured the personalities of the mohants in a very bitter and caustic style. Fakir Mohan Senapati, 'Dusty Baba', *Selected Short Stories* (New Delhi: HarperCollins, 1995), pp. 95–104. The same author drew another profile of a mohant (1915) who was initially projected as a man 'without a blemish on his character'. But he also 'collected and tamed pigeons and bulbuls, and founded an akhada club in the math', where 'a few cronies' would be 'smoking ganja and gossiping' until midnight. 'The affairs of twenty villages were at their fingertips. The Mahant had to know everything—he was the judge, magistrate, and moneylender of the area, all rolled into one.' Fakir Mohan Senapati, *Stories*, Paul St-Pierre et al. (trans.) (Bhubaneswar and Kolkata: Grassroots, 2003), pp. 62–3. Later on, a section of local students started agitating against the different mathas with the slogan

'*mathadhana kothakara*'. For a brief reference to the movement, see Gauranga Charan Sarkar, 'Mathadhana Kothakara', *Fakir Mishra Smaranika* (Puri: Fakir Mishra Smriti Committee, 1987), pp. 55–61.

72. For the Oriya politics of these years, see Nivedita Mohanty, *Oriya Nationalism: Quest for a United Orissa 1866–1956* (Jagatsinghpur: Prafulla, 2005).

73. For a further discussion on the politics of the Satyabadi School, see: Chandrasekhar Mishra, *Satyabadire Satabarsha* (Cuttack: Author, 1953). Radhakanta Barik, 'Gopabandhu and the National Movement in Orissa', *Social Scientist* 7, 3 (May 1978), pp. 47–8.

74. I have seen some of the old files of these newspapers preserved at the Utkal Sahitya Samaj Library, Cuttack. They provide a wide coverage of the Akali struggle of the period.

75. *The Samaj*, 18 May 1921.

76. Towards the closing years of his life, Gopabandhu Das became increasingly sympathetic towards the politics of the Hindu Mahasabha. Thus his attitude towards the matha system also changed. Some of his writings published in the literary journal *Satyabadi* also confirm his leaning towards the Hinduism of Lala Lajpat Rai. I owe this information to Krishna Chandra Bhuyan, Department of Oriya, Anandamohan College, Kolkata. Regarding the writings of Gopabandhu Das, see *Gopabandhu Rachanabali*, Vols 1–8 (Cuttack: Gopabandhu Smritiraksha Committee, 1976–1978).

77. The government was cautious in negotiating with the movement. The district magistrates and the subdivisional officers were instructed to take strong steps against those propagating the cause of non-cooperation in the countryside. A meeting was held in Puri on 8 March 1921 with the district magistrate on the chair. The mohants, landlords, and moneylenders of the locality attended it. The district magistrate instructed them not to extend any help to the non-cooperators. Gopabandhu's *Samaj* provides much interesting information about the role of the government of this period. Prasanna Kumar Rautray, 'Role of Press in Freedom Movement: A Case Study of Orissa' (Utkal University unpublished Ph.D. thesis, 2002), pp. 96–7.

78. These years were characterized by a long period of bitter rivalry between two Congress groups, one headed by Harekrushna Mahatab and the other by Nilkantha Das. The conflict continued even when the first Congress ministry was sworn in under the Government of India Act of 1935. I owe this information to Jatin Kumar Nayak, Department of English, Utkal University, Bhubaneswar.

79. For a brief biographical sketch of Bawa Kartar Singh, see Hardev Singh Virk, *Saade Vigyani* (Amritsar: Guru Nanak Dev University, 1990), pp. 21–6. Also see Hardev Singh Virk 'Bawa Kartar Singh' in Harbans Singh (ed.), *The Encyclopaedia of Sikhism* 2 (Patiala: Punjabi University, 1996), pp. 450–1. In this connection, we also need to remember the possible involvement of two other important Sikh personalities of the period. One was Bawa Ladda Singh Bedi, a leading contractor

from the city of Kolkata (then Calcutta). He was widely respected by the Sikhs of
Kolkata and played an important role in the gurdwara politics sponsored by the
Government of Bengal in the 1920s. The other name was Sundar Singh Majithia,
then an executive councillor and revenue minister in the Punjab government.
They might also have convinced the Bihar and Orissa governments in this regard.
Their names also appeared in an appeal issued by the Datan Sahib Gurdwara
Committee and were 'reportedly' published in the *Desh-Darpan* (a Punjabi daily
published from Kolkata).

80. Virk is not, however, very specific about Bawa's role in the Datan Sahib
Gurdwara episode of 1935. He has very briefly referred to it in a line. Hardev
Singh Virk, *Saade Vigyani*, p. 25. It seems from his writings that Bawa was not even
present in Cuttack at the time. But the deed of agreement signed in the Cuttack
court quoted by S. S. Sagar and R. S. Tak ('Departmental Notes: Guru Nanak in
Cuttack', *Journal of Sikh Studies* 2, 1, pp. 127–44) clearly brings out Bawa's presence
there. Besides, the marble plaque of 1938 still preserved in the old building of
the Datan Sahib gurdwara also carries his name. See also n. 83 below.

81. The Oriya nationalists of the Utkal Sammelani had generally been
maintaining a close relationship with the provincial administration. They also
tried to keep a safe distance from the non-cooperation movement and criticized it
on different occasions. When the Simon Commission arrived in India (1928),
the Congress issued instructions that it should be boycotted, but the Utkal
Sammelani sent representatives to testify to the Commission. The government
reciprocated with goodwill towards the Sammelani, sending the O'Donnell
Committee to Orissa (1931) to determine the boundaries of the proposed new
state of Orissa and in 1936, the state was established. For a detailed discussion on
the contemporary political situation in Orissa, see Bijoykumar Pradhan, 'National
Movement in Orissa (1920–1936 AD)' (Rabindra Bharati University unpublished
Ph.D. thesis, 1997).

82. For their literary contributions dealing with the history of Sikhism, see
Himadri Banerjee, *The Other Sikhs* 1, pp. 88, 90, and 112–13. All three of them—
Chintamani Acharya, Brajasundar Das, and Gopalchandra Praharaj—had a very
close relationship with the British Raj. In December 1995, Natabar Samantaray,
a noted Oriya scholar (now late) then residing in the old town of Bhubaneswar,
told me that in his younger days, the Oriya newspaper *Satya Samachar* of
Brajasundar Das (brought out in the 1930s) was universally regarded as '*mithya
samachar*' because it not only received regular official patronage, but also published
exaggerated information about the extent of success of the colonial administration
on different local issues. In his autobiography, Gopalchandra Praharaj referred
to his 'hobnobbing with top bureaucrats from the State Governor to the Viceroy'.
He was also 'decorated by the British Government of India'. Incidentally, Gandhi
also stayed with Praharaj during his visit to Orissa in 1927. See Gopalchandra
Praharaj's autobiography quoted in John Boulton, 'Autobiography in Oriya

1917–1976', *John Boulton: Essays on Oriya Literature*, Ganeswar Mishra (comp.) (Jagatsinghpur: Prafulla, 2003), pp. 127–8. Like Praharaj, Chintamani Acharya was also honoured with the title 'Rai Bahadur'. I saw it written on a marble plaque at the gate of his house in Telenga Bazaar, Cuttack (June 2002).

83. The marble plaque was still there on the walls of the older building of the Datan Sahib Gurdwara when I last visited the place in June 2002. I have with me a photograph of the marble plaque.

84. These days, many interesting attempts have been made to revive the folk theatres in Orissa; but often, these remain more of a ritual or an artificial reconstruction of the past. In recent years, I have had the privilege of witnessing some video-cassette performances of these folk dramas. In many cases, these reflect how the symbols of urbanism often dominate the so-called rural scenario. Sanatan Mohanty of Bhadrak has kindly drawn my attention to this point. He has long been actively associated with the revival of the *Mogal Tamsa* in Bhadrak.

85. For this, see S. S. Sagar and R. S. Tak, 'Departmental Notes', Annexure B, *Journal of Sikh Studies*, 1: 2 (August 1974), p. 139.

86. *Directory by Orissa Sikh Pratinidhi Board, 1998* (Cuttack: Gurdwara Guru Nanak Datan Sahib, n.d.), p. 13. According to its own estimate, the total size of the Sikh population of Orissa is around twelve thousand.

87. It was my privilege to spend a number of days with them when negotiations were on at different levels in Orissa and Punjab. They were initiated by a group of dedicated Sikhs who had been residing in Cuttack and Bhubaneswar over a number of years. They have set up a registered body in the name of Bhai Himmat Singh— the Bhai Himmat Singh Religious and Charitable Trust (Puri)—and devoted much of their time and money to the cause of the community. It would, however, be wrong to regard the Orissa Sikhs as a homogenous group. A few of my Sikh friends in Cuttack and Bhubaneswar have drawn my attention to inner differences regarding the method of gaining access to the Nanak Baoli at Puri.

88. I have come across the public notice hanging on the walls of the Baoli Sahib declaring its affiliation to the Udasin Panchayati Akhara, Allahabad. The mohant of the Mangu Matha also confirmed the point. I have a photograph of the notice.

Bhangra and the Project of Sikh Studies

Tony Ballantyne

Bhangra has played an extremely important role in the articulation of both Punjabi and Sikh identities over the last four decades. It has been a prominent element in the creation of a Punjabi regional identity in the wake of Partition, played a central role in the cultural life of diasporic South Asians in the United Kingdom, and functioned as a flexible expressive form that has connected the various Punjabi communities (both within South Asia and outside) into a shared, if highly uneven, cultural space. Equally important, bhangra has been a powerful medium in the projection of Punjabi and Sikh culture. Through lyrics, stage performances, cassettes, CDs and mp3s, music videos, internet discussion groups, and the press, visions of Punjabi history, Sikh identity, and the values of rural (especially Jat) Punjab have been widely projected within the nation state of India and beyond to the global stage.

In this chapter, I suggest that a close examination of forms of popular culture, such as bhangra, produces new insights into the performance and systematization of community identity and allows us to explore the relationships between technology, economic structures, and social formations. More specifically, a careful consideration of bhangra's histories offers particularly important insights for Sikh/Punjabi studies because it not only raises questions about the relationships between the 'homeland' and diasporic communities, but also forces us to grapple with the identity politics of Sikhism and its place in the political economy of global culture. By tracking back and forth between sites in Punjab, India, the United Kingdom, and to a lesser extent, the United States, this essay connects bhangra to the very different pressures that have moulded Sikhs in a range of specific locations, at very specific points in time. And by offering an extended discussion of the interfaces between Punjabi diasporic communities and the Afro-Caribbean populations of British cities, I attempt to unravel the complex cultural webs and networks that have moulded the development of Punjabi culture and Sikh identities within a global frame. In so doing, this chapter locates both bhangra and Punjabi culture at the cultural 'crossroads' identified by George Lipsitz as the improvisational, creative, but fraught sites where diverse people meet, engage, and define themselves.[1]

Ultimately my central concern here is bhangra's ambivalent and shifting relationship to both Punjabi and Sikh identities. I examine three particular moments of cultural reconfiguration, particular points when the forms, aesthetics, and politics of bhangra were reworked, producing lively debates over 'tradition' and the boundaries of community. I begin by sketching the history of bhangra within Punjab itself, examining its early history as a localized dance form and its utility in post-Partition India as a potent signifier of a pan-communal 'Punjabiyat'. This history of the re-territorialization of a local folk form as an embodiment of regional identity is typically occluded by cultural studies scholars and neglected in studies of bhangra's place in the South Asian diaspora. The middle part of the chapter assesses the new forms of bhangra that emerged within Britain between the late 1970s and the early 1990s, exploring both the aesthetics and identity politics of what I term 'black bhangra' before tracing the erosion of this tradition by more commercialized forms of bhangra and 'Indipop' in the mid-1990s. In the final section, I conclude by returning to Punjab itself, highlighting the ability of Punjabis 'at home' to access and assess these new trends. Within the Punjabi context, as I show, considerable effort has been devoted to a further reformulation of bhangra in an attempt to shore up 'tradition' in the face of the 'cultural imperialism' of 'disco, tango, or rock-and-roll'.[2]

Territorializing Bhangra as 'Punjabi'

Although the educational system, the print culture, and other literary forms of colonial Punjab were dominated by the ascendancy of Urdu—a hegemony initially sponsored by both the colonial state and influential Orientalists such as G. W. Leitner—rich vernacular traditions flourished despite limited state support. Most obviously, the reading of Guru

Granth Sahib by granthis and the collective performance of *kirtan* underscore the centrality of both religious observance and oral expression in Punjabi, both spoken and sung, in the cultural world of the Sikh communities in the nineteenth and early twentieth centuries. Beyond *bani* and kirtan, however, we can also identify a rich array of Punjabi expressive traditions. The folk-tales narrated by travelling *mirasis* (ballad singers) and village elders collected by Charles Swynnerton, for example, were an important manifestation of the persistence of the 'enchanted universe' that Harjot Oberoi has identified as characteristic of pre-colonial rural Punjabi culture.[3] Music was a central feature of this cultural world and a variety of folk musical traditions developed around the rhythms of agrarian production and the key points in an individual's life cycle, especially marriage, pregnancy, birth, and death. These celebratory folk songs co-existed with popular narrative ballads that were quickly established as staples of the print culture in the urban centres. But even as narrative ballads such as 'Hir' (expressed in its most refined form in Waris Shah's *Hir-Ranjha*) or the tragic tale of Sahiban and Mirza were being refined, reworked, and repackaged on Punjabi printing presses, oral versions of these tales remained popular in small villages, where they were frequently recited to the accompaniment of music.[4] The profound interdependence of the oral and literate traditions within the transformation of Punjabi expressive and musical traditions confirms Stuart Blackburn and A. K. Ramanujan's insistence on the constant 'borrowing' backwards and forwards between oral and written folk narratives within South Asia.[5]

One important element of this vernacular rural culture was bhangra. The scant body of source material on Punjabi folk culture before 1947 means that the early history of bhangra remains contentious and debates over its etymology, origins, and nature are common.[6] It is clear, however, that by the late nineteenth century, it had emerged as a dance typically performed to the beat of the large *dhol* drum (which was often accompanied by smaller *dholak* or *dholki* drums). It was the relationship between the vigorous and agile movements of the dancers and the dhol's beat that was at the centre of this performative tradition, rather than the lyrics (which typically celebrated fertility and the joys of harvest) sung by the accompanying vocalist or the supporting enthusiastic cries of the dancers and/or the gathered crowd. Bhangra rhythms were typically flexible, expressing a wide variety of moods: Iqbal Singh Dhillon suggests that in its ability to express the 'festive, virile, romantic and even the mourning', bhangra was and is the 'total dance'.[7] Traditional Punjabi folk dances like bhangra were always gender-specific: women might perform dances like the giddha, luddi, sammi, and pharuha, while bhangra itself, like the jhummir and bagha, was a specifically male dance form.[8] Prior to Partition, bhangra was not only gender-specific but, like other forms of rural popular culture, it was a highly localized performative tradition. It was locked into the particular social structures, economic patterns, and cultural forms of a specific space. In bhangra's case, it was principally associated with the Sialkot, Gujrat, Shekhupura, Gujranwala, and Gurdaspur districts of western Punjab and the bhangra of the villages of Sialkot was widely considered the purest and perhaps even standard form of bhangra prior to the massive upheavals that transformed the social and cultural landscape of rural Punjab from 1946.[9]

In the wake of Partition, bhangra assumed new importance as part of the projection of 'Punjabiyat' and in the articulation of a regional culture that transcended the deep divisions that were laid so bare in the violence of Partition. Within this context, bhangra became a ubiquitous feature of the province's culture within independent India. As *The Tribune* observed: 'The *bhangra* dance, today, is no longer associated with the Baisakhi festival alone. On any festive occasion, say *Lohri,* betrothal and marriage ceremonies, the birth of a son, cultural and sports meets, agricultural fairs, including cattle fairs, one can witness this dance.'[10]

Bhangra's transformation into an icon of Punjabi identity was carefully cultivated by the regional government. Refugees from the western parts of Punjab that were the cradle of bhangra were a crucial vector that carried bhangra east into the newly formed Indian Punjab. Dance was an important cultural glue within the turbulent context of Partition. It allowed displaced people to perform and reaffirm traditional ties, cultural bonds that transcended the turbulent politics of caste and religious community. In April 1948, a bhangra 'team' of refugees put together by Chaman Lal Rana entertained Jawaharlal Nehru and Lord Mountbatten at the Kurukshetra refugee camp. Soon after Partition, the Punjabi state began to sponsor bhangra as an emblem of a distinctive Punjabi identity within independent India. Revealingly, the first instance of bhangra as an organized spectacle for a mass public audience was sponsored by the PEPSU (Patiala and East Punjab States Union) government for the Republic Day parade in Delhi in 1955. In 1956 the Government of Punjab sponsored a female giddha team and a male jhummir team to perform on Republic Day and bhangra enjoyed a special status as iconic of Punjabi culture as a whole. By 1956 bhangra had appeared in Hindi films such as *Jagte Raho* and *Naya Daur*. Punjabi educational institutions, particularly Khalsa College and Punjab University, as well as a range of other schools and colleges, began to emphasize the importance of bhangra and organized bhangra teams and competitions. In this new staged form of the dance, a wide range of movements associated with other male folk dances were assimilated into tightly synchronized performances which displayed a great variety of coordinated movements at considerable speed. New dramatic elements were introduced into bhangra performances and teams were now judged on their movement, appearance, and 'choreography'. At the same time, new instruments (the *chimta* and *algoza*) were added to accompany the dhol, a new emphasis was placed on the singing of *bolis* by an accompanying singer (where the *laakri* [leader] would traditionally have sung prior to the performance of bhangra and during short pauses by the dancers), and 'coaches' emerged to drill their teams and to oversee the increasingly complex range of formations and forms used by the dancers.

It was through these innovations that bhangra, which had largely emerged in parts of Punjab which had now passed to Pakistan, became a way for Indian Punjabis to perform, project, and proclaim a distinctive provincial identity to the newly formed Indian nation. This emblematic role was not confined within South Asia, but also was projected on an international stage, with a bhangra team from PEPSU representing the province as part of the Indian Cultural Delegation to China in May 1955.[11] The Punjab state continues to identify bhangra as an integral part of a distinctive regional culture: indeed, bhangra is a prominent element of the Punjab government's web page, where it is depicted as embodying the 'infectious zeal for life' that is identified as both the state's key cultural feature and its chief marketable tourist commodity.[12]

We must recognize, however, that bhangra has a multiplicity of histories, as its development since World War II has taken place within a context of sustained Punjabi mobility both within and beyond South Asia. As an expressive form, it has developed *simultaneously* within Punjab and within diasporic communities in Asia, Africa, Europe, Australasia, and North America. While the remainder of this chapter attends to this simultaneity in bhangra's development within a cultural frame, it is important to closely examine its development in Britain during the 1980s and early 1990s, where bhangra was profoundly reworked in innovative and challenging ways by two generations of British Punjabis.[13]

The Punjabi Diaspora and the Transformation of Bhangra

The new wave of Punjabis who settled in Britain after World War II carried bhangra with them and bhangra's subsequent development has been very closely tied to the changing demographic profile and economic fortunes of these migrants. The sustained growth of the British Punjabi community in the 1960s not only created sizeable urban enclaves, capable of fashioning new social institutions and a complex mesh of cultural networks, but also began to equalize the gender ratio of the migrant community. With the resulting consolidation of the migrant Punjabi family and the foundation of community groups, the building of new gurdwaras and mandirs, and the proliferation of weddings, British Punjabi social life increasingly emphasized family activities (as opposed the hyper-masculine culture of the early migrants) and the maintenance of 'tradition'. Within this revivified social scene, bhangra emerged as a key marker of tradition, embodying the transplantation of the rural culture central to Punjabi regional identity.

It is almost impossible to underestimate the extent of the cultural transformations enacted within this transplantation. While bhangra was originally closely associated with Baisakhi, Baisakhi in Britain's fickle spring was far removed from the warmth and fertility of April in Punjab. Thus, fairly quickly, within the British context bhangra was uncoupled from the rhythms of the seasons and agricultural production that had initially nourished this form of expression and instead became a key feature of weddings, birthday parties, and various family or community celebrations. These transitions were more abrupt in Britain than in Punjab. This shift towards increasingly staged bhangra performances extended the transformation of bhangra in post-Independence Punjab itself.[14] Moreover, the very different material, social, and political underpinnings of diasporic life meant that bhangra was displaced from its specific locations (and attendant variations) within the landscape of rural Punjab to the community buildings and rented halls of Southall, Coventry, Birmingham, and Bradford. While prominent performers in this community circuit, such as Mohinder Kaur Bhamra and Bhujangy, adhered closely to many popular bhangra staples, others such as Deedar Singh Pardesi wove bhangra and ghazals together, while many smaller bands combined bhangra with *filmi* music, both old and new, in their sets. One key change that followed these transformations, which is now almost impossible to pinpoint in time, was the gradual shift in the usage of the term 'bhangra' itself, as it came not only to signify the dance, but also to refer to both the dance and the wide range of popular musical forms produced by Punjabi musicians.

Amongst these early performers the most important was Alaap, a group that has been identified in initiating the hybridization of bhangra.[15] Founded in 1977 in Southall, Alaap were prominent in the community circuit, playing weddings and other celebrations. Their 1979 album *Teri Chunni de Sitare* was the first album to be recorded by a British bhangra group and is widely recognized as marking the birth of the 'Southall scene'. In the early 1980s, Alaap worked closely with Deepak Khazanchi, who has been described as the 'Phil Spector of Bhangra', and the result of this collaboration transformed the aural scapes of bhangra. Khazanchi, an experienced musician and producer who had performed both in East Africa and Britain, introduced 'Western' instruments, especially bass, guitars, synthesizers, and drum machines into bhangra, to create a novel new sound that nevertheless remained tied to the conventions of bhangra transplanted to Britain.

In an important 1988 essay, Sabita Banerji described the impact of these recordings:

For perhaps the first time their [British Punjabi] original culture was being served up in a form that was not conservative and old-fashioned, but young, modern and western. It was, above all, their own—neither imitative of the West nor pandering to the tastes of an older generation; neither exclusively Indian, like film music, nor exclusively Western like pop. Thus Bhangra heralded the coming of age of a new generation and gave them a voice with which to tell their white compatriots who they were and what they were; not the shy, insular and conservative creatures they had hitherto been stereotyped as, but ordinary fun-loving young people.[16]

The success of Alaap and other pioneering British groups not only reworked the sound of bhangra, but also initiated a radical shift in the ways in which bhangra was performed, consumed, and circulated. Inherited traditions of performance, form, and style were reworked in major urban centres, especially Birmingham, Coventry, and London, and a generation of youths re-crafted bhangra as a fundamentally urban music. Just as the systematization of bhangra within the Punjab itself after Partition relocated the performative tradition from countryside to the stage, a later generation of British Punjabis moved the genre from the stage of the community centre or wedding hall to the streets and to that quintessentially modern, urban space, the disco.[17]

These innovative urban forms of bhangra had necessitated an important relocation of bhangra's social context. In the 1970s and early 1980s, bhangra enabled British Punjabis to perform 'traditional' community rites and rituals of identity, a function it continues to retain in smaller British cities and centres with smaller South Asian populations. As one young man from Newcastle, which had a small Punjabi population and lacked an energetic music scene, explained to Andrew Bennett, bhangra 'brings back memories... it's like tradition... it gives you a buzz to be doing something a bit traditional'.[18] One of Bennett's female informants underscored the importance of bhangra events in the performance of 'traditional' identities, especially for younger British South Asians who feel pressured to wear 'Western clothes' on a daily basis: 'Going to a bhangra evening is like the only chance to wear eastern clothes... Where I live there's like eleven people who are Asian... my mum will go into town with her Indian clothes on, but I wouldn't dare.'[19] There is no doubt that for many Punjabis bhangra, even in its new forms, continued to be seen as evocative of home and elicited these nostalgic feelings. But from the early 1980s, in British cities where Punjabis co-existed with substantial Afro-Carribean populations, radically new visions of bhangra emerged. In short, bhangra became an important performative tradition that allowed Punjabis in Britain to articulate distinctive identities, contest visions of Britishness, and craft new cultural alliances across the lines of language, religion, ethnicity, and race.

It is useful to term these innovative new forms of bhangra born in Britain's cities in the 1980s and early 1990s as black bhangra. This term offers some important insights and is more precise than some of the alternative terms. To term them 'British bhangra', as is common in internet chat groups and bhangra websites, is misleading because it defines these new traditions primarily through the nation state, when in fact these new forms reflected the collision, interweaving, and fusion between bhangra and black musical traditions that reach out beyond the nation of Britain to span what Paul Gilroy terms the 'Black Atlantic'.[20] 'Hybrid bhangra'[21] may offer a more theoretically sophisticated alternative which stresses the in-between-ness of these innovative forms of bhangra, but it generalizes processes of encounter and exchange between Punjabis and Afro-Caribbean peoples into an abstraction that actually works to obscure the very specific power relationships and cultural borrowings that characterize these relations. More precise terms such as 'Raggamuffin' and 'Bhangramuffin'[22] are extremely useful as they demarcate particular forms of expression fashioned out of the repertoires of reggae and bhangra, but these terms cannot capture the broad spectrum of new musics woven out of the encounter between bhangra and Afro-Caribbean musical traditions (including, but not restricted to, reggae, soul, R&B, and hip-hop).

Conversely, the term black bhangra is heuristically useful for three reasons. First, and most generally, it foregrounds the importance of Afro-Caribbean musics in the reshaping of bhangra from the mid-1980s, a cross-cultural engagement that is frequently elided or masked in popular writings on bhangra, particularly those produced from within South Asia. Second, and following on from this, by designating these performative traditions as black bhangra, we firmly locate them within the racial politics of the Atlantic world, specifically urban Britain under Thatcher and her immediate successors. Even though, as Modood has argued recently, the identification of British Asians with blackness was eroded in the later 1990s, the reformulation of bhangra coincided with the convergence of South Asian and black urban struggles against the British National Party and the National Front and, at a more general level, the centrality of race in debates over British identity and its limits in the 1980s and early 1990s.[23] Within this context, various South Asian performers, activists, and intellectuals embraced the category of 'blackness' as an important statement of their anti-racist politics. This move, as Sanjay Sharma has suggested, did not preclude or marginalize an individual's South Asian identity, but rather marked the articulation of a new 'strategic identity politics' that harnessed the particular cultural resonances and political power of blackness within post-colonial Britain.[24] Third, it suggests that recent bhangra emerged out of the interstices of two structures central in the formation of modernity: the 'Black Atlantic' and the 'imperial social formation' created by British colonialism in South Asia.[25] Although both black and South Asian diasporas can claim long histories within Britain, the influx of labourers from the Caribbean and South Asia after World War II meant that black and South Asian workers rubbed shoulders in Britain's industrial cities. Although black–South Asian relationships were frequently uneasy, these encounters initiated important cultural and musical exchanges which would ultimately transform the soundscapes of Britain and beyond.

The cultural significance and influence of bhangra within British soundscapes and cultural patterns was unevenly distributed and was profoundly shaped by demographic patterns and local contexts. The new politically aware and aesthetically innovative forms of bhangra that emerged in the late 1980s and early 1990s typically emerged from substantial Punjabi communities that lived alongside or in close proximity to large Afro-Caribbean populations. Southall in west London and Handsworth in Birmingham were two such locations where South Asian youths shared urban space, educational institutions, and class positions with British Blacks and were drawn into Leftist and anti-racist groups that aimed to fashion a new solidarity between Britons of South Asian and Caribbean origin. Even though such multi-ethnic and multi-confessional neighbourhoods were sometimes the site of tension, conflict, and violence, they were also sites of engagement, exchange, and creativity. Apache Indian, who fashioned a powerful mix of bhangra and reggae in the early 1990s, credits much of his musical style particularly to Handsworth's demographic mix: 'I had Indian influences because of my background but I loved reggae music. Handsworth had a lot of Jamaican influence.'[26]

Why did new expressive traditions that challenged this view of tradition develop in urban centres? The emergence of black bhangra ultimately rested on transformations in the demographic composition, community life, and cultural aspirations of Punjabi communities in Britain. In urban centres, especially London and Birmingham, Punjabi communities clustered together in working-class enclaves, where important elements of Punjabi culture were nurtured but also brought into dialogue with the culture of their working-class, largely black neighbours. In London, the concentration of Punjabis in Southall nourished the emergence of a vibrant bhangra scene in the 1980s. The steady flow of Punjabis (especially from Jullundur district) into Southall from the early 1950s, initially to work at Woolf's rubber factory, transformed the demographic balance of the Ealing–Southall area, and by the mid-1970s, Punjabis were the dominant ethnic group in Southall or '*chota Punjab*' (little Punjab).[27]

In centres such as Southall, Punjabi youth in the late 1970s and 1980s began to exercise greater freedoms. While at a broad level this reflected adjustment to the pressures exerted by British culture as a whole, it also emerged out of specific demographic and economic factors. Traditional family structures, especially the joint family, were not as prevalent amongst diasporic Punjabis in Britain. Because the main surge of Punjabi migration has come relatively recently, Punjabi families in Britain tend to have dense horizontal networks (brothers, sisters, and cousins) rather than the complex inter-generational structures that shape life within Punjab itself.[28] The resulting simplification of kin structures created greater space for some teenagers, as many households lacked the grandparents and the uncles and aunts who might supervise children while parents were working. Punjabi women, frequently identified as the upholders of tradition, were extremely active in the formal workforce (especially in the case of Punjabis who migrated to Britain from East Africa) and their participation rates eclipsed those of other South Asian women and British women as a whole.[29] While this strong engagement with the labour market inevitably devolved some domestic responsibilities onto daughters, it also meant that many Punjabi children were not under the direct motherly supervision that remained common in Punjab. This meant that some Sikh and Punjabi youths had greater freedoms to associate with non-Punjabi friends, to engage widely with their urban environments, and to explore other cultures. These inquisitive needs were deeply felt by many second- and third-generation Punjabi Britons. Reflecting in 1988, Harwant Singh Bains, a prominent Southall youth worker and anti-racist campaigner, observed '[a]mongst many of my friends, both boys and girls, there is often a yearning to escape from the confines of Southall... and to embrace the fugitive freedoms of the "outside world"'.[30]

Bains stresses that that 'outside world' was often hostile and racist; but we must recognize that it was also alluring. The new forms of black bhangra spoke directly to the cultural dilemma of migrants, blending 'tradition' with new and exciting elements borrowed from black British culture and expressive traditions. It functioned as an empowering way of sampling the exhilaration offered by this 'outside world', while retaining important affiliations to inherited identities and cultural forms. Equally important, black bhangra grew out of a rejection of the assimilationist aims that some older, more economically successful Punjabis articulated. Even if the desire for 'economic assimilation' identified by Harwant Singh Bains as a powerful force amongst the Punjabis of Southall persists until today, the racial violence of the late 1970s—from the murder of Gurdip Chaggar in 1976 to the Southall 'riots' of 1979 and 1981—and ongoing debates about the elasticity of Britishness certainly undercut any residual aspirations to 'Whiteness' that some Punjabis might have nurtured. Even if resistance to the National Front in Southall during 1981 did not trigger the widespread politicization of British Punjabis, it did reveal the reluctance of the British state to rein in British fascists and ultra-nationalists, groups whose agendas in the 1980s profoundly threatened the very future of the British Punjabi community. In light of this, diasporic Punjabis increasingly both emphasized their distinctive heritage and, where possible, their British citizenship.[31] Highlighting their multiple positions in relation to the nation state gave these diasporic subjects the ability to critique the British state from within (or at least from the margins). Within this context, the rapid embrace of new forms of bhangra by Punjabi youths was part of this rejection of assimilation and must be viewed as part of the contest over the nature of British South Asian identity and the limits of Britishness itself: as Gurinder Chadha explained, bhangra 'gave back something for ourselves, it had nothing to do with English people or white society. It consolidated the debate about whether we are Black, British or Asian'.[32]

Many Punjabis responded to these challenges by reasserting the primacy of 'tradition', upholding the unquestioned authority of the cultural forms that they had transplanted to Britain, and nurturing a powerful nostalgia for 'their Punjab'. A strong desire for 'traditional' bhangra over the new styles of bhangra fashioned in Southall or Handsworth was often an important element of this stress on cultural continuity, especially among older Punjabis or in towns with smaller South Asian populations. Within such contexts, hybridized bhangra forms did not develop locally and bhangra remained tightly tied to events that drew upon broad involvement from the local South Asian population, regardless of religion, regional origin, or age. Bhangra events in Newcastle, for example, were family occasions, where grandparents and grandchildren would participate alongside teenagers and young adults. This active family participation in Newcastle bhangra meant that, despite the efforts of some community activists and DJs to use bhangra as a forum for bringing young British South Asians into contact with Afro-Caribbean youths and cultural forms, bhangra was understood by many young Asian people in Newcastle 'as primarily as a form of folk music which draws upon and simultaneously promotes particular versions of traditional life'.[33] The new sounds and forms of self-presentation that were generated by black bhangra were frequently the object of conflict within families, as the explicit borrowings from Afro-Caribbean culture made many Punjabi parents (and some youths) nervous.[34] It is also important to note that while some young Punjabis, such as those encountered by Kathleen Hall in 1991, rejected the most explicitly hybrid forms of black bhangra, the groups that they upheld as embodying 'tradition' (such as Alaap) were in fact central to initiating the radical transformation of bhangra within Britain.[35]

These debates about Britishness identified by Gurinder Chadha were carried out through the lyrics, language, and personal style of bhangra artists themselves. In 1990, Gerd Baumann offered a succinct summation of the lyrical concerns of bhangra: 'these songs are celebratory in tone, and can focus on the beauties of the harvest season, on natural and human beauty, and on a range of usually male sentiments about attraction, companionship, friendship and love.'[36] Virinder S. Kalra has challenged this characterization, noting that it 'does not take into account the diversity that is present in the lyrics of the genre, nor give any credence to the way in which lyrics have been "re-invented" in the modernized form [of bhangra]'.[37] There is no doubt that the themes identified by Baumann have remained prominent in both Indian- and British-produced bhangra over the least two decades and such song texts remain particularly popular in certain contexts, particularly at weddings, parties, and among older Punjabis. But as Kalra insists, new lyrical concerns have emerged and have, as a result, fashioned a greater diversity of thematic concerns in bhangra lyrics.

Reflections upon migration, the loosening of community bonds in the diaspora, and a longing for the 'homeland' (concerns that did, potentially at least, connect with the drive for Khalistan) have been important features of these lyrical connections of these new forms of expression. Nirmal's lyrics to Kalapreet's *'Us Pradesh kee Vasna Yaarab'* are one striking example of these reflections on displacement. One verse asks:

My friend, what is the use of living in that land
Where love does not live,
Where every house looks at you with hate and laughs,
Where souls are cold as ice,
Where the soil is very bad?[38]

This song has achieved iconic status, especially after its powerful dramatization of British Punjabi's angular relationship to the nation and national identities was used to open Gurinder Chadha's 1988 short film *I'm British... But.*

Thus the quandaries of the diasporic condition were prominent in the bhangra of the 1980s and early 1990s. Johnny Zee's 'Why did I Come to Vilayet?', from his 1994 album *Spirits of Rhythm*, offered a humorous but poignant take on the conflicted position of the migrant, where a Punjabi father worries that his son has been alienated from the very basis of his Punjabi identity ('You've forgotten the taste of saag/ And sleeping on a string bed') and that he has succumbed to the temptations presented by alcohol and Western women.[39] Kalra's emphasis on the importance of diasporic themes of alienation and longing for a distant 'homeland' within the Punjabi lyrics of British bhangra is important, but we must recognize that the use of the vernacular as a vehicle for the evocation of loss co-exists with a complex mix of more hybridized linguistic forms and a very broad array of lyrical concerns. Setting aside the long-standing evocations of female beauty, love, and awakening sexuality that remain a powerful stock in trade of many bhangra artists, we can identify three other lyrical idioms that have emerged over the last two decades.

The most culturally vital form of lyrical innovation produced within the diaspora was the interweaving of bhangra and reggae, particularly in the work of Apache Indian.[40] While much has been made of the rhythmic affinities and exchanges between bhangra and reggae, the idioms and vocal style of reggae artists profoundly imprinted British bhangra from the late 1980s. This reflected the close co-existence of Punjabi and Afro-Caribbean communities in Southall and in Birmingham's Handsworth, a suburb that produced artist Apache Indian (a Punjabi named Steven Kapur) who has enjoyed great success in both the Caribbean and India in addition to Britain. The chorus to his single 'Arranged Marriage', wove together Punjabi with the Jamaican patois Apache heard spoken on the streets of Birmingham:

Me wan gal from Jullunder City
Me wan gal say a sooni curi
Me wan gal that say she love me
Me wan gal sweet like jelebee

The third verse concludes:

Say the gal me like have the right figure
In she eyes have the surma
Wear the chunee kurtha pyjama
And talk the Indian with the patwa[41]

A second aesthetic shift that also emerged out of the diaspora was the harnessing of hip-hop culture to powerful critiques of the prejudices at the heart of British life. This strand is best typified by Hustlers HC, three *kes-dhari* Sikhs who married bhangra rhythms, not to the creolized stylings of reggae, but rather to the gritty and violent urban narratives characteristic of gangsta rap.[42] By using English as their medium, Hustlers HC carried their message to both young British South Asians and to a wider British community that typically could not access the lyrical content of Hindi or Punjabi songs. Their 1994 single 'Big Trouble in Little Asia' foregrounded the rootlessness of the diasporic condition ('Homeless I've grown up, homeless I will roam') produced by British colonialism ('A jewel in the empire made of gold/Now it's raped and left out in the cold'), before exhorting the creation of a pan-communal anti-racist movement and the rejection of the quietism they saw as weakening the position of British South Asians:

The Hindu, the Muslim and the Sikh
United we stand, divided we are weak
Weakened the most by the coconut
The sellout to the white, the coward in the fight

The provocative English lyrics of 'Big Trouble' end by stressing the need to forcibly protect the community in the face of racist attacks:

I challenge the BNP to march on Southall Broadway
Big trouble comes and by any means
The blood will stain it and it ain't easy to clean...[43]

Following on from Hustler HC's merging of English gangsta rap narratives with anti-racist politics, the third and most recent reworking of bhangra lyrical forms has been incorporation of the verbal phrasings of hip-hop culture within songs with predominantly Punjabi lyrics. From the mid-1990s, bhangra artists have increasingly invoked the most depoliticized hyper-masculine traditions of hip-hop in the English introductions to their songs, choruses, and shout-outs where they style themselves as 'vocal assassins', who deliver the 'fresh flava' or the 'bad boy riddim', while remaining loyal to their 'crew' or 'homies'.

Although some artists continued to maintain aesthetics and performance identities heavily influenced by hip-hop (with names such as Punjabi Hit Squad), the shared political interests between Punjabis and Afro-Caribbean artists and activists took on a less political orientation in the mid-1990s. In part, this reflected the broader crisis in the strategic alliances between Blacks and South Asians that energized the British Left and anti-racist movements, but it also dramatized a broader shift in the position of South Asians within British culture at large. In the early 1990s, greater attention was directed to the success of South Asian entrepreneurs, and both mainstream and community media placed a renewed emphasis on the pursuit of material wealth and political influence, often at the expense of social justice and the protection of the community's welfare. At the same time, South Asian cultural forms were increasingly assimilated into the aesthetics of British middle-class life. By 1995, bindis, *mehndi*, South Asian food, and South Asian fashion had become extremely prominent in British youth culture as a whole: 'Asian Kool', as it was styled, was a key component of the partial repackaging of Britishness in Tony Blair's 'Cool Britannia'. The politics of Hustlers HC or Kalapreet's invocation of Britain as a land where 'souls are cold as ice' were out of step with this new context. The political allegiances and sensitivities of black bhangra were increasingly overwhelmed by new forms of bhangra where the connection with hip-hop and the aesthetics of the black Atlantic remained, but were now stripped of their political teeth and packaged for global consumption.

Sikhi and the Challenge of Bhangra

The work of Bally Sagoo, Apache Indian, and other British bhangra artists were not only crucial in bringing British music into closer connection with Caribbean and American musical traditions, but also played a central role in forging a strong connection between British and South Asian popular culture. This should not surprise us as George Lipsitz has stressed that '[r]ecorded music travels from place to place, transcending physical and temporal barriers'.[44] In the South Asian context, Peter Manuel has demonstrated the importance of 'cassette culture' over the past three decades. The sale, duplication, and circulation of cassettes has played a key role in linking new diasporic and Punjabi bhangra traditions: in 1996, for example, it was possible to buy the work of artists such as Alaap as well as Bally Sagoo and Apache Indian from stalls in Simla, Chandigarh, Amritsar, and Delhi.[45] Although it lacks the affordability and easy circulation of cassette technology, television has also provided an important link between the diasporic communities and their homelands. While the uneven nature of the global mediascape means that India-based artists have had (and continue to have) limited visibility in the Western media, television services in India have been a crucial forum that connect the homelands with the production of diasporic artists. The rise of Star TV has been a crucial vector for transmitting the work of British bhangra artists to South Asian elites, who can consume the music and videos of these acts alongside 'Western' pop, R&B, and filmi music. Music is also prominent in state broadcasting and non-cable commercial television, particularly within Punjab, where music-related programmes take up to two-thirds of the airtime.[46] Sacred music, Bollywood songs, Punjabi folk and pop songs, and diasporic bhangra jostle together in this rich sonic and visual world which stretches out well beyond the political boundaries of Punjab itself. More recently, the rise of the internet has become an important vehicle for disseminating bhangra and fashioning new forms of connection between the diaspora and the homeland. Of course, access to the internet within South Asia remains heavily determined by class position and educational opportunity, but this new technology has allowed certain sectors of India's elite to gain quicker and wider access to the music, art, and style that have been produced by diasporic South Asians, as well as facilitating their consumption of global popular culture more generally.

It is very clear that these media have worked to transform space and subordinate distance, meaning that Punjabis 'at home' are familiar with many of the innovative forms of expression produced within the diaspora.[47] And, of course, these innovations have fed into the transformation of bhangra in Punjab itself. A 1998 article in the *Tribune*, for example, noted important transformations in the gendered dynamics of Punjabi folk dances:

It is worth pointing out that in the past in most of the regions of Punjab group dances did not have men and women together, as the latter were confined to the four walls of their homes. They were forced to observe the *purdah* tradition by which they covered their face with *ghund, dupatta* or veil. They were, however, permitted to witness the *bhangra* and other dances of the menfolk but the menfolk were not allowed to watch the *giddha, luddi, jago* etc. But now there has been a sea-change in such traditions. Both men and women come together to perform folk dances in the vicinity of modern villages and on the cultural platforms in the towns and cities of Punjab. It is indeed a healthy trend in a state like Punjab where today men and women join together in all spheres of life to promote culture, education, agro-industrial economy, social welfare scheme etc for the benefit of society at large.[48]

These reworkings of bhangra have been subject to fierce debate, especially within Punjab itself. The emergence of nightclub-based bhangra scenes in the West, in Delhi, and, to a lesser extent, in major Punjab cities has caused deep concern about the undercutting of 'traditional' forms of bhangra. As Iqbal Singh Dhillon has stressed, a troubling change for many Punjabis is the shift away from the specific dances for each gender and the separate performance of dances by men and women to the culture of the contemporary bhangra competition and nightclub where the genders freely intermix.[49] A recent *Tribune* article highlighted this displacement of tradition in a much more anxious tone than in its 1998 discussion of gender:

The beating of drums, recitation of bolis, clamouring of chimta and kato and the quintessential physical gyrations that formed the basis of Bhangra, the traditional Punjabi dance, seem to have been replaced by a more free-flowing dance form performed to a stereotypical techno music.[50]

Against this backdrop of 'tradition in peril', the *Tribune* explored the establishment of the Nachda Punjab Youth Welfare Club 'not just for the revival of this traditional art form, but also for its promotion, especially amongst the younger urbanites in the state'. Avtaar Singh, the club's president, explained that the club was responding to the 'invasion' of 'disco, tango or rock-and-roll'. One club member, Bhupinder Singh, cast the club as both preserving traditional Punjabi culture and as a missionary organization as he thought that 'bringing the dance forms [bhangra, but also the gidda, jhummar, and jandua] to the forefront is a sacred mission. This is an inherent part of our ethos and committed efforts have to be made for its resurrection'.[51] Yet what is striking is that even if the Nachda Punjab Youth Welfare Club was staging a battle to preserve traditional forms against the cultural imperialism of 'disco, tango and rock-and-roll', it too was fundamentally recasting 'tradition' and the gendered dynamics of Punjabi cultural performance. The club had elaborated a new form of the traditionally male Malwai gidda where male and female performers perform the boli in a call-and-response format while performing the gidda together. But this innovation was not a response to the needs of the 'urbanites' the club was targeting, let alone the demands of the diaspora: rather, as Avtaar Singh explained, this new Malwai gidda 'is typical of the rustic family life, where there are a lot of verbal duels between a brother-in-law and sister-in-law, husband and wife or between daughter-in-law and mother-in-law'.[52] It is this innovation through the incorporation of the norms of 'rustic family life' that provides the Nachda Club with its defence against the 'Westernization' of bhangra. The club's Lakhwant Singh stressed that the club was fighting an important battle over the future of Punjabiyat and that its defence of tradition was vital to stave off the debasing effects of Western understandings of gender: 'efforts need to be made so that our culture is projected in its true form and not after it has been "westernised" to suit their need of attracting attention by portraying semi-nude models in Punjabi songs'.[53]

Throughout the twentieth century, Sikh reformers have exhibited a recurring concern with the morality of dance. As a particularly vibrant and performative expression of popular culture, dance has frequently worried some members of the Panth and they have expressed anxiety about the effects of dance both upon the dancer and, equally importantly, on the audience. Dance, it seems, has the potential (at least momentarily) to recast gender relationships, express sensuality in unsettling ways, and uncouple the body from the social, cultural, and religious structures that govern it. In the early twentieth century, Singh Sabha reformers were sceptical of the value of bhangra, giddha, and other folk dances and were particularly worried over women dancing. They strove to ban the performance of giddha even within households and were staunchly opposed to public dancing.[54] Even though British bhangra groups such as Alaap have performed in gurdwaras, many Sikhs are uneasy with the musical innovations and new forms of sociability that have emerged around bhangra since the 1970s.[55]

The most significant discussion of bhangra's place within Sikhism is an article entitled 'Bhangra & Sikhi: Is there a Connection?'. This essay has circulated very widely on the internet, being incorporated into the web pages of various gurdwaras, Sikh student associations, and Sikh women's groups. The anonymous author of this article distinguishes 'traditional bhangra' from 'Westernized bhangra' and carefully sets out the relationship between bhangra and Sikhi:

It was probably even normal for there to be similar dancing and singing on weddings and other joyous occasions. But there is no evidence in Sikh history to suggest that the Gurus had ever promoted it or that it had even ever been performed in their presence. In those days, joyous occasions were marked by Sikhs—by the reading of shabads and singing of shabads and also by the distribution of gifts and food to the poor and needy. In Gurudwaras today, occasions are still celebrated as such today, Bhangra dancing and singing is not acceptable in a Sikh Gurudwara... Sikhi does not promote Bhangra and therefore it is not correct to believe that Bhangra is a *Sikhi thing*. Yes it is Punjabi—and because the majority of Sikhs are Punjabi—Bhangra seems to have been classed as a Sikh institution over the years. Without entering into the argument as to whether Bhangra should be performed at Sikh weddings and whether a Sikh is a bad Sikh if he or she listens to Bhangra, this page only seeks to suggest that *Bhangra is not a Sikh institution, but a Punjabi one*.[56]

This argument enjoys wide currency, with the *Tribune* arguing that bhangra was entirely unconnected to religion:

Besides, like other prominent dances of the country *bhangra* has no religious theme as its basis. In fact, Punjab is the only state of the country where its folk dances completely diverge from religion.[57]

Yet some young Sikhs resist this rigid division between the religious and non-religious, seeing bhangra as an important part of their 'heritage' and an important way in which they might affirm their identity as Sikhs. This tension has been identified by Jacqueline Warwick's work on bhangra in Toronto and in my own discussions with young Sikhs in both Britain and the United States.[58] At a broad level, this situation is reminiscent of the debates over the representation of Sikhs in British textbooks, where the visions of senior members of the community of what a 'proper Sikh' is and what the components of Sikhi are diverge from the self-understandings of young Punjabis who define themselves as Sikhs.[59] And there is no doubt that that many non-Sikhs persist in seeing bhangra as having some connection to Sikhism, even if this is simply the result of the prominence of turbaned kes-dhari Sikhs on album covers, posters, and in bhangra videos. At the same time, however, many influential Sikhs perceive the new forms of bhangra as a cultural threat, a corrosive force that should be contained, resisted, and rejected wherever possible. This position fashions a rigid division between the religious and the secular, as well as cementing a generation gap between parents fearful of global popular culture and their children.

Conclusion

This chapter has argued that music and dance have played a key role in the performance of Punjabi and Sikh identities over the last century. These expressive traditions are, however, by their very nature porous and have been constantly remade, redefined, and reworked as bhangra artists have drawn upon cultural idioms from elsewhere in South Asia and, as Punjabis settled abroad, from the musics of Africa, Europe, the Caribbean, and the Americas. The evidence presented here reminds us that the Punjabi diaspora has never been entirely self-contained or hermetically sealed; rather, the networks, institutions, communities, families, and individuals that comprise the diaspora have productively engaged with the various urban environments and cultural landscapes they have encountered outside India. This chapter has placed particular emphasis on the encounter between the Punjabi diaspora and the Afro-Caribbean diaspora and the very real innovations produced from this cultural 'crossroads'. Understanding the processes of engagement, translation, adaptation, accommodation, and innovation that shaped these particular encounters seems a crucial project for Punjab and Sikh studies to pursue, particularly given that the current generation of Sikh children and teenagers are growing up in a world where black music and culture, from hip-hop to reggae, have become a potent cultural force and an important source of cultural identification for young people from Delhi to Dublin, Dallas to Dunedin.

More generally, reflecting critically on the multiple histories of bhangra produces some new insights into the performance and contestation of cultural identities. Throughout this essay, I have stressed bhangra's mercurial nature. It has been a potent vehicle that artists have used to project Punjabi / Sikh identities to South Asian and global publics; but as a cultural form, it has an ambivalent relationship to both territorially grounded notions of Punjabiness and to understandings of Sikh identity that are solely situated in notions of orthodoxy and orthopraxy. Here I have argued that bhangra has been territorialized and re-territorialized as an articulation of cultural identity. It seems that in pre-colonial times bhangra developed as a form of dance primarily in the vicinity of Sialkot and Gurdaspur, where it functioned as an important element within the popular culture of the countryside. It was only with the trauma of Partition that bhangra came to be seen as emblematic of the regional culture of Indian Punjab, as the provincial government sought out new ways to create a distinctive identity on the national stage that transcended the deep schisms unleashed by the political struggles, violence, migration, and exile of the mid-1940s.

But, as this essay has shown, in recent times of course this 'quintessential' element of Punjab's culture has been recast by diasporic communities who have produced radical renderings of bhangra which use digital technology, deploy the standard hip-hop techniques of sampling, looping, and cutting up, and that borrow widely from the style, content, and language of contemporary black musics. These innovations were underpinned by the specific demographic profile, class position, and racial politics of Punjabis in Britain, which encouraged a generation of young South Asian men to engage with black British culture. The new visions of Punjabiness, produced by artists as diverse as Alaap, Apache Indian, and Hustlers HC, were widely disseminated and have functioned as important cultural connections between Britain and other diasporic sites as well as circulating back to Punjab itself. These cross-cultural engagements and global cultural flows, however, have not been welcomed by some Sikh leaders, who have worked hard to insulate 'tradition' against these reinventions of bhangra and in some cases, they have gone so far as to dismiss bhangra as fundamentally un-Sikh.

These debates provide important vantage points on the maintenance, recreation, and policing of culture and the boundaries of religion, culture, and race. The basis of Sikh studies for the last three decades has been to assess the development of the Sikh textual corpus and to chart the relationship between texts and community formation. We can understand this project as an attempt to delineate the 'core' of the Sikh tradition, those beliefs, practices, and structures that have given Sikhism its distinctive and unique character. But in understanding the production of communities, it is also instructive in paying close attention to the maintenance of borders and boundaries. Harjot Oberoi has cast much light on the construction of religious boundaries in colonial Punjab, and thanks to the work of Kathleen Hall, Verne Dusenbery, Rashmere Bhatti, and Karen Leonard, we are beginning to develop a rich appreciation of the operation of religious and cultural boundaries in various diasporic locations. This chapter has been an attempt to traverse the colonial and post-colonial periods, offering a brief overview of bhangra's transformation in the twentieth century and a reading of its role in production of cultural boundaries. In bringing the cultural history of Punjab and its diaspora together, in exploring the connections between dance and religion, in charting the relationships between music and race, this chapter has been an attempt to highlight some of the richness, complexity, and texture of the global histories of Punjab and of Sikhism.

Notes

1. George Lipsitz, *Dangerous Crossroads: Popular Music, Postmodernism, and the Poetics of Place* (London: Verso, 1994). This essay glosses the arguments that I developed at greater length in my recent *Between Colonialism and Diaspora: Sikh Cultural Formations in an Imperial Age* (Durham NC: Duke University Press, 2006).

2. *The Tribune*, 13 September 1998.

3. Charles Swynnerton, *Romantic Tales from the Panjab* (London, 1903).

4. See, for example, Charles Swynnerton, *Romantic Tales*, pp. xvii–ix. Harjot Oberoi, *The Construction of Religious Boundaries: Culture, Identity and Diversity in the Sikh Tradition* (Delhi: Oxford University Press, 1994).

5. Stuart Blackburn and A. K. Ramanujan (eds), *Another Harmony: New Essays on the Folklore of India* (Berkeley: University of California Press, 1986), pp. 1–40.

6. The best discussion of these issues is Iqbal Singh Dhillon, *Folk Dances of Panjab* (Chandigarh: National Bookshop, 1998), pp. 66–71. For debates amongst Punjabis over these issues, see <www.punjabi.net>.

7. Iqbal Singh Dhillon, *Folk Dances of Punjab*, pp. 73–4.

8. Giddha was a dramatic dance based around clapping; luddi was a dance in western Punjab, based around circular movements; sammi a circular dance that was accompanied by songs and performed under moonlight; pharuha was a fast form of giddha particularly associated with the Malwa; jhummir is a male dance of western Punjab that was performed in a circle to the accompaniment of jhummir songs; while the bagha is a circular dance of south-west Punjab, based around the raising of the arms and thumping feet on the ground.

9. Iqbal Singh Dhillon, *Folk Dances of Panjab* (Chandigarh: National Bookshop, 1998), p. 79.

10. *The Tribune*, 13 September 1998.

11. Iqbal Singh Dhillon, *Folk Dances of Panjab* (Chandigarh: National Bookshop, 1998), p. 89.

12. http://punjabgovt.nic.in/Culture/culture.htm

13. The simultaneous development of bhangra in Punjab and the diaspora is stressed in Sabita Banerji and Gerd Baumann, 'Bhangra 1984–8: Fusion and Professionalization in a Genre of South Asian Dance Music', Paul Oliver (ed.), *Black Music in Britain: Essays on the Afro-Asian Contribution to Popular Music,* (Buckingham: Open University Press, 1990), pp. 137–52.

14. On bhangra and community occasions, see Sabita Banerji, 'Ghazals to Bhangra in Great Britain', *Popular Music* 7, 2 (1988), p. 208.

15. Ibid., pp. 208–9; 'Bhangra', Donald Clarke (ed.), *Musicweb Encyclopedia of Popular Music*, http://www.musicweb.uk.net/encyclopaedia/b/B112.HTM

16. Sabita Banerji, 'Ghazals to Bhangra in Great Britain', pp. 211–13.

17. On the street in bhangra, see George Lipsitz, *Dangerous Crossroads*, p. 130

18. Andrew Bennett, 'Bhangra in Newcastle: Music, Ethnic Identity and the Role of Local Knowledge', *Innovation: The European Journal of the Social Sciences* 10, 1 (1997), pp. 107–16.

19. Ibid.

20. Paul Gilroy, *The Black Atlantic: Modernity and Double Consciousness* (London: Verso, 1993).

21. On the imperial history of hybridity see Robert J. C. Young, *Colonial desire: Hybridity in Theory, Culture, and Race* (London: Routledge, 1995).

22. Bhangramuffin draws heavily from raggamuffin, a form of reggae that makes heavy use of digitised electronic instrumemntation and sampling.

23. Tariq Modood, 'Political Blackness and British Asians', *Sociology* 28 (1994), pp. 859–76.

24. Sanjay Sharma, 'Noisy Asians or Asian Noise', Sanjay Sharma, John

Hutnyk, and Ashwani Sharma (eds), *Dis-Orienting Rhythms: the Politics of the New Asian Dance Music* (London: Zed Books, 1996), pp. 43–4.

25. Paul Gilroy, *The Black Atlantic: Modernity and Double Consciousness* (London: Verso, 1993). Mrinalini Sinha, *Colonial Masculinity: the 'Manly Englishman' and the 'Effeminate Bengali' in the Late Nineteenth Century* (Manchester: Manchester University Press, 1995).

26. *Toronto Star*, 16 August 2002.

27. By 1976, Sidney Bidwell estimated that 30,000 of Southall's 52,000 inhabitants were South Asians and most of these were Punjabis. Sidney Bidwell, *Red, White & Black: Race Relations in Britain* (London: Gordon and Cremonesi, 1976), p. 5.

28. These structures are explored in Gerd Baumann, 'Managing in a Polyethnic Milieu: Kinship and Interaction in a London Suburb', *Journal of the Royal Anthropological Institute* 1, 4 (1995), pp. 725–41.

29. Parminder Bhachu, 'Ethnicity Constructed and Reconstructed: the Role of Sikh Women in Cultural Elaboration and Educational Decision-Making in Britain', *Gender & Education* 3, 1 (1991).

30. Harwant S. Bains, 'Southall Youth: An Old-Fashioned Story', Philip Cohen and Harwant S. Bains (eds), *Multi-Racist Britain* (Basingstoke: Macmillan, 1988), p. 235.

31. Kathleen Hall has offered a rich ethnographic study of these processes in Kathleen Hall, *Lives in Translation: Sikh Youth as British Citizens* (Philadelphia: University of Pennsylvania, 2002).

32. Cited in Sanjay Sharma, 'Noisy Asians or Asian Noise', Sanjay Sharma, John Hutnyk, and Ashwani Sharma (eds), *Dis-Orienting Rhythms*, p. 32.

33. Andrew Bennett, 'Bhangra in Newcastle', *Innovation* 10, 1 (1997), p. 111.

34. See Apache Indian's comments on the conflict in his family over reggae: George Lipsitz, *Dangerous Crossroads*, p. 130.

35. Kathleen Hall, *Lives in Translation*, p. 141.

36. Gerd Baumann, 'The Re-Iinvention of Bhangra: Social Change and Aesthetic Shifts in a Punjabi Music in Britain', *World of Music* 32 (1990), p. 90.

37. Virinder S. Kalra, '*Vilayeti* Rhythms: Beyond Bhangra's Emblematic Status to a Translation of Lyrical Texts', *Theory, Culture & Society* 17, 3 (2000), p. 85.

38. Kalapreet, *Us Pradesh Kee Vasna Yaarab* (Arishma Records, 1988).

39. This reworked Shaukat Ali's earlier 1974 version of the song 'Main Vilayet Kaanon Aiyaa?', Memories of Punjab.

40. Steven Kapur's stage name is a homage to the Jamaican ragamuffin star Super Cat, who is sometimes known as the 'Wild Apache'.

41. Apache Indian, 'Arranged Marriage', *No Reservations* (1991).

42. http://www.nationrecs.demon.co.uk/artistshtm/husler.htm Their publicity shots disseminated an explicitly Sikh image of the group—typical images pictured stern kes-dhari Sikhs—but their record label, Nation Records, heralded

the Hustlers HC as: 'the first Sikh rap crew to come out of the UK with a strong socio-political message. They did much to bridge religious divides in the Asian community as well as creating much respect for Sikhs in the Rap fraternity.'

43. Hustlers HC, 'Big Trouble in Little Asia' (Nation Records, 1994).

44. George Lipsitz, *Dangerous Crossroads*, p. 3.

45. See Peter Manuel, *Cassette Culture: Popular Music and Technology in North India* (Chicago: University of Chicago Press, 1993).

46. See Gibb Stuart Schreffler, 'Out of the Dhol Drums: the Rhythmic "System" of Punjabi Bhangra' (Santa Barbara: University of California, MA thesis, 2002), p. 10.

47. Paul Gilroy, *The Black Atlantic*, p. 194.

48. *The Tribune*, 13 September 1998.

49. Iqbal Singh Dhillon, *Folk Songs of Panjab*, p. 152.

50. *The Tribune*, 26 May 2000.

51. Ibid.

52. Ibid.

53. Ibid.

54. Iqbal Singh Dhillon, *Folk Songs of Panjab*, p. 152.

55. Kathleen Hall, *Lives in Translation*, p. 141.

56. http://www.sikhi.demon.co.uk/bhangra.htm

57. *The Tribune*, 13 September 1998.

58. Jacqueline C. Warwick, 'Can Anyone Dance to this Music?: Bhangra and South Asian Youth' (York University, Canada, MA thesis, 2001).

59. Eleanor Nesbitt, 'Sikhs and Proper Sikhs: Young British Sikhs' Perceptions of Their Identity', Pashaura Singh and N. G. Barrier (eds), *Sikh Identity: Continuity and Change*, pp. 315–33. Also see Eleanor Nesbitt, 'The Presentation of Sikhs in Recent Children's Literature in Britain', J. T. O'Connell, M. Israel, and W. Oxtoby (eds), *Sikh History and Religion in the 20th Century*, (Toronto: University of Toronto Press, 1988), pp. 376–87.

Tradition and History: Modern Communication and 'Sikh-Diaspora'

N. G. Barrier

Conflicting views of Sikh tradition and scholarship play an important role in the effort by Sikhs to grapple with immediate problems within the diaspora. The mixture of religion and politics prevalent in Punjab intellectual circles fosters particular claims of 'correct' interpretation and legitimacy, often for tactical or strategic purposes. Within the Sikh diaspora, however, the debate tends to be more complex and nuanced, reflecting the different cultural setting and the immediate conflicts that affect individuals and organizations. This chapter will survey how and why Sikhs are currently re-examining their past, and the role of scholars in that process, with particular attention to the implications of a rapidly expanding communication network that provides the basis for dialogue and a new understanding. As in the case of other religions, the internet, websites, and list servers are easily accessible vehicles for communicating ideas and attempts to reach consensus. In particular, the 'Sikh-Diaspora' online discussion group will be used as a source for examining how Sikhs debate issues and use sources, the historical record, and scholarly works. The concluding section of the chapter will suggest implications for Sikh public life and the ongoing interaction of Sikhs with Western-trained scholars.

Politics, Religion, and the Print Culture

Use of history, religious injunctions, and tradition is a prominent pattern in the public life of Punjabi Sikhs. Competing factions have their own self-proclaimed intellectual circles and organizations which meet regularly and issue resolutions filled with references to *maryada*, religious texts, and historical events. The Shiromani Gurdwara Parbandak Committee (SGPC) tends to rely on similar material to justify its edicts and decision-making process, as do the *jathedars* of the Akal Takht and the other takhts. Although primarily political in nature, the constant reference to historical precedents and real or imagined traditions is seen as vital to sustaining legitimacy for specific groups and organizations and to enhancing the authority of leaders within the Panth.[1]

The intensity and timing of concerted efforts to dominate the print culture of the Punjab with specific messages and interpretations depends frequently on political circumstance. A long-term crisis occasioned by events such as those in 1984 can affect discourses and conflicting views of the past for years if not decades. For example, the prevailing concern over 'Sikhism in danger' in the 1980s fostered intellectual witch hunts, selective use of earlier institutions such as the *Sarbat Khalsa* to seize and maintain power, and, in general, defensiveness toward dissenting views. The protracted campaigns, for example, against W. H. McLeod, Pashaura Singh, and Piar Singh are well known, but these are only part of a broader attempt by groups to capture and use public arenas for their own purposes. Similarly, the SGPC or provincial elections invariably evoke discussion of key issues of identity and tradition, such as the conflicts over *sahajdhari* voters, the role of the Akal Takht, revision of the 1925 Gurdwaras Act, and so forth.

The social, political, and organizational links between the Punjab and Sikhs within the diaspora has meant that Sikhs outside the region have been directly affected by events in the homeland. Much of the Khalistan campaign, for example, was rooted in diaspora politics, where once again claims about religious tradition and 'correctness' became part of the struggle for legitimacy and power. This also sustained the persistent and often shrill attacks on Western scholars and their associates. The twists and turns of political manoeuvring either within the SGPC or among central religious leaders such as the jathedars of the takhts have had a similar effect.[2]

More often, however, the particular features of the cultural and political systems within which diaspora Sikhs operate helped shape their discourse and priorities. The multicultural or 'religious liberty' policies in England, Canada, the United States, and Singapore, for example, have influenced the variation and timing of Sikh strategies and public activity. Moreover, local factions, institutions, and immediate issues either have influenced the differing interpretations of the nature of Sikhism or raised the questions of identity and tradition from local to national even or international prominence. Court cases over kirpans, turbans, gurdwara governance, and related matters almost invariably lead to claims about legitimacy based on perceived past practices, specific documents on rahit or conduct, history, and interpretation of the Guru Granth Sahib.[3]

The crises among diaspora groups and the resulting rhetoric and political struggles provide a fertile opportunity for Sikhs to re-examine their roots as well as offering opportunity for understanding the complexities of contemporary Sikh life. The initial US Sikh conference in 1978 and the four conferences at Michigan have attempted to provide scholarly insight into the process as well as generating case studies and comparative discussion. At the same time, individual scholars such as W. H. McLeod, Pashaura Singh, Paul Wallace, Harbans Lal, Arvind Mandair, and myself have been involved in legal issues surrounding controversies involving gurdwara disputes, the role of the SGPC and the Akal Takht outside of the Punjab, and, more consistently, disputes over the five Ks required for Khalsa Sikhs. One also finds these issues covered extensively on various websites and especially in *The Sikh Review* (Calcutta).

Some of the most fruitful research in Sikh studies has come from individual scholars concerned with different aspects of how diaspora Sikhs view themselves and their past. Venue Dusenbery's large corpus of writing, which spans discussion of ethnic and religious issues, is especially important in this regard. His early work was on Sikhs in Vancouver and the United States as well as the 3HO movement, before making a significant contribution to our understanding of the nature of the diaspora, and most recently he has documented the experiences of Sikhs in Singapore and Australia.[4] Brian Axel's research continues to shed light on images, history, and reconstruction of identity in response to crises and ongoing cultural challenges. Complementing his rich ethnographic and theoretical work on Maharaja Dhuleep Singh and Sikhs in the United Kingdom have been several case studies in Michigan conference proceedings and, most recently, the work of Tony Ballantyne in a monograph and various articles.[5] I also have focused on how Sikhs re-examine their past and reformulate history and tradition, beginning with some of the most creative publicists and intellectuals in the Singh Sabha/Chief Khalsa Diwan period, but also in a process that stretches well beyond the Punjab and that period. Louis Fenech's important examination of changing Sikh views on martyrdom have led to the study of other controversial areas such as conversion and the iconography of Uddam Singh. In his fundamental work on the Singh Sabhas, Harjot Oberoi raises key issues relevant to Sikhs in the modern world, and subsequently has explored the relevance of images and mass mobilization in terms of his personal experiences during the Delhi riots and the assault on him and the Sikh Studies chair at Vancouver. His student, Doris Jakobsh, has addressed women in recent Sikh history, linking the Singh Sabha attempts to reconcile traditional and Western approaches with the continuing dialogue on the topic within the diaspora and at the Golden Temple. Karen Leonard also has written major books and articles on Sikh identity and family in California, along with ongoing study of cultural trends and institutional changes. Bruce La Brack continues to contribute on Sikhs in California as well as on theoretical concerns. From another perspective, there is a close tie between how Sikhs and intellectuals in eastern India viewed both tradition and contemporary events and how similar processes unfolded in a non-Indian diaspora, a theme developed fruitfully by Himadri Banerjee for over a decade.[6]

Sikhs themselves grapple with the contemporary implications of identity, tradition, and cultural setting. Several notable examples jump to mind. First, Pashaura Singh has brought to his research and writing an intimate knowledge of Sikh scripture and tradition that gives his work a strong sense of authenticity and authority. His revised dissertation on the Guru Granth Sahib both explores critical issues of text and meaning as well as proceeding to showing the ongoing place of the scripture and its message among Sikhs today. His articles on rahit, custom, and contemporary Sikhism continue to provide scholarly insider perspectives. Similarly, Gurinder Singh Mann has produced two monographs that deal with textual matters and their relevance for contemporary Sikh discourse. In addition, he has facilitated dialogue through conferences and annual programmes in the Punjab. Darshan Singh Tatla has written a major history of the Sikh diaspora in North America and the United Kingdom as well as the basic reference guide to historical sources and literature. In his work, emphasis is placed upon the interaction of politics and religion, along with the role of communications in the lives of individuals and Panthic institutions. Shinder Singh Thandi has focused on diaspora politics and is working on a new book that will survey the Sikh experience in North America and the United Kingdom. Representing a new generation of scholars, Arvind Mandair, the holder of the Sikh Studies chair at University of Michigan, has studied the interaction between Sikh traditions and Western scholars. His dissertation on the Singh Sabha movement and the intellectual challenges that fashioned its programme and rhetoric is currently being revised. Another scholar trained in the United Kingdom, Jeevan Singh Deol has explored similar concerns. Representing an informed layman's perspective, I. J. Singh has been especially effective in providing an insider's response to a wide range of topics affecting the Sikh community. His three books, with more on the way, explore how Sikhs view themselves, their institutions, and their traditions.[7] And from yet another viewpoint, Puneet Singh Lamba has founded 'The Sikh Times' (www.sikhtimes.com), an invaluable source for provocative essays and news concerning Sikhism, the Punjab, and the diaspora.

The work of both Sikh and Western specialists emphasize the centrality of an emerging print culture in shaping discourse and focusing Panthic attention. Since the days of the Singh Sabhas, control of public institutions, public space, and especially the ability to influence the public through tracts, books, and newspapers has been a constant element in the ongoing revival and reformulation of Sikh history and tradition. This became quite explicit in the turbulent period of the 1980s, when supporters of militancy and Khalistan within the diaspora developed an effective communication network and tried, with some success, to control key Sikh institutions in the West. Activists used *The World Sikh News* and an expanding network of Punjabi journals to frame debates, attack opponents, and in general legitimize their religious and political perspective. The resulting campaigns in specific gurdwaras and a general mobilization of Sikhs against Western scholars is well known, as are innovations such as creating new intellectual groups to counter research judged anti-Sikh and the establishment of quasi-scholarly conferences that moved from place to place garnering support.[8]

While political rhetoric and agendas continue to be important in contemporary Sikh discourse, the medium has changed dramatically in the last decade. Information now is available almost instantaneously through internet editions of newspapers, most notably the Chandigarh *Tribune*. Articles and themes in the press then are duplicated throughout an expanding network of sites and sources. Several websites selectively choose material and add their own essays, such as 'Khalistannet'. Others such as 'The Sikh Times' and 'Sikh Sentinel' carry a wide range of stories from Indian and Western newspapers. One of the most systematic approaches to distributing news is the work of a librarian and prominent member of the Maritime Sikh Society based in Halifax, Canada: Jagpal

Singh Tiwana. Jagpal selects stories from North American and Indian papers and then posts them widely.

Circulation of news reports is only a small part of the rapidly expanding network of websites (over two thousand) and organizations who actively distribute material on current affairs, Sikhism, tradition, and a myriad related topics. Many Sikh list servers or cyber discussion groups create 'virtual communities' with participants who use the internet to explore culture and exchange ideas.[9] A recent count indicates that there are over three hundred Sikh discussion groups listed on Yahoo Groups. Among the most prominent are 'Sikh Net', 'Sikhe.com', 'Sikh Agenda', and 'Sikh Diaspora'. 'Learning Zone' has now emerged as the largest and often most contentious of the new sites, with an average 40 exchanges daily. In addition, participants often develop their own websites and put together elaborate essays and cross-references. One of the first and most distinguished of the sites is Sikh.org, a very professional source of information created by Sandeep Brar in 1994 and continually updated with useful and timely articles. Two other especially notable examples are surbut-khalsa.com (produced by Harjinder Singh, who includes a regular column 'The Man in Blue') and Devinder Singh Chahal's 'Understanding Sikhism' (chahal.info).

The quality of discussion and information varies with each site or group, often reflecting immediate crises or a specific news story. For example, by far the most traumatic experience confronting Sikhs in North America in recent times has been the effects of the attack on the World Trade Center. That generated new self-defence and political organizations, such as The Sikh Coalition and SMART (sikhmediawatch.org), and also led to an intense discussion on how Sikhs are perceived and should relate to different cultures.

The resulting dialogue through internet exchanges provides important documents on how Sikhs dealt with both attacks and misconceptions. More importantly for this chapter, these kinds of crisis evoke serious debate over identity and tradition. An obvious issue is the connection of Sikhism with Islam, which led to a detailed set of interchanges on Sikh history and the roots of the religion. Another involved images (what to project) which moved quickly to a discussion of kirpans and turbans, and amritdhari–kes-dhari–sahajdhari relations. Historical documents and scripture became sources of dispute, as well as criticism of individuals such as Yogi Harbhajan Singh and Khushwant Singh, who wrote articles or gave interviews on the Sikhs.[10]

Immediate responses to threats to the community and debates over identity underscore the importance of sustained exchanges among Sikhs and their associates in the new cyber environment. Obviously the frequent anonymity of participants and the self-selecting nature of each group make difficult generalizations about what Sikhs think and how they view themselves and the world around them. On the other hand, with appropriate care, students of contemporary Sikhism can find the sites, groups, and intellectual exchange most useful in understanding issues and challenging assumptions about Sikh attitudes. This is explored in Doris Jakobsh's article 'Constructing Sikh Identities: Authorities, Virtual and Imagined'.[11]

One approach to utilizing the internet sources to understand diasporic concerns might involve doing searches of specific terms or issues, such as the 'Akal Takht' or 'Sikh women', and then reviewing the literature. Alternatively, a specialist concerned with how Sikhs view tradition, identity, and the role of scholarship can track interchanges within one source. That permits following particular threads of thought and exploring patterns of commonality and disagreement.

The following section adopts that methodology, using the exchanges within a relatively small discussion group, 'Sikh-Diaspora', to evaluate general issues, perceptions, and controversy. As will be noted, 'Sikh-Diaspora' has its own history, parameters, and, to some degree, a self-selected group of participants who are very serious about what is happening to them and to their religion. 'Sikh-Diaspora' in no sense can be taken as reflecting general Sikh opinion; rather, it is an instance of how one set of individuals share their appreciable knowledge and concerns over time. The questions they raise and the way they organize material and relate to each other, however, suggest patterns and potential areas of knowledge that can be explored in the future.

Sikh-Diaspora: Approaches to Authority, Rahit, and Divergent Claims

Three Sikhs, formerly from Nairobi Kenya, formed the 'Sikh-Diaspora' online discussion group in February 2001. Two founders now form the management team: Tejpal Singh Thind in Montreal and Karamjit Singh Bharij in Northampton, in the United Kingdom. Bhupinder Singh Mahal left the group in early 2002 over editorial and related matters. The editors play a prominent role in the discussion and influence the tone and direction of the interchanges. In general, however, the messages tend to be freewheeling and reflect the individual concerns and ideological bent of participants. The membership has grown to approximately 850, with around 75 regular participants, and others who join in with questions or comments sporadically. When compared to other major discussion groups, 'Sikh-Diaspora' is very active.[12] Although detailed biographical information is not available, the experiences and informed opinions reflected in the discourse suggest that many are professionals with extensive contacts in the Punjab and their new cultural setting. Numerous members are in Canada, the United States and the United Kingdom, but Sikhs in South America, Africa, Europe, India, and East Asia often participate. Also associated with 'Sikh-Diaspora' are several Western scholars such as Doris Jakobsh, Owen Cole, Joy Barrow, and N. G. Barrier as well as at least one notable Sikh academic, Pashaura Singh at the University of California, Riverside.

'Sikh-Diaspora's policy and mission have gone through several revisions, but from the outset, the founders wanted to create a channel for open exchange of ideas in an environment fostering a sense of equality and mutual respect. The management tries to minimize personality and ideological clashes and especially prevents use of the forum to propagate ideologies and missions of cults, organizations, and 'clandestine' groups which 'seek to subvert the Sikh faith'. Within those parameters, there is considerable give and take, but the general tone is serious and, despite some attacks and sharp words occasionally, the exchanges tend to be high-minded and thoughtful. In rare instances, individuals attacking others or refusing to operate within the general guidelines have been 'unsubscribed'. The primary mission is 'to serve as a forum for the Sikh diaspora to preserve, enhance and share their cultural heritage and to encourage interaction with fellow Sikhs to advance and promote opinions and views on matters vital to Sikhs and Sikhism'. (Appendix A at the end of this chapter).

Participants in 'Sikh-Diaspora' cover virtually every topic relevant to contemporary Sikhism. Several specific issues will be discussed in the next section, but underlying the dialogue is a shared concern with the scriptural and historical roots of Sikhism. Discussion of the nature and content of the Guru Granth Sahib is central, as are debates over appropriate conduct and ritual as mirrored in the various rahit-namas and the most recent code, the Sikh Rahit Maryada, issued under the auspices of the SGPC and the Akal Takht. As in the case of any religion, there is attention not only to sources but also who can interpret those sources and tradition in general.

'Sikh-Diaspora' participants exchange ideas on authority, the role of the SGPC, the Akal Takht, and other prominent religious centres, as well as on divergent interpretations from groups and organizations such as the Akhand Kirtani Jatha. The discussions register a balance between respect for scripture and related traditions and their application and adjustment in a diaspora setting.

Like all Sikhs, participants in 'Sikh-Diaspora' view the Guru Granth Sahib as the inspiration and major source for their religious beliefs. Disagreement over continuity of thought among the first nine gurus tends to be minimal, although exchanges over the meaning of specific passages occur occasionally. One of the most recent interchanges has been on whether the gurus performed miracles. Some argue that the scriptures support such incidents, while others interpreted the texts as metaphors or allegory. All seem to agree that the essence of Sikhism involved personal growth and spiritual matters, and that whatever the arguments concerning specifics in the gurus' lives, their message was consistent and valid for all times. Similarly, one thread involved the divine nature of the gurus. Much of that discussion incorporated comparisons with other world religions.[13]

The major disagreements grow out of concern with Sikh identity and, within that context, the particular significance of the life and works of Guru Gobind Singh and the creation of the Khalsa. Sikhs in 'Sikh-Diaspora' struggle frequently over 'who is a Sikh' and the necessity of receiving amrit and adopting a defined lifestyle with the five Ks. This is not surprising, since such discussions can be found in the press, public arenas such as conferences and gurdwaras, and in many other internet sources. Unlike some of the rhetoric found elsewhere, however, 'Sikh-Diaspora' approaches these contentious topics with sophistication and an attention to the sources. Hearsay and generalized references to 'tradition' in support of a position are usually challenged quickly. Still, the threads sometimes evoke heated and personal references, at which point the moderators intervene by refocusing the topic or ending the discussion.

Participants in the group have attempted on several occasions to hammer out a consensus in defining Sikh identity. The spur for such efforts typically comes from incidents such as gurdwara politics, an honour awarded to a Sikh (especially if the Sikh was clean-shaven), or representation of authentic Sikh tradition in public meetings and court cases. Most 'Sikh-Diaspora' members agree on the importance of initiation and the creation of the Khalsa, but as almost invariably happens in such dialogue, the faultline between two sections of 'Sikh-Diaspora' involves whether the spiritual and religious teachings in the scriptures are sufficient or should be complemented by the discipline associated with Guru Gobind Singh.[14] Those most prominent in the dialogue tend to share the conviction that kes-dhari–amritdhari Sikhs cannot claim to be 'orthodox' or 'mainstream' and should not dominate public arenas and discourse. Non kes-dharis are seen as important in the presentation and daily affairs of Sikhism in a global context. Other groups and institutions, such as the Sikh Agenda group and the Institute of Sikh Studies in Chandigarh, hold quite different views.

Alternative approaches to historical events appear often in the spirited debates. 'Sikh-Diaspora' participants do not automatically accept the traditional views surrounding the events of 1699, using a wide range of documents and historical treatises to frame their arguments. Attempts to understand Guru Gobind Singh's message and mission have also led to revisiting a controversial aspect of Sikh tradition, the nature of the Dasam Granth. Most of the discussants believe that the Guru produced sections of the Dasam Granth, and that other parts were added later and did not reflect his views. A few felt that Hindu politicians are trying to manipulate the issue to divide Sikhs and underscore their commonality with Hinduism, while others argue that the Dasam Granth has to be understood within a cultural and historical milieu.[15]

As with many divisive issues on 'Sikh-Diaspora', the group struggled with the question of who could decide issues such as sahajdharis–kes-dhari–amritdhari relations, the importance of the Dasam Granth, and how cultural boundaries should be dealt with. Whether or not amritdhari Sikhs should provide the major leadership in Panthic organizations remains a theme that has been revisited over the last three years. Divisions remain, but the discussions gradually wear down or shift to other related topics. On these and other matters, Sikhs frequently refer to local practices and experience, balancing those with perceptions of tradition. Often in the face of sharply divergent views, attempts are made to evoke documents and institutions that may help resolve the disputes.

One important thread of argument revolves around the rahit-namas, the Sikh Rahit Maryada, and the legal definitions of 'who is a Sikh?'. Several members are quite conversant with the evolving rahit-namas' literature and use both documents and also critical studies such as those of W. H. McLeod to buttress arguments. Not surprisingly, some adopt the position that the rahit as portrayed by the Singh Sabha movement and later forming the basis of the 'official' Sikh Rahit Maryada promulgated by the SGPC in

1945 should be the normative standard for judging Sikh belief and daily life. Others question whether the document reflected a consensus of opinion when it first emerged in the 1930s. They argue that any single set of rules and boundaries now more than half a century old should be re-evaluated and adjusted to meet the new challenges and situations within the diaspora. A counter-argument and a criticism of some recent discussions on 'Sikh-Diaspora' by Bhupinder Singh Mahal are reviewed in the concluding remarks to this chapter.[16]

Prominent in the interactions have been two historical definitions of 'who is a Sikh', those in the 1925 Gurdwaras Act and the Sikh Rahit Maryada. The former has the simple injunction that 'A Sikh means a person who professes the Sikh religion'. If in doubt or for any other reason, they should affirm 'that I am a Sikh, that I believe in the Guru Granth Sahib, that I believe in ten Gurus, and that I have no other religion'. Opposing this rather general definition are those who argue that the Maryada definition should pertain: 'A Sikh is any person who believes (*nisacha rakhada*) in Akal Purakh; in the ten Gurus; in Sri Guru Granth Sahib, other works of the ten Gurus, and their teachings; in the Khalsa initiation ceremony instituted by the tenth Guru; and who does not believe in any other system of religious doctrine.'[17] Neither definition resolves the fundamental differences among 'Sikh-Diaspora' correspondents, but most tend to tolerate divergent opinions and share a concern that institutionalizing potential differences among Sikhs is divisive and could weaken the Panth. Boundaries and designation of 'orthodox' Sikhs as opposed to those who do not wear turbans or maintain hair are seen as creating political problems and limiting the size and effectiveness of the community in a diaspora setting. Also reflected in the discussion is the argument that within the diaspora, many clean-shaven Sikhs have and are providing leadership and resources. 'Sikh-Diaspora' discussants tend to try and balance strongly held views with the practical implications of living in a non-Punjab world.

Who should decide matters? Again, there has been no clear resolution of which institutions or organizations are seen as authoritative judges of tradition and controversial matters. One of the interesting features of the site is the marked degree to which current news and interpretations of events in Amritsar and the Punjab help frame issues and debate. All participants are familiar with the politics of the SGPC, the scandals associated with various jathedars and other leaders, and the relationship between some decisions made by the 'clergy' (the jathedars of the takhts and especially the Akal Takht) and turmoil within diaspora settings. The SGPC receives respect for its historic role in mobilizing Sikhs and protecting shrines, but very few 'Sikh-Diaspora' discussants envision it as a legitimate arbiter of issues. Adding to the confusion has been the persistence of self-proclaimed 'intellectual groups' and the calling of 'World Sikh Conferences' which challenge the legitimacy of the SGPC and criticize edicts from the Akal Takht.[18]

Although most Sikhs in the group honour the historic role of the Akal Takht and in general the 'clergy' (however defined), they tend to weigh its traditional authority against their own experiences and perceptions of recent developments surrounding the various jathedars. Some prefer that the Akal Takht make decisions affecting Sikh public life, either in isolation or more frequently, as the result of a transparent and careful deliberation. Others argue that in light of the current legal status of the jathedars, primarily serving at the will of the SGPC, which has legal authority over most Sikh shrines, decisions are too politicized and do not take into account the values and attitudes of Sikhs outside the Punjab. There seems to be general agreement that reform of the institution is necessary, with the jathedars being chosen on the basis of agreed high standards and then given the authority (in collaboration with other religious leaders and perhaps special committees) to make decisions on large issues. The incidents involving the use of chairs in Vancouver gurdwaras and the frustrated attempt of the jathedar to decide internal matters in the Fairfax, Virginia gurdwara are well known. The consensus seems to be that the many problems and issues growing out of local concerns within the diaspora cannot and should not be resolved through hukam-namas or edicts from Amritsar.[19]

The numerous threads on history, authority, and sources suggest several underlying dynamics. First, while individuals drop in and out of the discussions, less than a hundred engage on a consistent basis. Over the years, they have developed working relationships and often appreciate the perspectives of others. Second, some participants have associations with organizations and particular movements that help frame responses to issues. One of the most notable involves recently converted Sikhs, generally associated with the 3HO movement. These question the link between Sikh religion and Punjabi culture, question specific practices that seem to be entrenched in ethnic custom rather than the teachings of the gurus. Also, individuals either associated with or providing leadership for particular institutes or intellectual groups in the Punjab, such as

H. S. Dilgeer, express alternative opinions and add to diversity within the group. Sikhs associated with the Akhand Kirtani Jatha (with historical roots in the Bhasaur Tat Khalsa group and Bhai Randhir Singh) similarly present different approaches to women, Rahit Maryada, and doctrinal issues.[20] Third, younger Sikhs, either professionals or students, ask questions and then respond within the resulting thread. One gets the sense of an expanding universe of 'Sikh-Diaspora' membership with at least some diversity and varying perspectives. Sikh and Western scholars also share their expertise, but most prefer to engage only when requested or in light of their personal areas of research. As will be noted, the role of academics and Western observers within 'Sikh-Diaspora' and in general as interpreters of aspects of Sikh history and tradition constitutes a perennial thread of debate.

'Sikh-Diaspora' participants clearly are engaged in the difficult process of examining their historical and religious roots in light of Western education and cultural values. Alternative paradigms and experiences help shape their responses to questions of tradition, authority, and the relationship between religion and politics. They struggle with the tension between their rich spiritual heritage and other ways of explaining their tradition and self-understanding. In reflections on matters such as *piri/miri* (the relationship of politics and religion), Punjab politics, and the role of the SGPC, sensitivity to diversity and the separation of church and state within a Western context underpin arguments and certainly the tone of debate. A useful example of such questioning is found in Appendix C. There seems to be at least tolerance of divergent opinions on Sikh identity although some underlying issues are so divisive that sometimes individuals withdraw from the group. When the discussion moves from sources and views of religious belief to actual practice and very troublesome contemporary issues, however, the intensity and often the discord increase noticeably. Caste, the role of women, recent historical events and personalities, and specific symbols such as hair, the turban, and the kirpan lead the 'Sikh-Diaspora' group invariably into sharp divisions over matters that directly affect their daily lives.

Some Areas of Contention: Events, History, Caste, Women, and the Five Ks

The 'Sikh-Diaspora' discussion of controversial issues generally emerges in response to a specific incident, a news story, or a more general topic that evolves into a separate thread. The differing perspectives reflect the personal experiences of individuals and their cultural setting as well as the more universal theme of relating perceptions of the past to contemporary problems. Virtually every social and historical issue is reviewed, some periodically or on a regular basis. Although sometimes the arguments broaden and encompass or generate a spectrum of different threads, the moderators attempt to keep the focus on the theme and to work towards if not resolution, at least a common understanding of differences before interchanges are concluded. Sometimes the exchanges become so heated that a thread is summarily ended.

History and the role of particular individuals in the public life of the Panth are prominent concerns. The most traumatic of recent events, such as Operation Blue Star and the attacks on Sikhs after the assassination of Indira Gandhi, frequently form the backdrop for subtexts. Interpretations of who did what and the consequences are divisive, as is the debate over the role of Bhindranwale, the militants, and Sikh institutions such as the SGPC and the Akal Takht during and after the trauma of 1984. Personal recollections are often tangled with the issue of Hindu–Sikh relations, just as the temporary identification of Sikhs with Muslims or turbaned terrorists after 9/11 led to a re-examination of the influence of Islam and Sufi saints within early Sikhism. The US attacks on Afghanistan in turn fostered a brief discussion of the history of the Sikhs in the period of the last gurus, and subsequent campaigns by the various Sikh units and Ranjit Singh along the border and into Afghanistan. For example, wars between Sikhs and Afghans were discussed briefly in October and November 2001. The general conclusion, with some dissent, was that the events reflected border politics and not ethnic conflict. Often a discussion will begin with general comments, then evolve into questions about historical accuracy, and finally attempts by several informed individuals to weigh interpretations against a documentary backdrop.

Two of the most persistent threads involve the British period. First, members of 'Sikh-Diaspora' are familiar with the outlines of the Singh Sabha movement and, when examining a specific ideological or identity issue, bring in the perspective of how Sikhs first tried to address problems and then create solutions or institutions that would strengthen the Panth. Some see the Singh Sabhas as a positive element in the evolution of modern Sikhism, while other contend that especially the Tat Khalsa insistence on boundaries and emphasizing particular aspects of tradition has left a legacy of division and notable matters unresolved.

Attention to the 1925 Gurdwara Act, the need for reform of the SGPC, and the place of the Sikh Rahit Maryada consequently reflect interest in and ambivalence toward the Singh Sabhas and the Chief Khalsa Diwan programmes.[21]

The second concern is the Sikh role within colonial Punjab. Duplicating to some extent the divisions in how Sikh historians view the 1857 Mutiny and other turning points in Sikh–British relations, discussion reflects pride in Sikh bravery but also explores the wider implications of support for the Raj. Two defining events generate sharp debate, the heroism of Sikhs at Saragarhi and the role of Sikhs in the two world wars. In September 2003, a newspaper report on the Saragarhi Memorial Gurdwara in Ferozepur, which commemorated the heroism of 21 Sikh soldiers in Waziristan on 12 September 1897, sparked a discussion of whether the soldiers should be honoured or considered collaborators. One commentator summarized the argument succinctly: the Sikhs allied with the British against a return of Muslim rule and went on to become the backbone of the Imperial army. Should they have surrendered on the Frontier against hordes of Aghans? The answer is 'that they did the right thing to fight to the death. They should be honored... They fought as soldiers should. They took an oath when they were recruited that they will fight even if they have to die. They fulfilled their oath. Sikhs should be proud of this fact'.[22] The issue then expanded to an evaluation of 'imperialist' versus 'nationalist' views of the Sikhs. Over a dozen messages went back and forth on statistics for Sikh martyrs in India's freedom struggle. Sikh heroism in the current struggles in Kashmir is also discussed, often in conjunction with news of a particularly brave action by a Sikh soldier or regiment or in response to news about massacres of Sikh civilians.[23]

The attempt to create a 'Sikh hall of fame' has raised questions about the criteria for selection and also the perennial issue of 'who is a Sikh?'. Some question the inclusion of Sikhs (such as the first Sikh Congressman Dalip Saund) who are clean-shaven, while others champion individuals on all sides of the political spectrum in the Punjab. Khushwant Singh has become probably the most controversial candidate, with references to his ideas, image, and literary contributions appearing quite frequently. His two-volume *History of the Sikhs* (published initially by Princeton University Press in 1963) is both a reference for historical facts and interpretations and also a frequent target for 'Sikh-Diaspora' participants who dislike his persona and major role in interpreting Sikhism in the West and in India. Some foreign scholars, such as Max Arthur Macauliffe, also are quoted and recommended for recognition, although widening such discussions to include Western specialists raises additional controversy over the supporters and detractors of W. H. McLeod and others.[24]

Lack of consensus on Sikh identity also affects evaluation of distinct Sikh rituals, education, and Sikh festivals. Virtually everyone agrees on the centrality of a Sikh marriage ceremony (Anand), but the degree to which elements of Punjabi culture, heavy expense, and dowry affect arrangements remains controversial. 'Sikh-Diaspora' discourse also incorporates debates from India over matters such as edicts from the Akal Takht on marriage halls. The ongoing effort of diaspora Sikhs to accommodate Western and Sikh/Punjabi approaches to marriage appears occasionally in the group, as do frank discussions of open caskets and other changes in rites of passage. In a related area, most participants want to combine some formal education in Sikh tradition and Punjabi with the 'progressive' Western education necessary for the high professional standards of the community. Details about curriculum and means of instruction, however, evoke a range of opinions. The ongoing discussion of a distinctly Sikh calendar (Nanakshahi) is debated, especially in conjunction with the degree to which Sikhism shares common dates and festivals with Hinduism. Recently, there has been much interaction over whether Sikhs should celebrate Diwali and, if so, how the festival should be viewed in terms of Sikh rather than Hindu tradition.[25]

Over the last century, Sikhs both within and beyond Punjab have debated the significance of the kirpan and maintenance of long hair. Parallel threads have focused on the turban as a religious symbol. The Sikh struggle to legitimize acceptance of the five Ks in public arenas has produced many landmark court cases as well as stirring debate within the community itself. Within each country of residence, Sikhs have had to adapt to local custom and attempt to win recognition of their religious and cultural rights. The struggle is perennial, coming to a head sometimes with sudden crises such as 9/11 or the decisions of a local police force (most recently, the New York Police Department) or a country (the recent French decision to ban turbans and headscarves). Discussion in 'Sikh-Diaspora' circles goes on and on, sometimes repeating older claims and then adding new elements that involve scientific evidence or new court challenges. Members have struggled with the wisdom of wearing swords on planes and the size of kirpans. Balancing respect for the kirpans as a religious symbol with their occasional use as a weapon in gurdwara disputes raises the familiar theme of norms versus practice.[26]

Also running throughout the discussions is concern with maintaining hair and the related issues of turban, apostasy, and the concept of patit ('fallen', usually a technical term for an initiated Sikh who commits a *kurahit* ['serious sin'] but also used loosely to refer to kes-dharis who cut their hair). Threads go in many directions, again reflecting the diversity and legal–cultural setting experienced by individuals. Most recently, the decision of the SGPC to limit the role of 'patits' in religious ceremonies and musical events have stirred up a sharp exchange. Adding to the fervor have been reports of Sikhs removing 'patits' from family networks, which in turn has led to the discussion of the nature and legitimacy of the Sikh Rahit Maryada.[27]

Attention to daily conduct and limits on specific activities also has evoked disagreement over whether Sikhs should eat meat and, if so, whether that means only *jhatka* (an animal killed with one blow, an injunction drawn from the rahit-namas). Since many in the 'Sikh-Diaspora' group are physicians or scientists, arguments include references to research as well as evidence from the Guru Granth Sahib and subsequent treatises on Sikh conduct.[28]

Discussion of initiation, hair, and the turban are also found in the recurring debate over women, family, and the role of caste in contemporary Sikh/Punjabi society. Members are well acquainted with the potential conflict between the gurus' normative injunctions about social and gender equality and the realities of practice in Punjab and the diaspora. The rights and equality of women keep reappearing. Sometimes women involved in the 3HO movement or the Akhand Kirtani Jatha challenge segregation of females in worship services or, more frequently, in key rituals and gurdwara governance. Examples of women involved in *sewa* or service are used to counter generalizations about male dominance, although the patterns of patriarchy in Punjabi society obviously influence Sikh social practices. The issue sometimes is highlighted by developments in the Punjab, such as the thwarted effort of Sikh women to participate fully in activities within the Golden Temple complex and the resulting confusion and counter-charges among authorities over earlier edicts and what constitutes 'maryada'.[29]

Whether women should wear turbans has always been a source of disagreement among Sikhs, and that debate is repeated within 'Sikh-Diaspora'. Similarly, several threads follow history and the role of tradition in the use of the surname 'Kaur' as a parallel to males adopting 'Singh'. Dowry and especially the continuing troublesome pattern of female infanticide (either through neglect or new medical techniques) also appear in response to either a particular case of 'honour' killing and dowry death or to census reports highlighting the sharp discrepancy between the number of males and females in Sikh areas of Punjab.[30]

The arguments over women are inevitably tied to an ongoing debate over ethnicity and religion, a problem resurfacing as Sikhs evaluate their traditions within a diaspora setting. Marriage, identity by name, creation and control of institutions, and broad social and political networks—all lead to discussions of Sikhs and caste. The interchanges also tend to get a bit more testy and personal, although the moderators usually keep messages within reasonable bounds.

The numerous threads on caste can be broken into three categories. First, caste names and Sikh identification with organizations organized by caste (such as Jat or Ramgarhia associations) are often debated. Some argue that only 'Singh' should be used, while others feel that in a Western context, caste identifiers can be useful for surnames and do not damage basic concepts of Sikh equality. The prevalence of specific gurdwaras controlled by Jats or Ramgarhias sparks severe criticism of both castes as well as strident defence of ethnic histories and successes.[31] Second, 'Sikh-Diaspora' members frequently address the practical roles caste plays in everyday life, such as social and marriage networks. Some of the most heated rhetoric can be found in these debates, for example this very telling plea at the end of one message:

Why all this preoccupation with Jats and the separate issues of caste? Nobody has come up with concrete examples of where Jats are causing any harm, yet the air is thick with insinuations of pride... We should speak out against this sort of labeling and concerted attack on people frequently derided as simpleton farmers, but who have lent many of their ethnic ideals to what is recognized as the Sikh form today.[32]

Such discussions also lead to the evaluation of marriage outside the Sikh community, bringing together various references of historical traditions and rahit with the obvious patterns of intermarriage that are occurring in non-Punjab settings. Third, the role of Dalits and the importance of those judged by some to be marginal within the Panth appears occasionally, either in response to a news story or a discussion of political strategy. No one denies the mistreatment of lower-caste Sikhs in the Punjab, but opinion varies about how to resolve the issues of inter-dining, intermarriage, and participation in community activities and gurdwaras.[33]

Conclusion

Websites and groups such as 'Sikh-Diaspora' provide abundant information on contemporary Sikhism as well as suggesting important themes of Sikh experience within diaspora settings. The 'Sikh-Diaspora' example is not meant to be representative of all Sikhs but rather an articulate exchange of ideas and issues that can be explored and compared with other interpretations. Appendix C, for example, contains a wealth of questions and interpretive material useful for understanding at least one approach to the Sikh experience beyond Punjab. Similarly, a recent conference at Birmingham underscored the continuities between how Sikhs now and a hundred years ago are placed in respondent roles, not setting agendas but often having to react within Western paradigms.[34] The names of the 'Sikh-Diaspora' threads reflect that realization: 'Evaluating Western Values', 'Emulating Western Values', 'Sikh Terminology in Diaspora', or an especially detailed and rich interchange on 'Living with a New Sikh Culture in Diaspora'. This does not mean that all Sikhs are addressing such issues or refining arguments, but it does suggest that many Sikhs spread around the world are committed to serious evaluation of tradition and change, and want to share their perspectives. Several prominent members of the group actively engage with specific organizations and intellectual networks within the Punjab. Recently, for example, some associated with 'Sikh-Diaspora' joined in the seminars and *sarbat khalsa* in Chandigarh, which addressed timely issues relating to the nature of Sikh tradition, the Dasam Granth, the role of the SGPC and the Akal Takht.[35]

One interesting dimension of 'Sikh-Diaspora' involves its being cited in positive and negative fashion as Sikhs interact over contemporary issues. One of the most recent illustrations involves a detailed paper by Bhupinder Singh Mahal.[36] An original founder of 'Sikh-Diaspora', the author presents a thoughtful analysis of the 'Sikh-Diaspora' discussions on 'who is a Sikh', in which he challenges the current interest in 'identity' as a process that undercuts the centrality of initiated Sikhs and the historical significance of Guru Gobind Singh's creation of the Khalsa. He also raises legal issues and tries to make the case that the earlier gurus shared his concern with the five Ks and maintained hair. Using a naval analogy, he identifies the ship as Sikhism built on the plans of the architects (the ten gurus), bearing a Sikh 'quom' registry, and with a captain (gurdwara leaders, SGPC, other institutions) at the helm, elected by the crew based on experience, knowledge, and capabilities. Mutineers are pilgrims who have recanted, in essence become apostates because of their rejection of Khalsa identity. 'These are the people who have to explain to outsiders, time and again, why they profess to be Sikhs but do not look like a Sikh.' Those currently leading 'Sikh-Diaspora' are trying to defend their own adaptations to circumstances in a new cultural setting.[37] Other long-term members of 'Sikh-Diaspora' have voiced similar concerns in private correspondence, underlining the particular orientation of the group and rightly questioning whether it should be seen as representing current Sikh opinion.

Participants in discussion groups such as 'Sikh-Diaspora' are addressing whether and how to respond to multicultural initiatives. They are fully aware that often joint programmes force Sikh terms and traditions into modes of thinking that from the perspective of Sikhism are not accurate and do not do justice to the spiritual and closely held beliefs that permeate worship and to some degree daily practice. This was a major theme in both the recent Birmingham conference and the attempts to re-evaluate Sikh tradition at a London seminar several years ago.[38]

On the other hand, many of the Sikhs in 'Sikh-Diaspora' are trained in modern professions and have expanded their worldview and self-understanding in a non-Punjab context. One of the most important elements in 'Sikh-Diaspora' is a shared belief in process and method of argument. The questioning that goes back and forth is not a competition, as one sometimes finds in Sikh discourse and of course in the discourse of many world religions, but rather an engagement that involves examining sources, thinking about problems, and then trying to find basic agreement that will prove a useful base for action now and in the future. One finds dozens of illustrations of this method in 'Sikh-Diaspora', but a good example is the interchange over Sikh terminology. Individuals listed definitions from recognized dictionaries, the works of scholars such as McLeod, and the on-line Microsoft Encarta College Dictionary. Another useful shaping of argument combines the traditional method of question and answer with a juxtaposition of 'accepted wisdom' or 'standard interpretations' with references to history, the teachings of the gurus, and more modern versions of rahit.[39]

What can scholars learn from these interchanges and, in general, the rapid spread of virtual communities and exchanges of large amounts of information within the new communication networks? In short, a lot. My personal research agenda and, more importantly, the questions I ask are influenced almost daily by exposure to 'Sikh-Diaspora' and similar sources. I find new references, books, ways of organizing material, competing perspectives, and a range of ideas that are invigorating and sometimes a burden (especially when I am gone for a period of time and the messages pile up). The archives of 'Sikh-Diaspora' and other organizations such as Sikhe.com and the Sikh Coalition are filled with documents and cross-references to court proceedings, linked newspaper accounts, and other materials. Opposing views and interesting documentation can be found in several Yahoo groups including Punjab Forum, Sikh-Agenda, Learning-Zone, Khalistan, Sikh_news_discussion, and others.

Equally important are the expanding networks of friends and associates that are linked to 'Sikh-Diaspora'. I have not met most of them personally, but I know their arguments and they share their experiences in a very typically Sikh way, with open and welcoming dialogue. I—and others also—could easily write essays and pursue projects on the basis of the richness of local archives and personal experiences available in the lives and institutional settings of many of the participants.

This leads to a central question: what is the role of scholars in such dialogue and, in more general terms, in the very active attempts of Sikhs to re-examine their roots, their present circumstances, and their future? First, I would suggest we must be humble. At least a dozen Sikhs on 'Sikh-Diaspora' know much more about specifics in the history of the community here and in Punjab over the last half century than I can ever learn. The older 'Sikh-Diaspora' members have lived through and experienced much of recent Sikh history. They know the sources and the arguments from within the tradition, and share that information.

Second, we can provide scholarly material and historical perspective from our research. That helps inform discussion at particular junctures, as in the case of the evolution of rahit or the specifics of movements or events such as the evolution of the 1925 Gurdwara Act. In reviewing the record of 'Sikh-Diaspora' discourse, I realized that I had been a more active participant than I remembered. Generally, I dealt with factual material or interpretations growing out of the Singh Sabha and Chief Khalsa Diwan. Occasionally, I highlighted parallels between recent events or institutional decisions and those occurring earlier. Some of the responses were positive, others quite bitter. To engage in such discussion groups, even those that had a moderated discourse such as 'Sikh-Diaspora', opens up the possibility of charges of ulterior motive and personal attacks. Several times, for example, I have been challenged quite aggressively when I discussed areas in which I have some expertise, such as the Bhasaur Singh Sabha and the Chief Khalsa Diwan. Also, what from our perspective might be a straightforward presentation of fact easily becomes ammunition for argumentation. Some of the best examples include reviews of Hew McLeod's evidence in the Canadian Sikh turban cases, and the use of rahit-namas material from his book.[40] This underscores the need for caution and extreme sensitivity. Our contributions are supplementary and for all practical purposes, Sikhs themselves are at the centre of the dialogue. We participate as informed guests, always ready if requested to present an outsider's perspective.

Finally, western scholars especially should be sensitive to the seriousness of the dialogue and its ultimate purpose: Sikhs resolving their understanding of tradition and how that relates to their contemporary situation. Some of the most detailed threads address the issue of scholarship and the perils of using documentation. One clearly stated warning, from an informed discussant who generally is sympathetic to Western scholarship, summarizes the situation:

> We should be careful not to imply that scholars of Sikhism 'know' more about Sikh religion or history than those who practise the religion and live the history... this discussion forum is meant to complement academic discourse, not to follow it.[41]

Academics can contribute, we can learn, we can try and understand from the sidelines. Ultimately, however, scholarly contributions are only one of a series of considerations that Sikhs must address as they grapple with the significance of their traditions and what Sikhism means in the twenty-first century.

Notes

1. Background on the various uses of tradition and the mixture of religion and politics is documented extensively in the *Spokesman*, Chandigarh. A scholarly overview of themes and struggle over authority can be found in N. G. Barrier, 'Authority, Politics and Contemporary Sikhism', Pashaura Singh and N. G. Barrier (eds), *Sikhism and History* (Delhi: Oxford University Press, 2004), pp. 194–229.

2. See the summary of challenges and politics in Darshan Singh Tatla, *The Sikh Diaspora*, (Seattle: University of Washington Press, 1999); also, the review in N. G. Barrier, 'Controversy among North American Sikhs', *International Journal of Punjab Studies* 6, 2 (1999), pp. 217–40.

3. Case study and review of use of 'tradition' in N. G. Barrier, 'The Fairfax,

Virginia Gurdwara Case and Sikh Identity', Pashaura Singh and N. G. Barrier (eds), *Sikh Identity: Continuity and Change* (Delhi: Manohar, 1999), pp. 365–78.

4. Venue Dusenbery, 'Of Singh Sabhas, Siri Singh Sahibs and Sikh Scholars', N. G. Barrier and Venue Dusenbery (eds), *The Sikh Diaspora Migration and the Experience beyond Punjab* (Delhi: Chanakya, 1989), pp. 90–119. 'A Sikh Diaspora: Contested Identities and Constructed Realities', Peter van der Veer (ed.), *Nation and Migration: the Politics of Space in the South Asian Diaspora* (Philadelphia: University of Philadelphia Press), 1995, pp. 17–42. 'Socializing Sikhs in Singapore', Pashaura Singh and N. G. Barrier (eds), *Transmission of Sikh Heritage in the Diaspora* (Delhi: Manohar, 1996), pp. 127–64. Venue Dusenbery and Rashmere Bhatti, *A Punjabi Community in Australia* (Woolgoolga: Woolgoolga Neighbourhood Centre, NSW, 2001).

5. Brian Keith Axel, *The Nation's Tortured Body: Violence, Representation, and the Formation of a Sikh 'Diaspora'* (Durham, NC: Duke University Press, 2001). N. G. Barrier, 'The Singh Sabhas and the Evolution of Modern Sikhism', Robert Baird (ed.), *Religion in Modern India* (Delhi: Manohar, third revised edition 1995), pp. 192–223. 'Sikh Politics in British Punjab Prior to the Gurdwara Reform Movement', Joseph O'Connell (ed.), *Sikh History and Religion in the 20th Century* (Toronto: University of Toronto Press, 1988), pp. 159–90. 'Competing Visions of Sikh Religion and Politics', *South Asia* 23, 2 (2000), pp. 33–62. Tony Ballantyne, *Orientalism and Race: Aryanism in the British Empire* (Basingstoke: Macmillan, 2002).

6. Louis E. Fenech, *Martyrdom in the Sikh Tradition: Playing the 'Game of Love'* (Delhi: Oxford University Press, 2000). Harjot Oberoi, *The Construction of Religious Boundaries: Culture, Identity and Diversity in the Sikh Tradition* (Delhi: Oxford University Press, 1994). Doris Jakobsh, *Relocating Gender in Sikh History* (Delhi: Oxford University Press, 2002). Karen Leonard, *Making Ethnic Choices: California's Punjabi Mexican Americans* (Philadelphia: Temple University Press, 1992).

7. Pashaura Singh, *Guru Granth Sahib* (Delhi: Oxford University Press, 2001). *Bhagats of the Guru Granth Sahib* (Delhi: Oxford University Press, 2003). Gurinder Singh Mann, *The Making of Sikh Scripture* (New York: Oxford University Press, 2001); *The Goindval Pothis: the Earliest Extant Source of the Sikh Canon* (Cambridge, MA: Dept. of Sanskrit and Indian Studies, Harvard University, 1996). Darshan Singh Tatla, *Sikh Diaspora: Sikhs in North America* (Westport: Greenwood, 1991). Shinder Singh Thandi, 'The Punjabi Diaspora in the UK and the Punjab Crisis', Pashaura Singh and N. G. Barrier (eds), *Transmission of Sikh Heritage in the Diaspora* (Delhi: Manohar, 1996), pp. 227–52. Arvind Mandair, 'Thinking Differently about Religion and History', Christopher Shackle et al. (eds), *Sikh Religion, Culture and Ethnicity* (Richmond: Curzon, 2001), pp. 47–71. Jeevan Deol, 'Eighteenth Century Khalsa Identity: Discourse, Praxis and Narrative', ibid., pp. 25–46. I. J. Singh, *Sikhs and Sikhism* (Delhi, 1998); *The Sikh Way* (Guelph, 2001); *Being and Becoming a Sikh* (Guelph, 2003).

8. For background on early communication and networks beyond Punjab, see N. G. Barrier, 'Sikh Emigrants and Their Homeland', N. G. Barrier and Venue Dusenbery, *Sikh Diaspora*, pp. 49–9; Barrier, 'Controversy'.

9. Sikh-Diaspora message, 1 January 2004. References in this essay indicate the nature of the correspondence and date. However, for privacy purposes, the names of the members initiating the messages have been omitted. We received permission from the editors of 'Sikh-Diaspora' to utilize messages in this fashion.

10. 'Sikh-Diaspora' exchanges, September–November 2001. Especially useful are 'Sikh-Diaspora' 16–9 September 2001 and 'Sikh-Diaspora' 25–30 October 2001. Some charged Khushwant Singh with being pro-Hindu and personally not reflecting true Sikh values. Discussants reacted to an interview with Yogi Harbhajan Singh on CNN, in which he was addressed as 'Your Holiness', and to his claim to be the leader of Sikhism in the West. Several noted he could not answer even simple questions on Sikh doctrine and history. For example, 'Sikh-Diaspora' 18 September 2001.

11. *International Journal of Punjab Studies* 10, 1–2 (2003), pp. 127–42.

12. Karamjit Singh statistical tables, 'Sikh-Diaspora' 1 January 2004. 'Sikh-Diaspora' messages averaged between 400–500 a month in 2003; 'Learning Zone', 100–200; 'Sikh Agenda', approximately 300; 'Khalistan', 40–100; 'Sikhcyber Sangath', 200–300. This chapter reflects an assessment in 2004, but in the interim, the dynamics of cyber communication have shifted, with new sites but often the same patterns and controversies. The most notable shift has been in the prominence of 'Learning Zone' based in England, which attracts often heated messages and exchanges. A contrary perspective, questioning the freedom of exchange and divergence on 'Sikh-Diaspora', is found in Bhupinder Singh Mahal, 'Campaign to Recast Sikh Image by Sikhs of Diaspora: Disavowing the Import of Baisakhi of 1699', *Abstract of Sikh Studies* 5, 1 (2003), pp. 40–55. I appreciate his reviewing an earlier draft, and have tried to address some of his concerns. The final essay, however, reflects my own assessment.

13. Discussion in 'Sikh-Diaspora' November 2003. The issue of continuity of the gurus' thought and the nature of guruship runs throughout the last two years of discussion.

14. Debate has appeared continually over the last three years. Most recently, a thread involving 'patit' Sikhs and actions of the SGPC led to a renewed discussion of kes-dhari–amritdhari–sahajdhari relations. 'Sikh-Diaspora' January 2004.

15. The Dasam Granth issue has been discussed widely over most Sikh sites and groups, such as 'Sikhe.net', 'Sikh Agenda', and others. It is a perennial topic on 'Sikh-Diaspora', for example, threads of July 2003 and January 2004. A detailed review of 'Sikh-Diaspora' approaches to Guru Gobind Singh and the Khalsa tradition in Bhupinder Singh Mahal, 'Campaign'.

16. Major discussion, 'Sikh-Diaspora' October–November 2002. The various sections of the SRM are used in debates over issues such as who is a real Sikh, correct action, details of ritual, and family relations. Also useful is the review essay and documents in Devinder Singh Chahal, 'Apostasy of Sikhism or Violation of Rahit Maryada' ('Understanding Sikhism', Chahal website).

17. Background in N. G. Barrier, 'Authority' and 'Controversy'. In addition to the major effort to delineate an acceptable definition of 'who is a Sikh' (last months of 2002), the issue appears regularly in 'Sikh-Diaspora' threads. Mahal argues that only a small group within 'Sikh-Diaspora' dominates these ·discussions, but my statistical analysis and regular reading of messages suggests a wider attempt to iron out differences. The matter has really not been resolved, either in discussion groups or in other arenas such as gurdwaras, the Akal Takht, and the SGPC. Practice, rules, and edicts often conflict. The Spokesman is especially useful in highlighting the ongoing struggle in the Punjab. I participated in the 'Sikh-Diaspora' discussions, trying to summarize issues and provide a historical context: 'Sikh-Diaspora' 13 and 21 October 2002; responses in subsequent messages, especially 24 October 2002.

18. The parameters of the discussion have been evaluated in N. G. Barrier, 'Authority'. The issue appears repeatedly, usually in conjunction with specific edicts such as decisions about 'patit' Sikhs or granting honours to the families of individuals involved in assassinating 'enemies' of Sikhism such as Indira Gandhi. The World Sikh Conference was reviewed extensively in late 2003. Background can be found in the Spokesman.

19. These issues are discussed in N. G. Barrier, 'Fairfax'. Two of the most controversial issues that led to group discussion involved efforts to disenfranchise sahajdhari voters from SGPC contests and proposed revisions of the Sikh Gurdwara Act.

20. An example of a contribution by a Western Sikh convert is found in Appendix B. The document presents a fresh approach to Sikhism in the West, and is also part of a large dialogue on the relationship between Sikhism and Punjabi culture (a major theme running through three years of 'Sikh-Diaspora' debate).

21. Exchanges in January 2004. Background on the Arya Samaj–Singh Sabha relationship can be found in N. G. Barrier, 'Contemporary Sikhism and the Singh Sabha Experience', presented at the Sikhism and Inter-Religious Dialogue Conference, Birmingham, October 2003. On current perceptions of the Singh Sabha movement and its potential revival as a means of mobilizing Sikhs, see essays published in The Sikh Bulletin (Roseville Gurdwara, California).

22. 'Sikh-Diaspora' 11 September 2003.

23. One thread involved the contribution of Sikhs to the freedom movement. A dispute arose over statistics adopted from Abul Kalam Azad's India Wins Freedom that suggested most martyrs dying in anti-British activities were Sikhs. This also involved evaluations of various individuals, including Bhagat Singh,

and a revisiting of the nature of the Gurdwara Reform Movement, from which Azad apparently drew some of his statistical information. 'Sikh-Diaspora' September–October 2003. On Bhagat Singh and his representation in two new films, see 'Sikh-Diaspora' June 2002.

24. Discussion of the Sikh Hall of Fame appears sporadically, but the major exchange was during the last months of 2001. Similarly, McLeod and Khushwant Singh are mentioned frequently in a variety of discussion threads. The proposed Sikh Hall of Fame has not been institutionalized, probably because of conflict over identity, historical events, and the comparative contribution of individuals.

25. On the casket issue, see 'Sikh-Diaspora' November 2001. The debate on Diwali is especially important because of the attempt to evaluate historical documents in the light of contemporary practice. 'Sikh-Diaspora' November 2001. Other extensive discussions focused on the role of ritual in Sikhism, especially akhand path. 'Sikh-Diaspora' May–June 2002.

26. For example, 'Sikh-Diaspora' February 2002. The NYPD and French cases are ongoing threads, and are also covered in most of the Sikh discussion groups and websites. SMART has been playing a major role in the defence of the kirpan and turban in the US, while the Akal Takht and the Indian government are actively involved in the French situation. Apparently Belgium is about to pursue the same policy as France.

27. 'Sikh-Diaspora' January 2004. The issues of the younger generation, what constitutes tradition in specific terms and the representation of Sikhism in public arenas are hotly contested. One important question is whether non kes-dharis can defend symbols of the Khalsa (especially the turban and kirpan) in legal proceedings. 'Sikh-Diaspora' October 2002.

28. 'Sikh-Diaspora' October 2003.

29. 'Sikh-Diaspora' March–May 2003. Many articles from Punjab newspapers and other sources on this issue were regularly posted to 'Sikh-Diaspora' by Jagpal S. Tiwana. For example, a most provocative essay, 'Myths about Sikh Women and Seva' by Majindarpal Kaur, a law student from the UK who was involved in the incident where Akal Takht and Golden Temple authorities denied women's rights to sewa. The article is very articulate, challenges misuse of 'maryada', and buttresses arguments for women's rights by reference to documents and the Guru Granth Sahib. 'Sikh-Diaspora' 15 May 2003.

30. For example, 'Sikh-Diaspora' January–February 2002 and September 2003. One of the major participants in the discussion is Doris Jakobsh, a specialist on women and Sikhism. Her research is in *Relocating Gender in Sikh History* (New Delhi: OUP, 2003) and a major paper on the sewa issue and role of women in contemporary Sikhism at the Birmingham Conference, October 2003. On dowry and marriage issues, see 'Sikh-Diaspora' February 2003.

31. For example, 'Sikh-Diaspora' December 2001; February–March, 2002; December 2002; and June 2003.

32. 'Sikh-Diaspora' 6 March 2002.

33. For example, on Dalits and more general caste issues including inter-marriage, see the following threads: 'Sikh-Diaspora' December 2001; May 2002; December 2002; and November 2003. Also refer to the chapters by W. H. McLeod and John C. B. Webster in this volume.

34. Proceedings will be edited shortly by Arvind Singh Mandair, Hofstra University. Also more background on the conference may be found in my other chapter in this volume.

35. For example, Ishwinder Singh. Information on the conference and its implications are in the *Spokesman* October–December 2003, and reports in the *Tribune*.

36. Bhupinder Singh Mahal, 'Campaign to Recast Sikh Image by Sikhs of Diaspora: Disavowing the Import of Baisakhi of 1699' (Chandigarh: Institute of Sikh Studies).

37. Ibid. I also appreciate his critique of the initial draft of this essay, along with suggestions for revisions from a variety of other 'Sikh-Diaspora' members.

38. Edited proceedings in Shackle, *Sikh Religion*.

39. Some of these issues are evaluated in W. H. McLeod, *Discovering the Sikhs* (Delhi: Permanent Black, 2003). Examples of the use of McLeod's scholarship and dictionaries include 'Sikh Terminology in Diaspora', 'Sikh-Diaspora' 7 April 2002.

40. 'Sikh-Diaspora' 20 January 2004.

Appendices*

A. *Objectives of 'Sikh-Diaspora'*

To recognize and understand that the Sikhs in their diaspora face continuing evolution and shaping of all aspects of their society as a result of influences exerted upon them by the cultural and racial diversity reflected in their adopted environment.

To encourage expression and discussion of issues and challenges facing the Sikhs in their adopted lands to equitably participate in mainstream life and assist them in the elimination of barriers to such participation.

To foster dissemination of information and ideas dealing with religious, social and economic matters among Sikhs and in their interaction with communities of different origins.

To select and compile, from time to time, writings posted on the Sikh-Diaspora in book form for distribution to libraries or prospective readers.

*Source: Excerpts from 'Sikh-Diaspora'.

To condemn myths, bigotry, intemperance or discrimination associated with caste, creed, race, colour or physical handicap, and to censure ethnic jokes and racial slurs.

To promote within the forum a sense of equality and mutual respect for each other.

To disallow use of the forum for propagating ideologies or missions of cults or missions of cults or clandestine groups which seek to subvert the Sikh faith.

B. *Living with a New Sikh Culture: Views of a Convert*

I realized most of you do not realize I am a convert to Sikhism. Until this point, I didn't see a need to make that distinction. Allow me to give a little background since the subject of this thread is in calling for a more universal approach to Sikhism and in cutting the proverbial Punjabi umbilical cord.

I adopted Sikhi four years ago in an Amrit Sanchar of the Akhand Kirtani Jatha. My mother is a Slovak Catholic; my father was an American Native of the Cherokee tribe and could rightly be called a very devout pagan, meaning he worshipped all of Nature. I studied in Catholic schools and spent the final three years of high school in a convent. I studied theology at both undergraduate and graduate levels and went on to study to become a chaplain at a post-graduate level. In between these studies, I lived in Greece for three years, returned to the States, married and gave birth to a son. Shortly after my son was born, I converted to Orthodox Judaism, simply because I could not impart a Catholic/Christian teaching to my son. I did not believe Jesus was God which is the mainstay of Christianity... While in the final months of my residency studies for the chaplaincy, I was speaking with a Tanzanian patient, when the doctor interrupted us to tell the patient that he had an inoperable cancer. He accepted the doctor's words with no emotion whatsoever. He was a Shiite Moslem. In my profound stupidity, I thought he said he was a 'Sikh' Muslim. I became quite close with this patient and his entire family until his death three years later. I was so impressed by this man's strength of character and conviction, that I began investigating Sikhi, thinking that was his faith. It didn't take long for me to realize they were two different religions, but I was captivated by the absolute simplicity of Sikhi. So basically I discovered Sikhism because of a Moslem's faith and an error on my part.

Perhaps the greatest ill of Sikhism today is the fact that two people speaking cannot seem to listen to what the other has to say. Sitting in Sangat I wonder how long Sikhism will survive... As a convert to Sikhism, even though I may tie a turban as required by AKJ, or the fact that I may offer my prayers according to the longer Damdami Taksal version, [and an] in many ways an 'orthodox' Sikh, I am sickened by one group condemning the other [over] whether they abide by every tenet of Sikhism or not. A Sikh is a Sikh and until we stop this nonsense of one being closer to the 'truth' than the other, neither side will be able to approach the truth of Sikhism as laid down by Sri Guru Granth Sahibji, because each side will be too busy in pursuing the toppling of the perceived 'opposition'.

While I would not encourage Sikhs to cut their hair, remove their turbans or seek to lose their outward appearance, I would not be a Sikh if I condemned those who chose to do so. By the same token, we cannot judge Sikhs by the color of their skin, their gender or nationality. We must however continue to strive for unity among the Panth. An old saying says, 'United we stand. Divided we fall.' We must also keep in mind the tender age of Sikhism. I firmly believe we are experiencing the ongoing 'growing pains' of Sikhism.

(Source: Excerpted from 'Sikh-Diaspora', 16 July 2002.)

C. *Living with a New Sikh Culture in Diaspora*

The founding fathers of America wisely insisted on the separation of 'church' and state... Sikhs in modern Punjab have made a series of strategic political mistakes. Their interests are served by neither the 'secular' Congress party nor the Akali Dal. The reasons are complex, and I do not pretend to fully understand them. However, it has not served Sikhs well to equate religion with politics, just as it does not serve Muslims, Hindus, etc. Since most of us are in the Diaspora, we have a similar choice confronting us. I suggest that history (Sikh and other) should warn us away from lumping together our religion and our politics. Unfortunately this very situation is occurring in North America and UK currently. We must realize that being such small minorities, we will likely only gain lip service and tokens, rather than anything substantive, as a result of activist action. On the debit side, our politics will be identified with our religion and vice-versa. Aggressive groups claiming to represent us can therefore set the agenda, demand conformity, and draw us into conflicts that serve no larger purpose than to buttress egos, and provide incomes for a few. I believe our religion should not be utilized for political agendas; neither should erstwhile religious leaders represent us politically.

I propose we also consider separating Sikhi from culture. This combination of culture and religion can also be arguably blamed for the apparent ossification of religious practice. Many of the demands placed on congregants are of Punjabi origin, having little or no religious significance. These often serve as barriers to participation by non-Punjabis or young people of Punjabi descent, who are not attuned to Punjabi language, behavior and practices. While the Punjabi-ness of Sikhi practiced in the diaspora may be comforting for the majority, it may not be conducive to others who may have important contributions to make to our religion. We need new perspectives, fresh evaluations and youngsters to rejuvenate our practices. All religious practices need this nurturing input if they are not to become irrelevant. Sikhi in the diaspora is at such a turning point. We can by default allow it to become more like the tried and tested (and failed) type practiced in Punjab; or take advantage of a golden opportunity to foster pure Sikhi, unadulterated by cultural mores peculiar to one region alone. I might add that it was a region we saw fit to leave behind physically, why not culturally?

Concomitant with the above are the rights of the individual. The only way to guarantee true civility and tolerance is to elevate respect for the individual to a very high priority in our dealings with each other. We may even be able to stop bickering and produce something useful, getting beyond political affiliation, gender, caste, etc. I believe it is an attitude in line with the ethos of our religion. Beware, it will also be rejected by those interested in mass manipulation.

We have to begin to debate the separation of Sikhi from culture and politics in earnest and in depth. Organized, far-sighted and meaningful reform of the institutions of our community is one of the most pressing needs of the day.

(Source: Excerpted from 'Sikh-Diaspora', 18 June 2002.)

Sikhism and the Visual Arts[1]

Amrit and Rabindra Kaur Singh

As visual artists from a Punjabi Sikh background who have been working professionally in the UK for the past 12 years and who researched Sikh art as postgraduate students, we have observed the under-representation of Sikh art within the world of academia and we hope to establish a place for it on an international platform of serious critical debate within the fields of both global Sikh art and contemporary art studies.

We begin with the premise that, no matter how innovative, art does not exist in a vacuum, but is, rather, the product of the artist's experience, perceptions, and reactions to his or her environment; that the style and content of an artist's work as well as the circumstances surrounding its development can offer a unique insight into the developing social, political, and cultural character of a particular people, time, and place. It is an insight which while rooted in the 'individual' dimension of the artists' personal identity and experience, often reflects the 'wider' dimension or collective experience of the community, and, in turn, the society they come from. Since our own work is no exception in this respect, our intention is essentially to give a brief insight into its development over the past 12 years as a way of exemplifying how Sikh art can provide an invaluable resource for furthering Sikh and Punjab studies—exploring how our evolving style, themes, and iconography embody a Sikh heritage that is not only both rooted in broader Indian aesthetics and identity but also reflects the wider British Asian experience which has contributed to the continuing development of mainstream British art, identity, and culture.

We should clarify here that as artists who have struggled to avoid the kind of 'ethnic' compartmentalizing that undermines the status of culturally diverse art within the mainstream, we always describe ourselves as contemporary British rather than specifically Sikh or Punjabi artists. Having said this, our paintings have nevertheless been influenced by our Sikh heritage, sometimes consciously but more often than not subconsciously, as a natural consequence of who we are and as an expression of much that we take for granted about our cultural ideology and upbringing. At the same time, the fact that our work is not exclusively concerned with our Sikh or Punjabi identity is significant in itself within the context of Sikh studies—indicating how we, like many Sikhs, continue to define and redefine ourselves in relation to the world around us.

To begin with, our determined exploration of the Indian miniature style and our preoccupation with themes relating to issues of cultural identity in our early work hark back to the negative attitudes we faced during our first degree in art. While we were seeking to develop a personal style that was meaningful to our own heritage, there was constant pressure from tutors to comply with role models from contemporary Western art. Our perspective in the dissertation which emphasized the impact of non-European art on Western art—though described as of a high level—was refused for evalution by the tutors. We regarded our tutors' attitude not only as hypocritical but as an extension of the kind of institutionalized prejudice that we experienced as young Punjabi Sikhs growing up in a predominantly White British society still steeped in colonial notions of assumed Western cultural superiority. On a daily basis, this manifested itself through peer pressure, largely sustained by derogatory media stereotypes of Asian-ness, and the general expectancy of mainstream society that one should conform to Western values and lifestyles.

Against this background, our early works, like 'Wedding Jange II', are in style and content a political statement which assert the right to be accepted on our own terms both artistically and culturally. As an expression of pride in traditional values, right in the midst of Western society, they present positive images of Punjabi culture that challenge popular misperceptions about those traditions particularly derided in Western society and media, such as the arranged marriage and extended family system.

So in 'Wedding Jange II', for example, we find a typical scene from a Punjabi wedding where the groom's family are about to set off to the bride's house—it shows various customs being played out by the women of the house while family and friends dance the Bhangra in the street. If it were not for the backdrop of the Liverpool cityscape, it could easily be a scene from a Punjabi village. The celebration takes place on a stretch of roadway that is decorated like a Persian carpet and dominates the composition, just as our Punjabi Indian heritage dominates our own sense of identity even though we were born and bought up in the West. In the same way, a tree which divides the painting into two cultural zones of activity (East on the left and West on the right) is rooted in and blossoms only on the Eastern side. Neighbours (representing the curious West) observe the festivities with a mixture of intrigue and bemusement. While the general scene is one of friendly co-existence between cultures, certain details remind the viewer that this supposed 'harmony' is not something that can be taken for granted. As such, one of the neighbours reads the local newspaper which carries two stories about the 'turban on the buses' issue and our own battle with the university to have our degrees reinstated—thereby recording the British Sikh community's various, ongoing struggles to maintain freedom of religious and cultural expression. At the same time, it is an image about how diasporic communities, no matter how traditional, have not only had to adapt to their new environment but have also not hesitated to make use of the new opportunities it has afforded them. Hence, though the groom's family would traditionally have travelled to the bride's house in a procession of horses and bullock carts, here two coaches wait to take the family on their journey, while the whole event is captured on film by the obligatory cameraman, courtesy of Western technology. But ultimately this painting challenges the whole notion of wholesale cultural assimilation (an idea which was bandied about when we were growing up in a then still developing 'multicultural Britain', but which many Asians rejected as implying at best a dilution of their own traditions and at worse a total negation of any distinct sense of cultural identity in order to be accepted as part of mainstream). What the painting promotes instead is the concept of informed or selective integration and a multiculturalism characterized by the co-existence of diverse cultures, based on mutual respect for difference. The idea of assimilation versus selective integration is represented by the Concord (the ultimate tribute to Western technological advancement, symbolizing the positive benefits of Westernization) which flies past a mushroom cloud (conversely symbolizing the worst aspects of Western technology and a forewarning of the dangers of taking on board any culture wholesale). In short, this—like all our work—has many layers of interpretation that reflect the complexity of issues facing diasporic communities. In particular, it offers an alternative scenario to the dilemma facing second and third generation youth who often feel pressured to choose between two cultures, suggesting instead that it does not have to be a case of throwing the baby out with the bath water, can mean but having the best of both worlds.

'All Hands on Deck' depicts the cooking of our elder sister's wedding feast and shows all the family getting involved in the preparation process. One of the reasons why we focus a lot on family imagery and sense of community in our work is to counteract the almost obsessive emphasis on individuality in Western society. It is something with which we were particularly confronted not only as twins and Asian women (whose individuality was wrongly perceived as being suffocated by an oppressive, male-dominated culture), but more specifically as students working within an art establishment which advocated self-expression as the 'be all and end all' of being an artist and consequently had problems dealing with the fact that we shared a common interest in Indian art that resulted in us developing near-identical personal styles of painting. But coming from an Asian tradition, the idea of individuality was something that we did not value much because it was alien to the values of family and community which we grew up with as part of a large extended Asian family. So when we found ourselves being criticized for not being individual enough at school and art college, we felt it was not only an attack on our identity as twins and artists but as Asians. We started to use our work to expose what we saw as the hypocrisy of a Western attitude which seemed to value individuality, but only on its own terms, and to challenge the notion of individuality by reinforcing the role of family and community in Asian culture. We think as Sikhs this was especially important to us because Sikhism teaches the value of family in the process of spiritual awareness—as a training ground; a place where you learn to give and take and be less selfish; using the values you have learnt within the family, such as mutual responsibility, respect, duty, and care, and taking that into the wider community for the benefit of society as a whole. So 'All Hands on Deck' picks up on this by showing the equal importance, interaction, and interdependence of each member of the family, from the youngest to the eldest.

From the early- to mid-1990s, many of our more significant works deal with our experience as Sikhs born and brought up in Britain. As a documentation of contemporary Sikh life, these might be seen as continuing the Company School era of painting and Woodblock print traditions which depicted the secular day-to-day life of nineteenth- and early twentieth-century Punjab. And it is are very true that they do focus on showing the mundane activities that go on in daily life, but with a difference. Because rather than merely recording *how* we live in Britain, these works are a statement which asserts the *right* to live the way we do in Britain, against the strong pressure that we felt (particularly as young Asians) growing up in a predominantly Western environment to conform to Western values, traditions, and lifestyles. In this respect, they are also primarily about countering the negative stereotypes of Asian-ness we often see through the media.

So in our image titled 'Tel', we have a typical scene of the preparation of the groom with the Phulkari canopy being held over his head. It is very traditional in its format, with the various cultural rituals being played out by the women in a way that recalls the wedding scenes of Guru Nanak in the nineteenth-century janam sakhi murals of Baba Atal Gurdwara. We also have the contemporary element here with the young boys inside the house playing snooker, having no interest in the ceremonies that are being performed outside—making the point that it is the women who are the keepers of tradition. As such, one of the main purposes of this painting and others like it is to demonstrate the status, centrality, and importance of women within Sikh culture.

Our painting titled 'All That I Am' again continues the tradition of Sikh portraiture, but extends the genre further by presenting a narrative portrait which functions on three levels. First, as the individual story of our father's life—beginning at the top left with Amritsar (his birthplace); travelling through the period of Partition of Punjab, when the family first came to England; and following the other stages of his upbringing, education, and achievements around the painting until we get to the present day. Second, as an archetypal image which reflects the collective Asian diaspora experience in the 'rags to riches' scenario. Third, as a portrait of who we are as a result and reflection of our father's and his generations' efforts, sacrifices, and achievements.

Looking at an image whose content looks beyond our own personal experience as Sikhs in Britain towards the wider diaspora Sikh experience, 'Mr Singh's India' (commissioned in 1999 by the Glasgow Museum of Modern Art) is a painting which records the Scottish–Sikh relationship both through popular culture and historical links. Just to give a few examples, the setting for the piece is a Punjabi-owned restaurant in the heart of Glasgow (called 'Mr Singh's India'), which was decorated in typical Raj fashion but had Sikh waiters who greeted clients in turbans and kilts—a perfect example of how the Sikh community is happy to take on board and adapt aspects of a new cultural environment. And William Wallace (who most people will probably know better as Hollywood's 'Braveheart') is shown dining with his Sikh counterpart Maharaja Ranjit Singh. Many British Sikhs identified with the movie and the figure of Wallace because of the parallels they found in Ranjit Singh—here were two larger-than-life national heroes who successfully fought to keep respectively the English and British foreign rule at bay. Other elements in the painting point to the historic military connection of the Scottish Sikh regiments and the cultural exchange that has existed between Scotland and Punjab primarily through the Paisley shawl trade.

Moving on from a situation where we were essentially trying to revive the historic traditions in Sikh art, we began to apply certain characteristics of traditional Sikh art to contemporary contexts. 'Lesmahagow Durbar' is actually one in a series of paintings commissioned by the Royal Museums and Galleries of Scotland, Edinburgh. The series (collectively titled *The Iqbalnama*) is about Baron Iqbal Singh, who has become quite an established celebrity in Scottish circles and whose fame has reached further shores in more recent years. But as someone who is known for his patronage of Scottish heritage, he has become a symbol of the Scottish Sikh community, which is partly why the museums decided to commission the series about his life and how he has promoted what he feels is a part of *his* Scottish heritage as a Punjabi who has adopted Scotland as his home. The colour and motif of the border is typical of the Sikh school of miniature painting, while the format in general draws on the darbar scenes of courtly images. There is also a reference to Maharaja Dalip Singh and Princess Bamba, whose images flank the gilt framed mirror. Their inclusion not only symbolizes the nostalgia that many in the Sikh community have for the lost era and glorious past of the Sikh raj, but also serves to exemplify ways in which Sikh heritage has traditionally been documented through the arts as both images are copies of specific historical sources: the former is based on Winterhalter's portrait in the Royal Collection Osborne House and the latter on the c. 1887 photograph (from the Lahore Fort Collection) taken of Princess Bamba on the occasion of her formal presentation at court.

Our earliest contact with the rich artistic heritage of Sikhism began about 14 years ago, when we both took up postgraduate research into Sikh art. Initially we studied collections at the Victoria and Albert Museum, London, and elsewhere in Britain. Then in 1990 we had an opportunity to actually travel to India on a 12-month INTACH scholarship. During that period, the kind of art we were researching (namely, the janam sakhi manuscript traditions, illustrated Guru Granth Sahibs, and also, simultaneously, popular Sikh imagery or calendar art) inspired our work of that time.

For example, the painting titled 'The Enlightenment of Guru Nanak Dev Ji' represents an episode from the janam sakhis, or stories of the life of Guru Nanak. However, while much of the early Sikh images we studied were simplistic in their representation of the specific narrative they depicted, this work draws more on the Persian tradition of manuscript illustration to present a much more imaginative treatment and interpretation of the subject both in structure and content. It shows not just a single moment in the sakhi but a sequence of events that take place within the narrative as a whole. So here we have Guru Nanak bathing; then being taken up to the abode of God (which is in the upper register of the painting); and then receiving the nam or Word—all within the same painting. Although it is not shown here because this slide was taken before the painting was finished, in the bottom border of the original painting we have included the actual script of the sakhi itself, following the traditional janam sakhi convention of integrating text and imagery to enable the viewer to interpret the visual narrative more easily.

Just to place this painting in its proper context in terms of the chronological development of our art, one of the reasons why we decided to try and produce new work that in many ways sought to revive the historic traditions of Sikh art was because we became frustrated and annoyed by the reaction that we received from a lot of people when we first started to study Sikh art in India and in England. Very often we were confronted with comments such as 'what do you mean you're studying Sikh art?', 'the Sikhs have no art', or 'they have no artistic heritage'. And so we felt that by reviving this tradition and bringing it into a contemporary relevance it would re-open the debate about the heritage of the Sikhs particularly within the artistic context.

Again, drawing on the traditional narrative miniature format, our piece 'The Spiritual Enlightenment of Guru Amar Das' presents a visual interpretation of specific verses from the Guru Granth Sahib. It is one in a series of similar works which were done at a time when we were studying Sikh writings as part of our research into Sikh art and which were intended to communicate to the wider audience (and more importantly, the non-Sikh audience) something about certain aspects of Sikh religious thought and spiritual teaching. It shows Guru Amar Das as the central figure being blessed by Guru Nanak and it's all about the path to spiritual enlightenment—the nature and means of attaining this is represented in the various visual symbols which surround them. These in turn are based directly on our interpretation of particular literary descriptions and allegorical imagery used in the Guru Granth Sahib. To give one example, take the grouping of five horses. It's often described within the scriptures that to restrain one's ego (which is fuelled by the five senses) is as difficult as trying to restrain five wild horses. Now as the Guru is someone who has obviously managed to achieve this, the horses are shown in a very calm and static state, and each of them has a symbol on its forehead that represents one of the five senses. In fact, there is a tremendous amount of symbolism in this work. One of the things worth mentioning is the hierarchical composition, which in itself reflects the different levels of human existence. So starting at the bottom here, we have the state of mundane existence or the material world (symbolized by the globe) and as the process of enlightenment progresses, the composition moves to different areas of transcendence from this earthly plane and the further up the painting we go. So in the middle panel here, for example, you have a kind of intermediate state between earth and the heavens, while in the uppermost register, the state of Divine union is represented by an abstract decorative pattern and the Ik Onkar symbol behind Guru Nanak. We also have the symbolism of the lotus, which recurs in Sikh literature: Guru Amar Das is shown meditating on the lotus, the symbol of the pure soul, which is very much rooted in the earth but rises above the earth (or the temptations of worldly existence).

Still in the realms of portraiture, we were commissioned in 1999 by the Barber Institute of Fine Art to respond to a famous painting in their pre-Raphaelite collection, 'The Blue Bower' by the Victorian British artist Dante Gabriel Rossetti. The result was a series of works called *Facets of Femininity*, which focused on eight female icons of the twentieth and twenty-first century and explored not only the diversity of women as portrayed by the media in our modern times, but also how far removed perceptions of femininity had become from the limited Victorian ideal. All eight portraits are highly symbolic—from the patterned background to the objects and animals around them, to the flowers, animals, and colours chosen. The relevance of this series to how Sikhism has informed our work is evident in the portrait 'Margaret Thatcher', which illustrates the way in which we continue to be inspired by aspects of Sikh iconography even when dealing with non-Sikh subjects. For example, in Sikhism, the egoist is likened to the crane which remains with its head underwater seeking food, too engrossed with self-interest to be concerned with the world around it. So we personally felt this would be an ideal animal to represent the political ambition of Mrs Thatcher, whose policies we believe cultivated the go-getting 'every man for himself' attitude of the 1980s. The painting also demonstrates how we have been interested in trying to reinterpret, adapt, or extend the imagery inspired by our traditional Sikh heritage, to create a new context that gives it continuing relevance to new audiences. We mentioned the symbolism of the lotus and how traditionally the pure soul is likened to the lotus that blooms with its face towards the sky—that is, the upturned lotus. It appears again the background detail of Margaret Thatcher's portrait—it's hopefully not too hard to see why the lotus is turned *down* in this case, yet another indication of our 'passion' for her!

A similar example of how we have appropriated aspects of our Sikh heritage in the treatment of non-Sikh themes can be found in the image called 'The Greatest', which depicts the boxing icon Mohammed Ali (although in format it is actually based on one of the allegorical portraits of the Emperor Jahangir in the Smithsonian Institute, Washington, and plays upon the same kind of iconography). It is one of the 12 pieces that we completed in 2002 as part of the UK celebrations of the Commonwealth Games and in our capacity as official 'artists in residence' for this national event. The underlying theme of this series (*Sportlight*) was to explore the relationship between sport, media, and celebrity and hence the changing role of the sports personality. So the image of Mohammed Ali is not so much about him as a boxer (which is why the boxing ring plays a very minor part in the image itself) but how he used his boxing fame as a political tool. We related to the personality of Mohammed Ali as Sikhs because he was somebody who gave up everything, including his career, to fight for what he believed in. He put faith before his own material gain and his faith was very much the driving force behind his actions— namely, why he chose to take his fight out of the boxing ring onto the world stage and was so determined to fight prejudice against the Black community within America. It seemed to us that that particular spirit which he possessed had parallels with the Khalsa spirit—that is, the quality exhibited by the Khalsa which fought for the defenceless, stood up to be counted, and put their faith before everything else. And we wanted to reference this within the portrait. So for the border we used the typical

Wedding Jange II

All That I Am

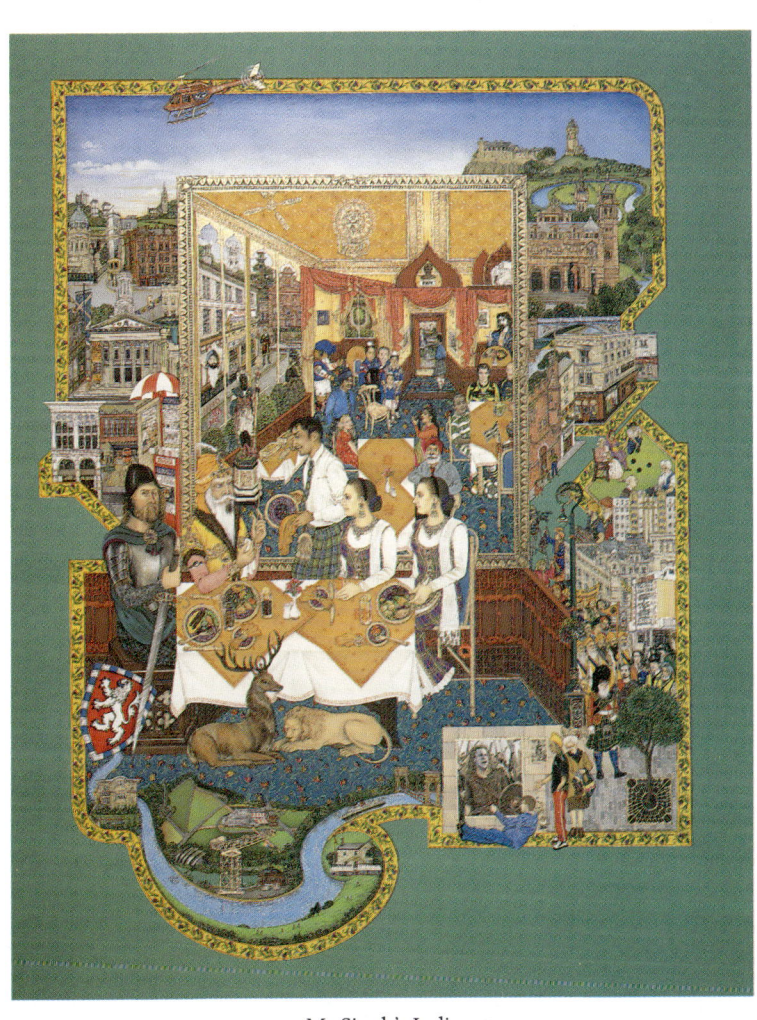

Mr Singh's India

The Beast of Revelation

Battle of the Giants

Forever in Our Hearts

All Hands on Deck

colours associated with the Khalsa—the saffron of sacrifice and the dark blue for steel and strength. It's a deliberate choice of colours to make a specific parallel.

By contrast, 'Forever in Our Hearts', portraying a very dear uncle who passed away in 1994, is completely innovative in its composition. It is a narrative contemporary portrait, which in keeping with the tradition of historical Sikh portraiture uses symbols or visual icons to represent aspects of the subject's personality and status. The symbolism comes from global sources—and there is really no boundary for us in where we take our inspiration from, because we believe Sikhism has always been an eclectic faith, born out of an open-mindedness from which we continued to draw confidence in taking freely from the aesthetic traditions of all the world religions. So there's a real mix here. For instance, the white elephant is the Buddhist symbol of compassion (representing one of the characteristics our uncle possessed), the strawberry motifs in the border come from Christianity (symbolizing a life of good deeds), while the lion (a universal symbol of bravery) represents our uncle's courage in the face of adversity and his strength of character. At the same time, it draws upon specifically Sikh imagery—such as the swan, which is popularly used as a metaphor for the pure soul in Sikh writings.

'Nyrmla's Wedding' depicts the mehndi ceremony of our elder sister's wedding. Again, themes around the wedding and family dominate this period of work because as young Asians growing up in the West, we were constantly faced with peer pressure and media stereotypes that undermined the institutions of arranged marriage and the extended family. They were inevitably the target of criticism and so we felt that something needed to be done to redress this. So 'Nyrmla's Wedding' is a very optimistic picture which shows the celebration taking place in a happy atmosphere and safe environment symbolized by the predominantly warm colours of yellow and red. But in the upper right part of the painting, we have a view through the window—a vision of the outside world which has become a threat to the traditional values that we hold, with Ronald McDonald and a Coca-Cola bottle symbolizing the multinational impact on traditional ways of life, and a landscape of global destruction and pollution symbolizing the pitfalls of blind economic and scientific progress fuelled by an ever-increasing individualistic, materially driven consumer society. This is very much a painting which speaks from a personal experience that is specific to the British or even wider diasporic Sikh perspective (as a community that is perhaps more fearful of losing the traditional cultural values that

Sikhs 'back home' might take for granted). But it uses this personal starting point to make a statement about a process of globalization and economic progress (often equated with Westernization and regarded as being in conflict with traditional values and lifestyles) that has universal relevance in echoing the experience of 'ancient' traditions globally—whether it be that of the aboriginal Australians, the native Americans, or the Amazonian Indians. In this context, the painting asserts the idea that what are often labelled as backward or outdated traditions and values by the West have continuing value in modern society; that we can learn something from them because they have existed for many centuries without causing harm to anyone else or the environment—in contrast to the whole idea of Westernization and globalization, which, although often sold on the back of civilization and progress, have proven also to be very destructive forces.

Having said this, the work also points to how Asians in Britain have embraced aspects of Western culture, using symbols of Western innovation like camcorders and stereos and objects of pop culture like the Batmobile or the Power Ranger and Jasmin doll. It is not all about rejecting the West, but also about making an informed choice and realizing that it is possible to be progressive and modern while retaining traditional values; the two are not necessarily incompatible. It is important to stress this because very often as British Asians the constant pressure to choose Western over Eastern culture is based on a general assumption that the former is superior to the latter. And it is a pressure that we object to because: First, since, culturally we feel we belong to both East and West, we want to choose the best of both worlds. Second, we apply the all-embracing outlook of Sikhism to life generally which means that all cultures have something positive to offer and you can be quite happy living in two, three, four, or more different cultures if you choose.

'Nineteen Eighty Four' depicts the storming of the Golden Temple and exemplifies how the diaspora community responds to events outside of the place of their settlement and maintains ties with their motherland. It is very much a statement against the misrepresentation of the event as we saw it on British television and what we really wanted to show was the extent of the atrocities and the kind of human disaster that this actually signified. So although it starts from a very personal perspective, it is an image which is really about universal issues of politics and political corruption, representing the idea that it is really the combined effects of corrupt politics globally which are responsible for the everyday man or woman in the street suffering to the degree that they do. The image draws on certain modes of established iconography within the genre of Sikh calendar art. For example, the familiar figure of Baba Dip Singh is taken directly from the classic representation associated with the Amritsar artist G. S. Sohan Singh (the original painting used to be displayed at the spot of Baba Dip Singh's martyrdom in the Golden Temple complex before being replaced in more recent times with a version by the popular Sikh artist Amolak Singh).

This image titled 'The Beast of Revelation' was actually based on a famous work by William Blake and it copies his composition, but the symbolism has been changed to give a contemporary context. It draws upon the Biblical Book of Revelations, which talks about the coming of the end of time: an age marked by Satan's reign (or the prevalence of evil) on earth through the tyrannical and corrupt leadership of worldly rulers. Now some people may ask what this image has to do with Sikh art. But for us, Sikhism has always been a religion of challenge and reform, a philosophy and way of life that critiqued the social and political environment that it grew up in, and we see this work and others like it very much in that vein. It's questioning the state of politics today within a context that projects an idea of evil in terms of the crimes committed against humanity and nature, caused by political greed, and the misuse and abuse of power—things like slavery, environmental exploitation, pollution, and irresponsible censorship, which have been a degenerate and destructive force in society. For us personally, Blake's original painting called to mind the words of Guru Nanak, which we believe continue to have resonance in today's political and social climate:

The age is like a drawn knife
Kings are butchers
And righteousness has taken wings and flown
In this dark night of falsehood
No moon of truth is seen to rise[2]

Similarly, 'From Zero to Hero', again from the *Sportlight Series*, shows David and Victoria Beckham as the ultimate icons of popular culture in the British media—the perfect union between the worlds of pop, fashion, and sport is another critique of contemporary society, this time representing how the secular has taken over the sacred in popular consciousness as material icons replace religious icons in a modern world obsessed with a self-image defined by designer labels and the cult of celebrity.

Before concluding, we would just like to offer some pointers in this direction that look outside our own practice. For example, within the study of early twentieth-century Sikh art, individual artists like Kirpal Singh, who is popularly heralded as the 'best exponent of the Sikh's history in pictures', pioneered the development of Sikh iconography in Western style through his epic scenes of Sikh history. While his paintings are well known within the global Sikh community, he is relatively unknown within the academic fields of art and cultural studies. Others, like Trilok Singh and G. S. Sohan, have been reduced to near-obscurity even within Sikh circles; yet the works of these artists not only defined a whole era of Sikh struggle and reform but inspired a new generation of Sikh artists who have gone on to reflect Sikh sentiments and values in a way that is relevant to their own times.

The area of Sikh calendar art or mass-produced printed imagery is, as we discovered during our postgraduate research into Sikh art, another vast resource that has been touched on in part but remains to be explored in depth despite being the most universal and widespread art form within the global Sikh community. Through this printed medium, Kirpal Singh's paintings (like those of other artists who found patronage from official Sikh organizations such as the Shiromani Gurdwara Parbandhak Committee, or SGPC and Punjab Sind Bank, henceforth PSB) have come to represent the collective consciousness and identity of the Sikhs presenting the 'official face' of Sikhism—or at least how this was defined and redefined, particularly since the early twentieth century, in the period of self-examination that was spearheaded by such reform groups as the Singh Sabha movement.

As well as studying the imagery itself, articles in the popular Indian press and Sikh journals of the time reveal how the growing popularity of Sikh imagery and 'commercial' art in particular was a matter of public debate. The arguments which are set out on both sides provide another dimension of research for furthering Sikh studies in that they contribute to our broader understanding of the issues that gave rise to the Singh Sabha movement (and others) and influenced perceptions of what constituted a distinct Sikh identity. Amongst other things, the objections to images of the gurus on the one hand and the need to establish an official standardization of Sikh iconography on the other, for example, appear to have been directly linked to a desire to establish an identity which increasingly dissociated itself from any Hindu influences— in reaction to what many reformists believed to be the systematic undermining of Sikh identity (and its 'distortion' through Hindu practices) and the subsequent denial of Sikh rights (as a separate religion) since Indian Independence.

Equally revealing would be a study of how Sikh imagery has been used both within and outside the community and what can be deduced from this in terms of how Sikhs perceive themselves and are perceived by others. Our early research into Sikh calendar imagery, for example, showed that for official Sikh organizations like the SGPC and PSB, art had a didactic function. It is essentially used as a tool not only for asserting and promoting Sikh identity and history, but for demonstrating its continuing relevance today to Sikhs and non-Sikhs alike. Consequently, such organizations maintain close control on what their artists paint and how they treat the subjects, adopting a sombre, generally Western realistic style that 'befits' the seriousness of the subjects. More often than not, these are circulated free of charge to be displayed in public and formal spaces—including offices, government buildings, and gurdwaras.

Within the general community, however, printed Sikh images take on a variety of functions (largely devotional, ritual, and social), which in itself reflects the diversity of practice and belief amongst the Sikhs at the personal and grassroots level. From time to time, they have also acquired a secular or political dimension. During India's fight for independence, for example, images of the modern-day freedom fighter Bhagat Singh, the Sikh gurus, and historical Sikh heroes such as Baba Dip Singh were all widely circulated and proved such potent tools of anti-Raj propaganda that they were banned by the British government. In some cases, Sikh heroes are depicted alongside non-Sikh heroes. In other cases, familiar Sikh iconography is reinvented within a non-Sikh context. For instance, a poster from the 1950s shows Bhagat Singh tearing open his chest to reveal the object of his devotion, Mother India—making an obvious parallel with a well-known episode from Hindu mythology where Hanuman tears open his chest to reveal the object of his devotion, Ram and Sita. Images such as these, which presented Sikh heroes as national icons and which were intended for the general market, exemplify how the Sikhs were perceived by the Indian masses.

Conclusion

Our Sikh heritage has had a significant impact on our work in terms of its aesthetics and ideology. As artists, it has always been important for us not only to value traditions of the past but assert their continuing relevance within the modern world. This has meant not just reviving historical formats and themes but pushing the boundaries of how Sikh art is perceived—challenging traditional definitions of Sikh art through a reinterpretation within a contemporary context that transcends cultural and religious boundaries. Ultimately, we believe that art is a universal language and that for Sikh art and Sikhism to gain wider recognition on an international platform, it needs not only to reflect the developing identity of Sikhism itself and respond to the new challenges presented to it in a global community, but must engage with important issues of social, political, and artistic debate that look beyond any finite Sikh perspective. In this respect, it is our view that Sikh art is not just about Sikhs, for Sikhs, and by Sikhs, as it is often categorized, but can be about everything, for everyone, and by anyone who uses the diverse languages of visual communication to analyse, reflect, and comment on the collective human experience through Sikh eyes. It is not just a record of how Sikhs view themselves and the world, but how the world views them. It is a resource which can offer valuable insights across the spectrum of academic study—social, political, cultural, and historical. It is a medium through which artists document, reflect, respond to, and redefine both an individual and collective heritage and an identity which is unique to their personal circumstances. As such, to neglect art within academic studies of Sikhs and Punjab is to miss out on a whole diversity of perspectives. So, if we are to explore new directions in Sikh and Punjab studies, we would like to encourage the wider integration of Sikh art within educational institutions that not only specialize in Sikh research but are also dedicated to global cultural studies—and we hope that our work will contribute in some way to that aim.

Notes

1. The images which are referred to in this essay but which are not reproduced here can be accessed through two publications: *Twin Perspectives: Paintings by Amrit and Rabindra KD Kaur Singh* (1999) and *Worlds A-part: Paintings by The Singh Twins* (2005).

2. Majh. p. 145. Translation from Inderjit Singh, 'Sikhism in a Secular World', *The Sikh Messenger* (1984–5), p. 32.

Contributors

Tony Ballantyne is Senior Lecturer in the department of history at the University of Otago. His most recent publication is *Between Colonialism and Diaspora: Sikh Cultural Formations in an Imperial World* (2006).

Himadri Banerjee is Professor of history at Jadavpur University. His publications include *The Other Sikhs: A View from Eastern India* (2003).

N. G. Barrier was Professor of history at the University of Missouri, Columbia. He has published widely on modern Sikh history, with his most recent collection (co-edited with Pashaura Singh) being *Sikhism and History* (2004).

Ian Catanach formerly taught history at the University of Canterbury. He has published widely on South Asian history, with a particular emphasis on economic and medical history. His publications include *Rural Credit in Western India, 1875–1930* (1970).

Louis E. Fenech is an Associate Professor at the University of Northern Iowa. His publications include *Martyrdom in the Sikh Tradition: Playing the 'Game of Love'* (2001).

Ian J. Kerr is Senior Scholar, department of history, University of Manitoba. His most recent publication is *Engines of Change: The Railroads That Made India* (2006).

W. H. (HEW) MCLEOD is Emeritus Professor of history at the University of Otago. He is a leading international authority on the history of Sikhs and Sikhism. His recent publications include *Sikhs of the Khalsa* (2003), *Prem Sumarag: the Testimony of a Sanatan Sikh* (2006), and *Essays in Sikh History, Tradition, and Society* (2007).

AMRIT KAUR SINGH AND RABINDRA KAUR SINGH are leading British artists. They have exhibited extensively in Britain and internationally. Their work has appeared in *Twin Perspectives* (1999) and *Worlds A-part* (2005)

PASHAURA SINGH is Professor of religious studies at the University of California, Riverside. His most recent publication is *Life and Work of Guru Arjan: History, Memory, and Biography in the Sikh Tradition* (2006).

JOHN WEBSTER has taught at several institutions in India and the United States. His publications include *A History of the Dalit Christians in India* (1992).